youth ministry

BOOKS BY LAWRENCE O. RICHARDS

A New Face for the Church
Creative Bible Study
Are You for Real?
How Far Can I Go?
Is God Necessary?
What's in It for Me?
69 Ways to Start a Study Group
Three Churches in Renewal
Reshaping Evangelical Higher Education
    (with Marvin K. Mayers)
A Theology of Christian Education

youth ministry

its renewal in the local church

lawrence o. richards

ZONDERVAN
PUBLISHING HOUSE OF THE ZONDERVAN CORPORATION
GRAND RAPIDS, MICHIGAN 49506

YOUTH MINISTRY — ITS RENEWAL IN THE LOCAL CHURCH
Copyright © 1972 by The Zondervan Corporation, Grand Rapids, Michigan

Library of Congress Catalog Card Number 79-189581

Ninth printing 1978
ISBN 0-310-31950-1

Grateful acknowledgment is made for permission to quote from the following
copyrighted material:

Creative Bible Study by Lawrence O. Richards, © 1971 by Zondervan Publishing
House.

The Living Bible, © 1971 by Tyndale House Publishers, Wheaton, Illinois.

Marital Counseling by Hirsch L. Silverman, © 1967, by Hirsch L. Silverman
published by Charles C. Thomas, Springfield, Ill.

The New Testament in Modern English, © 1958 by J. B. Phillips, published by the
Macmillan Company.

United Evangelical Action, official publication of the National Association of
Evangelicals.

Ways Youth Learn by Clarice Bowman, © 1952 by Harper and Row, New York, N.Y.

Young People and Their Culture by Ross Snyder, © 1969 by Abingdon Press, New
York, N.Y.

Printed in the United States of America

Contents

Foreword

"Renewal" is a word we often hear today. It's a word that calls both for a new approach to life in the church and for a return to New Testament patterns of ministry.

In both these senses, this book on youth ministry is a renewal book. In it I seek to draw from Scripture and to explore principles on which youth ministry can be confidently based. And in it I develop what seems to me a distinctive approach to ministering with youth.

The book itself is divided into several parts. The first explores contemporary youth culture, and hopefully will help you understand some of the ways of thinking and feeling about life that are characteristic of young people today.

Part two looks at youth as a time of life. Hopefully it will help you identify with adolescents. Although they are persons like you and me, they are under special pressures that we need to understand. The latter half of part two is a vital one, taking a look at leadership in biblical perspective. As I suggest there, this may be the most important part of the book, for it certainly examines a critical ministry area. Perhaps effectiveness in ministry does depend more on this one thing, *who you are as a leader,* than on any other factor.

The third part explores the primary processes of ministry. This is the heart of the book, attempting to explain those processes in which youth and adults must become involved to grow toward maturity as Christians.

Part four looks at programming and discusses both the structures (agencies, meetings, activities) of youth ministry and the organizing of youth for ministry.

The final and very brief section, part five, considers the goal and the result of an effective youth ministry: growth, together.

Together these chapters develop a philosophy of youth ministry, presenting a basic approach to youth ministry with an explanation of *why* we approach ministry as we do, and suggestions on *what* to do and *how* to do it. Although older teens (the senior high group) are primarily in mind as I write this book, the principles are also valid for, and have direct application to, young teens and college-age youth, with exceptions noted in the text.

Beginning with part two, this book will deal successively with the elements contained in the following diagram:

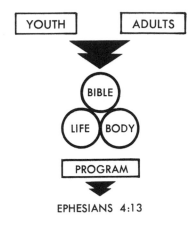

EPHESIANS 4:13

It is, I suppose, always rewarding to finish a book. As I complete this one I do so with the feeling that it may be the most significant book I've yet written. For, more than any other, it develops a pattern for ministry, one which I am convinced is both distinctively biblical and productive of exciting renewal — a renewal we desperately need, and need now.

LAWRENCE O. RICHARDS

Overview

In 1955 Elkin and Westley published an article in the *American Sociological Review* deftly titled, "The Myth of Adolescent Culture,"[1] in which they argued that the existence of a youth culture as a widespread and dominant pattern among adolescents in America should be questioned. Hardly anyone would write such an article today.

Not that "youth culture" is marked off by those characteristics adults often think of first: promiscuous sex, devotion to drugs, total rejection of adult authority, and so on. A recent interesting survey of 22,000 young people, sixteen to eighteen years of age, who were rated high scholastically, showed that:

1. 75% disapproved the use of marijuana, 21% would use it if it were legalized, and 10% use it now.

2. 96% disapproved the use of LSD, speed or heroin, 3% approved, 1% didn't answer.

3. 53% disapproved of premarital sexual intercourse, 42% approved, and 5% didn't answer.

4. 60% said they had not engaged in sex relations, 15% said they had, and 24% didn't answer.[2]

These may not be ideal results, but the responses certainly fail to show the existence of the depraved culture adults often visualize. In many ways youths' viewpoints and values reflect their parents' and show solidarity with the general culture.

Yet it is increasingly clear that there *is* a distinctive youth culture, marked off from the general culture in significant ways that are increasingly visible. And it is increasingly apparent, as, more and more, youth sense a deepening alienation from the local churches, that youth ministry *must* be built on an understanding of the distinctive ways youth experience and feel and view life.

While the characteristics of youth culture that call for our understanding are most easily seen in older youth, it is still true that, as John Snyder of the University of California at Santa Barbara has

---

[1]Frederick Elkin and William A. Westley, "The Myth of Adolescent Culture," *American Sociological Review,* Vol. 20, Dec., 1955.

[2]Report of a Merit Publishing Co. survey in *Youth Today,* Inter-Varsity newsletter, Nov., 1970.

pointed out, youth's alienation is often well-established before the student gets to college.[3] Indeed, the most significant elements of youth culture are increasingly felt on the high school and junior high school levels, and although not *every* young person will bear its stamp, the pattern of the culture is finding expression in increasingly significant numbers.

And so it is necessary to explore and mark out those elements of youth culture that underlie it as basic to youth's world-view. These basic elements must be grasped for our approach to youth ministry. For only when we understand the thought patterns of youth can we help them to "fight to capture every thought until it acknowledges the authority of Christ" (2 Cor. 10:5 *Phillips*). And only when we understand the ways youth experience life can we shape the ministries of the church to communicate with youth, and lead them toward discipleship.

It is to an overview of youth's distinctive culture, and a design for ministry with this decade's youth, that we turn in these first three chapters.

---

[3]Reported in *Youth Today,* Inter-Varsity newsletter, March, 1970.

Part One

YOUTH IN OUR CULTURE

1

a question of values

"I can't remember any basic decisions, actually," says an eighteen-year-old college freshman, thinking back over her life as a high schooler. "I just lived a day at a time, and did what seemed right and most fun at that time. A lot of times, though, what I did or didn't do depended on whether my dad would approve." Another older teen adds, "I think my main tendency was to take life as it comes. I don't think I really started using values that are uniquely mine until this, my sophomore year in college."

These quotes are characteristic of a large sampling of young people at a Christian college, and point up basic issues in Christian education of youth. Aware of them or not, high schoolers do make decisions. Aware of them or not, the values held by youth underlie their decisions. Thus the whole concept of values raises serious problems for the ministry of Christian education in the local church.

Today there is a popular awareness that distinct differences exist between the life-style of youth and that of the older generations. This awareness has been focused by such terms as "the generation gap" and "the NOW generation," as well as by the experience of many parents with their teens. Youth culture has also become a principal field of study for sociologists and anthropologists as well as Christian educators. The number of significant differences found between the generations[1] has led many, like sociologist Marcel Rioux, to believe that "intergenerational conflict" is "most significant" and of "fundamental importance" in any attempt to under-

---

[1] Among the differing orientations of youth and adult culture might be listed such things as experience-oriented vs. time-oriented perceptions, person-oriented vs. concept- or "thing"-oriented values, existential vs. linear perceptions, etc. Only those areas of direct relationship to this topic will be examined here.

stand the type of society which mankind is entering.[2] So also Allen Moore suggests that "young people tend to be precise indicators of what is going on within a culture."[3]

It is vital in planning for ministry with youth that we understand the styles in which youth tend to think and feel, and shape our ministries to what they *are*, not to what we might think they ought to be. It is particularly important when we examine the values of youth that we understand the cultural forces that affect them.

"lived a day at a time"

One of the most significant styles of contemporary youth culture is reflected in this simple phrase. To youth, life is lived a day at a time, an hour at a time, a moment at a time. What is significant is the existential *now*. Professor Erik Erickson, well-known identity theory psychologist, suggests several reasons for this trend.

> First, the past grows increasingly distant from the present.... Social changes that would have taken a century now occur in less than a generation. As a result, the past grows progressively more different from the present in fact, and seems more remote and irrelevant psychologically. Second, the future, too, grows more remote and uncertain. Because the future directions of social change are virtually unpredictable, today's young men and women are growing into a world that is more unknowable than that confronted by any previous generation. The kind of society today's students will confront as mature adults is almost impossible for them or anyone else to anticipate. Third, the present assumes a new significance as the one time in which environment is relevant, immediate, and knowable. The past's solution to life's problems are not necessarily relevant to the here-and-now, and no one can know whether what is decided today will remain valid in tomorrow's world; hence, the present assumes an autonomy unknown in more static societies.[4]

With the growing psychological emphasis on the *now,* and the receding significance of both past and future, immediate experience becomes of great importance. Thus Dennis Benson, in a book analyzing the nature and impact of youth music, notes that "the rock music of our time cannot be separated from the experiential and

---

[2]Marcel Rioux, "Youth in the Contemporary World and in Quebec," in *Folio* (department of Youth Ministry, NCC/USA, #5, New York, N.Y.).

[3]Allen J. Moore, *The Young Adult Generation* (Nashville: Abingdon Press, 1969) p. 16.

[4]Erik Erickson, in *Youth, Change and Challenge* (New York: Basic Books, Inc., 1962) p. 168.

14

spontaneous aspects of the *now* generation. . . . The *now* generation reflects this new orientation toward experience and spontaneity, particularly in its group activities."[5]

More than contemporary music reflects this new orientation to life. Keniston, in a study on *Drug Use and Student Values,* sees drug use for many students as "primarily a way of searching for meaning via the chemical intensification of personal experience."[6] Thus the many middle-class students in suburbs who try out drugs "just for kicks," may well be seeking such kicks because of a basic, though unformulated, belief that direct personal experience is of great value *in itself!*

Donald Michael, in a 1965 Random House publication projecting societal trends into *The Next Generation* has noted that advertisers have sensed this cultural drift. He suggests that "under these circumstances, novelty and sensation will be especially sought after" in the future, "even if the novelty is 'packaged only' and the sensation is for the most part vicarious or standardized or rapidly becomes standardized through the style-setting mass media."[7] Thus we have the prospect of an American culture capitalizing on the growing preoccupation of its population with the *now,* creating a whole system of valuing people and things in terms of their ability to provide for the individual a new experience or stimulation!

"what seemed most fun"

It's not surprising that "fun" should be highly valued by a person who is existentially oriented. Although in America "fun" has long been held to be a basic right of youth, Erickson points out that today within youth culture there exists an *"extraordinary* hedonism — using the word in the broadest sense — in that there is a desacralization of life and an attitude that all experience is permissible and even desirable." Yet Erickson sees "in their pleasure-seeking relatively little relaxed joy, and often compulsive and addictive

---

[5]Dennis C. Benson, *The NOW Generation* (Richmond: John Knox Press, 1969) p. 75.

[6]Kenneth Keniston, "Drug Use and Student Values," in *Background Papers on Student Drug Involvement,* ed. C. Hollander (Publications Dept., USNSA, Washington, D.C.) As Keniston notes, "The search for meaning through experiences is an important and valid search," yet "present experience in itself is (hardly) enough to provide the meaning of life."

[7]Donald N. Michael, *The Next Generation* (New York: Random House, 1965) p. 41.

search for *relevant* experience."[8] *Fun* has become part of youth culture's search for meaning, and so has lost its ability to provide joy!

Essentially related to this stance of youth culture is an underlying humanistic philosophy of life. In humanism the destiny of man is definitely placed within the very broad limits of the natural world, and thus "the chief end of thought and action is to further this-earthly human interests." So also "the watchword of humanism is happiness for all humanity in this existence."[9] In an existentially oriented world, *happiness* is consistently read as *pleasurable experience, now!*[10]

While older adults may be critical of youth for their open concern with happiness now, it ought to be recognized that this drift is characteristic of our whole culture, and is finding among youth, not its origin, but simply its open and honest expression. In discussing cultural aspects of delinquency, the well-known sociologist William Kvaraceus points out that "American living has been moving rapidly from a work-oriented to a play-oriented culture." He says,

> If the delinquent is sometimes viewed as pleasure-bent, riding heavily on a want-it-now track, it is because he is surrounded by elders who set the pattern . . . the adult lesson in self-indulgence is not lost on youth. Our technological culture is inventive and produces many gimmicks and gadgets that youth really do not need, but which they feel they must have after the hucksters get through.[11]

It is hardly surprising then to discover that a 1961 Gallup poll indicated no sense of goal or purpose for many teenagers, and that

---

[8] Erick H. Erickson, "Memorandum on Youth," *Folio* #5.

[9] The book quoted here, Corliss Lamont's *The Philosophy of Humanism,* is a strong defense and appeal for a humanistic view of life.

[10] A number of contemporary researchers, particularly British, suggest a future orientation in youth culture. The future is viewed with concern, as problems of ecology and overpopulation and threats of war seem to loom menacingly and hugely. But the impact of these views of and concern for the future seems in fact to drive youth to search for meaning in their *now,* as a way to avoid making hard decisions that force them to confront the future as reality. Youth culture turns to astrology and witchcraft just now, not as a way to deal with the problems that loom up in the future, but in an attempt to find a way to avoid facing them. Youth culture is not responding to the future by saying, Let's get to work, and prepare ourselves to straighten all this out. The future drives the culture back on itself, in a desperate search for a *now* experience that will blunt and dull the edge of the fear that concern for the future causes. And so the *now* is still the primary location of the experience and the identity of the youth culture, with nostalgic and futuristic tendencies building even higher the walls that capture so many in the frustrations of existential hedonism.

[11] Wm. C. Kvaraceus, *Dynamics of Delinquency* (Columbus, Ohio: Chas. Merrill Books, 1966) p. 15.

for those with some sense of goal, that mentioned most often was happiness. Realizing that values are carried by the culture and formed in interpersonal relationships (rather than by the presentation of words and ideas so relied on by most Christians), it is not even surprising to discover that a 1963 study of Missouri Synod youth indicated that "happiness is the life goal of most of the (churched) youth," with the primary hue of "happiness" basically hedonistic.[12] And it is not surprising to find that a 1967 study of youth in other conservative, evangelical churches showed the same![13]

"what dad would approve"

It hardly seems possible that the life style sketched thus far (one giving so high a priority to the *now* that both past and future considerations seem less and less important, and giving high priority to all types of direct experience) is one of which the older generation can approve. Parental disapproval does seem to limit the impact of youth culture on high schoolers who have strong ties to their parents, as did the girl quoted at the beginning of this chapter. Yet these ties, and parental approval itself, are losing much ability to shape behavior in high school today, and dissolve rapidly in a collegiate situation. Most significantly, while parental approval may restrict certain types of *behavior* during the high school years, the peer group has become more and more important in shaping the *values* of youth. These values may not seem to dominate observable behavior during the high school years; but the internalized values (which are observable in areas where direct parental pressure is removed) will be actualized in behavior later when external restraints are more completely removed!

Why is it that youth culture, and the values of the peer group, have such an impact on an adolescent — even on one from a Christian home and church? Researcher John Horrocks points out that

> the family — important as it is as a limiting and defining agency and as much as it is the central focus of any child's existence — nevertheless cannot usually transcend, or, indeed, in many cases even meet, the achievement of the peer group in shaping values and in providing perceived personal security as an individual.

Research has suggested that within the group situation the adolescent

---

[12]Merton F. Strommer, *Profiles of Church Youth* (St. Louis: Concordia Publishing House, 1963) pp. 76, 85.

[13]See chapter 12 of Zuck and Getz, *Christian Youth: an in-depth study* (Chicago: Moody Press, 1968).

can feel a sense of power, belonging, and security; he can make decisions in collaborating with his peers that he would never be capable of making alone. . . . Thus we may see the peer world, for most adolescents, as a tremendously important source of attitudes, the inhibitor as well as the initiator of action, the arbiter of right and wrong.[14]

Sociologist Muzafer Sherif notes that the adolescent's age-mates

become his *reference set* for sizing up his own problems, his own strivings, and his own abilities. . . . The actual movement toward age-mates during adolescence in modern societies is symptomatic of a general shift in psychological ties. For the time being, one's conception of himself is linked firmly with the domain of other adolescents, the ties with adults and children being proportionately less salient. Thus, adolescents, in certain respects, are much more concerned about how they stack up with other adolescents than with what their families, teachers, or other adults think about these matters. Other adolescents are a major reference set even for youth who are not members of clear-cut groups or cliques.[15]

Social psychologist James Coleman, reporting on an earlier study, noted in 1961 the emergence of an adolescent society which was significantly separated from the general culture. Speaking of the high schooler, Coleman wrote,

He is "cut off" from the rest of society, forced inward toward his own age group, made to carry out his whole social life with others his own age. With his fellows, he comes to constitute a small society, one that has most of its important interactions *within* itself, and maintains only a few threads of connection with the outside adult society. In our modern world of mass communication and rapid diffusion of ideas and knowledge, it is hard to realize that separate subcultures can exist right under the very noses of adults — subcultures with languages all their own, with special symbols and, most importantly, with value systems that may differ from adults. Any parent who has tried to talk to his adolescent son or daughter recently knows this, as does anyone who has recently visited a high school for the first time since his own adolescence. To put it more simply, these young people speak a different language. What is more relevant to the present point, the language they speak is becoming more and more different.[16]

Coleman's prediction has proven correct, perhaps fulfilled more

---

[14]John E. Horrocks, "Adolescent Attitudes and Goals" in Muzafer and Carolyn Sherif, *Problems of Youth* (Chicago: Aldine Co., 1965) p. 21.

[15]Sherif and Sherif, *Problems of Youth,* p. 15.

[16]James S. Coleman, *The Adolescent Society* (New York: The Free Press of Glencoe, 1961) p. 3.

quickly than he expected. The language youth speak today, the way they think and feel, the way they value and perceive life, has become more and more different. So different that today, to minister with youth, one must understand and accept youth on their terms — not his own. *Yeah, but you can't be 100% accepting*

"what seemed right"

It's an oversimplification of what actually happens in making choices to accept the statement "I just did what seemed right at the time" at face value. Sociologists, while not in full agreement on the definition of values, do tend to view them as "a selective orientation toward experiences, implying a deep commitment or repudiation, which influences the ordering of choices between alternatives in action." Values do lie beneath decisions as to "what seems right." It is important to note that these value orientations "may be cognitive and expressed verbally or merely inferable from recurrent trends of behavior."[17] Anthropologists also are "concerned with the values by which, explicitly or implicitly, the choices are made . . . in the society making the choices."[18]

Viewed this way, the idea of values is specifically related to the choices that actually are made — not to the value ideas that are professed. For instance, an individual who says, "I value the good of others," but who chooses to spend his time and his money on himself, obviously holds different values from those he professes. In the last analysis, the only true indicator of values is behavior. Only from behavior can we discover values, for "once a value becomes internalized it becomes, consciously or unconsciously, a standard or criterion for guiding action."[19]

How are the values that determine choices internalized (i.e. made part of the character of the individual)? I suggested earlier that values are carried by culture, and communicated through interpersonal relationships. University of Chicago's Robert J. Havighurst presents a helpful model of character formation (viewed as the integration of personality around values) this way:

---

[17]Donald N. Barrett, "Analysis of Values in Behavioral Science," in *Values in America* (Notre Dame, Indiana: Univ. of Notre Dame Press) p. 3.

[18]Raymond Firth, *Essays on Social Organization and Values* (London: Athlone Press, 1964) p. 178.

[19]Milton Rokeach, *Beliefs, Attitudes, and Values,* (San Francisco: Jossey-Bass, Inc., 1968) p. 160.

(1) *Character is learned through reward and punishment.* These rewards relate to the social environment of approval and disapproval, first from the home, then from the peer group. Through these pressures an individual is constantly learning moral values and habits.

(2) *Character is learned through unconscious imitation.* The first objects of imitation are the parents and other family members; this carries over to age-mates who have high status, and includes later imitation of an idealized self (a self-portrait of a person as he would like to be).

(3) *Character develops through reflective thinking.* This stage involves thinking about moral situations, tracing various kinds of behavior through to their probable consequences. At this stage reasoning and conscious choice of value ideas which have been generalized is essential.[20]

This model of value formation focuses attention on several factors in the life-style of contemporary youth, and the broad culture in which youth find themselves. Most significant are these: the loss of a clear-cut cultural (adult) model, and the trend away from reflective moral thinking.

Today we are quickly losing clear-cut value approval and disapproval patterns in American life. One study of adolescence points to the "shifting values so clearly observable in contemporary middle-class society" and suggests that "the weakening of conviction and belief in established value systems also contributes to the inconsistency between proclaimed attitudes and observable behavior" across our culture.[21] Such confusion has led to a distinct relativism. It is the style today for a young person who disapproves of premarital intercourse "for me" to hasten to add that this may, of course, be quite all right for others. Thus Liston Pope in 1961 called our age "a time of indecision, equivocation, and paradox — a time when ideals are clouded and values are confused." He added,

> We present to our young people a hazy picture of the very ideas on which they will base their lives. Belief in the essential goodness of man is tempered by recognition that man is a selfish creature capable of almost anything. Belief in social progress is still widespread in America, but we doubt that we are making any net gains except possibly in the field of mechanical gadgets. We continue to teach that

---

[20]Robert J. Havighurst and Hilda Taba, *Adolescent Character and Personality* (New York: John Wiley & Sons, 1949) pp. 6, 7.

[21]*Normal Adolescence.* The Committee on Adolescence, Group for the Advancement of Psychiatry (New York: Charles Scribner's Sons, 1968) pp. 230-1.

hard work is a great virtue, but the work week grows ever shorter. We praise virtues of frugality, temperance, and modesty, but we live as the most spendthrift and boastful nation in the world.[22]

Thus we live in a welter of conflicting values, with no clear-cut cultural patterns of approval and disapproval, and youth are cut adrift to find their own values within their peer group. But the pressures that exist in youth culture tend to support a relativism so pervasive that the strongest value pressures are the existential-hedonistic pressures discussed earlier!

But perhaps even more serious is the trend away from "reflective thinking," the behavior described by Havighurst which involves a generalization of value ideas and a conscious evaluation of behavior. With the *now* becoming the focus of youth perspective, and the past and future receding into a distant psychological field, the rational evaluation of choice-results seems less and less significant. With high values placed on direct personal experience as an end in itself, the trend is re-enforced. *The results seem to be a tendency for decisions to be made nonrationally, on impulse within a situational framework, and without conscious testing or extension of values.*

I recently asked 800 students of a Christian college to think back over their high school years, and complete a one-page questionnaire designed to bring to the surface their decision-making processes. The questionnaire included a series of ten items relating to decisions involving "what to do now," and ten items relating to decisions involving "what to do in life." The participants were asked which of these items were factors in their decision-making. Then they were asked to indicate the kind of decisions they had in mind while completing the check list, and finally they were given an opportunity to share an experience relating to decision-making.

One hundred and fifty-three of the returned questionnaires contained extended responses (responses of three sentences or more) in the space for sharing a decision experience. One of the most significant findings is the fact that of the one hundred and fifty-three, *thirty-four stated explicitly* that they did not think about decisions they made in high school: they "never went beyond the now." These students characteristically did not see themselves faced with significant decisions to make!

Only eight of the one hundred and fifty-three stated that they did

---

[22]Liston Pope, "Values in Transition," *Values and Ideals of American Youth*, ed. Eli Ginzberg (New York: Columbia University Press, 1961) pp. 230-1.

begin to make significant decisions in high school, and in each case their conscious application of values to decision-making was related to some particular conflict situation[23] which forced them to stop, to think, and to consciously decide which values were really important to them.

From this preliminary study, it seems tragically possible that the existential-hedonistic life-style of contemporary youth culture may significantly inhibit an awareness of the values by which youth operate. Nonrational, impulse decisions within a hedonistic culture should be of deepest concern to Christian education — not only because youth are making such decisions, but because we *all* are.

Conclusions

When we think of youth culture in Christian education we need to break away from visions of long hair and loud music. What is important to us is not merely the symbols of youth's difference, but the substance. And this substance consists of the set of values — the "what's important to me" — that lies at the root of their understandings and experiences of life, and at the root of their decisions and choices.

When we deal with these values and see relativism and the priority given to experience, we have difficulty in accepting their validity. As a philosophy, existentialism has proven an empty message of despair. And a thoroughgoing existentialist life-style seems to be a pathway to meaninglessness.

In an interesting study of social commitment among college students, Gelineau and Kantor describe the existentially oriented student as "one who is at the same time the most selfish and the most selfless of volunteers. He neither expects to gain any ultimate occupational advantage nor does he feel a traditional moral commitment. The responsibility he feels is to himself and to the exploration of experience. In this sense he is intensively concerned with self."[24]

Somehow the existentialist-hedonistic understanding of man, viewing an individual as responsible only to himself, and to himself as

---

[23]Conflict situations ranged from a broken home to the receipt of a large money gift, from the refusal of a parent to make a decision for his child to the sudden awareness of need for money for college. Each situation seemed to bring awareness of the need to make a significant decision, which in turn led to a rational evaluation of values.

[24]Victor Gelineau and David Kantor, "Pro-Social Commitment Among College Students," *Folio* #5.

a biological mechanism designed to explore experiences, is tragically shallow. No wonder Gelineau and Kantor view such individuals as persons motivated "from the overwhelming search for identity." The Christian Gospel places value on persons as created in the *image of God,* and thus bearing the timeless stamp of eternity. Such a person can hardly find his true self as a mere sampler of sensations!

The Gospel of Christ locates meaning in life outside the experience of personal pleasure, or the gaining of personal ends. The call to discipleship in the gospels demands that the believer "seek first the kingdom of God and his righteousness," not because God places a premium on human suffering, but because He knows that only within the framework of dedication to God and man can a believer actualize the person he truly is in Christ.

Yet it is important to ask one more question: is the existentialist life-style *itself* anti-Christian? That is, is it valid to value the *now,* and to value direct experience? These questions can be answered in only one way: *certainly this life-style is valid, and can be "Christian."* For Christian values can and should find expression as we decide to live our *now,* and the existentialist view is correct in that only the *now* is ever-present with us; only the *now* is the location of our choices and actions. Thus Christian values *must* be expressed existentially, and must be expressed in direct, personal response to experience. *May be going too far w/ this acceptance premise.*

The issue seems to rest in the distinction between the *cultural* pattern of existential decision-making and the *Christian* pattern of existential decision-making. The impact of contemporary youth's life-style, *as developed in youth culture* (particularly the tendency to live unexamined lives and the unthinking hedonism which controls so many choices), is of deep concern to Christian education. For the Christian man, a free moral agent invited to respond freely in all of life to God who meets us in Christ and calls us to a relationship of joyful obedience to Him, must live by examined values and by a conscious commitment of all of life to Christ.

Our task, then, in ministry with youth is now made more clear. To communicate to youth we must (1) understand the life-style of youth culture and recognize the value-impact of this life-style, and (2) effectively relate the Gospel to the life-style of youth today, both to facilitate formation of distinctively Christian values and to encourage their actualization in experience.

PROBE
case histories
discussion questions
thought-provokers

1. David Levy, Dartmouth College's highest-ranking graduate in 1971, gave a valedictory address full of despair. Among other things Mr. Levy said, "Take pity on me, those of you who can justify the air you breathe . . . send me letters and tell me why life is worth living. Rich parents, write and tell me how money makes your life worthwhile. Dartmouth alumni, tell me how the Dartmouth experience has given value to your life." And to the graduating class he said, "And if some one of you out there is also made like me, write me a letter and tell me how you came to appreciate the absurdity of your life."

   What relationship do you see between this youth's cry and the cultural elements discussed in this chapter?

2. Sometimes we wonder why youth aren't motivated by our exhortations. Take a look at three common attempts to motivate teens, and evaluate (1) what is basic to the approaches, and (2) why teens are not usually responsive to them.
   a. *from a high school teacher:* "Study, kids. There's a test coming in three weeks, and I'm warning you, it's tough!"
   b. *from a concerned parent:* "If you don't dig in and work in school, Jim, you won't be able to get into college when you graduate in two years."
   c. *from a youth sponsor or pastor:* "When the Lord comes back, you'll wish you'd gotten down to real dedication!"

3. Briefly describe in writing the settings in which most churches attempt to minister with youth. That is, spell out such factors as these: Where do they meet? What are the goals of the meetings? What happens at meetings? What are the adult roles? What are the youth roles? Etc.

   Then evaluate these settings in the light of three aspects of youth culture implied in this chapter:
   a. Values are communicated interpersonally, in a context of interaction and sharing of life — not through authoritarian announcements of "what is right."
   b. The peer group is the primary *reference set* of teens when it comes to lived values.
   c. Personal experience is viewed by youth as essential to testing and validating various ideas about life.

4. *Recommended reading*
   What's in It for Me? by Larry Richards (Moody Press: 1970) is an exploration of values, written for youth to help them understand their importance and function in life.

2

response to youth culture

Wherever the Christian Gospel went, people whom the Spirit touched turned away from their lifeless gods to serve the true God. And their relationship to Him was marked, where faith grew, by an increasing love for one another, and a steadfast, joyful obedience to the One they had come to trust as risen Lord.

It's striking that the greatest missionary to the non-Jewish world (a Pharisee who had once persecuted his own people when they dared to deviate and turn to Christ) moved so freely among Gentiles, whose culture and viewpoints repelled the faithful Hebrew. And that this man led the Church to its discovery that in Christ persons of every race and culture become one, and are to be accepted *as they are*, without demanding that one change to fit the other's view and style of life. When he was with the Jew, the apostle Paul "became Jewish" in thought and style of life; when with the Gentile, he "became Greek" that, by all means, he might win some. This was no compromise with the faith. For God's Word and Spirit find fresh expression in men of every place, of every age. Even in today's world of youth.

And it's no compromise with the faith if in our ministries we "become youth" and let the wildfire of the new life we so ignite burn, in its own way, in the world our world is fast becoming.

In the first chapter I sketched cultural forces which have led young people to operationalize values within an existentialist-hedonistic frame of reference. What does this mean in terms of human experience?

(1) In effect, this life-style encourages undue reference to factors in the immediate situation when making decisions. What a decision will mean for *now* is given weight far out of proportion to the weight given possible future meanings. The psychological focus on *now* elements of decision-making causes future elements (whether

25

the future is "tomorrow" or "next year") to recede into a psychological field of relative unimportance.[1]

(2) In practice, this life-style encourages the seeking of immediate personal experience. In consequence, the *authority* on which value judgments are accepted shifts from an external authority (the past, parents, societal institutions, or the church) to an internal authority: "I will not believe until I place my fingers on the mark of the nails." The youth of today are unlikely to be touched by appeal to tradition. They feel they must be allowed to find out for themselves.

(3) In practice, this life-style overemphasizes sensations as criteria for good/bad value judgment. Much of the unease of youth today, who have experienced a range of sensations unavailable to previous generations and failed to find *meaning* in them, seems to be a result of expecting to find in immediate experience that which only reflective consideration can provide: a sense of *right* to which one can be committed, and a sense of *wrong* from which one can consciously turn. As Werkmeister points out, "the immediacies of value experience, it is clear, must be transcended in value judgments, for without judgments, implicit or explicit, we can never rise above the immediately felt *as felt*."[2]

(4) In practice, this life-style has led to a kind of *spontaneous decision-making* which often fails to seek reference points within or outside of a situation, or which may consciously reject such reference points. "We did it for kicks" is a common way for youth to explain behavior ranging from innocent adventures to drug use and the most brutal of crimes. When spontaneity falls into an irrational pattern — or, as the Bible puts it, when "like animals they do what ever they feel like" (Jude 10, 2 Pet. 2:12 *The Living Bible*) — then a very serious denial of the nature and responsibility of man is implicit.

A Christian response

I suggested earlier that youth culture's life-style (in terms of its

---

[1]The implications of this factor for *situation ethics* has not, to my knowledge, been considered by either its proponents or its enemies. Yet this practice has great impact on the workableness of situation ethics, if not its theoretical base, for Fletcher and others insist that ethical decisions be made by reference to the consequences of any act. If in practice our cultural drift makes reference to consequences outside a limited immediacy mere wishful thinking, situation ethics is likely to become merely a way of justifying hedonistic responses.

[2]H. W. Werkmeister, *Man and His Values* (Lincoln, Nebraska: University of Nebraska Press, 1967) p. 107.

concern for the *now* and its emphasis on immediate personal experience) is not anti-Christian. What might a Christian response to each of the four practices sketched above be?

(1) *Undue reference to factors in the immediate situation.* Scripture seems to indicate a life-style in which there is a *balanced* concern for the now. By balanced I mean initially an awareness that the only segment of life for which we are responsible, and over which we have any control, *is* the now. James warns,

> Look here, you people who say, "Today or tomorrow we are going to such and such a town, stay there a year, and open up a profitable business." How do you know what is going to happen tomorrow? For the length of your lives is as uncertain as the morning fog — now you see it; soon it is gone.

The person who recognizes that his life is his *only* now will learn to depend on God for the future, and to say, " 'If the Lord wants us to, we shall live, and do this or that' " (James 4:13-15 *The Living Bible*).

So too Christ counsels us,

> Look at the birds! They don't worry about what to eat — they don't reap or sow or store up food — and your heavenly Father feeds them. And you are far more valuable to Him than they are! Will all your worries add a single moment to your life? . . .
>
> So don't worry at all about having enough food and clothing. Why be like the heathen? For they take pride in all these things and are deeply concerned about them. But your heavenly Father already knows perfectly well that you need them, and He will gladly give them to you if you give Him first place in your life. So don't be anxious about tomorrow! God will take care of your tomorrow too. Live one day at a time (Matt. 6:26-34 *The Living Bible*).

While we are to focus our concern and energies on the *now*, the freedom to live now rests, for the believer, on his trust in a God who controls the future. The Christian does not deny tomorrow, or discount it. Both Old and New Testaments are teleological documents: both have a strong sense of history and destiny. The God of the Bible is a God in control of history, working out all things for His glory and for our ultimate good. Thus Paul anchors his motivation and his values in God's planned consummation of history.

> I am still not all I should be but I am bringing all my energies to bear on this one thing: Forgetting the past and looking forward to what lies ahead, I strain to reach the end of the race and receive the

prize for which God is calling us up to heaven because of what Christ Jesus did for us (Phil. 3:13, 14 *The Living Bible*).

Peter too rejects the existentialist idea that *now* experience is valid and meaningful in itself, and as an end in itself. He warns that

> the day of the Lord is surely coming, as unexpectedly as a thief, and then the heavens will pass away with a terrible noise and the heavenly bodies will disappear in fire, and the earth and everything on it will be burned up. And so since everything around us is going to melt away, what holy, godly lives we should be living! . . .
>
> Dear friends, while you are waiting for these things to happen and for Him to come, try hard to live without sinning; and be at peace with everyone so that He will be pleased with you when He returns (2 Pet. 3:10-14 *The Living Bible*).

While the *now* is important to biblical writers, the reference points of value are *outside the now,* extending through time and eternity, and anchored in the nature and revealed purposes of God.

A major concern of Christian education, then, might be stated as *the extension of youth's reference points for "now" decisions beyond the immediate situation,* and a *relating of value ideas to a Christian understanding of God's purposes.*

(2) *Encouragement of immediate personal experience and consequent shift of authority.* At first many Christians will greet this whole idea negatively, particularly those who accept Scripture as final authority and who react strongly when anyone appears to be questioning its stated values.

But closer examination leads even the conservative believer to view this trend as essentially healthy. For too long conservatives have tended to view Scripture as only a *truth system.*[3] The logical extension of an emphasis on Scripture *truth* is to see Christian education's task as the communication of the true content of Scripture, and the appropriate response to Christian education an assent: "We believe it too."

Too little attention has been given by evangelicals to the *nature* of the truth they believe Scripture reveals.

Closer attention to Scripture itself shows that the truth revealed is essentially a *reality system.* That is, in the Word of God the Spirit of God has revealed the true nature of the world we live in, the true nature of man and of God, the ultimate consummation of

---

[3]I write, of course, from the historic conservative position, holding to verbal inspiration and propositional revelation.

history, the pattern of relationships and responses to God and to life which correspond with "the way things really are."

It is important to note that an entirely different pattern for Christian education results when the Scripture is viewed as reality structure than when emphasis is placed on it as a truth system. These patterns are:

theological emphasis	*communication pattern*	*appropriate response*
truth system ⟶	communicate content ⟶	accept it as true
reality structure ⟶	guide to experience it ⟶	discover it to be real

That Scripture reveals a reality structure seems to me to be the one great impact of Christ's answer to a disciple who asked, "Sir, why [after Your death] are You going to reveal Yourself only to us disciples and not the world at large?" The passage tells us that Jesus replied, "Because I will . . . reveal Myself [only] to those who love Me and obey Me. The Father will love them too, and We will come to them and live with them. Anyone who doesn't obey Me doesn't love Me" (John 14:22-24 *The Living Bible*). With this simple statement Jesus highlighted the fact that the reality of God can only be experienced, and that such experience is contingent on obedience —commitment to the reality Christ's commands reveal. By obedience the believer discovers for himself that the scriptural view of reality is real indeed.

When we give priority to the Christian faith as reality structure, the emphasis in youth culture on authenticating experience becomes extremely significant. Too long have older generations blindly rested on mental assent to a reality meant to be experienced, and made a fetish of defending a Word which they have not obeyed. The demand of youth to find out for themselves is in fullest harmony with the nature of the Gospel, and ought to be welcomed with joy, not greeted with criticism!

Thus a major concern of Christian education must become the *guiding of youth to discover the reality of the Christian faith by personal experience,* and by an experiential testing of Scripture's claim of authority. (See John 5:39, 40; 7:16, 17.)

No Christian convinced of the validity of his faith need draw back from such a test, or from such a direction in Christian education for youth.

(3) *Role given to sensations as criteria for good/bad judgments.* While it is good and valuable to savor the full capacity of man to feel and to enjoy, it is unrealistic to expect sensation to provide either a knowledge of good/bad or right/wrong, or to provide a sense of meaning and purpose in life.

If Scripture is accepted as reality structure, it becomes clear that the biblical view of man places on him the responsibility of evaluating his choices in life by far different criteria than the pleasure feelings various actions afford! As suggested earlier, youth who seek meaning in such experiences fall into an almost compulsive pattern of life, and experience at the same time a frustrating sense of identity loss. Man is not simply a pleasure machine.

Thus, (4) *spontaneous decision-making arising from existential feelings* is a most serious phenomenon, and one which Christian education must deal with directly.

The directions indicated for Christian education by an understanding of the nature of Scripture and of youth's decision-making processes seems relatively clear. A major concern of ministry must involve guiding youth to consciously evaluate their values as expressed in choices they make, and their feelings in the experiences they have. Along with this must come a deepening of youth's awareness of the decisions they do make daily, and a sharpening of their sensitivity to values these decisions express. We can no longer afford to let youth live out the high school years unaware that they *are* using values, daily, to make decisions. We can no longer leave them unaware of the cultural forces pressuring them away from a distinctively Christian style of life.

I have suggested, then, that in our culture, and in view of youth culture's trends, Christian education with youth must give attention to

> *extending youth's references points for decisions beyond the now*
>
> *relating value ideas to a Christian understanding of God and His purposes*
>
> *guiding youth to discover the reality of Christian faith by personal experience*
>
> *guiding youth to consciously evaluate values expressed in their decisions.*

Implximations for youth ministry

A person structuring an educational ministry with youth must make several basic decisions. Two are particularly significant. The first choice is one between attempting to "reduce the pervasiveness of adolescent society, and returning to a state in which each boy and girl responds principally to parents' demands" or to "take the adolescent society as given, and then use it."[4] Put simply, the choice is between *fighting youth culture* or *working within it*.

Actually, no such choice exists. We *have* to work with youth as they are. Horrocks points out that "excessive and uninvited adult intrusion into the adolescent peer world becomes highly non-facilitative and interferes with some of the most basic functions of the peer group as the adolescent wants and needs it to be."[5] Any attempt to force youth to accept the adult world-view breeds only resistance and rebellion, and distorts the positive contribution the peer group can make to the maturing personality. Not only this, but the Christian must affirm that believers are called to live *in* the world, not to withdraw from it. The world youth now live in (and must be equipped to live in) is the kind of world our whole society is fast becoming! The Christian in any culture must come to grips with his world, and learn to express the reality of Jesus Christ within it — and to it.

A second decision has to do with the relationship between adults and youth. Will the adults who minister seek a superior/subordinate relationship, and attempt to relate to teens as authority figures? Or will adults be persons *with* the teens? Will we grant young people equality of personhood — will we respect them, listen to them, and share ourselves with them as we ask them to listen to us and share themselves with us? Again, the Christian's response must be to extend true personhood to youth, to accept their differences and value them, and to extend to each the freedom to find his personal authority in God.

With these decisions made (made for us) (that youth culture and youth themselves will be accepted *as they are,* and that young people will be related to as *persons*), structural elements of a ministry with youth for our time can be sketched.

---

[4]This choice is suggested by Coleman (*Adolescent Society,* pp. 312-3) in relationship to strategy open to public schools.

[5]Horrocks, "Adolescent Attitudes and Goals," p. 25.

(1) *Ministry with youth must encourage questioning.* It has been the habit of Christian teaching to discourage questioning. Moore comments,

> The tragedy is that so many young adults never allow themselves to question beliefs or to be confronted with the searching demands of life in order that their religious cliches and moralisms can be fully examined. As Allport points out, there is probably no other region of the personality that claims "so many residues of childhood as . . . the religious attitudes of adults." For all too many young adults it is not the loss of faith which besets them but a superficial faith.[6]

If Christianity is a reality structure, it is vital that faith not be viewed as ideas planted in childhood and allowed to rest undisturbed till death! Instead, the issues of life and of the biblical revelation should be constantly probed and questioned, and deepening understandings tested in daily obedience to the call of God.

One serious finding of the college questionnaire mentioned in the first chapter was the limited awareness by many of the respondents of the many decisions youth do "make for now." Much of life seemed to the teens to be patterned for them by parents[7] or peers, and the only decisions which they were conscious of making for themselves were those involving what to do with leisure time!

Thus Christian education must structure occasions for searching and testing both life experiences and the Christian faith, and an attitude favoring such inquiry should pervade youth ministry.

(2) *Ministry with youth must stress direct experience.* The experiences of youth in suburban Christian culture are often limited, and the youth themselves isolated from the harsher realities of sinful human existence. A strong dose of reality can have a tremendous impact: "Cynicism and feelings of hopelessness alternate with renewed idealism as the repeated discovery of the discrepancy between the ideal and the real necessitates evaluation of the cultural institutions and of one's own values."[8]

Jack Mabley, editor and columnist, reports the impact of discovered reality on one conservative college student in a column, "What makes a student turn radical?"

---

[6]Moore, *Young Adult Generation,* p. 77.

[7]It's clear that youth ministry must also involve the parents in a thinking through of their role in helping youth toward responsible autonomy. This issue, too, is normally disregarded in structuring the ministry of the local church.

[8]*Normal Adolescence,* p. 89.

"I heard for the first time (on campus) some of the things about what makes a war, and who benefits. Near the campus is a ghetto. It was easy to see what dollars being spent on war could do in the slum. Everywhere I looked.there were autos, and here was this ugly ghetto. I was getting upset."

Day heard volunteers were needed at Chicago State mental hospital. "I didn't know what I expected to find in American hospitals," he said, "but the Chicago State shocked me. The stench almost knocked me over. I was helping in a geriatrics ward of about seventy women and there was very little I could do after changing sheets."

"Treatment was a joke. So-called medicine cabinets are filled with tranquilizers to be given in whatever doses are needed to knock someone out. The routine is endless, and all I saw were old women dragging around staring straight ahead or hunched over in metal chairs." . . .

He joined a peace march. "Two of my friends were beaten on the head. One is a beautiful girl who needed eight stitches in her head."

The change was clearly in motion now.

"I began to doubt everything I ever believed about morals or simple truth. When I heard stories about police brutality they were much more real to me."[9]

Before one reacts against the "radicalism" this kind of experience produced, it is far more important to ask, Why are so many young people allowed to grow up in our churches completely isolated from such experiences? Why do we avoid experiences which demand re-evaluation of the meaning of life, and which stimulate a personal commitment consistent with the Gospel? After all, it is God who calls us, if we love good, to hate evil, and to become a people "with cleansed hearts and real enthusiasm for doing kind things for others" (Titus 2:14 *The Living Bible*).

Certainly the Gospel calls for exposure of young people to the realities of our existence, and for opportunity to explore the meanings of such experiences in light of the Christian faith. This should be basic in our Christian education ministry.

In his study of beliefs, attitudes and values, Milton Rokeach, social psychologist, delineates several factors which determine the centrality of beliefs; that is, their impact on our personality, decisions, and behavior. He sees these as most significant:

1. *Existential versus nonexistential beliefs.* Those directly concerning one's own existence and identity are assumed to have more functional connections.

---

[9]Jack Mabley, in the *Chicago Daily News*.

2. *Shared versus unshared beliefs about existence and identity.* Beliefs shared with others are assumed to have more functional connections and consequences.

3. *Derived versus underived beliefs.* Beliefs grown from direct encounter with the object of belief are assumed to have more functional connections and consequences.[10]

Thus Christian education needs to stress learning situations which challenge the very identity of youth as Christians; learning situations in which they can share a direct encounter with the world that is, and share a personal response in terms of the reality portrayed in the Word.

Far too long we have called youth inside church walls to talk about our faith. Today we must move with youth, *as* the church, out into the world, to test the reality of our faith against the facts of human life and existence.

(3) *Ministry with youth must build on the "lived moment."* This concept of University of Chicago professor Ross Snyder is of great significance.[11] It asserts both the validity of the youth life-style, and the possibility of using the "lived moment" as the starting point in Christian education.

It is important to note that the "lived moment" includes its meanings. It is not just raw sensation. Snyder says that "interpreting firsthand experience is an important part of living it."[12] In his book Snyder suggests a number of ways to accomplish this interpretation. One particularly is helpful to us here, in focusing youth's awareness of values.

The first step Snyder suggests is to "describe as fully as possible exactly what happened *as it happened.*"[13] This description includes what went on inside us — the feelings we had as the situation developed as well as the objective data we perceived.

A second step is to *name* what happened. Snyder asks, "What *kind* of transaction was going on here? What would I name it? What made this the kind of lived moment it was?"

---

[10]Milton Rokeach, *Beliefs, Attitudes, and Values,* p. 5.
[11]Ross Snyder, *Young People and Their Culture* (New York: Abingdon Press, 1969).
[12]*Ibid.,* p. 33.
[13]*Ibid.,* p. 82.

It is natural for the conservative believer[14] to go on now to measure his experience and interpretation of it by Scripture's reality revealed, and to test that reality against his experiences. What really did happen in me? What insights does the Word hold? What new dimensions of understanding does this open up? What patterns of response are suggested?

Thus any experience becomes an occasion for Christian education: for testing and probing values and reality.

The experience may be that of a group of young teens who live a current musical recording, who discuss and analyze the sounds and words and meaning, and who express what hearing the song said in them. They may then turn to a Psalm, to experience its impact, and relate the two. What does each affirm about the world, about themselves, about relationship with God and others? Which is reality? To which will they commit themselves? Which will they value?

The experience may be a visit to a slum or hospital, a simulated quarrel between sisters, a shared involvement in ministry through a rural VBS. The experience may be anything — anything which involves youth in direct encounter, which encourages questioning, which is explored and related as a lived moment to the reality portrayed and promised in Scripture.

The experience may be anything — but it must challenge youth to a Christian commitment which is more than words; which is in fact a commitment to live and to test and to respond to Christ as He speaks, across the lived moment, to them.

Directions

I've suggested in this chapter that we need to understand and to accept the life-style of youth today, and that our ministry with youth should be shaped to communicate the message of Christ within that framework.

Essentially, this means accepting many of the differences of youth from us as valid expressions of life — as valid as our own.

---

[14]Snyder has a third step; using the insights he has gained to make generalizations about the *nature* of persons, of God, of love, etc. I have serious problems with the theological presuppositions of this step, and believe we must replace it with evaluating insights by Scripture.

It means approaching Scripture as *reality structure,* not emphasizing its nature as truth system.

It means placing priority in youth ministry on direct experience and involvement with youth in the challenging issues of life.

It means, for conservative evangelical Christianity at any rate, a jolting shift from programs packaged for the faithful few, who show up Sunday evenings for "youth meetings" to sit isolated from life and skirt around problems they never feel free enough to discuss honestly. It means a jolting shift from Sunday school lessons neatly outlined to communicate the doctrinal ideas we love (themselves torn from their context-of-life in Scripture). It means a willingness to meet with youth as equal persons, to go with them into their world and ours, and to put God's Word to the test by daring to act on it, rather than merely talk about it. And it means sharing openly with youth the impact of our experience in the world; submitting ourselves and our perceptions to the living authority of a Scripture we find authoritative by experiencing the reality it portrays.

To communicate a living faith to youth in a world like youth's today, we have no other choice.

PROBE
case histories
discussion questions
thought-provokers

1. Communication across generations is always distorted unless there is mutual respect for persons and for differences. When one person insists another think and feel exactly as he does about everything, terrible barriers to understanding are erected.
   Examine the following poem, written by a young friend of mine, Rick Christianson, and ask yourself: What is he talking about? Who is he thinking of? What are his feelings? Why does he feel as he does?

   My name is Allan

   now you know my name
   do you know what lies behind it
   what I am like
     and do you have the right
     to judge and preach
   when you live within yourself
                 outside of me

   Are you threatened

     by apparent loss of ideals of respect
                 authority

eking out delusion
that sincerity is all you need
that this is the essence of belief
                    in human value

You are sincerely wrong

to continue in your alley
of naive enlightenment
    subjecting others to your
    position of assumed authority
your reputation stumbles
surviving on what the fear of others
                    can do for you

With law and force

we make the body conform
but it's the mind
    you never control a thinking mind
your followers are controlled
when you control emotion
    set an atmosphere they can suck on
    and they follow
up and down the hills
of your manipulation until they fall
                into a deepened grave

Then to prove concern

[you have to try to prove it
it's never simply understood]
you have a cortège
of professional mourning
    a salute to hide your empty eyes
    and leave a flame to burn
symbol of a sacrifice
                not yours

2. *Balance and extremes.* In this chapter I suggested that the Christian, whether youth or adult, needs to develop a balanced concern for the now. By this I mean that we all need to recognize the importance of the present (and not be, as the old saying has it, "so heavenly minded that we're of no earthly good"), but guide our life within the present by the total reality — past, present, and future — revealed in God's Word.
Perhaps we can visualize the place given "now" experiences in persons' lives by drawing a continuum, each end of which represents an extreme (and distorted) view. If we do this, we'll find the older generation *tending toward* the right of center, and the younger generation *tending toward* the left. But most individuals in either generation will *not* be on the extreme ends.

---

only the "now" is important	*only* the future (or the past) is important.

Role-of-"now"-in-life continuum

To make this continuum conception more clear, take a look at the following expressions of viewpoint, and locate each where you believe it belongs along the continuum.

(1) Thirty years ago, one evening at 7:16, in the basement of old North Church, I became a Christian.

(2) I saved my money for thirteen years, skipping lunch and vacations, to have enough for this trip.

(3) That was last week. Now Jan's the one who turns me on.

(4) Did I tell you what the Lord showed me this morning?

(5) Tomorrow may never come, honey. Tonight is really all we have.

(6) You shouldn't take on so, friend. After all, you'll be together again in heaven.

(7) I really want to drop out of college and spend my time evangelizing. This going on to seminary — why, that's years!

(8) And when I realized the Lord really is coming, any time, I took a good look at the way I was living.

(9) Evangelism is getting people settled on where they will spend eternity.

(10) Evangelism is helping people turn their lives over to Christ right now.

With the various expressions ranged along the continuum, you may find it interesting to ask yourself, which part of the continuum seems to you to provide the most balanced, most biblical view of life?

3. The continuum concept helps to make more clear two important points about thinking of ministering *within* youth culture's framework.

(1) It helps us avoid dichotomizing. That is, in describing youth's understandings of life, we are not thinking primarily of the *extremes*. It's not as if an *either/or* choice is involved: "Either see life as youth see it (with youth characterized at the extreme end) or reject the 'sins of the world' and see life as we adults do!"

Neither youth nor adult needs to misunderstand the other's feelings and understandings of life, or characterize them as extreme.

38

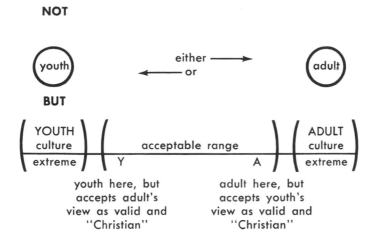

NOT

youth ← either → adult
or

BUT

(YOUTH culture extreme) (acceptable range
Y   A) (ADULT culture extreme)

youth here, but
accepts adult's
view as valid and
"Christian"

adult here, but
accepts youth's
view as valid and
"Christian"

Thinking in a continuum framework, each can begin to accept the fact that there is a wide range of mutually acceptable views which permit each to respect the other. If we avoid thinking that anyone who differs from us is automatically on the unacceptable, opposite extreme, we will be able to communicate much more helpfully with each other.

(2) It helps us see how to *approach* each group when communicating Christian truth. For instance, evangelism of those somewhere on the *left* side of the continuum above is most likely to be received if our initial presentation focuses on Christ as Savior of this present life, who enters our personalities to make life meaningful and joyful. Evangelism of those toward the *right* side of the continuum above is most likely to be received if we focus on Christ as the Savior who assures of eternal life in heaven.

Ultimately, evangelism finds its balance by leading believers to discover that both are true: Christ came to be our Savior in time *and* eternity. And Christian growth should bring us to a balanced life, in harmony with God's revelation of total reality through the Word.

But where persons are in their ways of looking at and experiencing life determines our initial approach. This is why it is so important to understand youth and to communicate with them in their frame of reference — not to demand that they accept ours before we can even begin to speak of Jesus.

4. You can develop other continuums to help you analyze other aspects of youth culture difference. For example, here is a continuum line on the role of experience as "authority." Try to develop for

yourself a series of statements (as in PROBE 2, above) that you can fit along this line.

Only through personal experience can		Only through the wisdom of some authority
I know right/wrong, true/false.		can I know right/wrong, true/false.

5. *Collateral reading*
   Ross Snyder's book, *Young People and Their Culture* (New York: Abingdon Press, 1969), is very helpful in sketching significant ways youth perceive life, and important aspects of youth's distinctive culture.
   My book, *Is God Necessary?* (Chicago: Moody Press, 1970) shows how basic Christian truth can be communicated with an approach that accepts and works within youth's feelings and viewpoints.

3

christian "education" of youth

In a recent book on the anthropology of education, John Middleton points out that "education is the learning of culture. The various activities that we in Western industrialized societies refer to under this rubric are only part of the educational process." Indeed, "the major parts of any educational program concern the inculcation and understanding of cultural symbols, moral values, sanctions, and cosmological beliefs. In our own society we separate out these parts from the 'formal' education. . . ."[1]

Our tendency to think of "education" merely as the teaching of concepts or skills in the classroom has led to tragic results. And we are forced to note that, no matter how much we stress truths dealing with, for instance, personal evangelism, and no matter how often we meet in church to role-play witnessing situations and to memorize approaches, neither youth nor adult is likely to respond with an enthusiastic witness in daily life! Somehow a classroom education, isolated from life, has succeeded in communicating ideas, but has had little effect on values, on personality, and on behavior.

But how effective the general youth culture has been in shaping the thoughts and feelings of our churched youth — even when it runs directly opposite to our classroom teaching from the Bible![2]

It is certainly time to rethink our approach to ministry with youth, to recognize the weaknesses of the classroom's intellectualization of our

---

[1]John Middleton, ed., *From Child to Adult* (Garden City, N.Y.: Natural History Press, 1970) p. xiii.

[2]I refer here to such things as relativism (It's wrong for me, but it may be all right for him; each person has to do what's right for him) as contrasted to a biblical absolutism (Right and wrong are defined, and revealed, by God, who knows them accurately). Tragically, although many Christians recognize the biblical viewpoint when it is presented, the "feel" and their lives express the cultural viewpoint, which has been more effectively communicated to them through the culture than we have communicated the biblical through words.

faith, and to seek to communicate life in Christ through an education viewed as "the learning of culture" rather than "the learning of ideas." To do this, to build a Christian education that communicates life and living, we will need to focus on the locations where that kind of learning takes place — locations marked by depth of interpersonal relationships, and shared "real" experiences.

I have spent most of the first two chapters sketching elements of "youth culture" — parts of the pattern of values and beliefs and feelings about life which increasingly characterize each fresh generation of our young people.[3] And I've suggested that understanding certain key aspects of youth culture is very important to us, giving us insight into more fruitful approaches to communicating the Gospel.

For instance, two months ago a friend told me of a Sunday school class that she attends with her fiancé, but which completely turns her off. The teacher is well-prepared, speaks interestingly, is concerned about the college students he teaches, and says nothing with which she disagrees. He has been giving good, accurate, Bible teaching. But somehow she feels totally frustrated by the class.

I told her I thought I could tell her—without knowing the person or the class — something about the kids who came, and then explain why she feels as she does. I suggested that the class is (1) made up almost completely of freshmen and sophomores who (2) are all from very traditional, conservative churches. She was surprised that my guesses were accurate. She and her fiancé are the only upper classmen present, and all are from the background I described.

We then talked about communication patterns that "fit" the cultures of "adult" and "youth" generations.

The adult generation is oriented to answers, and tends to seek a specific solution or point of view which satisfies. To get to that solution the adult characteristically *eliminates* alternatives, usually without feeling the need to explore them fully. Thus a person teaching the Bible from this orientation seeks to move in a straight line toward a previously worked out solution, arguing rather logically, and rejecting alternative views quickly and decisively. The process looks something like the cone below; it's a process of *narrowing down to the right answer:*

---

[3]There are many more aspects of youth culture which might have been mentioned but were not. Some of these will be touched on in later chapters of this book.

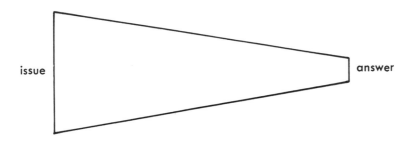

And once the "right answer" is found, the quest is over, the seeker satisfied.

The youth generation is oriented to questions, and tends to want to explore all points of view. To find a solution that satisfies a young person, rather than eliminating alternatives, will tend to *generate more* alternatives and develop a need to explore them all as carefully as possible. Thus a person teaching the Bible from this orientation would seek to move outward, keeping open to new insights and ideas, holding off decision until alternative views are explored, trusting and expecting the Holy Spirit to guide to living and vital truth. The process is the reverse of the one above; it's a process of *opening outward to the right answer:*

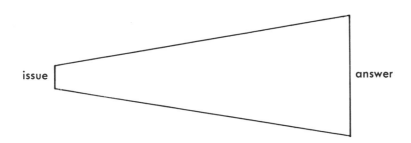

And once the "right answer" is found, it needs to be tested in experience, while yet holding open the future in prospect of an even better solution.

It was on the basis of this understanding of communication patterns that I guessed the class makeup. For young people from conservative, traditional backgrounds, who have to a large degree been cut off from contact with their peer group in school, will usually feel as uncomfortable in the "opening" pattern as the average adult. *But once out of the home environment, such youth tend over two or three years to shift toward the general youth culture's orientations!* So upperclassmen, even those from similar backgrounds, would tend to be unhappy with the kind of class described.

It is important to note here that *both* orientations and approaches can lead a person to a biblical view of life, and to a commitment to Scripture's revelation of reality. One approach is not "more Christian" than the other. But one *is* in harmony with youth culture's pattern; the other in harmony with adult culture.

Often the responses persons make to our attempts at ministry are made more to our approach than to our message. Thus the teen who was so enthusiastic about the new youth room in his church because it had a private entrance that avoided the sanctuary and "you don't have to get any of that horrible atmosphere!" wasn't necessarily being "unspiritual." It's far more likely that he was simply expressing something he felt but could not have explained even to himself; that the worship and preaching that took place in the sanctuary were in a pattern that did not communicate to him. Something in his personality, shaped by youth's culture, blocked his hearing and his response.

Approaching ministry

The fact that differences in culture make necessary different approaches to persons is only part of the reason that I suggested in the preceding chapter that we need to restructure youth ministry. It is true that approaching Scripture as a reality structure, modifying teacher/learner roles, etc., actually gives a closer fit to youth culture than do the approaches we now take. It is also true that placing priority on direct experience rather than the classroom discussion of ideas also fits youth. And certainly meeting youth as coequals (rather than speaking down authoritatively to them) is a necessary adjustment if we are to be heard at all. But these same changes in approach to ministry are demanded by that different understanding of *education* which I outlined in this chapter's introduction.

We must begin to think of Christian education as the teaching and learning of Christian faith as culture — not merely as the communication of true information about life and the Bible.

In my writings I cannot break away from the first comments in Scripture on communicating the biblical faith (Deut. 6:5-7). This passage declares that the communication of faith is marked by several utterly basic characteristics. First is that the faith be experienced as a life commitment by adult models. Second is the expression of that faith-life in words. Third is communication of that faith-life in both concrete and abstract form, through adult modeling and verbal teaching in the context of shared experience. The biblical faith has always been meant to be communicated as a culture, as a total way-of-life, in the context of personal relationships and shared experiences.

> You shall love the Lord your God with all your heart, and with all your soul, and with all your might. And these words which I command you this day shall be upon your heart; and you shall teach them diligently to your children, and shall talk of them when you sit in your house, and when you walk by the way, and when you lie down, and when you rise (Deut. 6:5-7 *RSV*).

Strikingly, this is the way *any* culture is communicated. Persons who understand and are committed to experience life a certain way communicate their understandings to others by expressing their commitment verbally and through their lives, as they live together and share life's experiences.

To communicate as a life a faith that involves a distinctive way of understanding the world and ourselves through God's revelation, we dare not divorce words from experiences, or intellectualize truths which we must feel as whole persons.

Meyer Fortes, in "Education in Taleland," points out the difference in psychological emphasis between an education that takes place naturally, through the ongoing experiences of life, and a training which takes place in classrooms rather than "real" situations.

> The training situation demands atomic modes of response; the real situation requires organic modes of response. In constructing a training situation we envisage a skill or observance as an end-product at the perfection of which we aim and therefore arrange it so as to evoke only motor or perceptual practice. Affective or motivational factors are eliminated or ignored. In the real situation behavior is compounded of affect, interest and motive, as well as perceptual and motor functions. Learning becomes purposive. Every advance in knowledge or

> skill is pragmatic, directed to achievement of a result then and there, as well as adding to a previous level of adequacy.[4]

Put simply, Fortes is saying that when we learn in the context of life we learn as whole persons, with our motives and desires shaped in our learning as well as our understanding, but that training, whether in working arithmetic problems or mastering Bible doctrine, has little power to mold motives, and thus little power to shape personalities.

But it is toward just this goal, the reshaping of personalities into the image of Jesus Christ, that Christian education must be directed! The man of God is not the person who can recite the Word of God for hours on end, but the man who lives the Word, motivated by a deepening love for Jesus Christ. So Paul writes to the young Timothy, "See that they look up to you because you are an example to them in your speech and behavior, in your love and faith and sincerity" (1 Tim. 4:12, 13 *Phillips*). So too John reminds us, "Obedience is the test of whether we really live 'in God' or not. The life of a man who professes to be living in God must bear the stamp of Christ" (1 John 2:5, 6 *Phillips*).

And so this book, which is based on the conviction that youth ministry must be redesigned, not on the model of Western class-room "education," but on the model of culture communication, life to life. And so too our task in the body of this book, to see *how* we can build a ministry with youth in the local church that can lead a generation to "bear the stamp of Christ."

Design for ministry

I've suggested that the classroom model of education, dominant in secular Western culture, is not a helpful model for the church. This is, however, a model on which most of church ministry has been developed. And so we desperately need another model, developed on a broader, culture-communication concept of education. Such a model must provide central roles for the three basic elements of culture communication outlined on page 45: there must be those who model the faith-life; there must be expression of faith-life's understanding in words; there must be communication of faith-life in "real life" situations.

The diagram on page 47 (Figure 1) shows the process through which these elements are blended into a plan for ministry with

---

[4]Meyer Fortes, "Education in Taleland," *From Child to Adult,* ed. John Middleton (Garden City, New York: Doubleday and Company, Inc., 1970) p. 38.

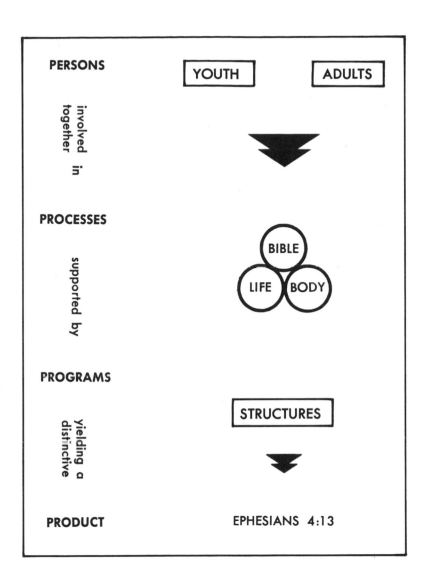

FIGURE 1
MODEL FOR YOUTH MINISTRY

youth. And this diagram shows those elements of the youth ministry which I believe must be understood and lived by the youth worker.

Persons The new model for youth ministry views youth and adults involved together in several processes. But a number of important questions and issues need to be settled before such involvement can take place. For instance, we need to explore what the young people we hope to so involve are like. By this I don't mean so much the marks of youth culture as the distinctive aspects of adolescence as a time of life.

Youth are moving in adolescence through a variety of developmental experiences, gaining in intellectual powers, struggling with a growing yet uncertain self-image, reaching out toward emotional independence from parents, learning new ways of relating to other youth of the same and of the opposite sex, etc. These developmental characteristics mark adolescence off as a special and stressful time of life, and significantly distinguish youth from adulthood. What I am getting at is simply this: while the basic processes of Christian ministry with persons cuts across the generations, youth cannot be treated in the same way as adults. Young people need to be understood as they are: growing, learning, discovering, suffering — all in their special ways. So when we plan an educational ministry with youth, it is important to take time to understand *them*; individually, of course, but as individuals who share many common "growing up" characteristics.

So in this book, chapters 4 through 6 examine youth as persons, sketching some of the special aspects of adolescence that one ministering with them needs to keep in mind.

At the same time, however, one ministering with youth needs to understand his own role as "leader" and the relationships between himself and youth which facilitate ministry. Among the questions that must be answered here are those relating to the nature of that authority which youth recognize and to which they respond; the biblical concept of leadership; relationship with the group and individuals; the counseling relationship; how to establish and maintain a relationship of mutual respect, etc.

These issues are dealt with in chapters 7 through 9, and a portrait of the leader and his ways of leading is drawn. In the long run, the effectiveness of ministry with youth may depend more on understanding and accepting who youth are, on who the leader is, and on the relationship between them, than on any other factors.

Processes Three primary concerns for ministry with youth are highlighted in the ministry model, and reflect my conviction that youth and adults must be involved together in Scripture, in building relationships as members of the Body of Christ, and in living Christ's life in the world.

The chapters on Scripture (10, 11) explore the meaning of the Bible as God's revelation of reality, which believers are invited to experience in Christ, and shows how we can communicate the Bible as His fresh, life-pervading Word.

The chapters on Body relationships (12, 13) explore the biblical concept of the believer as joined with others, and committed to others, in Christ's Body. They show how the Body functions to support the communication of Christian faith as life. The Body of Christ, functioning as Scripture reveals, is an utterly essential means the Spirit of God uses to transform and to imprint on human personality the stamp of Christ.

The chapters on life (14-16) explore ways in which commitment to Christ and His Way is expressed in the world, in witness and in service. The Word and the Body, when focused together on life, support the development of a distinctive Christian culture, a community of believers who find their citizenship in heaven and who, as ambassadors in a foreign world, live in joyful allegiance to a Lord whose ways are not the ways of men around them.

Programming Only when the persons and the processes involved in Christian education of youth are understood can we deal, in chapters 17 and 18, with programming for the local church. Thus this topic, which typically has become the main concern of many books and most ministries, is reserved for the subordinate role it deserves. And the criteria by which programming for ministry in the church is to be evaluated is a simple one: "Does this support, or inhibit, the involvement of youth and adults in the central processes of ministry?" In these chapters, too, examples and principles for developing programs that will be means, not ends, are given, and the role of such normal features of church life as socials critically examined.

Product Finally, in chapter 19 the product of a restructured youth ministry is reviewed, and the whole approach related to the biblical imperatives that must direct our thinking, and give all our ministry its purpose.

When cultures collide

So far I've spoken of two cultures (youth and adult) and implied a third (a "Christian" culture, a community of believers who live within a society but express in their lives values and understandings which are derived from Scripture, not from the world of men around them). In speaking of the first two I may have been misunderstood as defending youth's culture and demanding that adults accept — or even adopt — American youth culture's way of understanding and living life. I must admit that many of youth's ways of seeing life, holistically rather than dichotomistically, experientially rather than intellectually, etc., appeal to me. But I do *not* suggest that all adults must begin to feel life the way teens and twenties do. I only suggest that adults seek to understand the ways youth think and feel, and accept these ways as valid for them. I do not suggest that we must in any sense accept the *extreme* extensions of youth culture's approach to life. In fact, the relativism and existential hedonism toward which this culture tends must be decisively rejected in favor of a different, biblical perception of life. But so must many categories in which adults view life, when these categories are not in harmony with reality as revealed by God's Word. No, ultimately the goal of Christian education is not to accept cultures uncritically as they stand, but to shape within every culture a distinctively Christian expression of it, with those elements that have been twisted into strange shapes by sins awful artistry brought again into harmony with Christ.

When the Bible speaks of the lost as borne along on this world's ideas of living, and lost in a world of illusion (Eph. 2), it points out that we stand in need of both individual and cultural transformation; of a drawing together into a company of persons committed to Jesus Christ to work out, in individual and corporate life, the divine transformation.

Coming at Christian education from the point of culture is not a surrender to this world's ways of life; it is a challenge to express the life and love of God while living *in* this world, by being distinctively not *of* it.

A cultural approach, then, suggests three important things.

(1) *Understanding culture guides our approach to persons.* As I stressed in chapter 2, when we understand the ways persons and groups think and feel and experience life, we know better how to introduce the Word. We know better in terms of content which

viewpoint to emphasize (as was illustrated in the preceding chapter in PROBE 3), and we know better in terms of method how to proceed (as illustrated in this chapter with the two cones showing "narrowing" and "expanding" ways of seeking truth (page 43). So understanding significant cultural features makes definite differences in the ways we shape our ministries to reach people.

(2) *Understanding culture broadens our concept of education.* When we see culture as a whole complex of feelings and understandings of life, with ideas and beliefs and values and attitudes and behaviors *all* vitally significant, we see the weakness of an education that majors only on communication of beliefs and ideas. And we see the weakness of a Christian education that builds around sermons and classrooms, with adult "teachers" telling youth what to believe without sharing their lives.

A look around us at our churches and our young people reminds us all too stridently that the world is more effective in communicating its way of life than we are in communicating God's. We shouldn't be surprised. Since the creation of man, culture, as a complex of values and beliefs and understanding of life, has been communicated life-to-life, bound tightly in close interpersonal relationships and shared experiences. Today both adult and young believers in America are far more "American" in values and perceptions than "Christian." While the biblical faith has been talked at us, we have been involved in living life with others whose attitudes, values, and behaviors are hardly Christian. While we've worked in churches to impress the mind with biblical truth, the personality has been shaped through relationships with those (both saved and unsaved) who hardly have God's word "in their hearts."

The response we must make to this is not withdrawal from association with non-Christians and from believers who don't make our grade. Nor need it be redoubled effort to teach more doctrine.

The response must be to develop an approach to ministry that involves the carriers of culture.

To develop an approach to ministry that centers on building relationships with those who *do* have His word in their hearts, and who thus can both model and speak it as, together with young and growing Christians, they seek to build a transforming community, a true church, in which the Word of God is not only heard but lived. Understanding the carriers of culture gives us the direction we need to restructure ministry with youth.

(3) *Understanding culture helps us understand our goals.* For too long Christian ministry focused its efforts on the individual. Certainly it is individuals who are, and become, Christian. It is individuals who grow in the faith. But to transmit and nurture the faith-life, we should *not* gear ministry to individual response alone. We should not ask individuals to leave their groups and swim upstream *alone*. When we do, we violate something basic in the human personality. And we go against revealed reality.

How tragic when our efforts in Christian education are focused on telling young people, "Go witness," and then we leave each one to move, alone, into his high school world, charging him to fight against all that that society supports. God lays on us many imperatives. But He does not ask us to live out His Word alone.

God created His church — not as a place where lonely people might go weekly to hide their loneliness and failures from each other and talk of a better world, but as a community of believers who love Jesus Christ and one another, and who share their lives so meaningfully that all support and minister to the rest. The church is to be a culture, a community where transformation and obedience are supported and motivated by the sharing of life among those who experience the Word and can express its reality in their flesh and blood.

It ought to be clear from Scripture that the Church of Jesus Christ is to be a culture, God's colony on earth, and that in the context of personal relationships that love creates within His Body, Christ Himself works His change in men.

And so the goal of our ministry with youth is not merely to reach individuals, to establish Joe in Bible study, or to see Karen off to college in God's will. It is to build a community of youth and adults who are together committed to Jesus Christ and His understanding of life, and who seek daily to reproduce in themselves the reality His Word reveals.

Conclusions

Can a distinctive Christian culture be created? And among youth? Will teens and twenties desert youth culture's view of life when these are out of harmony with life in Christ?

Surely!

We see examples in many places. We see it in a current symbol of the Jesus People; a simple poster advertised in the Hollywood

Free Paper of a hand with one finger raised, symbolizing Jesus as the *only* way to life. Will youth desert their questioning and probing, their unwillingness to commit themselves to one way in this world of many ways? Thousands of youth in California and across the country answer, "Yes! Jesus is the only way. Come live by His Word."

We see the power of a counter-culture in Life's report of youth revival in Rye, New York, where teens reject their culture's views of sex and work and even its insistence on examining the many options life always opens up. This group of kids even rejects the newspapers, because "newspapers lead to relative thoughts which poison the mind. We just feed our minds by imbibing the great truths of the Word, so we can be *positively* positive!"[5]

When cultures collide, something new can be formed.

But when in a spate of words we hurl an intellectualized faith against a culture, the words, even when they draw assent, seldom transform.

And so we must move on to restructure our youth ministries, shaping them to build and to communicate a way of life.

PROBE

case histories
discussion questions
thought-provokers

1. I'm aware that when I speak in this chapter, arguing for an educational system built on a cultural rather than classroom model, it's difficult to grasp. Perhaps an illustration will help, one you can think through yourself before going on to see why I feel it's a good illustration. Here it is.

    The best example of a cultural approach to education may be found in the way a child learns his native language.
    The corresponding classroom approach is, of course, the way a school child is taught a foreign one.

    Now, what do you think are the *significant* differences in these two approaches to learning?

---

[5]Jane Howard, "The Groovy Christians of Rye, New York" *Life,* May 14, 1971.

NOTES

If you've jotted down your thoughts, I'd like to share mine now. The child learning his own language learns it naturally, by imitation, in a context where he and others use it constantly. He learns it by being fully involved in situations where it is being used, by *needing* it to get along. Every tone, inflection, emotional nuance, is felt and experienced as well as understood. The child learning a foreign language in the classroom has no multiple models, and learns especially by drill. He does not use the language in life situations where he and others are fully involved, and the tones, inflections, and emotional cues to meaning are lost on him. He feels more at home *reading* the language than *speaking* it, and although he can decode it if given enough time and such tools as dictionaries, it is not something he can comfortably live.

What I've been suggesting in this illustration is that we need to develop ministries with youth that teach our faith as a child's native language is taught. Ministries through which youth can learn naturally the realities of the biblical faith, seeing that reality in others, becoming fully involved in situations where that faith is lived. Every truth, every doctrine, is to be felt and experienced as well as understood. When one learns this way, personality is shaped. Where one learns as in the classroom, by drill, the learner is not being equipped to *live* what is taught.

Christian education with youth needs to involve, and minister to, the *whole* person.

2. A few years ago Dave Roper, minister to youth in California's Peninsula Bible Church, sent at my request a tape recording describing how he motivated young people to witness. Here is a transcription of his tape. As you read, check out his approach by measuring it against the three *essentials* of *culture-communication* given on page 45.

HOW TO MOVE TEENS TO WITNESS
by Dave Roper

We have taught classes on evangelism, we have scolded, we have pushed; we have done everything that we could possibly do, and we've never had any kids doing personal nose-to-nose evangelism until about two years ago. What forced the issue was that we finally decided that we had to start taking kids out with us — literally hanging them up and sticking them out there and *making* them witness. So we started using Campus Crusade's Community Surveys. We'd go out to the park and down to the beach and over on to Stanford Campus and Foothill Junior College Campus. We took different kids with us as we had opportunity and just witnessed to people "cold turkey." Kids began to trust the Lord, and it was just amazing. In a period of about three months, we had over fifty college and high school kids that accepted the Lord; it was really exciting to see what the Lord was doing. The same thing has happened again this year. We're finding that some of our own kids now are taking their friends out, and they're beginning to survey and witness on their own.

At first I was not much in favor of Campus Crusade's materials, but I am gaining a greater appreciation each day for their approach. We just teach kids to memorize the Four Spiritual Laws and we use their procedure right down the line with very little modification. All I can say is that it's done the job; we have kids who are vital and they are effective in their personal evangelism. They're fruitful, and this is just a real encouragement to all of us. We have had at Log Cabin in the past six months about seventeen or eighteen boys trust the Lord.

It has been due totally to the ministry of our own young people. I frankly know of no other way to motivate teens to witness than to go out with them. What we do the first couple of times is let them sit in and then about halfway through a presentation we'll turn to one of the kids and say, "Now Joe, what does Jesus Christ mean to you?" Kids turn pea green and try to fall through the floor, but they *have* to witness and they stammer out something and it is usually pretty bad and it comes out pretty heavy and not too effective, but at least they have said something! They come away from there all excited — "Man, that's great! Let's do it again!" About three or four times like that and they're ready to take someone else out. We tell them after about the second trip out that we want them to memorize the Four Laws, and we drill them to make sure they know what they are talking about before we turn them loose. We also want to build into these kids the whole concept of their spiritual life and the witness of the indwelling Christ through them. Otherwise, it just becomes another effort in the flesh.

So we find that there are two corollary points that are kept in balance all the way through, and that is, not only do we want them out there witnessing to their friends, but we want their witness to be the overflow of a life that God has filled.

3. There have been many statements of goals of Christian education of youth. Here are three sets of goals stated by well-known evangelical Christian educators. In view of what we've been seeing in these first three chapters, how would you evaluate each set of goals? How would you modify them? What would *your* list of goals for ministry with youth look like if you stated them at this time?

GOALS OF YOUTH WORK

1. Get into Word and prayer
2. Get into Christian service for testimony
3. Relate to the Body of Christ (including $, gifts)
4. Train for leadership
5. Train for Christian home
6. Know how to find the will of God
7. Develop social and mental responsibility
8. Prepare for worldwide Christian service
9. Develop creativity
10. Provide activity in cooperation with home, school

Rev. Howard Hendricks[6]

1. Personal relationship with teens
2. Respect for God's Word as relevant, contemporary
3. Develop devotional life

---

[6]Howard G. Hendricks, from class notes, "Christian Education of Youth," Dallas Theological Seminary, 1961.

4. Lead to worship
5. Self-discovery connected with moral living
6. Guidance in doctrine, understanding their faith
7. Witness
8. Put God first in their lives

Rev. Donald Aultman[7]

1. Christian conversion
2. Christian knowledge and conviction
3. Christian living
4. Christian attitudes and appreciations
   (God, meaning of life, self, others, world)
5. Christian worship
6. Christian service

Rev. Elmer Towns[8]

---

[7]Donald S. Aultman, *Guiding Youth,* (Cleveland, Tennessee: Pathway Press, 1965), pp. 71, 72.

[8]Elmer Towns, *Teaching Teens* (Grand Rapids: Baker Book House, 1965).

Part Two

PERSONS IN MINISTRY

YOUTH AS PERSONS

ADULTS AS LEADERS

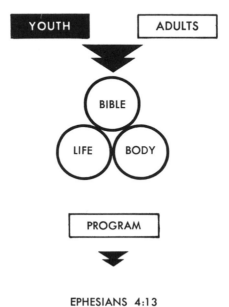

EPHESIANS 4:13

YOUTH AS PERSONS

4

the emerging self

I no longer know myself as a teenager. I remember some things. I remember a shyness that made me cross the street or look away if I met a girl I knew on the streets of our small town. I remember embarrassment when, all too regularly, a giant pimple would form on the tip of my nose, announcing its coming with hourly reddening until the whole pustule had formed. I remember the clumsiness that frustrated me in sports; for all my six-feet-two. And I remember quiet walks at night, moved by the pattern of warm and cool shadows to reverent wonder at the world, at being.

I remember, but I no longer feel these things. Somehow today I'm a different person, shaped by youth's experiences, of course, but no longer able to enter fully into the frustrations and the joys I knew.

And there's no way back.

All the texts and readings on adolescent development, all the theories of adolescence, all the empirical studies, can never recreate for me a world through which I — and most of you who read — have passed.

Yet this is what we need far more than grasp of theory and facility with psychological terms. We need a sympathy that grows from knowing deep within that youth is a special time of life; from seeing beneath behavior and quickly flying words to understand, accept, and care about persons who are emerging from childhood, changing shape before us, and becoming adult.

So in these chapters on the young as persons I hope to avoid the clinical and the impersonal, to build a portrait we can feel together rather than an academic sketch that may well sharpen insight, but all too often treats the teen as object, stripped of his humanness, stretched on a sterile slide for our examination.

To me this approach is important. Whatever else we say of ministry with youth, we must insist that every teen be valued, respected, and in every way related to as fully human, a person we are privileged in Christ to love.

Framing our thinking about youth as persons around the concept of the "emerging self" has, of course, much precedent. David L.

Lehman, summarizing sixty years of study by European and American psychologists, suggests agreement that "the fundamental task of adolescence is 'ego identity' or 'self-definition'."[1] This, of course, does not mean that youth entering adolescence have no sense of "self." Various writers express their understanding of what happens in young people during the adolescent years in different ways, that together sketch a picture we ought to have in focus before going on to see how this process feels to those going through it.

Friedenberg calls the process self-definition. "Adolescence is the period during which a young person learns who he is, and what he really feels. It is the time during which he differentiates himself from his culture, though on the culture's terms. It is the age at which, by becoming a person in his own right, he becomes capable of deeply felt relationships to other individuals perceived clearly as such."[2] Douvan and Adelson express the same understanding in these words:

> Identity does not begin in adolescence. The child has been formulating and reformulating identities throughout his life. . . . At adolescence, however, the *commitment to an identity* becomes critical. During this period, the youngster must synthesize earlier identifications with personal qualities and relate them to social opportunities and the social ideals. Who the child is to be will be influenced (and in some cases determined) by what the environment permits and encourages.[3]

Thus identity-building is not unique to the years of youth, but it is of vital, lifetime importance. Adolescence does not "mark the birth of a 'new self,' but it is true that the achievement of self-identity is not fully realized until the conflicts and problems of the adolescent period have been lived through."[4]

Although it would be wrong to picture the teen years as marked only by storm and stress, it should be clear that coming to terms with who one is, and who one wants to be, is hardly conducive to great calm and stability. Particularly when all sorts of concerns exert pressures on the emerging personality. James Adams lists a

---

[1]David L. Lehman, "Current Thinking in Adolescent Psychology," *Readings in Adolescent Development,* ed. Harold W. Bernard (Scranton, Penn: International Textbook Co., 1969) p. 73.

[2]Edgar Friedenberg, *The Vanishing Adolescent* (Boston: Beacon Press, 1964) p. 9.

[3]Elizabeth Douvan & Joseph Adelson, *The Adolescent Experience* (New York: John Wiley & Sons, 1966) p. 14.

[4]William C. Bier, *The Adolescent: His Search for Understanding* (New York: Fordham University Press, 1963) p. 140.

number of problems that are felt by high schoolers as "the biggest personal problems which may be causing you some difficulty."[5] Problem categories (in order of frequency of mention) along with explanatory comments as to the types of problems which young people reported were these:

1. School — academic difficulties, extremely few negative comments about teachers
2. Interpersonal problems — getting along with one's peer group and other people
3. Maturity — recognition by others (mostly parents) and oneself
4. Emotions — lack of understanding one's emotions, moodiness, fluctuations
5. Work — finding a job, deciding on a vocation
6. Sports and recreation — athletics, dancing, driving, use of leisure time
7. Health — skin blemishes, weight problems, mental and physical health of self and family
8. Ethical and moral problems — in dating behavior, religion
9. Family — parents, siblings
10. Habits — smoking, drinking
11. Finances — personal financial needs, family, college
12. Unclassifiable problems
13. No answer
14. No problem — often stated apologetically

Strikingly, many of these are directly related to the question of the emerging self. What are my limits and abilities academically? Can I see myself as more advanced than others? Or a failure? Who am I in my relationships with others? Popular? A leader? Recognized as valuable and worthwhile? Am I ready now to take responsibility for myself? Or do Mom and Dad still see me as a child? Why do I feel so uncertain, so moody? Am I really an unstable person? Can I make up my own mind? Make my own way?

Young people emerging into adulthood have to ask these questions, and give at least tentative answers, during adolescence.

Whether the process is viewed as a reorganization of one's hierarchy of values[6] or as the achievement of self-identity, it is clear that this time is one of extreme importance to young persons, and to Christian education. For if the years of youth truly are years of

---

[5] James F. Adams, ed., *Understanding Adolescence: Current Developments in Adolescent Psychology* (New York: Allyn & Bacon, 1968) pp. 5-7.

[6] See a discussion of this theory of Spranger by K. Bruno Beller, "Theories of Adolescent Development," *Understanding Adolescene,* ed. J. F. Adams.

transition, of forming the person and personality, then these are crucial years for introducing youth to the fulness of life in Christ — crucial years to help teens discover who they are, and can become, in Him.

Those ministering with youth, then, desperately need to understand what is happening in the fellows and girls they serve, not only in order to sympathize with them and feel with them as they know pressures we only dimly remember, but also to recognize the role Christian ministry can have in guiding youth to define themselves as Christ's persons, to help them crystallize, as their own, values and attitudes and personalities that bear His distinctive stamp.

That guy in the mirror

It's striking how much impact a youth's physical characteristics and appearance have on his self-image. In fact, the first adolescent feelings for the self are probably rooted here. One writer notes that "it would appear from autobiographical material (submitted by both high school and college-age youth) that the adolescent not only is acutely aware of every physical variation from his concept of what is normal or beautiful or handsome, but that this is perhaps his most frequent frustration."[7]

This shouldn't surprise us. Physical growth doesn't strike all youth with measured regularity. Jack may spurt up in height far beyond his age-mates, so fast that his coordination and physical integration lag behind. Looking almost collegiate, his clumsiness causes burning embarrassment as he tries futilely to catch a football or execute a play. Ken, on the other hand, lags far behind. As a high school sophomore he is mistaken for a sixth-grader, and retreats into quietness, hoping only to remain unseen in a society where delayed puberty makes him feel a helpless misfit. Growth comes unevenly to fellows and to girls during early and middle adolescence, and this alone leaves a definite mark on a teen's perception of who he is — a mark that often refuses to fade away. Thus psychologist Harold W. Bernard points out that of 10 early adolescents (ages 12 to 14) of low strength, six will show shyness and later adjustment problems.[8] So too, "the boy who is accelerated in physical development is socially ad-

---

[7]D. Gottlieb & C. Ramsey, *The American Adolescent* (Homewood, Ill.: Dorsey, 1964), p. 113.

[8]Harold W. Bernard, *Psychology of Learning and Teaching,* 2nd ed. (New York: McGraw Hill, 1965).

64

vantaged in the peer culture. In adulthood the same success pattern continues. He is poised, responsible, achieving in conformity with society's expectations."[9] And girls who develop faster tend to have greater prestige among their peers and thus generally greater self-confidence and assurance.[10] One's body gives early and powerful impressions of the self.

Physical deviations of any sort can cause anxiety and uncertainty, and have a negative impact on youths' feelings about themselves. How prevalent this is is shown by the fact that of a number of adolescent girls (who characteristically enter puberty earlier and develop more rapidly than boys) over half have felt intensely that they were "too tall," while over half the boys of the same age-group have been concerned that they are too short! Both are troubled by blackheads and pimples, and many girls become convinced that they are disfigured with a nose too large or some other feature that makes them homely.

The rapid, uneven growth of early adolescence creates many wide variances within the age-group that, to teens suddenly sensitive about their bodies, seem to be terrible deviations from others and from the peer group's ideal of strong, athletic males and attractive, well-developed girls.

Of course, this time of wide variation is one that passes. Boys like Jack who spurt up too fast at last recover their coordination; the Kens who lag behind catch up and gain strength. And in time girls take the shape that God intended, ripening toward womanhood.

Often, by the high school and college years, no sign of the earlier "distortions" that were so intensely felt remain. When we look at older teens, coming to the end of high school years and ready to step into the wider world of college or of job and marriage, we may see a vibrant health of body and attractiveness that makes it hard for us to believe these youth could be anything but confident and proud. How wrong we often are! For all too often the shame that gripped the growing youth as he looked in his mirror and compared himself with others has been planted deep within. Often a teen does

---

[9]Mary Cover Jones, "Psychological Correlates of Somatic Development," ed. Hill and Shelton, *Readings in Adolescent Development and Behavior* (Englewood Cliffs, N.J.: Prentice-Hall, Inc., 1971) p. 22.

[10]Margaret Siler Faust, "Developmental Maturity as a Determinant in Prestige of Adolescent Girls," *Readings,* ed. Hill and Shelton, p. 50.

not see himself as you or I see ourselves, but he sees a self still warped by what he once felt himself to be.

This is one reason why we need to be sensitive to the physical makeup of youth. *It matters to them.* It matters intensely, for one of the first pictures of the emerging self is drawn from the way a person sees his body, and the way he feels about what he sees. When a young person is ashamed of what he sees, his whole personality, his whole way of responding to life and other people, can be deeply affected.

So we must resist the temptation to look at a young person, and relate to him on the basis of what *we* see, confident that the girl we find attractive will see herself that way, or that the young man we see as a leader, quick and intelligent, will have this same image of himself. We need to wait, to discover who each person believes himself to be, and meet him there with an invitation to become.

This is a lesson Lorraine, a student of mine, learned from Jan, an attractive, busy fifteen-year-old. A "normal American girl," Jan worked hard at school, found summer and holiday jobs, played at tennis and in her school band, and found acceptance with a group of guys and girls at church. But appearances were somehow deceiving, as Lorraine learned in a relationship that grew and lasted over several years. In letters to Lorraine,[11] letters we'll be looking at in this and other chapters, Jan showed her friend a personality that no casual observation would reveal. A "self" that did not match what Lorraine and others saw, but which was all too real to Jan.

Take a look at this first letter, reproduced here without comment, and jot down in the margin any words that seem to you to describe how Jan feels about herself.

10/7/65

Dear Lorraine

I'm sorry I didn't get these pictures and sketches to you sooner. Beth betrayed me, she wouldn't do them. So I decided to try once more and see what I could do. Well, not so hot. I just can't draw people. Lets face it I can't draw. I should of return the pictures sooner so you could decided what to do with them. I'm sorry . . . You always helped me out on songs that I can't play, and not only that, put spiritual promblems. So I figure I could repay you back, but I guess it didn't work out that way.

We won that football game last Saturday against Wilson North. I

---

[11]Although the names in the letters have been changed, these are the actual letters written by the girl I've called Jan. The situations described are also actual situations.

didn't see anyone from the other side that I thought I might know. Oh, Well . . .

We've to play for Northwestern this Saturday. That's going to be real nice. We have to live about 7:30 a.m. and we won't get home until 6 or 7:30 at night. We get to watch the football game free.

Then on Oct. 12, Columbus Day, the band was invited to attend in the Columbus Day parade. It's going to be televise and the band members get out of School. The other kids has to go to school. What ashame . . .

Don't forget about that stakeing date, Oct. 23 or 30 . . . So far Hellen, Jenny, Eve, and me, can go.

How's your tennis coming along? My gym teacher wants me to join the tennis team, but my mom says no . . . I come home every night limping. My leg, that got tangle with the tobagon, gets weak so I can't hardly walk. I don't know whats the matter, it's been almost year now; it should of healed by now. When I'm on the trampoline and then when I get off; it seems like all the muscles in that leg tighten up, it aches. It's redicules.

I joined the premet club at school again this year. That's about medicle stuff. We get some inventations from hospitals asking if we would like to take a tour of their hospitals and listen to lectures about medicle stuff. Last year we were invited to Hinsdale Hospital, it was real interesting and fun.

Well, I better sign off for now. I'm sorry about those sketches. I'll see you in church.

Love,

Jan

P.S. I hope you can
read my typing. My
fingers were numb.

Age of turmoil

This is what one writer calls early adolescence, those years when jolting bodily changes are accompanied by surging feelings that youth can hardly understand. Most of adolescence is marked by some inner turmoil, some sense of the grip of feelings and moods that lift to heights and suddenly drop to agonizing depths.

Lorraine was jolted one Sunday afternoon when Jan's emotions broke through her control as several girls practiced a musical number. Jan burst into tears, then rushed from the church. That night a letter was slipped into Lorraine's hands; the letter showed her the turmoil inside — a turmoil that could sweep over Jan for no apparent reason. Here's that letter.

Dear Lorraine

I know this is the cowards way to say I'm sorry. I should tell it to you instead of writing it. But I wasted too much of your time this afternoon. I mean I could tell you after the Lord's supper, but I'd be here all night and all tomorrow.

I know the scene I put on this afternoon wouldn't prove to anyone that I was a Christian. I guess I still have that "old nature" in me. I don't know, I guess I was tired and too edgy (I think that's spelled right). I notice all this week I felt like harpen (I think that's spelled right) everybody — I just didn't feel like myself. I had so much to worry about. I mean my job, if I could do good, so they would keep me after the Christmas holidays, also. But then I have to go and make that charge account wrong — now I figure I would get fired and wouldn't get enough money for my Christias presents. And then keeping my grades up in school, handing in my homework, and, also, keeping the title of 1st trombone in band and in school. And even thinking about the war over in Viet Nam, so many young men being killed, and the women and children, also, being killed over there. But my biggest worry is that my friends, some, will boing to the "Lost Eternity" — In seminar they talk about happiness and joyfulness, but they never realize that the Lord is coming soon, and they'd have to face hardness and deceitfulness instead of these lovely times so far. I ask myself, why should I think of other people of why should I think of the war over in Viet Nam, its not here, I'm still alive, I've got enough food to eat, a lot of clothes to wear, and shelter to keep warm and protected. But who else realizes this, who else cares, who else feels the same way I do. Nobody, and if there was, there's very few in this world.

But its really no excuse for this afternoon. All I can say is I'm sorry. But that's not enough, Lorraine, I'm jealous of Jenny. I have been ever since I've known her. I don't know why, she's always been a good friend to me, maybe too good. I don't know. It seems like every time when I like someone a lot she has to like that person a lot, also. And it seems like that person shows more affection and kindness, even love, toward her than me. Jenny can sing, play instruments, and get better grades in school than I do. Well, she deserves every talent she has, because she was willing to earn it. But it seems like I can't always realize this. And all I can say to her is, I'm sorry. So I try to stay away from Jenny and especially when shes around that special person. So I won't cause any commotion.

All I ask from you and Jenny is forgiveness. I'm sorry. If it still is possible, I would like to sing with you and Jenny this coming Sunday. We can still have a trio. You pick the song and I'll try my best to get every note right. I'm *tired* of giving up, I'm tired of putting it off, I know I can do anything and everything just as well as the next persson. Please, Lorraine, forgive me.

Now you really know what kind of Christian I am. I *promise* I'll change and do anything you or anyone else ask of me the best of my knowledge and will power.

Please try to understand me. I don't know. I guess I'm a mixed up little kid. Yes, a kid. That *can't* grow up and realize what I have and what I can do, until I lose it.

I'm sorry. Iwant to show my life to the whole world as a Christian but I guess I'm going at it the wrong way. You want to know why I was crying Sunday. I was lonely, I didn't think anyone would care about me, I didn't think I deserve to be baptize with Diana, Jimmy, Carrie and Jenny. Because I didn't show my life, my attitude towards God, like they have.

Oh, theyr's a lot to say, but so hard to express. So hard to understand someone else.

Christmas is coming up. The season to be happy and to show forth love. I'm sorry.

Can we try that trio for next Sunday? Maybe even a quartet, Hellen can help out. I don't care, but *I* want to be in it, this coming Sunday.

Write when you have time.

Jan

PS If I can't get every note, I'll keep silent. Please.

To call youth a time of turmoil doesn't mean we must picture every moment as a time of agony, or every action irrational, controlled by feeling. Certainly not. But it does mean that we need to be deeply sensitive to youth's moods, and realize that many behaviors are symptomatic of inner struggles they, like Jan, feel deeply — struggles with forces they do not yet understand. Often youth's moodiness, criticalness, giggles, sulkiness, quarrelsomeness, brashness, daydreaming, argumentativeness — all behaviors that tend to irritate adults — signify not character but special needs.

Many factors, like those we see in Jan's letter, can heighten insecurity: lack of harmony between parents, competition for their love, conflict of values between home and school and church, an inability to "keep up" in clothes and activity, major or minor physical difficulties. Insecurity grows with the awful fear that feelings may surge out of control, to cause a quarrel or sudden outburst, followed by agonizing guilt expressed in a pitiful "I'm sorry" — or by an angry feud as fear of oneself forces a bitter defense. In an age of turmoil teens need a constant example; adults who face life with quiet confidence in God, who feel and share their feelings, but who mirror a faith that carries a person beyond himself and his inadequate resources.

Youth need ministers who can live with youth without anxiety, with the ability to accept and love persons who have not yet grown to love or to accept themselves.

PROBE
case histories
discussion questions
thought-provokers

1. I noted in this chapter that the physical can have a definite impact on self-image. Often a very different impact than another might imagine. This is illustrated in the following conflict situation between Jack and Miss Giles, which I've described in my book, *Are You For Real?* (Moody Press, 1968).

   As you read the sketch, note first of all how Miss Giles' image of Jack was formed — and how Jack's own image of himself reflects deeply felt physical inadequacies.

   Note also how each person's image of "Jack" affects behavior. Then, after reading, think about the "questions for you" that follow.

Miss Giles was nervous. *If only Jack were more dependable,* she thought, glancing around the room all prepared now for her junior high youth group's yearly parents' program.

She couldn't help liking Jack, a big, strapping fourteen-year-old. He had a ready grin, a wild sense of humor, an almost puppyish clumsiness. And he was intelligent ("sloppy" his teachers called him, yet they always gave him high grades), as well as a natural leader.

But Jack was also something else: undependable. Miss Giles noticed it when she took over the youth group in January. Give him a part, and he always seemed to forget. Or he'd get stubborn and refuse to do it. Or he'd start clowning, and get the whole group roaring. Twice he hadn't even bothered to show up. *No wonder I feel a little nervous,* she thought. But then that magazine article had said, "The cure for irresponsibility is responsibility." And Jack had so much potential! So — out on a limb she went and gave Jack the major part for tonight's parents' program. *Oh dear.* She twisted uncomfortably in her chair. *I wonder where Jack is now.*

Jack, on his way to church, was feeling rotten. He hated it, and he hated his folks for making him go, and his thoughts bubbled in anger. Just for a moment, slip into Jack's mind and feel with him.

That stupid Miss Giles. I wish she'd drop dead! . . . Now, why did I think that! I wish I didn't slip into thinking bad things. Why can't I keep from doing things like that?

Really, I can't do anything right. He picks up a stone and throws it at a telephone pole. *Missed! I knew I would. Some kids are good at sports, but I'm not. I'm clumsy. Can't hit a baseball. Fall over my own feet at football. Can't do anything.*

Stomach is hurting more. With every step toward the church, he feels sicker. *Why didn't I look at my part this week? When that postcard came from Miss Giles to remind me, I tried. But it all looks so hard. And even if I did learn it, I'd just make a big fool of myself.*

Why do I always have to blurt out some stupid thing when I get in front of the kids? Then they all laugh at me, and I feel so stupid. And then I just can't seem to stop. I grin and laugh and act stupid and silly. . . .

There's the church.

How can Miss Giles do such an awful thing to me? She must know I can't do the part. She must hate me a lot. I can tell from the way she's been acting lately. She gets real sarcastic when I say anything in planning group on Tuesdays.

She must know I can't do the part. She's about as nasty as they come. It'll serve her right if I make a fool of myself and spoil her silly old program. It'll serve her right if I don't even stand up — not in front of all those people. And she'd better not try to make me!

Questions for you

   (1) How much of your expectations of the teens you minister with is based on your impression of their physical appearance?

   (2) How can you tell if you see each teen as he sees himself?

   (3) What clues might you expect in an individual's behavior to his view of himself?

   (4) Can you think of any individuals who have puzzled you, whose behaviors and attitudes might reflect a poor self-image?

   (5) How important for an effective youth ministry is getting to know teens so well that they share with you the same kind of things that Jan shared with Lorraine?

2. Youth need to work toward emotional stability. The following were suggested by a graduate class of mine as guidelines for promoting stability. What's your reaction to them? How would you change them? Or, more important, how might you implement them in your ministry?

   (1) Set a good example of consistency.

   (2) Help each youth build confidence by accepting him, giving him a sense of security. Be liberal in praise, sparing in criticism, and avoid all ridicule. Create an atmosphere of security, love, and valuing of each individual.

   (3) Give each a standard to live by. Every youth is working toward a philosophy of life — something to give life meaning and make it worth living. Show your teens that the Christian life centers in Jesus Christ, and is His life in us, not an imposing and unreasonable set of "don'ts."

   (4) Impress each teen with his personal importance to God, and demonstrate his importance to you. Each teen needs to know that someone cares about him as a person. He needs to realize that you, and God through you, value him as a unique, one-of-a-kind person.

3. Even in ministries where the atmosphere facilitates the growth of emotional stability, outbursts will occur. One such is reported in this experience of another student of mine, who handled it creatively and well.

   Read her report, and see what principles of dealing with emotional outbreaks you can draw from her description of the situation.

The place is a church during Sunday evening youth group. Tom, a fairly large boy for his age (fourteen), and Bill, small for his age (also fourteen), often have spiffs. As I walked in this evening, Tom and Bill were at it as usual and Tom looked quite angry.

"OK, fellas! Break it up!"

"But Miss Lind! Tom. . . ."

"What's the problem?"

Bill was always the first to say something and I thought that Tom was just a big bully.

"I'd like to see you after the meeting, Tom, . . . and you, too, Bill."

Later, in the pastor's office, alone with Tom:

"Tom, what was the real problem tonight when you and Bill were cuffing one another?"

"Aw . . . he's a fink."

"Why? What does he do that makes him a fink?"

After talking awhile, I ferreted out that Bill was the source of the problem. Unaware to me, Bill had goaded Tom for a long time, teasing him constantly about being a big bully and calling him a fumbling moose. Tonight he had cruelly told Tom that his dad was dumb and even though he had grown up he hadn't grown out of his awkwardness and Tom would be a social misfit, too.

When I learned about that, Tom and I talked about *why* Bill would say this (because he was so small), and then talked about patience and how to avoid his attacks.

Then, after church, I had a chance to discuss the outburst with Bill. He told me that Tom was so big and always bullying him. I asked specifically what had been said, and he said he couldn't remember. From there I started talking with Bill about school and his activities. He told me all about it, relieved that I had let off talking about the fight; he told me about the school play he had tried out for, and that another fellow had got the part because he was bigger, even though the teacher had told him that his expression was better.

From there I asked Bill if he would like to direct the play that we were going to put on for the Passion Week services. Eagerly he took it up.

I made it a point to find how to involve Tom in something he felt confident in, too. In his case it was making props for the stage.

4. I noted in this chapter that Lorraine's association with Jan continued over a period of years. Here is her evaluation of Jan and her growth over these years, and the ways Lorraine tried to minister to Jan as a person.

AN EMOTIONAL PROBLEM IN A CHURCH CONTEXT

Jan and Jenny were both in my Sunday School class of twelve- and thirteen-year-olds, and were very close chums. They sat together, shared a locker at school, confided in each other, played softball and rode bicycles together. They frequently talked nervously and excitedly about going to high school.

Following graduation from eighth grade both girls entered high school as freshmen. Within two months Jan refused to speak to Jenny. If Jenny joined a group where Jan was present, Jan would promptly separate herself or, ignoring Jenny completely, become very sulky and silent. When Jenny made attempts to reach her in any way, Jan would jerk away. The growing feud between the two made its presence felt in the class and among the young people in general, since one was almost forced to be on one side or the other.

Knowing both girls quite well and something of their background, I shall speak for Jan, expressing what I think her feelings were — anger toward Jenny who suddenly seemed to overshadow her in every way. The result was that Jan felt she had lost status in the group.

"I hate Jenny. She thinks she is so smart and can do anything. She thinks she's better than I am. Just because she gets mostly A's in school and I get mostly C's. And she plays the piano, flute, and violin and owns her own instruments, while I only play the trombone and have to rent it from school. She takes private lessons, too.

"She has a lot of pretty clothes because her grandmother sews for her. And her clothes always look good on her. I have only a third of the clothes she does and besides, they're old and some don't fit right. My mother doesn't know anything about sewing and I don't have any money to buy new clothes. I tried to get a job at the Tastee Freeze last summer but they said I wasn't old enough. It just isn't fair.

"Last summer we were good friends; but since we started high school, Jenny is so stuck up! She's always talking so nobody else can get a word in edgewise. She always has her hair fixed nice, too — mine just sticks out all over. I wish I knew how to fix it.

"She's always asking me what the matter is and why I'm so touchy. Why should I have to talk to her if I don't want to? I've got other friends besides her.

"She thinks her family is better too because they live in a nice brick house, and her father works in an office, and her mother visits and plays bridge. My mother works six days a week in a factory and my dad runs a gas station — when he's sober, that is. Our house is little and old and ugly and the street isn't even paved out front — it's full of holes. I'm embarrassed to have anyone else come along when Lorraine drives me home.

"I'll never speak to Jenny again!"

HOW LORRAINE TRIED TO HANDLE THE SITUATION

1. Made efforts to maintain friendship with both — generally felt this was successful.
2. Didn't try to push the two together by force or convincing.
3. Tried to take every opportunity to compliment Jan on changes of her hair style, dress, etc.
4. Encouraged her to talk about current hair and dress styles in school.
5. At times was able to offer specific suggestions which she experimented with.
6. Suggested she work up a song on her trombone to play for the Sunday School.
7. Spent time accompanying her on the piano as she practiced her trombone.
8. Occasionally wrote her brief letters during the week.

9. Invited her with a friend to the *Messiah* at college last Christmas — they accepted.
10. Tried to find opportunities to use her budding drawing skill.

RESULTS APPARENT THIS FALL

1. Jan and Jenny friendly with each other and a larger group.
2. Marked improvement in Jan's grooming.
3. General improvement in social skills.
4. Regular attendance at church twice each Sunday.
5. Active participation in Bible study — attends older girls' club from church.
6. Talks freely of friends and activities at school.
7. Grades in school now mostly B's.
8. Relative gave her a used trombone.
9. Invited me to have Sunday dinner with her and her mother in their home.
10. I don't pretend to have brought these changes but I do feel I was able in some measure to be used by the Lord in helping Jan.

Jan was growing through the age of turmoil.
How are the youth you minister with growing?

5. *Collateral reading.* If you're interested in more thorough explorations of adolescent development, and the role of the self's emergence, you might look up the following books:
   James F. Adams, *Understanding Adolescence* (New York: Allyn and Bacon, 1968)
   Elizabeth Douvan and Joseph Adelson, *The Adolescent Experience* (New York: John Wiley & Sons, Inc., 1966)
   Don E. Hamachek (ed.), *The Self in Growth, Teaching, and Learning* (Englewood Cliffs, N.J.: Prentice-Hall, Inc., 1968)
   Rolf E. Muus, *Theories of Adolescence* (New York: Random House, 1962)
   M. Rosenberg, *Society and the Adolescent Self-Image,* (Princeton, N.J.: Princeton University Press, 1965).

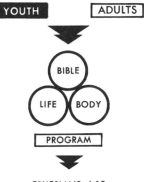

YOUTH   ADULTS

BIBLE

LIFE   BODY

PROGRAM

EPHESIANS 4:13

5

the social self

Teens move out of early adolescence into a time of relatively steady physical growth. Usually adjustment to and acceptance of their bodies has come, though often, as I noted last chapter, real scarring of the self-image may remain. Still, with movement into the high school years the focus of youths' growth in personhood shifts to the social and interpersonal.

In our country, these years involve a striking shift of dependency from adults to peers. Gottlieb and Ramsey suggest three factors in our society that move teens toward their peers and away from adults. "The increase in social activities and programs which demand peer group participation is the first. This concentration of activities reaches its maximum point during the high school and college period. The clarity of adolescent expectations as opposed to the vagueness of what adults want from adolescents is the second structural factor. Again, adolescents make clear that which is needed for status and prestige within the youth society, while the adult society presents a variety of conflicting expectations. The third element leading to greater peer involvement stems from the fact that adolescents are rarely allowed to enter the adult world until they go through certain rites of passage. Even here, however, there is a lack of agreement between adults as to when a young person is officially ready to take on adult roles. . . . The fact that we have no precise time or act which signifies completion of the transition from youth to adulthood adds to the continuation of a youth society."[1]

In shaping youth ministry it's vital to understand the impact of the social environment on the emerging person, to be sensitive to the pressures and needs of youth, and to develop a Christian community in which a distinctive Christian understanding of persons and a distinctive pattern of Christian relationships exist.

---

[1]Gottlieb and Ramsey, *American Adolescent,* p. 198.

The area of personal relationships deserves a whole chapter in this book, not only because this is an area which deeply concerns the young people with whom we minister, but also because in and through relationships with others a person's set of values, his very sense of who he is, takes shape.

Put academically, we might say it as Anderson does: "The psychological self-image is formed early in life as a result of the succession of experiences of the child with significant people in his environment. It is built out of interpersonal experiences for survival."[2] This point of view has been expressed most strongly by Sullivan, who is explained by Jersild:

> . . . the "self-system" has its origins in interpersonal relationships and it is influenced by "reflected appraisals." If a child is accepted, approved, respected, and liked for what he is, he will be helped to acquire an attitude of self-acceptance and respect for himself. But if the significant people in his life — at first his parents and later his teachers, peers, and other persons who wield an influence — belittle him, blame him, and reject him, the growing child's attitudes toward himself are likely to become unfavorable. As he is judged by others, he will tend to judge himself. Further, according to this position, the attitudes concerning himself which he has thus acquired will, in turn, color the attitudes he has toward other persons.[3]

Although this is an *inter*personal process (none of us is merely wax on which others plant infallible imprints), it is easy to see why personal relationships are so significant for teenagers. During adolescence teens are struggling toward a fresh, yet lasting understanding of themselves. How others respond is particularly important to youth; often one's sense of worth as a person is tied to the acceptance and approval of others. As "the work of Cooley, Mead, and James makes clear, the individual's self-appraisal is to an important extent derived from reflected appraisals — his interpretations of others' reactions to him."[4]

The importance of others to teens helps explain why so many of the symbols of youth culture that irritate adults, the fads in hair

---

[2]Camilla M. Anderson, "The Self-Image; a Theory of the Dynamics of Behavior," *The Self in Growth, Teaching, and Learning,* ed. Don E. Hamachek (Englewood Cliffs, N.J.: Prentice-Hall, Inc., 1968), p. 6.

[3]Arthur T. Jersild, *Child Psychology* (5th Ed.) (Englewood Cliffs, N.J.: Prentice-Hall, Inc., 1960) pp. 116-126.

[4]Morris Rosenberg, *Society and the Adolescent Self-Image* (Princeton, N.J.: Princeton University Press, 1965).

length, in clothing, in music, are of such concern to the young. To be a part, to be approved of by the group with which most of life is lived, reflects directly on a youth's sense of worth and personhood.

Parents and the emerging self

It is obvious that during the earliest and so-called "formative" years of a child's life mom and dad have the greatest influence on the developing personality. Many studies show relationship between parental attitudes and behaviors and the characteristics of their children. Even though during the adolescent years there is a distinct shift toward the peer group as a reference set for many values and decisions, we should not get the impression that the high school and college years are marked by a total rejection of the parental way of life. One recent study by a Chicago psychiatrist leads him to believe that most middle-class American teens grow up with a desire to become a part of the suburban culture into which they were born. In a longitudinal study of "average" teens, those not disturbed or suffering economic or emotional deprivation, Dr. Daniel Offer found that "the boys admired their parents and shared and reflected their values; success in school was of utmost importance to them, and more than 90% wanted to marry and have families like the ones in which they were raised."[5]

Other studies show a similar impact of the parents on attitudes held by teens toward love,[6] and that certain kinds of choices teens make during adolescence persist in being parent-conforming even while other kinds of choices are peer-conforming.[7] An interesting (unpublished) study of college students by Dr. James M. Lower, Professor of Education at Wheaton College, showed that in the sophomore year young people still tended to see themselves as having the same personality traits as the parent or parents they designated as an *influential other.* Only later did self-descriptions

---

[5]Reported in *Science News,* vol. 96, 27 Sept. 1969.

[6]David H. Knox, Jr., "Attitudes Toward Love of High School Seniors" *Adolescence,* Vol. 5, No. 17, Spring 1970, pp. 89-98.

[7]Clay V. Brittain, "Adolescent Choices and Parent-Peer Cross-pressures," *Readings,* ed. Hill and Shelton, pp. 201-209. Brittain concludes that peer-conformity dominates in making choices in areas in which social values are changing rapidly, as opposed to areas in which social values remain relatively stable, and in areas where immediate consequences are anticipated in contrast to those where the emphasis is on long-term effects.

tend to become less related to the student's perception of his parents, and more distinctively his own.[8]

So, with all our concern for the peer group in Christian education of youth, and with all our awareness of the growing isolation of teens from significant personal relationships with adults (including parents!), we must not confuse youth's identification with other teens as rejection of parents or their values — or with a lessening of youth's need for the right kind of parental guidance.

The need for a "right kind" of parent/teen relationship is something most young people and most parents are acutely aware of. Particularly as growth into adolescence brings conflict. Probably, as Schaimberg suggests, "some level of adolescent-parent conflict has been virtually a constant factor in human societies."[9] But it is also probable that conflict is greater in our society, largely because extension of the adolescent period into the early (and sometimes late) twenties puts unique strain on young people who feel a great need to discover who they are as persons in their own right, yet who at the same time are forced to remain economically and emotionally dependent on parents. Sadly, very few parents understand adolescence as a time of self-definition, when a young person needs the opportunity to develop a sense of identity and personal competence. Most seem to struggle to retain the same pattern of relationship established when their child was younger, and to demand a similar decision-making role in his life. Rather than provide the kind of guidance that helps a young person make his own wise choices, too many parents insist on retaining the right of fiat decision, and use disciplinary patterns which, though appropriate to childhood, have much less validity for adolescence. So conflict arises. A conflict that grows out of the young person's deeply felt need for an independent identity and parental uncertainty as to how to react to this demand.

It's not possible here to work toward a definition of the parent's role in helping his teen away from dependence toward a healthy independence (actually an interdependence) that marks maturity.[10]

---

[8]James M. Lower, "The 1966 College Student: His View of Himself," Faculty Workshop Program, Wheaton College, Wheaton, Illinois, September 8, 1966.

[9]Lawrence Schaimberg, "Some Socio-cultural Factors in Adolescent-Parent Conflict: A cross-cultural comparison of selected cultures," *Adolescence,* Vol. 5, No. 15, Fall 1969, pp. 333-341.

[10]A good book for parents is Haim Ginott's *Between Parent and Teenager* (paperback). I hope also in the next few years to develop a book for parents of teens, writing from a distinctively Christian perspective.

But it is important to note the impact that relationships with parents can have on the young person's feelings about himself. This is illustrated by the experience of a former student who had extremely good relationships with her parents, but who felt deeply the impact of a particular experience on her sense of worth as a person. Her evaluation of the overall relationship shows a sensitive awareness of the issue we're discussing.

Accepting the adult authority of my parents was always one area of development I thought I had under control. Of course, my parents made it easy for me, since most of their rules were reasonable and helped instill in me a sense of right and wrong. The rules were never really spelled out, but were understood nonetheless. My parents never found it necessary to inflict punishment by taking away the car or any other privileges like dating or school activities. They never had to because, quite frankly, I never did anything "bad" and I shared with them everything I did. Actually, I was afraid to do anything bad, not because of the punishment I might receive, but because of what it would do to my parents' image of me.

Some people said I lived a "sheltered life" — thought I was a "white knight." Such comments never really bothered me because I didn't want to be the way everyone else was — so self-concerned, boy-crazy, manipulated, insecure, and unstable. Perhaps my "sheltered" life and high standards kept me from doing a lot of things with the crowd, but they were things I would have felt out of place doing.

Then came an experience which I shall never forget and which has made things a little different ever since. During my junior year in high school I became interested in dramatics. Kenyon College, a men's school nearby, always relied on "home talent" for its female roles. They needed a May Queen: just a young girl to look pretty and say two lines. I tried out and was given the part. Being in a college play was just what I needed at the time. I loved dramatics and felt much more at home in the college age group. My parents sensed that I was more mature than most of my peers and were glad that I had the chance to develop my interest. However, for the first time they spelled out a rule. "You can be in college plays, but you can't date college men." The rule never pleased me. I was excited about Kenyon men as *people* with so many different personalities and goals. They made me feel like a queen on stage and off. I continued to share my good times with my parents; they knew almost as much about the different boys I met as I did. *And* they knew that I especially liked Rory Rogers.

And so it seemed perfectly natural and right for me to accept Rory's offer to "drop in" for a little while on a fraternity dance one Friday night after rehearsal. Rory said he could take me home, so I told the lady I came with to go on, and then I decided I'd better call my parents and let them know that I'd be home an hour late. In my mind, I wasn't having a date with Rory. I'd never been to a fraternity dance

79

before and considered the evening more of an adventure with a good friend.

I called home.

"Hello, Dad? This is Rhoda. Rehearsal was over early and Rory asked me if I'd like to go over to his fraternity party for about an hour. He has a car, so he'll bring me home. OK?"

"NO! Stay where you are. I'll be right there."

"But, Dad!"

"I said no. Stay where you are. I'll be right there."

Click.

I was numb, completely confused, and so very frustrated and humiliated. As I explained what had happened to Rory, I found myself getting madder and madder at Dad. Why? Why was Dad all of a sudden saying NO!? It didn't make sense. I thought they *trusted* me — they had no reason not to!

Rory waited with me until Dad came. I didn't say a word on the way home — I just sat there feeling very much like the defeated foe submitting to his conqueror. I was bitter and spent the whole night and following day in tears up in my room. My room. For the first time they were forcing me to voluntarily ostracize myself up in my room. I just didn't want to ever see either of them again. They had humiliated me in front of Rory, a member of the one peer group I did want acceptance from. They had as much as said, "We don't trust you. You can't make wise decisions." And worst of all, they had made me feel *immoral* — as if my intentions had been dishonest and sexual!

I was beginning to feel a real communication barrier between my parents and me. I recognized and even *welcomed* their authority over me as long as their demands were understandable and explainable. But just a cold NO!?

I never quite overcame that experience. Of course, time took away my humiliation, but it never really gave me back my former self-confidence, or sense of self-worth. I know now that it was best that my parents ended my relationship with Rory before it ever had a chance to begin. But the way in which they went about it caused a resentment to grow within me that probably did more harm than dating Rory ever could have caused. Suddenly I felt that if my parents couldn't trust me, why should I continue to trust them? Should I even trust them with my thoughts?

I can look back now on the experience more objectively. I now know that it wasn't me they mistrusted, but Rory. How much it would have helped heal my injured self-image to have known that then! My parents' authority over me guided me through adolescence — but such unquestioned obedience on my part has left me a little less sure of myself now and capable of unbearable and quite unnecessary guilt complexes when I do act independently.

Helping hands

One factor that reinforces the importance of age-mates for the high schooler is his need for support in the struggle to understand himself as an individual apart from his family. The Smarts see "one of the basic functions of the crowd" as providing "a group identity which separates adolescent from parent, a 'we' feeling apart from the family. Thus the adolescent strengthens his own sense of identity by being a member of a group which defines his difference from his parents."[11] The same point, that being a member of the peer group is felt by youth as an important hand up toward independence, is made by others. Coleman sees adolescence as a unique transitional period when a boy or girl "is no longer fully in the parental family, but has not yet formed a family of his own, and close ties with friends replace the family ties that are so strong during most of the rest of life. He is moving out of the family he was part of in childhood, not yet within the family he will be part of as an adult."[12]

Whatever the reasons, young people do see themselves as being different from adult society, and like other youth. And the sense of not belonging in the adult world (at least not as a person in one's own right) makes it extremely important for the young person to belong in the world of youth. For many teens, belonging and acceptance in the peer world is felt as an intense need. I remember clearly one student explaining how in high school he let his grades drop from A's and B's to D's because he felt he must conform to his friends to be one of them. That this is not unusual is illustrated by another student, a girl, who shares this story of her conflict:

> In Junior High, wow, how I yearned and tried and struggled to be one of the "in crowd." I tended to do anything, say anything, go anywhere so that I might be accepted and thought highly of. An incident which caused me difficulty related to school. I liked school. I did most of my work and more. Kids in my class were not as academically inclined as I. They liked to goof off, and didn't care what their grades were. One of my friends directly tore me down because I didn't do as they did. I remember even physically fighting with her! I went home in tears. What should I do?

---

[11]R. C. and N. Smart, *Children: Development and Relationships* (New York: Macmillan Co., 1967).

[12]James S. Coleman, *The Adolescent Society* (New York: Free Press of Glencoe, 1961) p. 174.

This need to belong with one's age-mates is so strong in our culture that when churched teens in one study expressed their values and goals the goal ranked number one was: "Being a person well-liked by everyone."[13] Other social values (such as making a happy marriage and enjoying good times with others) shared the highest priority.

The adolescent attempting to "disengage"[14] from dependence on his family is far from being able to stand on his own. Still involved in the process of self-discovery, still dependent on others to confirm and support his emerging perceptions of himself, the teen is driven by deep need to seek identity with the peer group. And in the world of youth, identity with the group is normally gained through conformity.

Bell points out that

> the adolescent often sees himself as deviating from adult society. He often thinks of himself as an individualist. But he is not. There are probably few subcultures more demanding of conformity than that of the adolescent. What he fails to see is that the subgroup deviates from the adult world, but that the value of conformity within the subgroup is extremely strong.[15]

When we understand the need felt by teens for identification with other youth and for social support in their struggles toward maturity, we can see several warnings and directions for Christian education.

A Christian education that seeks to force young people to reject identification with other teens "for Christ's sake" (as we evangelicals have been known to do!) puts unknown pressures on the forming personality (as well as distorts Christianity itself, for our faith calls for a redemptive *involvement* with others — not withdrawal). And certainly a Christian education of youth which fails to build toward a strong Christian peer group will never achieve maximum impact. Once we realize the vital importance of interpersonal relationships to teens, we will make it a definite emphasis of our ministry to help them build the kind of relationships with each other that will support growth toward Christian maturity and provide that

---

[13]Merton P. Strommer, *Profiles of Church Youth* (St. Louis, Mo.: Concordia Press, 1963) pp. 71, 72.

[14]This term is used by Douvan and Adelson in an excellent discussion of the family in *The Adolescent Experience*.

[15]Robert R. Bell, *The Sociology of Education* (Homewood, Ill.: The Dorsey Press, Inc., 1962) p. 108.

sense of security[16] so important to healthy feelings about oneself. It also goes without saying that, if the values of the individual reflect the values of the group to which he belongs,[17] development of a peer group in which Christian values are expressed and transmitted is one of the most important ministries we can perform for individuals.

In Christian education of youth, helping teens develop the kind of personal relationships with other teens and with parents that facilitate the formulation of Christian personalities is of central concern. Not only can Christ's own values be best transmitted in a context of close personal relationships, but definition of oneself as a maturing Christian person demands just this context. Rather than fighting the natural dependence of teens on age-mates, struggling to break up cliques and other natural groupings, we must recognize these phenomena as evidence of personal needs, and as opportunities for creative ministry.

Yet, while youth need each other in their search for identity, many factors in adolescent relationships hinder rather than facilitate growth. I have just mentioned *conformity* to peer expectations as the unadvertised price of belonging. For many, this means a painful struggle to appear to be something they are not; a struggle to maintain a façade of that which, in time, they may actually become. My own research with high school and college-age youth has revealed how terribly hesitant they are to say what they truly think and feel. Uncertain about how they will be received, fearing the pain of rejection or ridicule, most adolescents cut themselves off from the very support they cluster together to find! Even more significantly, establishing relationships on the basis of one's performance (and this is exactly what conformity involves — the buying of acceptance through expected behavior) is completely contrary to the Christian approach to relationships and to the Christian understanding of persons. Although this topic has been discussed in depth in my book, *How Do I Fit In?*, and demands more extensive development than I can give it here, a brief orientation is important because a particu-

---

[16]Morh and Despres in *Adolescence: The Stormy Decade* (New York: Random House, 1958) point out that high status in the peer group is not necessarily the key to security, but that security comes with a warm, close friendship. "Individuals who had no status in their peer group, but did have one or two close friends, came through the adolescent years well. Status belonging and friendship belonging are not necessarily the same things" (p. 121).

[17]A great number of studies and much theory establishes this view. For good discussions see several chapters in *Group Dynamics Research and Theory*, 3rd edition, ed. Dorwin Cartwright and Alvin Zander (New York: Harper & Row, 1968).

lar concept of the Christian person and of Christian interpersonal relationships underlies the approach to ministry this book suggests.

Self-acceptance

Scripture portrays one class of people Jesus' ministry of love was unable to win to discipleship. These were the Pharisees, who, the Bible tells us, trusted in themselves that they were righteous. They conformed to all the outward standards. As Jesus put it, "Alas for you, you hypocritical scribes and Pharisees! You are like white-washed tombs, which look fine on the outside but inside are full of dead men's bones and all kinds of rottenness. For you appear like good men on the outside — but inside you are a mass of pretense and wickedness" (Matt. 23:27, 28 *Phillips*). These were men who had made careers of constructing façades, forcing themselves to pretend with each other and the general populace until they were unable to be honest even with themselves. And so we see the Pharisee in the temple thanking God that he is "not like other men — especially that sinner over there —" and going away as alienated from God and from himself as ever. While the sinner, seeing himself as he was and realizing his need, cast himself on God's mercy and went away forgiven and restored.

Surprisingly, the first step toward a truly healthy self-image and that kind of self-love Jesus commanded[18] is to reject, as a measure of worth, all performance (whether outward conformity to divine law and human tradition or conformity to whatever standards one's society and peer-group establishes) and to face the surging forces of sin within. For sin mars the best we do, with pride and selfishness and envy, and makes us all aware of our guilt and shame.

The Bible's strident insistence that each of us take our place before God, recognizing himself as a sinner, and the fact that God's generous dealings with us as well as His judgments are meant to lead us to the confession of sin and repentance, point out that God's way to a healthy and mature Christian personality requires honest evaluation and acceptance of all that is bad within us.

But the Gospel goes far beyond the demand that we recognize ourselves as sinners. The Gospel message asserts that, though we have fallen short of what we ought to be when measured by God's

---

[18]This is, of course, implicit in the command to "love your neighbor—as yourself."

law, *God still loves us.* God asserts that we are valuable as persons — incalculably valuable. And "the proof of God's amazing love is this: that it was *while we were sinners* that Christ died for us" (Rom. 5:8).

Our sense of worth is not to be anchored in performance, but in the Gospel's assertion that we are loved and valued by God for ourselves.

When we take this divine point of view, we are freed to love and accept ourselves as God does — and to have this same attitude toward others.

Thus youth culture's pattern of demanding conformity as the price of acceptance, while utterly human, is tragically un-Christian. Young people, like all of us, are to accept and love one another freely, because of Christ's love, valuing and appreciating each other as persons because God asserts each person's infinite value and worth.

Strikingly, the Bible presents this kind of self-acceptance and acceptance of others as the key to growth toward Christian maturity. When all self's energy is stimulated to maintain the façades behind which shame impels us to hide, we close ourselves off from God and His Spirit. But when Christians, in an atmosphere of mutual love and acceptance, step out from behind the façades, personalities are open to the healing ministry of the Spirit as He works through the prayers and support of others as each seeks to bear his brother's burden. Grasping the fact that, as the Bible says, we *have* peace with God through our Lord Jesus Christ frees us to enter confidently into a new kind of relationship, one of *grace,* and to take our stand here in happy certainty that God has glorious things for us in the future as He remolds us to be more and more like His Son (Rom. 5:1, 2).

This theme will be developed further in chapters on Body ministry, but it is important to point out here that a major thrust of youth ministry must be to help teens break out of performance-based, conformity-producing relationship patterns. To help them learn to be and express themselves with others in an atmosphere of acceptance and love. Helping young people accept themselves and others freely, to assert their worth as persons apart from what they do or at the moment are, and to express this conviction of the worth of persons in a community of love and care, is utterly basic to meaningful ministry with youth.

PROBE
case histories
discussion questions
thought-provokers
resources

1. Developing a biblical understanding of persons and acceptance-based relationships, and *experiencing* this as self-acceptance and a way of living with others, is vital to ministry with youth. You might want to look at my book, *How Do I Fit In?* (Moody Press, 1970), which is written to youth for this purpose. The book can be used in a variety of group situations as well as for individual reading. A guide to teaching it and other YOUTH ASKS books is available from Moody Press.

2. Recently an achievement motivation approach to relationship-building has been adapted by some Christian men. Their work not only communicates theory but also suggests a variety of group experiences which can help open up communication lines and develop good interpersonal relationships. If you are interested in checking out what they have as resource help in ministering with your teens as persons, write to

   Achievement Motivation Program Headquarters
   1439 S. Michigan Avenue
   Chicago, Illinois 60605
   Telephone: (312) 427-2500

3. I noted in this chapter the importance of the parent in the adolescent's growth toward maturity. Because parents do play a vital role in development, our ministry with youth definitely needs to include a ministry to parents.

   Look over the following *goals* which might be set for this aspect of ministry with youth. Which seem most important to you? Which are you actually working toward now? How might each be implemented?

   ### GOALS IN WORKING WITH TEENS/PARENTS

   I. *Education*
   (1) Equip parents for the responsibilities in Christian nurture.
   (2) Help parents understand adolescence and their own teenager(s).
   (3) Work toward agreement on a community of standards (hours, etc.).
   (4) Help parents understand the nature and approach of the church's ministry to teens.

   II. *Involvement*
   (1) Involve parents in the ministry of the church to teens.
   (2) Involve teens in the overall ministry and goals of the church.

   III. *Communication*
   (1) Help parents and teens keep open lines of communication on feeling as well as idea levels.
   (2) Keep parents informed of church-sponsored activities and involvements of teens.

(3) Keep communication lines open between church workers, parents, and teens.

4. I have held several parent/teen seminars in which we worked toward several of the above goals, particularly that of helping parents understand adolescence and their own teenager(s) and that of opening the lines of communication between adults and teens.

I am including an outline of a 6 session seminar (which is best conducted in a retreat setting or on a single weekend at home) which has been developed for these purposes. While much of the material is given only in outline, it may be helpful as an illustration of the kind of thing you may want to try in your own ministry.

PARENT/TEEN SEMINARS

It is the purpose of these seminars to promote the development of relationships between parents and teens that will support youth in their transition from childhood's dependence to a mature Christian interdependence. Several factors seem important for the existence of such support: (1) an atmosphere and experience of *intelligent love;* (2) an effective *guidance role* for the parent, as perceived by both parent and teen; (3) an *open communication* situation, which facilitates honesty and trust.

For the purposes of the seminar, these factors may be defined as:

Intelligent love.........a desire for the benefit of the one loved which issues in behavior which actually does help (rather than harm).

Guidance role.........an awareness by both parents and teens that the *directiveness* of parental authority has been replaced in most situations by a guidance that extends freedom to make choices within limits set by parents, and extended as the teen exhibits a developing maturity.

Open communication....the sense of freedom within the home that permits all members to express themselves freely to others, assured of acceptance if not agreement, without threat to self. This does *not* imply that each member of the family must communicate everything to the others: it implies rather an atmosphere of confidence.

The approach of the seminars is to work toward these goals by involving adults and teens in meaningful interaction, not by "preaching at" or "lecturing to" them. While content is introduced in the sessions, it is so introduced as to make more meaningful the interaction between the parents and teens involved.

MECHANICS

Parents/teens come to seminars together.

Each family is given a copy of ARE YOU FOR REAL? (Moody Press, 1968) before seminars, and asked to read it individually.

Interaction is stimulated in a variety of ways on a variety of levels, with content input used primarily to stimulate interaction and build understanding.

Time: 2-hour sessions are desirable.

Situation: a retreat or week-end setting is best so that there will be attendance by the group members at all sessions.

The leader is expected to "play by ear" in guiding the interaction and discussions which develop.

SESSIONS OUTLINE

Communication

1. Who, me?
2. What, listen?

Intelligent Love

3. White pedal pushers? Never!
4. Here's how *I* felt about . . .
5. Product and process.

Guidance

6. Freedom now! (?)

Session 1

To help participants begin to share themselves significantly with each other.

Process

(1) Seminar goals (p. 87) are shared with the group, time is given for questions and expression.

(2) Show filmstrip "Members One of Another" and briefly discuss what it is saying. The filmstrip is produced by Christian Education Press, 1505 Race Street, Philadelphia, Pa. It is also available from 1720 Chouteau Ave., St. Louis, Mo.

(3) Give each participant large sheets of paper and crayons, and ask him to use the colors and shapes to draw his real "self" — to creatively express his personality as he sees himself.

(4) Divide the group into teams of six or eight, mixing adults and teens as evenly as possible, but *not* placing any teens with their own parents. Then ask each group to explore in depth the "self portrait" each has drawn — beginning with each person's explanation of his drawing, and continuing discussion until each feels he is beginning to understand the others.

These teams of six or eight should be retained whenever the larger group is asked to break down into working units.

Session 2

To help participants see how their responses to each other can open up or cut off communication.

Process

(1) Point up in introduction the need for listening to one another, and "hearing" what is said. This session will help participants listen and respond so as to keep communication lines open.

(2) Pair an adult with a teen to listen to typical youth statements and practice the following kinds of response.

Advice-giving

Reassuring

Understanding
Self-revealing
Discuss the implications of each type (see pp. 139-141).
(3) Have a panel of teens discuss which kinds of responses they prefer in various circumstances.
(4) Break into family groupings to discuss what kinds of response seem to each member to characterize their lives together, and their daily communication.

Session 3

To help parents and teens distinguish areas in which high schoolers can make good decisions, and areas in which both believe parents ought to exercise guidance or control.
(1) As participants come in, give each the appropriate one of these two questionnaires to be filled out. (Results should be collated as session continues.) Leave plenty of space for answers, of course.

FOR PARENTS

1. List those things you do in your relationship with your high schooler because you love him (or her).
2. List things about your teen that you particularly appreciate.
3. List things about your teen that particularly bother or upset you.
4. Complete the following sentence:
"I attempt to guide my teen by——."

FOR TEENS

1. List those things in your relationship with your parents that indicate to you that they really love you.
2. List things about your parents that you particularly appreciate.
3. List things about your parents that particularly bother or upset you.
4. Complete the following sentence:
"My parents could help me most by——."

(2) Introduce the session by stating that although in the last session the group talked about relating to one another, it is important to remember that they are persons in a particular relationship: a parent-teen relationship.
  This session will help define that relationship more clearly, and work toward a spelling out of the responsibilities of a parent to a teen, and a teen to parents.
(3) Discuss adolescence as a transition from dependency to independence; the teenager's task of becoming a real person in his own right. (You can use material from these chapters, particularly the next, and from the book, ARE YOU FOR REAL?
(4) In the process of working toward maturity, it's vital for parents to know what they can do that will help, and what will hurt. Lead the group to discuss together the following (true) story:

"My daughter's always been responsive; I can't understand what's happening!" the distraught mother blurted out.
  Of course, she had been shocked when her 16-year-old had come home and announced that she wanted to buy white cord

pedal pushers. "They look so . . . hoody!" her mother had protested ("hood" being then the current term for the socially undesirable kids). The girl had reacted violently. "No, they aren't! Why, my friends all have them. Besides, I *know* what's hoody at my school."

Both were hurt and upset at the other's reactions. And neither would give in."

Ask the group to discuss: "What would intelligent love do in this situation?" And: "Who really knows what is hoody?"

(5) Break down into small groups (established at the first session) to discuss how each (adults and teens) feels about the following ten items which research has shown to be a cause of conflict in the home. Remind them that in the groups they are to treat and listen to each other as equals — no authoritarianism allowed.

PARENT/TEEN CONFLICTS[19]

(showing percentage of boys who checked each item as seriously disturbing their relationship with their mothers)

a. Won't let me use the car 85.7%
b. Insists that I eat foods I dislike 82.4%
c. Scolds if my school marks aren't as high as others' . . 82.4%
d. Insists that I tell her what I spend money for 80.0%
e. Pesters me about table manners 74.8%
f. Pesters me about personal habits and manners . . . 68.5%
g. Holds my sister or brother up as example 66.9%
h. Objects to my riding in car at night 65.7%
i. Won't let me follow vocation of my interest 64.5%
j. Complains about neck or fingernails being dirty . . . 55.7%

(6) Reassemble for briefing on results of initial questionnaire. Leader comments on any significant results, such as adult/teen difference in perception of what shows love, relationship of "things that bother" to "things parents do to their children because they love them."

Session 4

To help parents and teens better understand the pressures that motivate actions.

(1) The last session pointed up conflict areas between parents and teens. Introduce this session by saying something about the need for insight into how teens and parents *feel* in conflict situations — even where the points at issue are relatively inconsequential.

(2) Pass out the following information gathered when Christian teens were surveyed. Discuss: "What does this suggest about teens' feelings and needs?" And also give teens in the group the opportunity to say which advice seems most significant to them.

"WHEN TEENS TALK BACK"

Recently I asked a group of several hundred teens to complete an open-ended statement. The statement (below) encouraged high

[19]Larry Richards, *Are You For Real?* (Chicago: Moody Press, 1968) p. 79.

schoolers to give advice to parents, expressing anonymously and honestly what they would like to say in person.

Here's the statement, and some of the most common completions. *"I'd like to tell all teenagers' parents to —"*

make sure they remember what they did when they were kids before they pass judgment.

don't be overprotective; get to know your teenagers; discuss things concerning the family with teenagers; give your teenager some responsibility in the home.

realize kids are not living in the same day and age *they* did — really try to understand.

not let their kids do everything they want to.

not be too strict, but to care what their child is doing.

try harder to understand that we are living in another generation than they did. I wish they would practice what they preach.

try to understand their teens. Little by little you can see that they want to become independent, but make sure it's with God.

stop nagging their kids.

talk to their teenagers like they were adults and not forget that they're still teenagers.

talk to their kids instead of telling them what to do — don't give kids straight "no" for an answer when they don't want kids to do something — discuss it with them instead — explain why they don't want them to and let the kids make their own decision. In other words, cut the apron strings.

not be so sheltering *but* not too lenient.

talk to their teenagers and try to understand their viewpoint, but explain to them how you feel on the situation, too.

try to understand your teenager and help him whenever he needs your guidance and to show him love always.

try to understand teens' problems, and set down adequate standards (rules) that they must obey to avoid misunderstanding.

let the teens make some decisions and *mistakes* of their own.

love their teenagers and be something they can respect.

(3) Suggest that a skit may give insight into *why* the teens gave the kind of advice they did — and why parents may at times need that advice! Ask that while watching the skit, the teens listen to see how Karen feels; the adults listen to see how mom feels. In the discussion following, let each group share their insights. But keep the interaction focused on the feelings of each — not on the rightness or wrongness of either's actions.

KAREN CONFLICT

M. Karen, I thought you were doing your homework. You certainly don't have your reports ready, do you?

K. Mmm, no. I'll do it in a minute, though. I'm still working on this party.

M. Oh yes, I meant to tell you. I got a new recipe from Hazel Carrelson. It's for a delicious pineapple and chocolate cake. So I thought we could make that up for the kids. Her family is crazy about it.

K. O mother, I told the kids we'd have pizza. They go for that more than cake.

M. Pizza! Karen, do you realize what pizza for that crowd would cost! Plus all the pop they drink! You'll just have to tell them you changed your mind. We can't afford it.

I'll make up that recipe and it will do just fine. If I know *your* friends, they'll eat anything.

K. Mother —

M. You know they'll eat anything.

K. But mother, I want this to be a *nice* party.

M. Well, we can't afford it, Karen, and that's that.

By the way, I saw Mrs. Dawson at the beauty shop the other day, and I mentioned you were having some kids over, and that it might be a good chance for her daughter to get to know some of them. I thought you could call and invite her.

K. Marilyn Dawson! Oh, Mother! How could you? You don't know what the kids think of her. I couldn't ask her. The girls would just hate me.

M. Well, what's wrong with her? Mrs. Dawson says none of the girls pay any attention to her.

K. No, but the *boys* do! You should see the way she throws herself at them. It's sickening.

Mother, I just can't ask her to come. The girls would never forgive me. We can't stand her. She'd just wreck the whole party.

M. Well, I told Mrs. Dawson that you'd contact her. She even gave me her phone number. I don't think it would hurt your reputation to ask her to one party. Besides, she's probably a very nice girl. She just needs some friends.

By the way, just who *are* you asking?

K. Oh — well, if you have to see it —.

M. Roger Darby. Karen, you know what your father and I think of this boy. I don't think he's the kind of boy you should be hanging around with. He's no good influence. And he so often sways the crowd.

K. Mother, please stop interfering. I can take care of myself. Roger's the life of the party.

M. Karen, it's only because we care about you we feel this way. Your father and I try to do so much for you. I think the least you can do —.

K. Mother, I'm not a baby any more. You and daddy don't understand teenagers. Why can't I plan my own party — why don't you just leave me alone?

M. Oh, Karen, we're only trying to help you! It seems like you don't even want your own parents around anymore. We love you and want to have a part in your life.

(4) When both points of view have been discussed and appreciated through the reports of adults and teens, ask the whole group (adult

and teen) to try to identify with mom's feelings, and give some advice for teens.

Put parents together in small groups, to develop answers to "I'd like to advise all teenagers to —." And put teens together, to develop answers *as they believe the adults will complete it.* Come together to compare.

(5) Conclude with a Bible study of *Ephesians 6:1-4.* In view of the seminar studies so far, what seems to them to be involved in "honoring parents" and "not provoking children to wrath"?

Session 5

To help participants understand factors that contribute to growth toward Christian maturity.

(1) Have the group discuss together how best to describe the *mature* Christian person. What is he like? Follow this with a brief review of adolescence as a transitional period, and the goal of adult/teen relationships to aid in this transition.

(2) Develop a lecture covering material indicated on the personality types chart below, which comes from Robert J. Havighurst and Hilda Taba, *Adolescent Character & Personality* (New York: John Wiley & Sons, Inc., 1949).

PECK & HAVIGHURST

Factors & Focus
in Character Development

CONFORMER	EXPEDIENT
"consistent authoritarian" makes . . .	"parents support without demanding obedience or love"
+ Regularity, Rules — Autocratic control	+ general support — no clear cut right-wrong pattern
+ Trust, approval — Severe discipline	— laissez faire
R — ALTRUISTIC	**AMORAL**
"well-integrated, mature, internalized moral principles on which he acts, rather than on 'rules'"	"typically a rejected child"
+ Consistency + Mutual participation + let make decisions + trust & approval + consistent (lenient) discipline	— distrust — inconsistency — rejection — harsh discipline

(3) Break into family units for evaluation of home atmosphere. All participants at this time should be able to accept each other's evaluations and feelings, without necessarily agreeing. Discuss presence or absence, strength or weakness, of factors listed on the chart.

(4) Open question/answer time, with leader handling questions or reflecting them back to group for discussion.

Session 6

To help parents and teens define areas within which they sense a need for parental rules and guidance.

(1) Read from ARE YOU FOR REAL? the story of Jan (pp. 72-73) and discuss her ambivalent feelings.

Point out that youth are not asking for *complete* freedom, and that parents should not feel free to give it. But teens do need freedom. And parents need to fulfill their parental responsibilities. The goal this session is to seek a balance, and provide guidelines for both adults and teens.

(2) Parents and teens divide into separate groups, to discuss: "What areas should be controlled by clear rules and standards set by parents?"

The points of view of each should be shared in the whole group.

(3) Break into mixed groups (established at the first session) to attempt to work out guidelines for expectations in each area indicated by parents or teens as calling for parental involvement.

(4) Conclude with general discussion of the guidelines worked out in the small groups.

(5) Ask each family to go home and sit down together to set goals for their life together, developed from insights gained in the seminar.

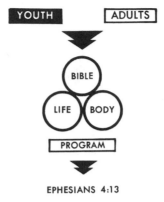

EPHESIANS 4:13

6

the responsible self

Growth toward maturity is marked in adolescence by the increasing capacity of young people to function as adults. Ability to think and understand shifts from childhood patterns to those that mark adulthood.[1] But seldom is a teenager given the opportunity in church or society to develop his capacity into ability. Instead, in most areas of life, adults withhold responsibility. Loukes, in discussing youth's passage to maturity, comments,

"Today we make our children economically dependent long after the age when we can call them 'children.' Our complex society demands a long period of initiation, when we dare not trust the young with the power of decision. And so the process of initiation becomes a long exclusion from initiative. The young must learn *how* to do, but they must never *do*. For us, therefore, the grant of 'freedom' becomes a kind of game. We deny the young real responsibility, and try to compensate them by giving them 'free time,' in which they can 'do what they like.' But human beings, curiously enough, do not want to 'do what they like.' They want to exercise responsibility, to make real choices, to engage in real human relations. We deny them real relationships with adults, and insist on their being content with the pupil-teacher relationship. So they respond by making their peer-group relationships which are, in a limited way, 'real,' with real risks and real choices, and so digging of the ground of human existence."[2]

While there is certainly reason to withhold some kinds of responsibility in a culture as complex as ours, there is little excuse for our practice in the church of withholding from youth the opportunity to live responsibly as Christians. And there is no excuse for our failure to concentrate on helping youth move toward a responsible living of their faith. But this we *have* done, in our classes where we insist on acceptance of what teacher

---

[1] See David Elkind, "Cognitive Development in Adolescence," *Understanding Adolescence*, ed. J. F. Adams.

[2] Harold Loukes, "Passport to Maturity," in Bernard, *Readings*, p. 167.

says, and in our replacement of initiation into responsibility with socials and entertainment.

We need to look again at our young people. And to see them as growing into — and in desperate need of — responsibility.

There are many ways we withhold — or seek to withhold — the power of decision from youth. One of the clearest examples is often found in classes where the Bible is studied. Look, for instance, at these descriptions of the Sunday school given by Christian teens:

> Week after week, we would go to the class, sit down, and listen to the teacher talk. The teacher would give the lesson, using little variety in the presentation, and without challenging us to think. There was little practical and personal application with which we could identify or practice during the week.
>
> Teacher talked *to* not *with* the class . . . teacher was more interested in giving his ideas than letting students develop their own . . . class topics were not relevant to the needs of the class . . . students had no interest, and attendance was a problem.
>
> Inevitably, after he had read the Scripture portion, he used this text as a sounding board for all his pet peeves against young people. And he would talk on in this fashion for about forty minutes. There was never any discussion. I do not remember anyone asking a question. Occasionally he would ask us a question, but it was like pulling teeth to get us to answer.

And from a visitor to a youth class:

> When I saw the teacher take out a little book and proceed to read from it, I saw each of the others there simultaneously settle back and tune out. When one of the guys raised his hand to make a comment, the teacher ignored him and droned on. Finally the boy interrupted, made a fairly perceptive statement, and got some interaction going, but this was soon squelched by the teacher who had to make it through the whole lesson before the time was up. I felt cheated.

Although of course it would be wrong to characterize *every* teen class by these descriptions, it is important to note that in none of the classes described (in fact, not in most classes in our churches) are teens treated as *responsible* persons — persons with the ability, and right, to think through issues for themselves.

Yet adolescence marks a definite growth in ability to consider issues, and also the development of a special need to do so. Garrison describes the impact of youth's growing ability to think critically, and the consequent generation of doubts, in this way:

> Many adolescents, especially those whose early training has been dogmatic in nature, become very skeptical of all problems not concrete

and not specific in nature. As the growing, developing youth increases his realm of knowledge and develops better habits of thinking, he is led to question many of the things he had formerly accepted uncritically. The youth coming into contact with more of life's realities assumes more mental and moral independence. He is thrown upon his own initiative and required to make decisions for himself. He comes to learn that many of the things he had been taught earlier and uncritically accepted are not in harmony with facts as presented at school or in his everyday readings. Early faith, so firmly entrenched, thus receives a serious setback when the child learns that the answers to many of his questions are not based upon almost obvious fact.[3]

So doubts come naturally to the adolescent. Sensing their growing ability to think, skeptical and demanding the right to test all things in order to know what is genuine, desiring reasons for their faith and better able to judge the validity of their own and others' reasonings, teenagers need a special kind of guidance — guidance that grants the right to think responsibly about faith and life.

The experience of a former student shows how deeply youth may feel about taking responsibility for their own actions.

> It has been in the church where I have had conflict over accepting adult authority. I don't have trouble accepting someone's authority over me; it's with the authority of the adult rules that I have had the conflicts.
>
> Ever since I can remember, as I was growing up in the church, we have always been told the many "don'ts." When I was in primary and junior high days, I never gave a second thought about them. Now that I am a teenager, I am reacting differently. I am thinking about these "don'ts" and making my own convictions about them. I believe it's between you and God to set your guidelines.
>
> When I began to question these many "don'ts" the attitude I got from adults was, "Don't question them, just accept them." Yet I couldn't do this. I wanted to know *why* I had to stay away from these sinful things.
>
> One conflict stands out in my mind. In our Youth Group at home, I was vice-president. Our youth director did not care for rock and roll. As a group we had had many discussions on the issue, but he seemed so narrow-minded. He wouldn't realize that there is a wide variety of rock and roll — from folk rock to hard rock. We knew not all the songs were clean, and we felt you should do your own distinguishing in listening.
>
> One Sunday our youth director decided anyone who wanted to hold a top position as leader or committee head had to give up rock and

[3]Karl C. Garrison, *Psychology of Adolescence* (Englewood Cliffs, N.J.: Prentice-Hall, 1965), p. 179.

roll. Of course, I was upset. But I prayed about it. In all honesty, I felt nothing was wrong with rock and roll, so I decided to resign rather than be a hypocrite.

Our whole youth group seemed on the verge of breaking up. Our Pastor became aware of the situation, and after a talk with our youth director, the restriction was lifted. It took several weeks before our group united once more.

To me, it seems as if the church is putting more emphasis on the "don'ts" of Christianity. I feel they should concentrate on God's love and how He can become real in your life. Once a teenager reaches this plateau, many of his activities may just go.

As I am growing, I am seeking God's will in my life. I am trying to live as I feel He would want me to live. At the same time, I try to understand why adults have set up these "don'ts." Only by realizing why, can I evaluate why I believe differently and see if I may need to make some revisions.

Ministry with youth demands not only that we recognize the young person's capacity to accept such responsibility for his own actions, *but that we actively encourage it.* The Bible exhorts believers to "live life . . . with a due sense of responsibility, not as men who do not know the meaning and purpose of life but as *those who do*" (Eph. 5:15, 16 *Phillips*). Abdicating responsibility in our life with God, acting uncritically on what others say we need to do to please Him, is completely unscriptural. And ministering with youth in such a way as to encourage such irresponsibility fits neither youth's characteristics nor Scripture's portrait of that maturity into which we want to guide them.

A letter written to teachers, parents, and sponsors by a man who served as youth department superintendent in a large evangelical church describes something of what is involved in treating youth responsibly. And it describes ways in which adults seek to withhold that responsibility for which teens' growing capacities fit them.

Dear friends,

The situation among some young people in our church is serious. Many of them are dissatisfied. A few have begun attending another church. Others are starting an organization through which they hope to find something they are not getting here.

Those involved are upper classmen, primarily seniors. They are, as a rule, our *best thinkers and leaders.* They are doing a good job of spreading discontent among *all* our young people.

There are many reasons for today's youth problems, which is by no means limited to our church. But one, which is very relevant to an evangelical church, has to do with the *inability of some parents, teachers, and sponsors to tolerate disagreement on the part of young people.* We often do not give our kids an opportunity in a climate of acceptance and understanding, to say what they really think and to ask the questions that really trouble them.

It is essential that we grant young people, without reservation, *the right to reach their own conclusions* — even when these conclusions are wrong. No matter how much we want to, *we CANNOT think for our young people,* nor can we compel them to accept our convictions. Only God can do that — and the sooner we accept this fact, the better. All *we* can do is to encourage them and *provide a climate that will be conducive to right conclusions.*

When young people don't accept our views, we must *encourage them to talk about their differences of opinion.* You don't change a person's mind by closing his mouth. If our kids don't talk in our hearing, they'll talk elsewhere — often without the presence of understanding adults who could help them think through to the logical conclusions of their ideas. *By being unwilling to listen, we are driving our kids underground.*

Our young people need our love. It will not do merely to act as though we love them, while really we are annoyed and upset. They are highly allergic to phony love, which includes only those of whom we approve. God can give us a genuine love — and ability to communicate it in words, actions, and attitudes. Our young people need our understanding and our acceptance *as they are* — not as we want them to be.

Otherwise, we'll soon be wondering where our young people have gone.

It would, of course, be wrong to suggest that youth have no need for adults in their re-examination of faith. For all their growing powers, youth are often idealistic and unrealistic. Judgment comes with an experience of and involvement in life which they usually lack. As a result, youth's examination of faith often breaks down at points where all critical thinking may go astray: failure to comprehend the problem, failure to gather enough information to draw meaningful conclusions; failure to organize information and insights appropriately. In all of these processes, adult guidance is often needed. But it must be, as my friend points out, the kind of guidance that treats youth as responsible persons; that grants them "the right to reach their own conclusions — even when these conclusions are wrong," and maintains a relationship of genuine love.

Competence

So far in this chapter we've looked at youth's expanding intellectual powers; their ability to think and question. Growth in ability to function on the "idea level" marks an increasing capacity to function as a whole person — not only to think about issues, but to express conclusions by living them out in experience.

Students of youth culture often pointed out that although young people speak out idealistically, they are slow to become involved in the crusades they criticize adults for not having undertaken. Young people have ambivalent feelings about responsibility: they want it, yet they are uncertain about their ability to handle it. As a result, youth who call most loudly for freedom and responsibility at the same time evade it, blaming and projecting responsibility onto parents, teachers, and other authority figures.[4] However, this trait is often due in our culture to the fact that young people are seldom given opportunity to test their competence and adequacy.

Friedenberg points out that youth have a tremendous respect for competence, and see it as one of the primary characteristics that distinguishes them from adults.[5] But, as Kvaraceus notes in *Dynamics of Delinquency*:

> Too often and too long American youth have been limited in their participation in important and worthwhile adult-like activities by law, by sentiment, and by overzealous adult-planning for youth. As a result, youth are too often relegated to passive participation roles or to the role of recipients of services rendered by adults in such areas as recreation, social and civic activity, religion, and schooling. . . . Locked out of meaningful and worthwhile adult-life tasks and activities, youth will try to fill in this waiting period with some kinds of maturing activities even though these may be along disapproved and delinquent routes. The emerging independence-seeking concerns of youth would tend to indicate that high school students are more ready to accept responsibility for adult-like tasks than the grown-ups are ready to provide opportunities for such experiences.[6]

Two general approaches to solving problems created by failure to develop competence have been suggested. One is to stop isolating youth from the problems and challenges adults face. Arguing from this approach in the *Journal of Marriage and the Family*, Ethel Venables notes that "one of the worst aspects of any alienation of young people from the adult world is that they are cut off from discussion of adult problems. To live through these is an essential preliminary to making responsible decisions when these are faced

---

[4]Ray Moore, "Helping Adolescents Achieve Psychological Growth," *Adolescence*, Vol. 5, No. 17, Spring 1970, pp. 37-54.

[5]Friedenberg, *The Vanishing Adolescent*, p. 17.

[6]Kvaraceus, *Dynamics of Delinquency*, p. 237.

on one's own . . . Young people must not be 'protected' from the troublesome aspects of civilized living — they need to be prepared to face them; and in this writer's experience, they are ready to respond to any overture which welcomes them into the adult community and indicates a genuine desire to hear their opinions."[7]

Certainly a similar approach is open to us in Christian education of youth. We need not protect young people from the challenges of Christian life and ministry to the world. Rather we need to let them share involvement with and concern for others. We need to let them participate with us in all that being Christ's disciples means. For too often the image of "irresponsible" teens (who, in one church I served were so characterized because they didn't fulfill assignments to bring potato chips and dip to one of our too-frequent socials!) is one we ourselves have fostered by cutting them off from activities that all but the youngest must view as childish.

Graham Blaine suggests a second and related approach: involving young people in hardship experiences which give each youth a "chance to prove his adequacy earlier in life, hardships to overcome in childhood, and a chance to act on his own."[8] Blaine feels this might enable young people who suffer emotional problems in college because of a sense of inadequacy to work toward maturity. While Blaine seems to think primarily in terms of physical endurance (like those provided in the "outward bound"[9] type of experiences), the concept of providing youth with a challenge through which they can both prove and develop their competence is appropriate to the emotional and spiritual challenges of disciplined living for Christ.

What I am suggesting, then, and will develop in later chapters, is that we structure youth ministry to involve our youth in real life, not to *protect* them from it; and that youth be guided toward maturity by helping them accept responsibility for their own growth and activities, under a distinctive adult leadership that at all times treats teens as responsible persons.

Toward interdependence

In thinking of the emergence of youth as responsible and disci-

---

[7]Ethel Venables, "Proposed Affinities in British and American Perspectives on Adolescence," *Journal of Marriage and the Family*, May, 1965.

[8]Graham B. Blaine, Jr., *Youth and the Hazards of Affluence* (New York: Harper and Row, 1966) pp. 103ff.

[9]A number of Christian organizations, including Wheaton College and Youth for Christ, are using such stress experiences in efforts to develop Christian leadership.

plined persons, it is important to see adolescence as *the* time of transition — the time when each young person is working toward a new and lasting definition of who he is as a person. When we see our youth in this framework, our ministry goals shift from those involving external conformity to those involving character formation. We want young people whose values are distinctively Christian, who live responsibly with others in church and world, and who in dependence on God make wise and mature choices.

During the adolescent years, those years of physical, emotional, social, and intellectual transformation, children grow out of their childhood and toward the kind of men and women they will become. Since adolescence is the time of the emerging self, the time of becoming, *the way we understand and guide our young people has the greatest of impacts on the kind of Christian persons they become.* Understanding their feelings and needs, the pressures that operate within their personalities and their culture, we can better relate to youth as persons, and better provide the distinctive kind of ministry they need.

Perhaps the sharpest impression that I have from my study of and experience with youth is that they need *facilitating relationships:* relationships with their parents, marked by openness of communication and willingness to explore one another's feelings and viewpoints without condemning or demanding change; relationships with other adults, marked by the adult's growing respect for the young person as a responsible person, and certainly in the later high school years marked by treatment of teens as fully responsible persons, extending to each the right of decision-making, and involving each in discipleship; and relationships with other teens in which needs and feelings and perceptions are honestly shared, and in which support and love and — where needed — forgiveness are extended.

The context of supporting, helping relationships permits a growth toward maturity that is *growth into interdependence* — not independence. For none of us is truly independent. We need others. As Christians we stand in particular need of other believers, who with us form Christ's Body. For it is in and through the Body that Christ's Spirit works our individual transformation, and guides us corporately into the will of Christ, our Head. The mature Christian is an interdependent man, who ministers to others and is ministered to, and who through lifelong involvement in such supportive relationships increasingly truly reflects and represents his Lord.

But along with facilitating relationships, young people need an honest experience of life. Christian interdependence is not designed to protect the individual from the challenges of life, but to equip him to meet them. Christian life is far better represented by the soldier than the sheep, and by terms like "disciple" and "witness" and "servant" than by "child." For the Christian is called to live vigorously in the world that *is*. Equipment for such active involvement for Christ demands the opportunity for the young Christian to develop competence. How foolish to withhold from youth the chance to function as Christ's disciple during the growing years — and then expect on the arrival of a birthday or on graduation from a school some sudden appearance of traits of character we never permitted to develop! If the "self" that develops during adolescence is to be the competent, responsible Christian self we see portrayed in Scripture, then our ministry during the transition years needs to be geared to developing just that competence with which adulthood is to be marked.

PROBE
case histories
discussion questions
thought-provokers
resources

1. Earlier I provided a list of goals of ministry with youth, developed by three Christian educators. Look back over these last three chapters, and in view of youth's characteristics and the nature of adolescence as transition toward adulthood, re-evaluate the listed goals. And try now to develop your own set of goals, keeping in mind that goals state *what* we want to do, not necessarily *how* we expect to do it.
   For example, in this chapter I suggested two goals which loom large in my own thinking about youth ministry. I feel we must help youth develop the ability to function in <u>interdependent personal relationships,</u> and we must provide opportunity for youth to develop <u>competence in living the Christian life</u>. I'm sure there will be other goals you will want to add.

2. I mentioned in this chapter the need to treat young people as responsible persons in view of their growing mental powers. Several illustrations I used may have given the impression (which I have) that in most of our talk about our faith adults do *not* view or treat youth as responsible persons. As a result, many questions and doubts of youth are forced underground, and many conclusions

103

they reach might well have been different if their thoughts had been accepted and the issues discussed with others.

3. A very creative and enthusiastic friend of mine, Mr. Dick Muzik, who has been associate Dean at Wheaton College and is now working on his Ph.D. at Michigan State University, has had an extensive retreat ministry with teens. One of the areas he has focused on is that of helping teens open up to each other as persons, and begin to share their perceptions and feelings. As this is an important step toward the development of interdependence in the peer group, I am including with his permission a retreat schedule and samples of some of the tools Dick has developed.

SCHEDULE

FRIDAY NIGHT

5:30 pm	Leave church.
7:00	Arrive at camp (unload and find a bunk).
7:30	Free time
9:30	Snack (Pizza)
10:00	Meeting: "DDT" (Dick's Discussion Time)
11:00	ACTIVITIES (Marathon)
1:00 am	Lights out! Mouths shut! Sleep!!! (Are you kidding?)

SATURDAY

7:00 am	Roll out
8:00	Wheaties (Breakfast for Rejects!)
8:30	Free "BURP" time (Counselors meet)
9:00	COMMUNICATING TIME! "Sometimes I feel like a BLOB." (Film) Break time TOPIC continued: "Quit staring at ME!"
11:30	Free time
12:30 pm	"GRUB" (Eat!)
1:00	Free Time (also organized confusion)
5:30	Banquet (Funniest formal wear)
6:30	COMMUNICATING TIME: "What does God the Father Look Like?" Break time TOPIC continued
8:30	Free time
9:30	Snack (Go ahead — buy that candy and rot your teeth!)
10:30	Candle Lighting Service (Devotions)
11:00	Lights out

SUNDAY

8:00 am	Let's shake it.
9:00	Ugh! EGGS!
9:30	Re-adjust dirt in cabins.
10:00	COMMUNICATING TIME: "Parent-Teen Relationships" Break time TOPIC continued
12:00	Free time
12:30 pm	STEAK (Well . . . it looked like steak.)
1:30	Start packing the bus with your OWN things.
2:00	COVENANT SERVICE
2:30	ADIOS AMIGOS!

"HOW I RELATE"
(Presented to Youth Group the Sunday Before the Retreat)

AGE: _____

SEX: _____

Rate yourself as to how well you relate in the following
areas by checking the right box:

SCALE: A. Relate well
              B. Relate above average
              C. Average
              D. Difficult relating
              E. I don't relate

	A	B	C	D	E
1. I understand myself					
2. I relate well to non-Christians					
3. I get along with my brothers or sisters					
4. I am accepted by Christian young people					
5. I get along happily with my parents					
6. I can relate closely with 1 or 2 other teens					
7. I am being accepted in school					
8. I can stand up to pressure by other teens					
9. I have meaningful friendships with adults					
10. I am being accepted as a mature person at church					
11. I have a close relationship with God					
12. I can make and keep close relationships					
13. I can settle disagreements with my parents					
14. I have healthy relationships with the opposite sex					
15. I am respected by my parents as a mature person					

NOW, put the number 1, 2 or 3 next to the following topics that you
would like to have discussed in that order on the retreat:

___ Relating to myself
___ Relating to non-Christians
___ Relating to my brothers/sisters
___ Relating to my parents
___ Relating to Christian kids
___ Relating to other adults
___ Relating to others at school
___ Relating to others at church
___ Developing close friendships
___ Developing a close relationship with God

Dear God,
    I want you to help me on this retreat to . . .

(This section is filled out, detached and sealed in an envelope by teenager;
handed back at the end of the retreat. This is a check to see if God did
what they asked Him to do before the retreat.)

(Kick-off Friday P.M.)

"COMMUNICATING WITH MY CHRISTIAN FRIENDS"

(HUMOR)

THOUGHT PROVOKERS:

Who or what is that person sitting next to me?

What is a friendship? How does it affect me?

Do I need Christian friendships?

Why do we have so many surface relationships with others in the youth group?

When was the last time you made a special effort to get to know someone deeper than the "Hi, how are you? Just fine" level?

Who was the last Christian friend you really shared your real self with?

Am I sensitive to the needs of each individual in our youth group? Or do I deliberately give certain people the cold shoulder?

Why do we form cliques? Why is there so much group pressure?

What's it like to be an "outsider" or "loner" in the group?

(POLARIZE FEELINGS)

EXPERIMENT:

Circle — backs to each other — close eyes — discuss: "Who in my group is most like me and why?"

Turn around and express your feelings in one sentence to the group.

(Recorder writes down observations by the group.)

Why do I feel this way?

Next, the person you named to be most like you is to share why he or she is or is not most like you.

GENERALIZATIONS:

Acceptance, need for belonging

Sensitivity to others' needs

Sharing, being honest with others

Love

Care

SCRIPTURAL PRINCIPLES:

Another church group: I Corinthians 11:17-22

Biblical fellowship causes deep personal relationships:

Matthew 20:26-28	Galatians 6:2
John 13:34	Hebrews 10:24
Acts 2:1, 20:35	James 5:16
Romans 15:1-2	1 Peter 3:8

RECONSIDER OPENING QUESTIONS

CHALLENGE AND SILENT PRAYER

(Presented Saturday A.M.)

SELF-IDENTITY

"COMMUNICATING: RELATING TO MYSELF"

"WHO AM I?"

(HUMOR)

THOUGHT PROVOKERS: Have you ever asked yourself these questions:

Why do I get into lousy moods?

How can a person find himself?

Why am I doing the things I do?

What makes me so prone to temptation and putting God last when I know better?

I like myself. Is this wrong?

Who am I? Does how I think determine what I am? Am I weird in the way I reason and think?

I seem to be changing all the time and I think it's hard to understand myself, my actions, and my feelings.

How can we like ourselves if we can't even understand or cope with ourselves?

Why do I do things? Why do I sin when I don't want to?

EXERCISE: Character study: "Sometimes I Feel Like a Blob!"
or Film: "Charlie Churchman & Teenage Masquerade"
Question: Why do teens wear masks? (Feedback)

SPEAKER'S COMMENTS: How I see myself and the forces involved.

BREAK

DISCUSSION: "QUIT STARING AT ME!"

ENCOURAGEMENT:

Say what you really feel in your group.

Gain group acceptance and respect.

Take your work together seriously.

EXERCISE:

Hand out the following questionnaire. Let the young people answer individually. Then have each member in the group try to guess the self-evaluations of the other members. This will provide a positive opportunity for each person to hear how the other members see him.

SELF-IDENTITY

"COMMUNICATING: RELATING TO MYSELF"

"WHO AM I?" (cont.)

"HOW I SEE MYSELF"

AGE: _____

SEX: _____

Check the box that best fits the way you see yourself.
Really be honest with yourself.
SCALE: A. All the time
             B. Most of the time
             C. More than usual
             D. Sometimes
             E. Never

	A	B	C	D	E
1. I am concerned with my appearance					
2. I want others to respect my opinion					
3. I get mad easily					
4. I am eager to get along with others					
5. I like working around the house					
6. I have a meaningful relationship with God					
7. I can express my feelings and thoughts easily					
8. I like to be alone					
9. I don't mind what others say about me					
10. I like to talk about myself with other people					
11. I am afraid of failure					
12. I like to read the Bible					
13. I like to enter into discussions with those my age					
14. I am critical of others					
15. I don't understand myself					
16. I like to study					
17. I like to just "shoot the bull" with the gang					
18. I like to go places with my parents					
19. I put on a good "front" to others					
20. I need to be with people					
21. I like myself, but I am also self-critical					
22. I am sensitive to the feelings and needs of others					
23. I like to be with my brothers and sisters					
24. I feel relaxed around my minister, teacher, etc.					
25. I make friends easily					

SPEAKER'S COMMENTS: How others see me.

TIME OF SILENT REFLECTION AND MEDITATION.

"SOMETIMES I FEEL LIKE A BLOB!"

HOW I SEE MYSELF:

I can't get a clear picture of myself. Who am I?

I need a better self-understanding of my feelings.

I tend to downgrade myself.

I want to understand what forms my self-concept.

INNER FORCES:

Physical, mental, sociological, emotional, and spiritual changes involved in growth.

The old nature is active.

    Study Jeremiah 17:9

           Romans 7:13-20

           Psalm 19:12

HOW GOD SEES ME:

Read Proverbs 16:2

     1 Samuel 16:7

     1 Corinthians 4:3, 4

God accepts us as we are. Philippians 1:6 "And I am sure that God who began the good work within you will keep right on helping you grow in His grace until His task within you is finally finished on that day when Jesus Christ returns."

Be honest with yourself. Romans 12:3b; 12:2

This uncertainty of who I am is normal.

Self-examination and self-doubt hurts for a while, but it is necessary.

A person tries to be what he thinks he is, and can end up being a phoney all his life; but who wants to be a phoney?

He can develop false fronts and try to be like his friends; but no one can be someone else.

You've got to be yourself! And accept yourself for the time being as you change.

"QUIT STARING AT ME!"

HOW OTHERS SEE ME:

I change to fit any situation.

I become what others want me to be.

I can "psyche" anyone out.

OUTER FORCES:

Other people can mold our self-concept.

Like a compass placed in the center of four magnets, our personality needle would go crazy. CONFUSION!!!

People form pictures of us; so we act to fit the picture; but what happens when we have to form more than one picture at a time? FRUSTRATION!!!

REFLECTIVE PROCESS: "Seeing ourselves the way others see us is a big part of the way we form our self-concept." But it is an unconscious process. Sometimes the pictures others reflect to us are cloudy and often warped ones.

HOW PERSONALITIES ARE FORMED: We learn to fit others' expectations; we imitate other people; we decide for ourselves by applying self-chosen principles.

We want to be liked and accepted by others (e.g. at school); we don't want to be laughed at. We respond to our feelings and not necessarily to the real facts. It is here and now that we live.

Other people's values are built into our lives.

WHAT DO I DO?

Accept your limitations.

Realize that part of your self-image is shaped by others; but be careful of their pictures, for they may be wrong.

Understand the change taking place in your life and that it is only for a little while; keep your mind up to date with your physical changes.

Evaluate your strengths and don't spend all your time thinking about your weaknesses; we tend to downgrade ourselves more than we should.

Examine your values.

The criteria for your self-concept should be based on Scripture:

1 Samuel 16:7	"Man looks on the outward appearances, but the Lord looks on the heart."
Romans 12:17b	"Do things in such a way that everyone can see you are honest clear through."
2 Timothy 1:7	"For the Holy Spirit, God's gift, does not want you to be afraid of people, but to be wise and strong, and to love them and enjoy being with them."
Ephesians 4:16	"Under His direction the whole body is fitted together perfectly, and each part in its own special way helps the other parts, so that the whole body is healthy and growing and full of love."
Romans 8:28, 29	"And we know that all that happens to us is working for our good if we love God and are fitting into His plans."

"COMMUNICATING WITH THE TRINITY 'FAMILY' "

THOUGHTS:

What does God the Father look like?
God has revealed Himself through nature, Bible, Christ, and man.
We are created in His image (Gen. 1:26).
  It is a spirit image (now we have a distorted image).
  We have everything that God has, but in a lesser degree. (Example)
  Our spirit image was placed in a shell called a body.
  Have you ever stepped out of your shell and taken a good look at the
    real you?
  God has made us so that we have feelings and moods; so does God.
  The body has no senses when we are not in it.
Let's examine this "Spirit Body" of God the Father.

"SPIRIT BODY" OF GOD:

1 John 4:12	No man hath seen God.
Exodus 33:11, 20-23	Face to face
John 4:24	"God is a Spirit; and they that worship Him must worship Him in Spirit and in Truth."
Genesis 3:8	Voice of God
Proverbs 15:3	Omniscient (all-knowing at any time [eyes])
Psalm 139:7-12, 17	Omnipresent (everywhere at one time [hand, thoughts])
1 John 1:5	Light
Psalm 89:14	Holy, Righteous, Just, Good, Truth (face, throne)
1 John 4:8	Love
Genesis 17:1	Omnipotent (all-powerful at any time)
James 1:17	Immutable (unchanging)

ANTHROPOMORPHIC WORDS are picture words of nonhuman elements;
e.g., eyes, face.

THEOPHANIES are appearances of God in human form. They cease with
the Incarnation of Christ.

GROUPS SHARE THEIR CONCEPTS OF GOD THE FATHER:
  Pass out form for drawing God's Spirit Image. Include the above verses
    and leave space for drawing.
  Have each group study the Scripture verses and form a group concept
    of God.
  Draw concept and have someone ready to explain the group's concept.

BREAK TIME

"COMMUNICATING WITH THE TRINITY 'FAMILY' " (cont.)

THOUGHTS:

Have you ever heard yourself thinking these thoughts:

Man, I have a hard time praying; it seems like my prayers bounce off the ceiling sometimes!

God seems like He is way out there some place; He is just a concept to me and not a real Person interested in my life.

There are times when I don't want to have devotions; I am not in the spiritual mood.

Sometimes the Bible is dry and dull when I read it; it doesn't mean that much to me.

God won't have fellowship with me when I feel this way or when there is sin in my life.

Sometimes I want to communicate with God, but I have no motivation! I want to, but can't!!

GROUPS DISCUSS THE FOLLOWING QUESTIONS:

Why can't I and why don't I communicate with God at times?

Record your observations and be ready to share them with the whole group.

FEED BACK TO THE WHOLE GROUP

GENERALIZATIONS (They should be interesting!):

Form the parallelisms between their pictures of God the Father and the observations to the questions.

No communication because of a distorted concept or lack of concept of who God is.

Share a few concepts and reasons for not communicating.

SPIRITUAL PRINCIPLES FOR APPLICATION:

Romans 8:19-28   (The Holy Spirit for the spiritual motivation vacuum. We just don't realize how much God wants to have fellowship with us. Cf. teens shutting out parent.)

Luke 15:11-32   (God's acceptance, grace, love, forgiveness, reward. Spiritual mood? Sin? Yes, He will have fellowship with you; but what kind of relationship?)

Hebrews 12:5-14   (How God trains and corrects us; horizontal and vertical relationships compared.)

God accepts us: even when spiritually dry.
even when living in sin.
even when out of fellowship with Him.
just as I am, as a unique individual.

Christian life is   If you try it by the yard, it's hard;
a step at a time: But if you try it by the inch, it's a cinch.

CHALLENGE TEENS ON THESE PRINCIPLES:

Relationships
Questionable things
Spiritual dryness
Salvation

SILENT REFLECTION & MEDITATION (Invitation)

"COMMUNICATING WITH THE TRINITY 'FAMILY' " (cont.)

CONCEPTS OF GOD

Casper the Holy Ghost
Arm with hand (bird, flower, strength, love)
Fog — Omnipresence
Sphere — perfect shape, can see all around
Big Brother — always watching
Air — You can't breath the same air too long
Space — a vacuum
Light — penetrates darkness (sun rays)
Hand, heart, world (protection)
Wave — constantly flowing
Uncle Sam wants you
Sallman's picture of Christ
Sign of infinity
Cube — all sides visible, structure
Cloud
Man with blank face
Tank
Big eye
Mountain range
Whirlwind
Flame of fire
Pinholes in space

REASONS FOR NOT COMMUNICATING

Sin and guilt
Don't need God
Not aware of Him as a Person
Stubborn
Wrong attitudes and concepts
Afraid
Don't read His Word
No devotions
Don't feel it's important
Mind wanders
Too busy
Lazy
Don't like to admit wrong or sin
Fear of disapproval
Temperamental
God's a last resort to get me out of trouble,
    fear, problems or to get me something I want

(Saturday P.M. Devotional)

CANDLE-LIGHTING SERVICE

(Room dark with one big candle lit in the center of room; people sit in circle; no talking.)

RETREAT AND POSSIBLE AFTER-EFFECTS:

Hilltop experience
 Place away from home, school, church, and the gang.
 Time set aside for spiritual growth.
Back home
 All gingersnaps for a while and then . . . zap!
 School and the gang pressures
 Home discouragements with parents, brothers, sisters, chores, etc.
 Spiritual dryness sets in; laziness; no devotions; no talk with God.
 Satanic attacks
 Finally, back in the old rut before the retreat advance.

RETREAT AFTER-GLOW:

Development of support groups with friends
 Sharing our hidden self with each other
 Being open
 Building honesty
 Developing confidence, sincerity, proper self-image
 Caring for each other's needs
Now to continue and build your support group at home
 Prayer
 Sharing problems and joys
 Healing each other's wounds
 Witnessing (sharing Christ with others)

SCRIPTURE:

Acts 1:9-14; 3:42-47   (After Christ leaves the disciples)
Hebrews 10:19-27   (God's command)

SYMBOLISM OF LIGHTED CANDLES:

Each candle represents a Christian.
Through the pressures of life, they go out; but we have other Christians to relight our candles.
Go forth in your group to your cabins, stopping along the way to light any candle in your group that may have been blown out. (Light candles before leaving.)

WARNING:

No talking back in the cabins; get ready for bed.
This time of silence is for you and your counselor to talk.
Make sure you are not responsible for causing someone to miss an opportunity to get a spiritual problem worked out with God.

(Presented Sunday A.M.)

"COMMUNICATING: PARENT-TEEN RELATIONSHIPS"

(HUMOR)

ENCOURAGEMENT:
Say what you really feel.
Gain group acceptance and respect.
Take your work together seriously.

THOUGHT PROVOKER:
It is a known fact, even in Christian families, that there are personality tensions because of various personal views of life happenings within the family. This becomes very noticeable in parent-teen relationships.

PASS OUT PARENT-TEEN RELATIONSHIP FORM
TO BE FILLED OUT: (See next page.)
Discuss individual observations in the group and the following questions: "Why do you think this area seems so important to your parents? To you?"

BREAK TIME

FEEDBACK OF OBSERVATIONS (symptoms of greater problems)

SCRIPTURAL PRINCIPLES TO BE APPLIED TO
THE PARTICULAR PROBLEMS

Philippians 2:3-9	unselfishness, concern for another's interests
Psalm 133:1	unity
Romans 12:9-10	love
Ephesians 4:2-3, 32	patience, peace, forgiveness, consideration
Proverbs 12:17, 19, 22	honesty
1 Timothy 4:12	responsibility, trustworthiness
Ephesians 6:1-4	respect, obedience.
(Other principles)	communication, listening
	understanding, rapport
	give and take, sharing of problems, joys, etc.
	growing interdependence
	desire for a degree of freedom
	respect for others' opinions
	desire to make own decisions.

CHALLENGE TEENS ON THESE PRINCIPLES:
Respect, Responsibilities, Relationships — Eccl. 12:1-2, 6-7, 13-14

TIME OF SILENT REFLECTION & MEDITATION
(Discussion on questions . . . interject Scripture suggestions above.)
Optional—use candle lighting service if this talk is presented Saturday P.M.

"COMMUNICATING: PARENT-TEEN RELATIONSHIPS" (cont.)

AGE: _____

SEX: _____

The following topics are some of the areas where tensions develop in the home. Check the box that best describes your family situation as you see it. Please be very honest.

SCALE: A. Excellent — no problems here.

             B. Good — we usually get along.

             C. O.K. — sometimes it is a problem, sometimes not.

             D. Not so hot — quite a bit of trouble over this topic.

             E. Bad scene — we don't get along at all on this topic.

TOPICS:

	A	B	C	D	E
1. Dating					
2. Going steady					
3. Choice of friends					
4. Hours I come in at night					
5. Use of spare time (goofing off)					
6. Way I like to dress					
7. My hair					
8. Chores around the house					
9. Money matters					
10. Use of car					
11. Brothers					
12. Sisters					
13. Choosing a career					
14. Choosing a college					
15. Pressure to go to church					
16. Pressure to get involved in church					
17. Music I listen to					
18. Dancing					
19. Movies					
20. Smoking					
21. School					
22. Grades					
23. Use of telephone					
24. Authority					
25. Discipline					
26. Study habits					
27. T.V.					
28. Temper					
29. Talking back					
30. Family discussions					
31. Places I go					
32. Working (job)					

Write down the principles found in the verses on the previous page that will ease the tensions in your family.

(Sunday P.M.)

COVENANT SERVICE
MY COVENANT

Many influential Christians recommend to young people that they make a written covenant with God concerning their future. Betty Stam once made a covenant at a youth retreat. She was later called upon to be a missionary martyr for the Lord. Some years earlier, Dr. A. B. Simpson entered into a covenant with the Lord. He later became the founder of one of our smaller denominations. Printed below are both of their covenants. Read them over carefully, then, using the questions on the bottom of this page for a guide, enter into your own covenant with God. Write it out as you would a letter to a friend. No one else will ever see this unless you show it to them, but it will be a solemn promise to God which you will never forget. Sign your name to the covenant and put it in the envelope. Address the envelope and seal it. This covenant will be mailed to you in two to four months so that you can see how you have progressed since this day to then.

BETTY STAM'S COVENANT

"Lord I give up all my own plans and purposes, all my own desires and hopes, and accept Thy will for my life. I give myself, my life, my all utterly to Thee to be Thine forever. Fill me with Thy Holy Spirit. Use me as Thou wilt; send me where Thou wilt; work out Thy whole will in my life at any cost, now and forever."

A. B. SIMPSON'S COVENANT

"I am from henceforth a soldier of the Cross, a follower of the Lamb, and my motto is, 'I have one King, even Jesus.' Support me and strengthen me, and be mine forever, O Lord. Place me in those circumstances thou mayest desire; but if it be thy will, give me neither poverty nor riches. Now give me thy Spirit and thy protection in my heart at all times and then I shall drink of thy rivers of salvation, lie down by still waters, and be infinitely happy in the favor of my God."

QUESTIONS

1. What is my purpose in life?
2. How will I honor God in my life?
3. What part of my life has been given to Him? Have I yet given my all to Him?
4. What price am I willing to pay for His will to be done in my life?
5. What do I want God to do for me? Through me?
    (These questions may help you in writing your covenant.)

TO THE COUNSELOR:

(This is the last service before going home. It pulls the strings together and solidifies God's working over the weekend in the teens' lives. Seal the covenants in separate envelopes and after two to four months mail them to the ones who wrote them so that they may make a personal check-up.)

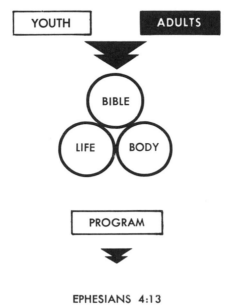

YOUTH ADULTS

BIBLE

LIFE BODY

PROGRAM

EPHESIANS 4:13

ADULTS AS LEADERS

CHAPTERS

7

being a leader

Earlier I suggested that we need to think of youth ministry as "the involvement together of youth and adults in three processes which are basic to maturing in the Christian faith." In the preceding three chapters we looked at youth, trying to see them as persons, distinct individuals certainly, but at the same time individuals who share developmental experiences common to all. In these next three chapters we will look at the adults who minister with youth. We want to see them as leaders — to understand what, biblically, a Christian leader is and how he ministers. We want to see them in relationship with youth — to understand the nature and quality of the person-to-person contact leaders must develop to be effective ministers. And we want to look at adults as counselors — an often misunderstood role, which requires redefinition.

Strikingly, leadership in the Church of Jesus Christ differs drastically from what the world thinks of as leadership. As Christ pointedly reminded His disciples, "You know that the rulers of the heathen lord it over them and that their great ones have absolute power? But it must not be so among you. No, whoever among you wants to be great must become the servant of you all, and if he wants to be first among you he must be your slave — just as the Son of Man has not come to be served but to serve, and to give his life to set many others free" (Matt. 20:25-28 Phillips). The implications of this active, servant style of leadership has seldom been understood in the church. Rather than become the servant and do, church leaders, like secular leaders, have tended to grasp at authority and tell others to do. But "it must not be so among you." Christian leadership — and especially leadership with youth — finds its distinctive pattern in the servant.

I noted last chapter that one of the ways youth feel adults differ from them is in their *competence* — their ability to function effectively.

It is clear that even within youth culture, competence is highly

121

regarded. The athlete is respected for his competence on the sports field; the friendly, well-liked boy or girl is admired for social competence. Because both physical and social skills are highly valued by youth, admiration is shown in imitation. The admired person, the competent person, is imitated.

Recently the role of imitation and the importance of the social model in learning and character development has been stressed in the social sciences. Roger Brown, in discussing the acquisition of morality, points out that "observation of adults" produces much more change in behavior than "direct reward."[1] It is more important to see attitudes and values expressed in life than to be "told" what to do, and be rewarded for specific behaviors.[2]

This concept is one definitely tied into the Bible's teaching on leadership, not only as implied in the concept of the servant (one who acts and *himself* performs necessary tasks rather than telling others what to do), but also as shown in the example of Christ and Paul, and in exhortations to young leaders. We are all familiar with Christ's method of leading: He took His disciples with Him as He taught and healed; He explained His actions and teachings when they were alone together; He sent them out to act as He had, listening to their reports and correcting them; after His resurrection and return to the Father He gave them the responsibility of acting as He had acted in this world.[3]

The apostle Paul also put much stress on living in such close relationship with his converts that they could see the Christian life made concrete and practical in him. He did not hesitate to put himself forward as a model. He told the Corinthians, "In Christ Jesus I am your spiritual father through the gospel; that is why I implore you to follow the footsteps of me your father" (1 Cor. 4:15, 16 *Phillips*). He exhorted, but when he called for a particular attitude marking spiritual maturity he said, "Let me be your example here, my brothers: let my example be the standard by which you can tell who are the genuine Christians among those about you" (Phil. 3:17 *Phillips*). And in another place he called on his converts to imitate him, as he himself imitated Christ.

---

[1]Roger Brown, *Social Psychology* (New York: The Free Press, 1965) p. 387.

[2]See also the discussion by A. Bandura and R. H. Walter in *Social Learning and Personality Development* (New York: Holt, Rinehart & Winston, 1963).

[3]Christ surely had this type of leadership in mind also when He said to His disciples not long before His ascension: "As the Father has sent me, even so I send you" (John 20:21 *RSV*).

When we understand the need all learners have of a model to imitate, we can grasp the significance of Paul's advice to young ministers: "Keep a critical eye both upon your own life and on the teaching you give" (1 Tim. 4:16 *Phillips*). The *life* is mentioned first! For the reality, the truth, of the words of the Gospel are to be incarnated in the person — the character, the behavior — of the Christian leader. Thus something of the meaning of Paul's statement linking words, life, and spiritual power becomes more clear. "The Kingdom of God," he says, "is not a matter of a spate of words but of the power of Christian living" (1 Cor. 4:20 *Phillips*). And Christian living, incarnating in the person and behavior of the leader all those realities God's Word calls us to experience, is utterly basic to leadership with youth.

Young people have been shown to overvalue and to idealize adults — to have a much higher opinion of them than is realistic. Particularly liked and appreciated are adults who have some leadership relationship with youth and who are perceived by them as considerate, fair, and reasonably capable.[4] Simply put, young people respond to adults who minister with them, and if they are not turned off by a leader's personality or incompetence, *will* model themselves after him.

To a large extent, the impression young people have of the nature of the Christian life will be gained not from our words but from our example.

Thus the first criterion for selecting a person to minister with youth is his *competence as a Christian*. He must, in fact, model the attitudes, the feelings, the values, the enthusiasm, and the dedication which he seeks to develop in youth. The concern for who the leader is overrides any other in youth ministry.

The place of the example and the servant nature of leadership in Christian ministry specifies those situations in which adults are to be involved with youth. Too often in the contemporary church youth and adults come together only within church walls, or on occasions where they *talk about* the Christian life — not live it. And so very often we develop young people who can talk a good faith, but who have no capacity to express faith through their life in the world. We have such young people in large measure because they

---

[4]Ethel Lawin, *Later Childhood and Adolescence* (New York: The Macmillan Co., 1963) pp. 200ff.

have had opportunity only to hear adults talk their faith — not to see them live it in the real world.

So the processes in which youth and adults need to be involved together *must* include "real situations" — situations in which adults serve as models of Christ's life, Christ's love, and Christ's concern for others in those very arenas where the ground of our existence is probed. So, too, no adult who ministers with youth dare relate to teens only in the formal situation of class or meeting. *He has to go out into the arenas where their lives are lived, to be with them on their "home turf," and there demonstrate the power of Christian living.*

Leadership and authority

Probably there is little that irritates and concerns adults more about young people these days than youth's apparent rejection of authority. While much of this reflects youth's struggle for independence, other reasons are rooted in their view of authority itself. In the church very often our conflict with young people is due to our own failure to come to grips with the implications of Christ's warning about the wrong kind of leadership, and His parallel presentation of the servant as a leadership model.

For one thing is sure about a servant: he hardly *commands* the obedience of those he serves!

Yet there is in Scripture a definite authority invested in leaders. Paul writes to the Thessalonians, "Get to know those who work so hard among you. They are your spiritual leaders to keep you on the right path. Because of this high task of theirs, hold them in highest honor" (1 Thess. 5:12, 13 *Phillips*). Other passages give insight into the fact that keeping others on the right path involves a variety of ministries — including rebuking, exhorting, and opposing a person who has strayed, even bringing a believer before the church for the whole group to discipline by withdrawal of fellowship. Scripture gives a distinct impression of vital and aggressive leadership in the church. There is no wishy-washy withdrawal from conflict or from contact when things within the church need to be set straight.

Yet the central place of leaders in the life of the church gives, in itself, no indication of *how* their authority is exercised — of *how* the leader leads and "keeps others on the right path."

We see more of the "how" in Peter's words as an elder to other elders:

Now may I who am myself an elder say a word to you my fellow elders? I speak as one who actually saw Christ suffer, and as one who will share with you the glories that are to be unfolded to us. I urge you then to see that your "flock of God" is properly fed and cared for. Accept the responsibility of looking after them willingly and not because you feel you can't get out of it, doing your work not for what you can make, but because you are really concerned for their well-being. You should aim not at being 'little tin gods' but . . . examples of Christian living in the eyes of the flock committed to your charge (1 Peter 5:1-3 *Phillips*).

And to this leader, who acts out of concern for his flock and who serves as an example of all that being a Christian means, believers are to "submit" (see 1 Peter 5:5).

It is important to note that in his word to leaders Peter gives no *(Paul did)* hint of pulling rank, or insisting that others do as leaders say. These things are simply not within the leadership style of the church. Leaders are servants. They do not command or demand. But as servants Christian leaders have the most compelling of all authorities: the authority of example, the imperative of competence.

The confusion that is generated in the church between the generations about leadership and authority isn't really too surprising. The idea of "authority" is a complex one, one capable of encompassing contradictory ideas. But the confusion may be reduced by thinking about different dimensions of authority.

The base of authority There are several possible bases for the exercise of authority. Among them are open coercive power, the institutional role, and ability.

A person or organization can command obedience and regulate obedience because it has the power to punish those who disobey. We see this in government, which can fine, imprison, or, in the last extremity, execute those who break its laws. Through its coercive powers governmental authority is *enforced*.

Another base for authority is seen in the institutional role. Here persons are organized together for the accomplishment of some purpose, and to better achieve that goal different functions are assigned to specific offices. We see this in a business, with its president, comptroller, personnel manager, department heads, foremen, etc. Each of these *offices* has certain powers to reward or punish behaviors that aid or inhibit the reaching of organizational goals. A person who is late for work may be docked an hour of pay; a person who fails to perform well may be given low efficiency ratings, or fewer raises, or he may be fired. The right of an individual to so reward or punish resides in the office he holds, in the functions that office is assigned within the organization. The authority resides in the job, not the man.

A third type of authority base is provided by ability. Because a person is recognized by others to have a special degree of competence, they follow his lead. Sometimes this competence is recognized by giving him a particular job (in this way organizational and ability bases of authority may coincide). But the response to his leadership and direction is still one which rests essentially on recognition by others of competence. I saw an example of this among youth this year when a group of teens working in a grocery disregarded the directions of an adult supervisor in planning and carrying out their work in the stock room, and followed instead the informally given suggestions of another teen. He clearly knew more about the operation and had better ideas than the supervisor. His companions recognized his authority, one of competence, and rejected the organizational authority of the adult.

Authority context The context in which authority based on open coercive power is exercised is essentially an impersonal one. Laws, rules, and regulations are stated, and the person under authority is to respond *to them.* When laws and rules are broken, power to punish or enforce behavior is exercised, again in an essentially impersonal way.

The context in which authority derived from the organizational roles is exercised is also impersonal. A boss just doesn't become too friendly with his employees. There may be much more interaction between persons in the organizational context, and loyalty to a good leader may develop. But there is still an overriding concern for the goals of the organization, and a use of impersonal sanctions to produce conformity.

But the authority which I've described as ability-based exists *only* in the context of relatively close interpersonal relationships. Only when ability and competence are demonstrated, and the evidence of competence is maintained through continued contact, will an ability-based authority produce response.

Authority impact It is interesting to look at the impact of various kinds of authority. Open coercive authority, resting on power and expressed in rules and laws, may be obeyed and even appreciated. But at the same time there is always a tendency to reject and to rebel on the basis of situational and personal variables. For instance, we all generally agree that it's best as well as legally demanded that we stop our cars at a red light. But in every situation? What about at night, when there's no car in sight for miles? What about when we are really rushed — we just *have* to be somewhere? As long as there is a basic trust in the rightness and helpfulness of the laws, there is conformity. But when, as with many youth today, there is a *distrust* of laws and of those who administer them, the kind of authority which rests on open coercive power is more likely to stimulate rebellion than obedience.

The inability of that authority which rests on the organizational role to produce conformity has also been clearly demonstrated in classic sociological studies of bureaucracy. In every office and branch and bureau people find ways to circumvent directives they do not *want* to obey. The indirect coercive power of the employer is totally unable to produce the desire for total obedience.

But here ability-based authority is distinctively different. *By rejecting all coercion, and by relying totally on recognition of its validity by others, ability-based authority produces a conformity that is characterized by an inner desire to respond.*

I think it should be clear by now just what I'm driving at. When Christ presents the servant as the model of Christian leadership, He removes all possibility of direct or indirect coercive power. A servant has no power to enforce. The servant can only *do.* When Paul speaks of the "power of Christian living" and when Peter urges leaders to "be examples of Christian living," both are pointing to the most exciting authority that can ever be exercised: an authority of ability, an authority gained by the quality of one's life as a Christian and freely granted by others who, knowing the leaders well, *want* to be like him.

Here, too, the importance of the model is reinforced. Young people will not *want* to grow in Christ only because of what they read about the Christian life, or because of what we *say* about Christian experience. Their motivation to grow toward maturity will be created and maintained by what they see of the reality of Christ in us.

Today in youth culture we are seeing a distinct shift away from responsiveness to authority based on coercive or organizational powers — a distinct shift toward response to ability-based authority. Young people are searching for models. Young people want to know and grow close to those whom they can respect as competent and real. The adult in the church or society who stands off in the distance and insists that youth obey his rules and his lists of do's and don'ts earns only contempt and produces rebellion. The adult who steps out from behind the protection of rules to demonstrate in living with youth the reality of Jesus Christ, the power of His love, and the excitement of total obedience to Him, finds youth eager to respond to him and to his authority.

The primary way that leaders function in the church, then, is by providing an example of Christian character and living which awakens a responsive desire in other believers to follow. The dynamics of this kind of leadership is interpersonal, and it is self-authenticating.[5] It does not rely on any coercive power to cause response; it relies entirely on the working of the Holy Spirit through the power of example in Christian living and love of others. The servant life is the key to servant leadership.

Selecting leadership

Understanding the nature of spiritual leadership helps us avoid common mistakes in selecting adults to minister with youth. Too often selection is based on verbal skills ("He sure can preach a good sermon," or ". . . lead songs enthusiastically") or on skills in ful-filling organizational roles ("He's a good administrator, knows how to function on a committee, and can really 'get things done' "). The leader youth need is not primarily a talker or organizer. He is a model, a person who by the power of his own Christian example motivates dedication to Jesus Christ. Youth leaders — as all Christian leaders — are to be selected on the basis of Christian growth and character.

Understanding the nature of spiritual leadership also helps us in "organizing" the youth group. Probably the most common approach in youth ministry today is to set up youth officers, group leaders, or committee heads, and to divide up among them the task of planning and carrying out activities of the youth group. I'll have more to say about this later under programming (chapters 17 and 18), and will in fact suggest an "organic" concept of organization very unlike the structures which the church seems determined to model on those

---

[5]I have used the term "self-authenticating" to describe the nature of Christian leadership elsewhere. For more on this important subject, you may want to refer to chapter 8 of my book, *A New Face for the Church*, (Zondervan, 1970).

of the business world. But for now it's important to note simply that leadership in youth ministry is *never the exclusive role of the adult.*

Youth have among them peers who are leaders, and who function in exactly the same way adult leadership is supposed to function — by serving as models.

In an interesting study of adolescent social structure Dexter C. Dunphy examines the stages of group development in adolescence (Figure 2, below), and points out that crowd and clique leaders develop who do not "boss the others around" but who often rather lead "simply by virtue of superior social skills" and the fact that they

LATE ADOLESCENCE

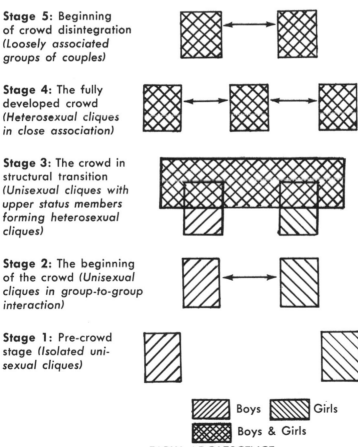

Stage 5: Beginning of crowd disintegration (*Loosely associated groups of couples*)

Stage 4: The fully developed crowd (*Heterosexual cliques in close association*)

Stage 3: The crowd in structural transition (*Unisexual cliques with upper status members forming heterosexual cliques*)

Stage 2: The beginning of the crowd (*Unisexual cliques in group-to-group interaction*)

Stage 1: Pre-crowd stage (*Isolated unisexual cliques*)

Boys   Girls

Boys & Girls

EARLY ADOLESCENCE
FIGURE 2
Stages of group development in adolescence

"embody personality traits admired in the group."[6] These natural leaders are normally *not* the highly visible, well-liked "life-of-the-party" persons adults often assume to be the leaders! The true leaders are most easily marked out by being overchosen on sociometric instruments,[7] being advanced in boy-girl relationships, and often by having a number of others designated by their name: "Rod's group," and "Julia's crowd."

Because this crowd leader is often not visible to adults, and often will lead in non-directive ways, he may be overlooked when attempts are made to develop "leadership" within the youth group. And because the natural leader's approach to leadership is through modeling and example, he may not be suited for the kind of leadership adults who work with youth often expect! Too often in the church young people are forced into leadership through the organizational role. And as group after group has found, even those capable of providing effective informal leadership by their example may be rejected when they are forced by their "office" to urge, cajole, push, pressure, and command other teens to help keep a youth program going.

The solution for adults is to turn again to the biblical teaching on spiritual leadership. For leaders are not called by God to stand behind a program and push; they are called by God to go before their brothers and *lead.* They move others by example, not by the power of their office.

Many working with youth in extra-church agencies have recognized the significance of locating natural leaders among groups of youth and building personal relationships with them. It is important for those *within* the church to develop ministry on this same principle, and to realize that leadership in youth culture is very often far closer to the biblical concept than the church's own approach! While the "how" of organization must be developed later, it is vitally important to realize that the distinctive style of leadership on which adult ministry must be built is the same style of leadership that we must develop among the youth. Far too often our "presi-

---

[6]Dexter C. Dunphy, "The Social Structure of Urban Adolescent Groups," *Readings,* ed. Hill and Shelton, pp. 214-25.

[7]Sociometry in its simplest form is the pattern of selection by individuals of other individuals when asked such questions as "who do you like best," "who best likes you," "who would you choose if you could only have three friends," etc. The interrelationships between choices made by members of groups has been found to give valuable insights into a number of group dynamics and relationships.

dent" and our "committee chairman" and our "program leader" roles hinder rather than aid in this important task.

PROBE
case histories
discussion questions
thought-provokers
resources

1. If my emphasis in this chapter on the modeling task of leadership and the centrality of example in fulfilling it seems overstated, consider these three passages of Scripture taken from the translation by J. B. Phillips. How much of what is said deals with *who* the leaders are, and how much with particular skills or abilities? What does the emphasis you note suggest to you about the leader?

    "It is quite true to say that a man who sets his heart on holding office has laudable ambition. Well, for the office of bishop a man must be of blameless reputation, he must be married to one wife only, and be a man of self-control and discretion. He must be a man of disciplined life; he must be hospitable and have the gift of teaching. He must be neither intemperate nor violent, but gentle. He must not be a controversialist nor must he be fond of money-grabbing. He must have proper authority in his own household, and be able to control and command the respect of his children. (For if a man cannot rule in his own household, how can he look after the Church of God?) He must not be a beginner in the faith, for fear of his becoming conceited and sharing the devil's downfall. He should, in addition to the above qualifications, have a good reputation with the outside world, in case his good name is attacked and he is caught by the devil that way.
    Deacons, similarly, should be men of serious outlook and sincere conviction. They too should be temperate and not greedy for money. They should hold the mystery of the faith with complete sincerity" (1 Tim. 3:1-9).

    Elders are "to be men of unquestioned integrity with only one wife, and with children brought up as Christians and not likely to be accused of loose living or lawbreaking. To exercise spiritual oversight a man must be of unimpeachable virtue, for he is God's agent in the affairs of his household. He must not be aggressive or hot-tempered or overfond of wine; nor must he be violent or greedy for financial gain. On the contrary, he must be hospitable, a genuine lover of what is good, and a man who is discreet, fair-minded, holy and self-controlled: a man who takes his stand on the orthodox faith, so that he can by sound teaching both stimulate faith and confute opposition" (Titus 1:6-9).

    Paul's own style of leadership is described in this significant passage. "Our message to you is true, our motives are pure, our conduct is absolutely aboveboard. We speak under the solemn sense of being entrusted by God with the gospel. We do not aim to please men, but to please God who knows us through and through. No one could ever say, as again you know, that we used flattery to conceal greedy motives, and God himself is witness to our honesty. We made no attempt to win honor from men, either from you or from anybody else, though I suppose as Christ's own messengers we might have done so. Our attitude among you was one of tenderness, rather like that of a devoted nurse among her babies. Because we loved you, it was a joy to us to give you not only the gospel of God but our very hearts — so dear did you become to us. Our struggles and hard work, my brothers, must still be fresh in your minds. Day and night we worked so that our preaching of the gospel to you might not cost you a penny. You are witnesses, as is God himself, that our life among you believers was honest, straightforward, and above criticism. You will remember how we dealt with each one of you personally, like a father with his own children, stimulating your faith and courage and giving you instruction. Our only object was to help you to live lives worthy of the God who has called you to share the splendor of his own kingdom" (1 Thess. 2:3-12).

2. Leadership by example involves an entirely different approach to ministry than is common in our churches. Chuck Miller, minister to youth at Lake Avenue Congregational Church, in Pasadena, California, is one exciting young youth minister who has just this kind of ministry. His simple description of the role of the leader, a role he has himself fulfilled with great blessing from God, is this:

> First, the leader does it *for* the youth.
> Next, the leader does it *with* the youth.
> Then, the youth do it *with* the leader.
> Finally, the youth do it *without* the leader.

What Chuck is expressing is the simple fact that young people need to experience through an adult's ministry to them the reality he is trying to communicate. They need his example, to make God's truth and way of life real. Then the young people need to become involved with the leader to see *how* he ministers to others. Then the youth need the opportunity to begin to minister as they have seen their leader minister to them and others, with his support expressed through his presence, encouragement, and additional instruction. Through this personally involved, example-leadership, young people grow to the place where they are able to minister on their own.

There is a great difference between the leadership tasks and approaches appropriate to example-leadership and those used by program-leadership. Let's suppose there are two leaders, one who adopts the philosophy expressed in Chuck Miller, and the other an "old school" leader, who organizes programs and studies and people. In general, one *shows*, the other *tells*.

Now, *how will each leader attempt to reach each of the following goals?* Spell out as clearly as possible the steps each will take, and why.

132

Goal one: to have our kids really love each other.

Goal two: to have our kids pray for and support each other.

Goal three: to have our kids take an interest in and show love for non-Christian friends.

3. The following are lists of responsibilities of various "youth leadership" offices suggested for youth group organizational structure by several Christian educators. Look them over, and compare the responsibilities of office and the kind of leadership needed to fulfill them with the responsibilities and leadership behaviors that I've suggested in this chapter as appropriate to Christian leadership.

    What conclusions do you think might validly be drawn from your comparisons?

The *president* of your youth group holds a place of honor, because his election indicates a trust placed in him by the members of the youth group. The president should be a person of integrity and high Christian standards.

The president should be one of the older Senior Highs who will be looked up to by other members. He should have some leadership ability, although he can learn this as you work with him behind the scenes.

The president should:

1. Preside at all business meetings of the youth group.

2. Serve as ex-officio member of all committees. He should attend as many committee meetings as possible, or have each committee chairman report to him at the cabinet meeting.

3. Know the activities of the planning group at all times. Work with the sponsor and the planning-group leaders in making assignments to these groups.

4. Work with the sponsor in steering the entire youth group, implanting enthusiasm and inspiration in the other members.

5. Plan projects for the Training Hour, together with the sponsor, and work out these plans through his planning-group leaders and committee chairmen.

The *vice-president* works as an assistant to the president. He is responsible for membership and enlistment and may have a committee to work with him, if your group is large enough. The vice-president should be a person who is interested in people and is not afraid to speak to newcomers and visitors.

The vice-president should:

1. Preside at business meetings in the absence of the president.

2. Greet visitors and make them feel at home in the group.

133

3. Know when members are absent and let them know that they were missed. This may be done by mail or by personal contact.

4. Keep an up-to-date record of all regular and active members of the youth group. Take attendance each week.

5. Work with the sponsor in contacting prospects through phone and home calls.

The *secretary* should be a person who is faithful in attendance and diligent in keeping records.

The secretary should:

1. Take minutes at all official meetings of the officers.

2. Keep accurate records of activities of the youth Training Hour for the church's annual report. This should include records of programs presented by planning groups, names of committee members, missionary activities, projects, socials, and attendance at meetings.

3. Take care of all official correspondence of the youth group, sending for materials and books needed, writing to missionaries, and sending thank-you notes to speakers and others who do special favors for your group, such as parents who help in programs.

4. Order materials and equipment at the direction of the president and planning-group leaders.

5. Keep a yearbook containing snapshots and a history of youth activities.

The *treasurer* should be a person who is vitally interested in stewardship and capable of keeping accurate records of the finances of the youth group.

The treasurer should:

1. Keep an accurate record of all incoming and outgoing money and prepare a monthly report for the youth-officers cabinet.

2. Open a bank account and deposit all money of the youth group in the bank.

3. Pay all authorized bills promptly by check. Bills paid in cash should be receipted.

4. Plan special projects for promotion of stewardship. Keep the group informed of expenses and missionary giving. Remind them of their financial responsibilities.

5. Prepare charts to show amounts given for special projects.[8]

I. The General Organization
   A. General Officers and Committees

---

[8]Roy B. Zuck & Fern Robertson, *How to be a Youth Sponsor* (Wheaton, Ill.: Scripture Press, 1960) pp. 19, 20.

1. The general officers of the Young People's Endeavor will consist of a president, vice-president, general secretary, and general treasurer. These form the Executive Committee. The officers should be appointed by the Board of Christian Education.

2. Duties of General Officers
   a. *President.* He will preside at all general sessions of the Endeavor. He will, with the pastor and Board of Christian Education, make appointments of the Family Training Hour directors, sponsors, and officers.
   b. *Vice-President.* The vice-president will assist the president and perform the duties of his office in his absence.
   c. *General Secretary.* The general secretary will keep all accurate records of all business meetings and will make monthly reports to the State Sunday School and Youth Department.
   d. *General Treasurer.* The general treasurer will hold all the money of the Endeavor and will disburse, with the consent of proper authorities, such funds as may be authorized.

B. Duties of General Committees

When the Family Training Hour groups are formed, it may be desirable to dissolve the general membership, visitation, missionary, and publicity committees in favor of the formation of the same committees in each group. This will necessarily be true of the program committee. Hence, no mention is made here of this committee. The program committee is discussed later.

1. *Executive Committee.* The executive committee should be composed of president, vice-president, secretary, and treasurer. It shall have power to act upon all matters pertaining to the groups as a whole between meetings. It shall, however, be subject to the authority of the pastor as well as to the will of the whole group.

2. *Membership and Visitation Committee.* The membership and visitation committee shall encourage all young people to become members of the Young People's Endeavor. It shall see that regular attendance is encouraged and that absentees are visited. It shall endeavor to promote a wholesome, friendly spirit. It shall see that all strangers are made welcome.

3. *Missionary Committee.* The missionary committee shall make arrangements for participation in a missionary project (YWEA). It shall appoint one of its members as corresponding secretary, whose duty shall be to correspond with missionaries on the field.

4. *Publicity Committee.* This group will publicize meetings with posters and special announcements. Each department should be represented and the special events of each group should be promoted.

II. Family Training Hour Organization
A. Three Divisions

Children	Youth	Adult
*4-11	12-Marriage	

B. Four Divisions

Children	Jr.	Youth	Adult
*4-8	9-11	12-Marriage	

C. Five Divisions

Children	Jr.	Jr. Hi	Sr. Hi
*4-8	9-11	12-14	15-Marriage

Adult[9]

---

[9]Donald S. Aultman, *Guiding Youth* (Cleveland, Tennessee: Pathway Press, 1965) pp. 71, 72.

8

developing facilitating relationships

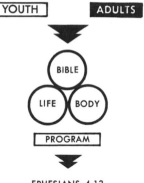

EPHESIANS 4:13

Few youth today have significant personal relationships with adults who are not their parents — and many have decidedly poor relationships with mom and dad!

Yet the nature and quality of personal relationships between youth and the adults who are involved with them in the three processes (in Scripture, in Body relationship, in Life) leading to spiritual maturity are vitally important. The Bible demands, as we saw last chapter, that the leader *be with* his "flock," and demonstrate in the real world the power of Christian living. Only here is the imperative authority of example truly communicated. But the nature of the interpersonal relationships in which such leadership is exercised is just as distinctive as the leadership itself.

Perhaps the central element of the context of personal relationships that facilitates growth and ministry is that all enter and maintain the relationship as co-equals. Adults who minister must minister as *persons with* youth, both respecting and being respected as individuals. The lack of this attitude toward youth is perhaps the greatest hindrance to effective ministry in our churches. In a series of "talk backs" with youths and adults in evangelical churches, Wheaton College anthropologist Marvin K. Mayers[1] found that youth were irritated about a number of adult characteristics. Among them were "lack of respect for the younger generation," "lack of willingness to listen to youth," "pessimism about new ideas," "absolutizing their own norms," "overprotectiveness," "feeling of need to control youth," etc. Each of these indicates that youth feel adults attempt to relate to them as *superiors* to *subordinates*. Such *relating down* to youth is tragically destructive, distorting and destroying the relationship context in which a truly biblical ministry must take place.

Understanding which relationships are facilitating, the adult attitudes and behaviors that underly them, and how they are developed is vital for all of us.

---

[1]Results of "talkbacks" on the part of youth and adults conducted by Dr. Mayers in 1968.

In a recent study of the generation gap as viewed by teenagers, four of five "refer to failures of communication and understanding or both."[2] Why does communication between youths and adults so often break down? It is easier to understand when we look at some common conversational response patterns, and see their impact on communication.

Before we look at the response patterns we need to sketch the setting in which we're going to see them. That setting is *not* a "counseling" setting where a young person has come to an adult for help. The setting is informal and conversational. It's talk between a young person and an adult that may take place in a living room, or leaning against a car in the church parking lot, or drinking a coke at the corner hangout. The setting is one in which two people are simply trying to communicate.

In this informal setting we're going to suppose that the teen makes some self-revealing statement. This itself needs some explanation. Two nights ago I was leaning against a car in a church parking lot here in Scottsdale, Arizona, where my family and I are summering. It was after a really exciting time of sharing with a half-dozen kids in a small group, where we had got down to examining together where our lives are being lived. One of the guys had shared his concern over his perfectionism, feeling that this was something about which Christ might ask him, "Do you want to be healed?" (cf. John 5:1-9). As a musician he felt constantly driven to be better, and falling short. When he and his pastor had sung together in church the week before, their failure to be as good as he felt they should have been made him angry and frustrated. Another teen expressed his sense of need for closer relationships with more kids; the kind of relationship in which he would feel free to say and be what he was. In the group these young people had revealed something of themselves — honestly, trustingly, expecting trust and concern in return. But now, leaning against the car, something else was happening. A different boy, who had been in another group, was talking to me in a constant stream of words. He was telling about the scout camps in Arizona he had been to, the way it had rained, and the size of the drops, a recent float trip down the Salt River, how far they had gone that compared to the distance

---

[2]Reported by Herzog, Sudia, Rosengard, and Harwood in *Youth Reports No. 1: Teenagers Discuss the Generation Gap,* U.S. Dept. of Health, Education, and Welfare, 1970.

they had covered the week before at the same time, and so on. And in all this spate of words there was nothing *personal;* nothing that revealed anything of who he was as a person, how he felt, what he valued. Even when I asked simple questions, like "I guess you enjoy your scouting, huh?" he could only nod and hurry on with his description of circumstances.

When at the beginning of the last paragraph I said that in the informal setting the teen "makes some self-revealing statement," I was specifying something important. In conversation, he says something about *himself.*

How we respond to communication on this personal level is the key to facilitating relationships.

Many of us have learned to talk endlessly about nothing, using words that may be full of sound and even fury but that signify nothing. But drawing close to another person, trying to understand and appreciate him, this is significant.

We have our setting then. It's informal (not "counseling"), and in the talking together self-revelation occurs. The young person makes a statement, communicates something, that reveals a little about himself. The critical issue now is, *how do adults respond?*

Over the past three years, in dozens of meetings with youth and adults, I've presented four patterns of possible response for analysis. *In every case* the evaluation of the teens has been the same. The four patterns of response[3] which I've suggested the group think of are *advice-giving, reassuring, understanding,* and *self-revealing.* To get the feel of the relational impact of each, and to clarify the way I'm using these terms, let's suppose that an adult is talking to one of the fellows I just wrote of (we'll call him Mark), and hears him say,

> What bothers me is this feeling that everything's got to be perfect. I mean, I can play with my band or sing like with pastor last Sunday, and when it doesn't go just right, I go off and when somebody says, "What's wrong?" I snap at 'em. I get mad at myself and other people, too.

The adult might respond to this personal sharing in any of the four ways.

---

[3]The four keys to response patterns which I am using in this chapter are not original with me. They come from Ross Snyder and have since been produced on tape by the Methodist church and used in an interesting approach to training youth workers. I have however used and tested these concepts in the way described in the chapter, with dozens of groups of youth and find invariable the results catalogued in the chapter.

Advice-giving This, according to the teens, is the most common adult response to such personal communication or sharing. An advice-giving response to Mark might go something like this:

> Mark, when you feel that way, you've just got to remind yourself that nobody is perfect. Keep saying, "Nobody's perfect," over and over again, and see if that doesn't help.

or

> Mark, the thing you ought to do when you feel down isn't go off by yourself — it's get right in there with the others. Chances are they won't have noticed the things you thought were poor, and start telling you how good it was. Try that next time, and just see if I'm not right.

Both these responses illustrate an attitude that underlies all advice-giving. "I've got the answer. I can help you. You do what I say." The one giving gratuitous advice presents himself as strong, and represents the other as weak and inadequate.

Reassuring Reassurance is quite similar to advice-giving. It also implies that the reassurer has greater insight into the problem than the one who is living it. Reassurance seems to imply that the feelings and problems revealed are unimportant, but are best shoved aside as unworthy of concern.

For example, let's look again at Mark's statement, and then at a couple of reassuring responses.

> What bothers me is this feeling that everything's got to be perfect. I mean, I can play with my band or sing like with pastor last Sunday, and when it doesn't go just right, I go off and when somebody says, "What's wrong?" I snap at 'em. I get mad at myself and other people, too.

Reassurance

> Why Mark, you're so much better than anyone else around here, it's wonderful. You don't need to feel bad — you're just great.

or

> Don't worry so much about it, Mark. You're young yet. You can't expect to be as good as you're going to be in a few years. So take it easy. With more practice you'll be right up there.

Whatever else the reassuring response implies, it says loud and clear that the thing that bothers *you* isn't very important to *me!*

Understanding A third kind of response is one that expresses a desire to understand. It's not condescending, but questioning. It's one way a person tries to say, "If something is important to you, it's important to me, and I want to understand."

This kind of response is an invitation for further communication. In some ways it's an inadequate invitation, because it invites the other person to come closer while you stand still and wait for him. But it does show concern.

Recalling Mark's expression of feelings, what might an understanding response to him be like?

> You really feel frustrated when you're not as good as you want to be.

or

> You mean, you feel you fall short all the time, or just when you really mess it up?

Again, whatever may be said about this response type, spoken sincerely, it does show an interest in Mark and a willingness to accept his perception of his problem.

Self-revealing While the understanding response invites the other person to come nearer, the self-revealing response itself takes the first step closer. What Mark has said reveals something of himself; it's his reaching out as a person for acceptance and care. In making a self-revealing response, the adult identifies with his feelings and perceptions, and says in effect, "Yes, I think I understand. I'm human, too I share your experiences and feelings about life." The self-revealing response is an attempt to meet the other *person-to-person,* to identify with him as bound up together with you in the common bundle of life. The self-revealing response says, "I am willing to meet you where you meet me."

What might a self-revealing response to Mark be when he says,

> What bothers me is this feeling that everything's got to be perfect. I mean, I can play with my band or sing like with pastor last Sunday, and when it doesn't go just right, I go off and when somebody says, "What's wrong?" I snap at 'em. I get mad at myself and other people, too.

Perhaps this:

> You know, even now in my job I feel like that sometimes. Sort of driven to keep at it till it's done perfectly — and really upset when I don't have time or something goes wrong.

Self-revealing, then, involves searching your own experience of life to find a common ground; an area in which you share as a human being the other's feelings and needs. When you find that common ground, rather than hiding your humanness, you take a step closer to the other person by revealing yourself to him just as he has revealed himself to you.[4]

The impact of response

I mentioned that in thinking about these patterns of response with groups of young people, each group has agreed in their evaluation of them.

For one thing, young people agree on the frequency with which they get each type of response. When they were asked, "From your experience, which response are you most likely to get from adults you know when you make a personal or revealing statement?" the overwhelming answer has been: *advice-giving*. The most common way adults respond when youth express their feelings or perceptions in a conversational setting is with advice. In descending order, the frequency of other responses, according to the youth, is *reassuring, understanding,* and finally, least frequently, *self-revealing*.

I don't suggest that any one of these patterns of response is appropriate to *every* situation. There are times when advice-giving will be the best response. *But it is serious when youth hear adults trying to relate to them primarily through advice and reassurance.* We can see why this is so serious when we picture the relationships implied in each response. I have asked young people to show, diagramatically, *where* the adult who gives each response *places himself* in relationship to the one who makes the personal statement. They have consistently come up with a uniform analysis. (See figure 3, p. 143.) Advice-giving places the adult above and far away from the teen. Reassurance still places him above, but perhaps a little closer. Understanding responses are felt by the kids as an attempt to be on their level, but as still a little above. And self-revealing

---

4"Common ground" does not necessarily imply that one has experienced feelings and perceptions of life that are *exactly* like the other person's. The Bible says of Jesus: "He was tempted in all points like as we are, yet without sin." This does not assert that *every* human experience was His. He never experienced the pain a woman can inflict in rejecting her husband, or the dragging agony of years spent as an invalid. But He *was* tempted and tested in every area of human experience: He knew rejection by His own people and the physical exhaustion of constant wearing travel and emotion-laden situations. Common ground for us does not require that we be in the exact situation of another, but that we have in our own unique experience of life known experience *like* his. It means that in our humanness and vulnerability to people, to physical and emotional and spiritual strain, we truly *are* like them.

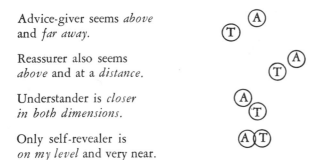

Advice-giver seems *above* and *far away.*

Reassurer also seems *above* and at a *distance.*

Understander is *closer in both dimensions.*

Only self-revealer is *on my level* and very near.

What distance and position does each type of response indicate?

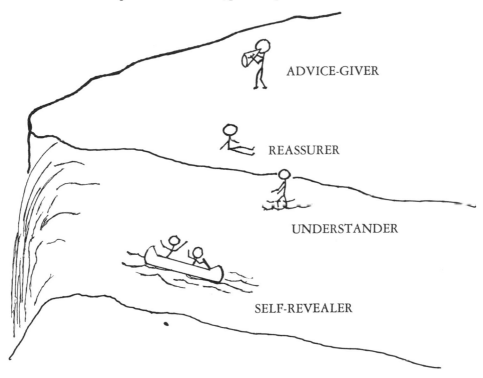

ADVICE-GIVER

REASSURER

UNDERSTANDER

SELF-REVEALER

Where is each in relationship to the person in the canoe heading for the falls?

Two representations of the relational implications of adult responses to youths' personal communications.

FIGURE 3

responses are felt as being on the same level, and very close or overlapping.

Shifting the analogy to picture the person who makes the initial statement as being in a canoe, drifting toward the falls without a paddle, the advice-giver is seen by youth as standing way up on shore, shouting through a megaphone. The reassurer is on the beach, seated and relaxed, looking over his shoulder. The one attempting to understand has begun to wade out into the water, usually with a rope that's too short. And the self-revealer has swum out and is sitting *in the canoe* with the person who shouted.

Leaving aside for the moment the question of which position is best for ministry (an important question, certainly, as many are afraid that to be in the same canoe necessarily means you're without a paddle too!), we need to ask *which of these relationships facilitates communication.* That is, which response is most likely to free the young person to keep on sharing; to make him want to move closer to you as a person? Here, too, the kids' response has been clear. *When youth are talked down to, as in advice-giving and reassurance, they have no desire to keep on sharing.* There is little motivation to develop a relationship in which you do not feel yourself an equal.

Anyone who has served as an enlisted man in one of the armed services knows what I mean. Your buddies are men from the ranks, like you. *You don't seek out and develop friendships with officers.* With *them,* no matter how fine they may be as persons, you always feel your subordinate position. Friendships demand give and take between equals, and thus are reserved for those who you feel view and treat you as an equal.

A relationship with young people in which adults characteristically *relate down* to them, responding to their self-revelation with advice and reassurance as a superior to a subordinate, is a *relationship which will not support or permit a truly biblical spiritual ministry.* The context of relationships which permits spiritual ministry, and makes it effective, is one in which each person is perceived and treated as a responsible, valuable, and equal person.

Strikingly, the *characteristic* response pattern that communicates such equality and plainly says, "I respect and value you as a person like me" is the self-revealing pattern — the response that communicates willingness to speak with youth "on the same level" — to admit that we sit with them in the same boat.

144

With a paddle

I've suggested that a ministry-facilitating relationship is one in which the adult admits and expresses his equality with youth as persons by encouraging mutual self-revelation and in which youth and adult each learn to trust the other with his thoughts and feelings and experiences, knowing that he is valued and respected.

This approach, this seeking to identify on a personal level with youth, bothers many adults — and some young people, too. Perhaps the most common objection is this: "But how can I help a person unless he thinks I've got answers?" The thought seems to be that self-revelation necessarily involves admission of weakness (and it does), and that this admission destroys confidence in the leader (which it does *not!*). To answer this common objection, we need to go back to our understanding of the Gospel, and of who we are as Christians. Lutheran theologian Merton Strommen says it well in a 1966 *Eternity* article. He suggests we live with youth as those experiencing *simul justus et peccator.*

> That Latin phrase, "simultaneously justified and a sinner," is a key one. It refers to a truth basic to the Christian life, but one that is difficult to teach conceptually. It must be experienced.
>
> The experience is one which comes when youth hears his pastor admit to his struggles as well as releases; his rebellions as well as realizations of God's guidance. It is the experience of having a parent apologize or ask forgiveness. It is the frank realization that we, young or old, must live in the forgiveness of God.[5]

Living constantly in God's forgiveness is central to the reality presented in the Gospel. God has not accepted us and called us His sons because of our accomplishments. In fact, Scripture is very blunt in insisting that the person who says, "I have no sin," face the fact that he lies. Walking in the light necessarily involves honest recognition of who we are. Only when we are ourselves with God, and confess rather than hide our sins, is He free to "forgive us our sins and cleanse us from all unrighteousness" (1 John 1:5-10 *KJV*).

We are then *both* saint and sinner; actually participants in Christ in the divine heredity, falling short of Him, yet in the process of becoming like Him. As Paul puts it, Jesus was "raised from the dead by that splendid revelation of the Father's power so that we too might rise to life on a new plane altogether. If we have, as it were,

---

[5]Merton P. Strommen, "I Can't Get Close to My Young People," *Eternity,* October, 1966, p. 22.

shared his death, let us rise and live our new lives with him!"
(Rom. 6:4 *Phillips*).

Our lives, then, are lived in a tension between who we are and
who we are becoming. We are saints, yet sinners. And the wonderful
truth is that, while we are still burdened by aspects of our old life
that cling to us, we are different from what we were! We are in the
process of becoming.

When we understand this, and are assured of God's love, we do
not have to hide either the sinner or the saint. Confidence in His
love and acceptance frees us from fear, and we know that whatever
we may be like now God is at work, forming Christ within our
personalities. As the Bible says, "Love contains no fear — indeed
fully developed love expels every particle of fear, for fear always
contains some of the torture of feeling guilty" (1 John 4:18
Phillips). Because we love God and know His forgiving love, we
can accept even our imperfections. In spite of them, God loves and
values us, and in fact He is working in us to remove all that blocks
His free expression of Christ through us.

The Christian who accepts himself as *simul justus et peccator* is
free to be himself with God. No false fronts are necessary. And it
should be clear too, because this *is* the Gospel, this good news of
Christ's forgiving and transforming love, *that we need to be ourselves with others. Only as they see us as we are, human and needy,
yet becoming through the power of God's Spirit new and different
persons, will others understand the Gospel and the great gifts God
has given us in Christ.*

I personally become very disturbed by those who say, "You
mustn't get too close to people you minister to," or "Don't reveal
your weaknesses, or people will lose confidence in you." The
Christian who ministers with others is not trying to lead them to
confidence in *him*. He is instead seeking to lead them to confidence
in *God* — by his example. Only by living with others as one who is
in need, yet who constantly finds that Christ meets need, can trust
and confidence and dependence be shifted from the human leader
to the Lord.

Self-revealing, as I've presented it in this chapter, *does* mean the
leader exposes his humanness, and identifies with the youth. He
seeks to meet young people person-to-person, and to step into the
same canoe. *But he does not come "without a paddle."* He comes
instead with a confident awareness that Christ living in the human

personality is our glorious hope for everything that is to come, in this life and eternity. He comes with the willingness to expose his weaknesses so that all can see that the power, the love, and the discipline that also mark his life are found through Christ.

In reality, the leader who presents himself as strong is never able to minister to others. As he stands before them wrapped in his own strength and hiding his weaknesses, he appears different from those who are burdened with a consciousness of needs and failures. And as *different* he stimulates despair. He is what I can never hope to be, for he is strong, and I am weak.

The leader who presents himself authentically, willing to reveal his weaknesses and needs and willing as well to reveal what Christ has done to transform him does not burden, but inspires. He is a living testimony that God can take the weak things and the despised of this world, and miraculously reshape them for His glory. Like Paul, who saw himself as chief of sinners and who never hesitated to reveal his sense of need or his times of discouragement, the authentic man is a leader whom others can trust and model themselves on. Only the authentic person, the self-revealing person, can serve as a living demonstration of the grace and power of God.

And so we see something of the relationship pattern that must exist in ministry. A relationship that might be characterized by saying that the leader always takes his place as a *person with* the others.

The adult who has discovered that the Gospel gives freedom to be authentic with others creates, by who he is, the relational context for spiritual ministry. Freed, as Paul was, to express himself in utter honesty ("We should like you, our brothers, to know something of what we went through in Asia. We were completely overwhelmed; the burden was more than we could bear; in fact we told ourselves that this was the end"), we are freed to present Christ as He is for us ("Yet we now believe that we had this experience of coming to the end of our tether that we might learn to trust, not in ourselves, but in God who can raise the dead" 2 Cor. 1:8, 9 *Phillips*).

The adult who sees youth as brothers, who speaks to them and listens to them as responsible and free human beings, expecting and giving acceptance, is the leader youth need. The adult who opens up his life to youth, extending and receiving forgiveness, granting and accepting that love that "covers a multitude of sins," can serve with youth as an example of the authentic Christian. Such personal involvement is the context in which spiritual ministry takes place.

Building relationships

It should be clear from what I've said about the relational context in which spiritual leadership can function that *this context does not exist in most churches*. Too often youth and their leaders get together in formal situations, where the leader is cast as a "teacher" or program "director." In these roles the adult is placed in a *superior-to-subordinate* position. And too often on these occasions the group involved is large; too large for interactive self-revelation to take place.

Other contexts in which leaders and youth commonly come together also fail to permit building the *"person with"* relationship. Socials and recreational activities, while they do let kids see the adult leaders out of their authority roles, are hardly conducive to self-revealing conversations. Committee meetings and officers' business meetings deal with business — not persons. *All too often formal and informal-superficial contact situations make up 90 percent of teen/leader interaction!*

This says much about our programming of youth ministry. It says that we need to restructure, to give priority to contact situations where mutual self-revelation is encouraged and can take place — situations in which teens can come to know adult leaders as persons, and where the adult can stand with youth as equally human, meeting on the common ground of shared need for experience of God's grace and His transforming power.

PROBE
case histories
discussion questions
thought-provokers
resources

1. Here are several statements that were made to me at various times by teens. To develop sensitivity to the several responses you might make to teens who share something with you, jot down a couple responses of each type (advice-giving, reassuring, understanding, self-revealing).

   I prefer not to talk to my parents, because they are very intolerant of ideas they feel are wrong, and I like to avoid fights.

   I've got more conflicts right now over religion than ever. I know I must accept many teachings by faith. But I still have many doubts.

   The biggest problem for me has been my parents and my church forcing a Christianity on me that just doesn't agree with what Christ advocated. Why is everyone so sure dancing and movies are wrong and judging and gossiping aren't? It's no wonder Christianity has a bad sound to the world when all they see is negative — don't smoke, drink, play cards, dance, go to movies. It's all no good if you don't love.

2. One concern of persons who object to adopting a self-revealing relationship pattern with youth is that no helpful or corrective ideas will be introduced. It seems to me that there are two important considerations in responding to this viewpoint.

   The first is this. Which relationship/response pattern creates a willingness to listen? . . . . a desire to continue communicating? Look back over the different responses you made to the teen quotes above. Which responses *if given to you* would have made you want to keep talking? Which would have killed motivation for future expression on your part?

   A second consideration is this. Which relationship/response pattern is most likely to give a young person the feeling that the adult really understands his situation, and perhaps has something to contribute? Look back over your hypothetical responses to the three quotes again, and ask yourself which response *if given to you* would give you some confidence that the adult who made them might actually be able to help you?

3. One very valid concern of evangelicals is epitomized in the question, "But is this viewpoint biblical?" This is a primary concern for me too, and I am convinced that both the origin and justification for what I am saying in this chapter and in the book as a whole is biblical and theological. God's Word says much about church life and leadership, and on this we need to base our ministries. If you're interested in the biblical principles concerning this you may want to see chapters 5 to 11 of my book, *A New Face for the Church* (Zondervan, 1970).

   You may also want to undertake a study of Paul and his style of relating to believers. 2 Corinthians is very revealing, and I believe this epistle shows clearly that Paul related to the various churches as a *person with* them, seeking to build mutually revealing and respecting relationships.

4. In the concluding thoughts of this chapter I pointed out that most "ministry" situations in which youth and adults come together *inhibit* rather than encourage the development of a personal relationship. While implications of this fact will be developed later, it is important to note now that even the formal ministry situation is *not necessarily characterized by a teacher/student, superior/subordinate relationship.*

   I mentioned earlier in the chapter the situation in which I talked with Mark. To describe it a little more fully, Mark and five other teens and I were sitting or lying on the floor of the preschool classroom at his church, studying the Bible together. In this situation I was *not* "the teacher." I was a *person with* the teens, submitting

149

myself as they submitted themselves to the Word of God, revealing as they revealed what its searching light disclosed. The following is the "lesson" we studied together, taken from Lyman Coleman's *Serendipity* (Christian Outreach, Huntington Valley, Pa.), it illustrates how we can be involved in the Word interpersonally, and are not necessarily forced into the formal pattern so common in our churches.

I believe that there are ways to personalize nearly all ministry settings, *and that we must begin to personalize immediately!* The church of Jesus Christ must once again develop the relational context in which spiritual leadership can be exercised.

An Exercise in Sharing (One Hour)

Preliminary Exercise (15 Minutes)   (in small groups)

1. In silence read John 5:1-9, pausing after each sentence to let your imagination recreate the situation for you.

2. Put yourself in the shoes of a psychiatrist who has been studying the behavior of the crippled man with a view to helping him and read over the passage a second time. Take special note of the dialogue between Jesus and the crippled man, beginning with the question of Jesus, *Do you want to recover?*

   Then, on the basis of your own examination of the evidence, write out a "case history" report on this man.

   The easiest way to get started is to imagine yourself as a psychiatrist who has interviewed this man before his encounter with Jesus to get his basic history (that Jesus seems to allude to in His first question) . . . and has interviewed this man again after his encounter with Jesus at the end of the passage.

   Simply start out your report with the words *"This man is—"* and proceed to describe what you feel was wrong with this person . . . and what happened to him in his encounter with Jesus Christ. For instance, you might say, *This man appears to be afflicted with a terrible sense of self-worthlessness and self-pity, stemming back to his childhood . . . etc.*

3. In the remaining moments of silence, think back over your own life and ask yourself this question: *If Jesus came to me in the same way that He came to the crippled man at the pool of Bethesda and asked me the same question that He asked the crippled man, what would He be referring to in my life? Or, to put it simply, Where do I need to experience the release of Jesus Christ from the hurts and pain in my life?*

   For instance, for one of you, it might be a childhood memory that is keeping you from opening up in your small group; for another, it might be a sense of bitterness.

   Whatever you do, be honest.

Small Group Interaction (30 Minutes)

1. Gather together in small groups and move your chairs in close.

2. Go around and ask everyone to share what he wrote as the psychiatric report for the crippled man . . . and explain why he feels as he does about his analysis.

3. Go around a second time and ask each person to share, if possible, what came to mind when he faced his own life with the same question; that is, that area of hurt or distress in his own life that needs to know the healing of Jesus Christ — physical, emotional, or spiritual. In particular, face with each other the question *Do you want to recover?* (Some of us would prefer to lick our wounds and soak up the pity that comes with sickness, rather than seek the Great Physician for His release and healing.)

    Some of the small groups will have difficulty with this kind of sharing until they have reached the point of trust and acceptance that is really deep.

Celebration   (15 Minutes)

1. In each small group, ask each person to think in silence of a gift that he would like to give in the name of Jesus to the other members of his small group — something for each person who has opened up his life and shared any hurt or pain in his past.

    For instance, if someone in a group has opened up his feelings of hurt at the sudden death of his dad when he was a boy, one of the others in his group may want to give him a gift of *understanding* of God's ways; and another may want to give him the gift of *tears* or the ability to cry; and the third may want to give him the gift of *love* . . . and accompany the words with a great big bear hug.

    After a minute to collect your thoughts, break the silence and give out your gifts.

2. In each small group, move up close together and join hands or put your arms around the shoulders of one another like in a football huddle . . . and in this posture, look each other in the eyes and thank each other for the gifts that have been given to you. And if you wish, close your session in song and prayer.

3. When your small group is through, slip out quietly without disturbing the other small groups that are finishing up.

9

counseling

YOUTH ADULTS

BIBLE

LIFE BODY

PROGRAM

EPHESIANS 4:13

These days there's a great emphasis on counseling in many schools training young people for ministry. To an extent this disturbs me, because counseling can never be the heart of an effective ministry. Growth toward maturity, and the healing that often must take place in persons before they are free to grow, comes essentially through involvement with others in the processes of ministry — particularly through Body relationships and Scripture. The church of the New Testament is a transforming *community,* and transformation is a community transaction, not primarily a transaction between two persons — especially when they are cast as *counselor* and *counselee.*

This point of view is not distinctively mine. Many behavioral scientists believe that under conditions of rapid social change, it is more important to pay attention to social structures and processes than to individual therapy in guiding in-person changes. And this is true whether they speak of increasing motivation in school or of reducing discrimination or of any other value- or personality-rooted concern — or, I would add, of guiding young people toward Christian maturity.

None of this is to suggest that there is no place for the Christian psychologist or psychiatrist. Obviously there are individuals in the church who need professional help. But in the normal situations of ministry, "counseling training" is not as important as an understanding of the interpersonal dynamics that free people to grow. And often "counseling training" is harmful. For the spiritual dynamics of change cut directly across the grain of many counseling theories and methods to rest, as every aspect of the Christian leader's ministry, on the impact of the "*person with,*" whose personality is stamped by the authority of example.

The pictures that the term "counseling" can conjur up in people's minds are interesting and varied. Some see it almost as "consoling." Here is a young person overwhelmed by troubles who sits, pouring out his heart to a sympathetic adult. The adult reflects his feelings,

153

and nods his head encouragingly, until the youth, relieved by the chance to express his emotions, says with surprise: "Why, I feel better now!" With warmest thanks he leaves the office, while the grateful adult, glad to have been of help, sits back in his easy chair to stare contemplatively at the wall until the next troubled teen appears.

Too often counseling does operate something like this, with the emphasis on expression of feeling, and with the greatest value for the counselee the release of emotions. Then he goes back into the real world, and finds himself faced with the same situations that tied him in knots in the first place, and discovers that the same feelings and frustrations are building up again. Building up, until the comforting adult is sought out once more.

Another picture, much like the first, has the adult gently questioning and probing, helping the young person understand why he feels so inadequate. Perhaps mom rejected him when a new baby appeared? Has his failure to get the grades his older brother was able to get left a psychic scar? When he understands himself, this wise adult counselor nods; now he'll be able to accept himself and perhaps the intensity of his unhappy feelings will be reduced.

Neither of these pictures of counseling is particularly helpful in youth ministry — or Christian ministry as a whole. For each approach treats the counselee as a truly inadequate person. One who actually cannot help himself. So each develops, not personal responsibility, but personal irresponsibility. Rather than responding to life, persons treated in these ways find ready excuses for their failures.

The Bible makes some amazing demands on Christians — demands that would be totally unreasonable if God himself did not infuse in us His power to change. Paul speaks of the dynamics of release and power when he writes,

> You *belong* to the power which you choose to obey, whether you choose sin, whose reward is death, or God, obedience to whom means the reward of righteousness. Thank God that you, who were at one time the servants of sin, honestly responded to the impact of Christ's teachings when you came under its influence. Then released from the service of sin, you entered the service of righteousness.

So now, Paul goes on,

> give yourselves to the service of righteousness — for the purpose of becoming really good (Rom. 6:16ff *Phillips*).

The Christian is *not* an inadequate man. The Christian is released from the control of sin which expresses itself in every aspect of the human personality, and *can* "give himself" to the service of righteousness.

So Christian counseling demands far more than the release of feelings and an accommodation to circumstances. *Christian counseling seeks to free persons to choose that freedom which is ours through obedience to God.* Christian counseling focuses not on emotions, but on the will.

A pastor friend of mine made a perceptive comment recently. Speaking of classroom training for the ministry, he noted that it is essentially "intellectual-spiritual." That is, the biblical view of life is studied to be presented primarily in an intellectual framework in sermons and teaching. But the ministry itself, he said, is essentially "emotional-spiritual." The biblical portrait of reality has to be communicated and grasped where people live; communicated as life to life so that it can be felt as well as understood.

In saying a moment ago that Christian counseling focuses on the will rather than the emotions, then, I am not suggesting that the intellect is the basic avenue of approach in counseling. Instead, as this chapter will show, I am convinced that the emotions provide a better avenue of approach to the will than the intellect. People do not live "rational" lives. We are not merely minds. Emotional and intellectual components are complexly blended in the human personality, and that personality must be touched and motivated as a whole.

Focus on the whole person eliminates one other portrait of the youth counselor that commonly comes to mind. This is the picture of the answer man, who sits behind his desk with files full of psychological and vocational preference tests, helping kids decide their future. "Which college shall I go to?" "Who has the best journalism program?" "Is a Christian or secular college best for me?" "What kind of jobs are open these days?"

Such contacts are information-seeking and information-providing. Although in conversation more personal concerns may surface ("How can I tell God's will for my life?"), the contacts still usually remain oriented to information. In effect, the young person is asking the adult to supply or point out facts that he needs in order to make a decision. Certainly there is a place for such vocational or educational counseling. But this is not our primary concern or orientation in this chapter.

When speaking of "counseling" in this chapter, I want to focus on what *is* our primary concern, and suggest an approach which will enable the adult ministering with teens in the local church (normally without counseling training) to understand what his counseling role is, and how he can best fulfill it.

When we counsel

I've sketched several portraits of what counseling is not. Let me sketch one or two portraits of what it is, for this book at least.

Rich drops into your office. He's slow in talking, but soon his feelings and his story come pouring out. For one thing, he's afraid — afraid that God is going to push him into the one way of life he doesn't want: being a missionary. And there's this girl he's interested in. He's afraid God isn't going to let him marry her. In fact, he feels as though he's in a box, squeezed together, tighter all the time. What difference does it make what he wants or doesn't want? Isn't God going to make him do what *He* wants?

And Rich keeps talking, to tell you about the Sunday school class of boys he's just quit teaching. Somehow, suddenly, all the words about God he's been brought up on and all the words he's been telling the kids seem unreal. He doesn't believe them anymore. They're empty — and so he had to stop teaching. He couldn't be a hypocrite.

There are others.

Debby's mother drops in, all upset. Her daughter's been such a good girl, and now, suddenly, they seem to be strangers. It all happened with those white cord pedal pushers (see pp. 89-90). Debby wanted them, but mom is sure they look like what the hoods wear. Debby strikes back: "All the girls have them. I *know* what's hoody!" But mom won't give in. Debby, usually so open and relaxed with mom, feels terribly hurt and cuts her out of her life.

So now mom tells you she wants to make an appointment to bring Debby to you, at 2:30.

At 2:30 you go outside, and there's Debby, angry at being forced to keep an appointment she never wanted to make, looking at you defiantly.

And there are others.

There's Jan, a girl you've noticed losing interest recently, growing distant from her Christian friends. Jan drops in, talks small talk, and seems unable to say what troubles her.

It was tough to decide to talk to Mr. Jack. But there wasn't anyone else to talk to now. It has been tough, all this past semester. At first Bob was just a nice fellow, someone to chat with in the halls, maybe even get to young people's or talk with about the Lord. That was the motive behind those first dates.

But soon it became more. Bob wasn't a Christian, but he was nice. He was exciting, too. Somehow more alive, more real, than the kids at church. He didn't swear or anything like that. And even that occasional smoke and talk of some beers now and then with fellows when she wasn't around didn't seem so important.

Of course, there was less time for church. Then the kids started pressuring her. Telling her she shouldn't date Bob. When the folks found out, dad really hit the roof. It wasn't fair, jumping on Bob like that when they didn't even know him.

Then it got worse at home. And at school, Bob was the only one to turn to But now — this was more than anyone had expected. Just a week ago they'd gone away and gotten secretly married. Even now no one knew about it.

The next day, with that sinking feeling that grew and grew, it was clear it was wrong. All wrong. But who could she tell? Not her folks. They'd never understand. Or the kids. There was no one. No one but maybe Mr. Jack at church.

But would he understand? Maybe he'd condemn her too. "I'll have to be careful. See what he thinks about — about kids like Bob." Maybe he'd think it was all right to see unsaved fellows and witness to them. Maybe he'd understand how a girl could get pushed by family and friends into even marrying an unsaved fellow. Maybe he wouldn't. "Maybe just not commit myself. Just feel him out.

"But just got to tell someone. Someone must help."

And there are others.

Kids like Mark, bound by his perfectionism. Kids like Sherrill, disturbed by conflicts at home, uncertain how to respond. Kids who are facing life, eager to live it meaningfully and well, but somehow uncertain, bound, sensing their inadequacies and looking for ways to live responsibly.

Sometimes the problems are really big ones, Like Jan's. Sometimes they seem smaller. But in each case the central need is not for release of emotions, or for an explanation of present bondage in terms of the past, or a dispassionate presentation of facts. *In each case the central need is for decision; for response to the situation that is adequate and will be freeing* — if not freeing from the situation, at least freeing for the personality.

The Bible tells us this kind of freedom is found in obedience. Not the sullen obedience of one forced against his will, but the joyful obedience of the believer who trusts God and trusts Scripture's revelation of what is right and best. Obedience is what Jesus speaks of when He says, "If you are faithful to what I have said, you are truly my disciples. And you will know the truth and the truth will set you free" (John 8:31, 32 *Phillips*).

Counseling situations, then, are those in which young person and adult wrestle together to find freedom through obedience to God. *Counseling focuses on the choice to obey.*

This clarification helps us see more clearly what must be accomplished in a counseling situation. For one thing, the problem which is at the root of the counselee's present inadequacy must be identified. There also has to come an understanding of God's evaluation of the situation, a grasp of reality as revealed in Scripture on which to base the obedient response. And finally there needs to be motivation to act.

Most secular counseling approaches are inadequate for the accomplishment of these three necessary tasks. We must seek understanding of how to "counsel" not in counseling theory but in the scripturally revealed dynamics of Christian leadership.

Approaches to counseling

There are various approaches to counseling which attempt to deal with (or have ignored) the three tasks which I have suggested must be accomplished. I'm aware that any attempt to simplify and sketch must lead to unfair distortion. Yet it seems necessary to highlight certain suppositions and patterns in various approaches as background for the counseling approach I will suggest. So, with apologies to proponents of other views for the unfairness that simplification must involve, I'd like to compare and evaluate three distinctive approaches.

Directive counseling The pattern of directive counseling is quite clear and simple. Although the process that a skillful directive counselor may use will be far more subtle, the philosophy underlying the approach is something like this. The counselee comes with a problem, which he reveals to the counselor. The counselor provides the answer. The counselee is expected to go out and act on it.

Diagramed, with the counselor's part boxed, directive counseling looks something like this:

REVEAL   PROVIDE   CHOOSE

PROBLEM   ANSWER   AND DO

There are several drawbacks to the directive approach. Given even that the counselor is a wise man, and knows the right answer, an externally imposed solution, like advice, is unlikely to be followed. I mentioned earlier that an intellectual-spiritual ministry is unlikely to move people. Simply telling another person what is best for him usually is inadequate to motivate action.

But now, how about our supposition that the counselor is a wise man? Can even the wisest of men play God to others? Most counseling situations do not face us with a clear-cut moral issue, where the biblical imperative, "Stop!" applies. In most situations the individual needs the personal guidance of the Holy Spirit in showing him just how to apply relevant biblical principles. A directive approach, in which the counselor tells the counselee what to do, puts the counselor in the position of playing God — often with tragic results. For as human beings we cannot know just in what way, how, and when God wants another to act.

But even if the counselor were correct in his solution and his instructions, would he help the counselee grow as an independent, responsible person? His counseling is far more likely to lead the other to depend on *him* rather than on God! Even the best directive counseling tends to establish a dependency relationship between counselee and counselor — a relationship that does not foster growth toward maturity.

Although it is relatively easy to introduce biblical content and the biblical perspective in the directive situation, doing it effectively, to motivate acceptance and response, is very difficult.

Non-directive counseling The pattern of non-directive counseling is significantly different. In non-directive counseling the counselor does not provide an answer: instead, he views his role as listening and reflecting feelings, so helping the counselee understand his own problems. With the issues clarified, the counselee is expected to come to his own solution, based on his own personality, perceptions, and values.

Diagramed, with the counselor's role again boxed, non-directive counseling looks something like this:

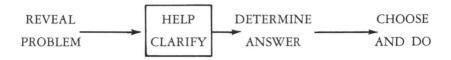

REVEAL → HELP → DETERMINE → CHOOSE
PROBLEM CLARIFY ANSWER AND DO

While non-directive counseling avoids the "playing God" aspect of directive counseling, it has other problems. One of these is the difficulty of introducing new information and insights. The non-directive counselor essentially stands *outside* of the counselee. He is concerned, but distant. His job is to feed back to the counselee his own feelings and perceptions about the problem until the counselee is able to come to his own solution, based on his own values and ideas about life. In non-directive counseling the counselor does not intrude his own values, or his solutions.

This is an extremely difficult position for the committed Christian to take. Believing firmly that Christ provides the answer for each human need, convinced that the biblical revelation must be understood if we are to have an adequate guide to knowing God's will or understanding life, the Christian *has* to introduce distinctive biblical values and perceptions in counseling.

While many of the techniques of non-directive counseling are valuable and used by counselors of every school, the underlying concept, that one must stand outside and, out of respect for the integrity of the counselee as an individual, not share himself or his values, must be rejected.

It is important to notice the relational aspects of both directive and non-directive counseling. *In each the counselor stands apart.* In neither does he seek to establish a relationship, described in the last chapter, that marks the context for ministry. In neither is he a *"person with."*

Identification counseling A third approach, which I have called identification counseling, is represented in the ministry of Swiss psychiatrist Paul Tournier. Rather than standing outside, to reflect or direct, Tournier seeks to share himself with the counselee as the counselee shares, and when each senses his identification with the other, to share solutions he has experienced in Christ.

This last approach harmonizes with what we've been saying in the last two chapters, for it permits the counselor to serve as a model who is trusted because of his humanity. I believe this is also what the apostle Paul speaks of to the Corinthians, when he talks of God as the "source of all mercy and comfort." He goes on to say that God

> gives us comfort in our trials so that we in turn may be able to give the same sort of strong sympathy to others in theirs. Indeed, experience shows that the more we share Christ's suffering, the more we are able to give of his encouragement. This means that if we experience trouble we can pass on to you comfort and spiritual help; for if we ourselves have been comforted we know how to encourage you to endure patiently the same sort of troubles that we have ourselves endured. (2 Cor. 1:3-8 *Phillips*)

The common experience of trouble provides the basis from which we can speak meaningfully to the troubles of others, and share that which was comforted and enabled us.

If we were to diagram identification counseling as we have the other two, it would look something like this, with the counselor's actions again boxed.

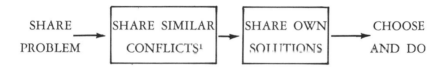

This process has been diagramed in greater detail by Bill Gothard, director of Campus Teams, whose analysis is presented in figure 4, p. 162, and explained on the next.

---

[1]See footnote 4 of chapter 8 concerning the nature of common ground.

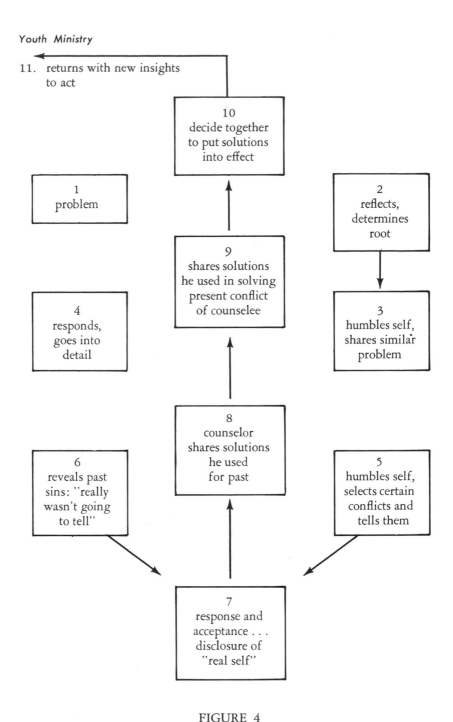

11. returns with new insights to act

1
problem

2
reflects,
determines
root

10
decide together
to put solutions
into effect

9
shares solutions
he used in solving
present conflict
of counselee

4
responds,
goes into
detail

3
humbles self,
shares similar
problem

8
counselor
shares solutions
he used
for past

6
reveals past
sins: "really
wasn't going
to tell"

5
humbles self,
selects certain
conflicts and
tells them

7
response and
acceptance . . .
disclosure of
"real self"

FIGURE 4

The Process of Identification
Counseling

Steps

1, 2   Most counseling processes seem to start here, with the counselor using non-directive technique to encourage the counselee to express his problem. The chart shows the purpose of this process in identification counseling to determine the "root" — that area common to human experience from which the problem arises.

3   Contrary to other counseling approaches, this approach accepts self-revelation, and the premise that the counselor must become a *person with* the counselee. When the counselor locates what seems to him the problem area, he humbles himself, and shares a similar problem, seeking common ground with the counselee.

4-7   These steps show the process of mutual self-revelation that gradually works down to mutual trust and acceptance. More than one conversation may be represented here, though if the counselor has established in his ministry with the young people the relational context described in chapter 8, the whole process may take place in a single meeting, including resolution of the problem.

8   With counselor and counselee in a mutually accepting, open relationship, the counselor is able to introduce the solutions he has found to the conflicts they have had in common. In biblical terms, the counselor has revealed the trouble he has experienced; now he is able to share the comfort and keys to endurance God provided for him. *The biblical perspective, then, is shared not in an intellectual-spiritual setting, but in a deeply personal, emotionally real, whole-person setting: "this is what I have experienced."* With rapport established, the content shared is acceptable to the counselee, and wins the hearing it might not have had if presented in another setting.

9, 10   The biblical perspective and experience of the counselor are then used by both to re-evaluate the counselees' situation and needs, leading to a shared decision as to how the counselee will respond. The impact of shared decision is not to reduce responsibility, but to support the counselee in his determination to act.

11   The counselee returns to the life-situation and acts on the new insights gained, the decisions made.

How identification counseling works

I noted earlier in the chapter that there are three tasks that must be accomplished if counseling is to have its desired impact. The counseling relationship must free the counselee to reveal and explore his problem; it must permit the effective introduction of God's perspective on the problem; and it must facilitate decision to act. In other words, the counselor must help his counselee express the problem, must introduce biblical content, and must motivate an obedient response to God.

The goal of counseling is important to keep clearly in mind. Counseling is not concerned so much with words as with life — with behavior. The New Testament speaks without apology of behavior. "No more evil temper or furious rage," Paul warned the Colossians, "No more evil thoughts or words about others, no more evil thoughts or words about God, and no more filthy conversation. Don't tell one another lies any more, for you have finished with the old man and all he did and have begun life as the new man, who is out to learn what he ought to be, according to the plan of God" (Col. 3:8-10 *Phillips*). The Christian is called to go on in life *as the new man:* to find in Christ the power to break the chains that bind him. *Counseling in Christian ministry is not to help a person understand himself, but to become himself.* And the Christian becomes himself by choosing whom he will obey: the demanding insistency of the sin and inadequacy that bind him, or God, who calls us to transformation through obedience. The goal of counseling is to help a person respond to God, to find freedom in the words and power of Jesus Christ.

How does identification counseling work toward this goal and seek to accomplish each task that lies on the pathway?

Discovering the problem Most persons who seek help are hesitant about revealing their problems. They are deeply concerned about how the other will respond, if the counselor will still accept them and like them. When the counselor makes himself vulnerable by sharing his own conflicts, he demonstrates acceptance and trust. He shows that he views himself as on the same level as the counselee, and takes his stand with him not as his judge, but as *simul justus et peccator.*

Sensitive self-revelation[2] normally encourages additional revelations by the counselee. I've noticed that even when I fail to grasp the root problem, self-revelation encourages further explanation. "No," I've been told. "It's not like that. It's like this. . . ." Self-revelation lets the other know that we are meeting *person-to-person:* that there is no "relating down."

Introducing content The difficulty in introducing the biblical perspective so vital to Christian solutions to life problems is not in making that perspective clear but in creating a willingness to hear. I noted earlier that ministry is not so much intellectual-spiritual as emotional-spiritual. We need help to grasp on a basic, common-sense level what God's way of life means, not merely help to crystalize concepts and doctrines. To some extent, any presentation of biblical truth that is divorced from experience comes across as intellectualized, idealized. But when God's truth is seen incarnated, fleshed-out and realized in the personal experience of others whom we see as being like us, it has the ability to grip and to compel.

Identification counseling seeks to build a personal relationship on that real-life, common-ground level. In the initial process of mutual self-revelation, each person has come to know and appreciate the other and to trust him as one who understands — as someone who is real. *When rapport has been gained, experience of the reality of God's Word can be shared as well as one's essential vulnerability to life.* In the rapport relationship, the biblical perspective comes across as more than theory, more than doctrine, more than "faith." It comes across as reality.

This may be one reason for Paul's great "if." "If we ourselves have been comforted we know how to encourage you." Only someone who has himself experienced the reality of God's comfort and guidance when in trouble is qualified to counsel. For counseling, like leadership itself, is the sharing of oneself so that in the servant-leader's example others also might find inspiration and trust to respond to God, in full obedience.

Motivating response While each person must be treated as a responsible individual, it is important to remember that responsibility is *not* independence. The most responsible of us need others to

---

[2]I recommend the reading of my book, *How Do I Fit In?* (Moody Press, 1970) for important background on this process. Self-revelation is a mutual process, which can proceed only as fast as each person is ready for it. *How Do I Fit In?* goes into greater detail as to the background and nature of building relationships through self-revelation.

support and encourage us. The identification process first links counselor and counselee together through mutual self-revelation, until rapport and trust are established. Then the counselor is free to share the divine perspective, revealing how the biblical truth has infused and transformed his experience and provides a basis for solution of his conflicts. So the biblical perspective has been explored by both as a basis for solving the counselee's problem, too. Ideally, the counselee has made a tentative decision to act on God's truth; to seek through obedience release and freedom.

At this point, where both directive and non-directive counselors leave those who come to them, the identification counselor continues in relationship. He prays for and with the counselee; he shows that he continues to care; he encourages. He helps the counselee realize that he is not alone. God is with him, and in the person of the Christian friend God demonstrates His continuing love.

PROBE
case histories
discussion questions
thought-provokers
resources

1. Many who work with youth suggest that rather than waiting for teens with problems to come to them, the leader needs to set up preventative personal conferences. Bill Gothard suggests several objectives for such a session. The following material has been adapted from unpublished notes of his "Basic Youth Conflicts" lecture series.
   (1) show personal love and concern
   (2) build genuine interest in his life and future
   (3) put him at ease to share personal problems
   (4) discuss where he is in spiritual growth
   (5) stimulate faith by setting reachable spiritual goals
   (6) establish a bond of prayer
   One of my friends suggests a different format for the initial personal conference. The conference is preceded by asking the teens in the group to write on a card: *three areas in which I would like to change.* These then become the general topic for conversation in the first counseling interview.
   I may note here that, although I have used the terms "counselor" and "counselee" throughout this chapter, I really do not like them. They seem to me to imply that superior/subordinate relationship which is so deadly to ministry. My own commitment is very much to the identification process; so much so that when young people or others come to talk with me I tell them I am *not* a counselor, or someone with answers. But I am more than willing to share, person to person. And very often in the process God shows His grace in

meeting needs. I much prefer to think of such situations as simply times to share, and to seek God's guidance together.

2. You may be interested in some modern theories of counseling which parallel quite closely what I have said in these chapters. Interestingly, some of them also spring from a theological base. Here are summaries of two, presented by Alexander Bassin in *Marital Counseling*.[3]

BASIC CONCEPTS OF INTEGRITY THERAPY

Any wrongdoing, past or present, that an individual decides to keep secret causes him to become walled-off from others in various ways. He feels he is on guard all the time to keep from being exposed as a type of person he doesn't want to be. He feels anxious, ill-at-ease, uncertain, depressed, always uncomfortable because of his dread of what others would think of him if they knew the facts of his behavior. Integrity Therapy insists, however, that what the person must do is work up enough courage to admit frankly to others the mistakes he has made — and he will frequently find that they accept him more completely than he ever thought possible — and he will then begin to feel better himself. The more he actually begins to practice honesty with others, the easier life will become, and his symptoms will slip away. He will also be surprised to notice that others become more open to him — that they also have been holding secrets of their own which they would like to get off their chests and thus feel better, too. One person dropping a curtain of secrecy encourages another to do likewise.

Listen, say the Integrity therapists, to that "still, small voice" within us, because what it "tells" us will help keep us psychologically satisfied. Unfortunately, this "voice" can be throttled to such an extent that it grows all but silent. Then we have no internal gyroscope to guide us, and we are in trouble. All sorts of symptoms emerge with the message: "Get back on the integrity track!"

Integrity therapy emphasizes the need for self-revelation, confession significant to others. It also insists that confession must be followed by restitution and good works. Mowrer has explored the history of primitive Christianity and notes how frequently public confession was a required ritual of group living; and he believes the original vitality of early Christianity may well be related to this procedure which insures honesty and integrity in interpersonal relationships. He notes how frequently the most effective of the self-help groups — Alcoholics Anonymous, Gamblers Anonymous, and others — succeed where more conventional approaches fail dismally in rescuing a victim from a life of shame and despair (p. 105).

REALITY THERAPY

Reality Therapy, the main component of which is emphasis on

---

[3]Alexander Bassin, "Integrity Therapy in Marriage Counseling," in Hirsch Silverman, *Marital Counseling* (Springfield, Illinois: Charles C. Thomas, 1967).

responsibility, is the brainchild of Dr. William Glasser, an extraordinarily warm, friendly, unassuming young psychiatrist.

THE REALITY THERAPIST

The therapist within the framework of Reality Therapy suffers some of the difficulties experienced by our righteous swami described earlier. He must be a highly responsible person — tough, involved, sensitive and human. He must be willing to fulfill his own needs and must be willing to discuss some of his own struggles so that the patient can see that acting responsibly is possible, even though difficult. He is neither aloof, superior nor sacrosanct, nor would he ever imply that what he does or what he stands for or what he values are unimportant. He must have the strength and courage to become involved, to have his values tested by the client, and to withstand intense criticism by the very person he may be trying to help. He must submit to have every fault and defect of his picked apart by the patient. He must be willing to admit that, like the client, he is far from perfect, but he is a person who can act responsibly even if it takes effort.

THE TECHNIQUE OF REALITY THERAPY

In various addresses, Dr. Glasser has explained the methodology of his treatment procedure. He warns, however, that, in contrast to conventional psychiatry, the theory of which is difficult to explain but the practice easy, Reality Therapy has a simple, fifteen-minute theoretical base, but a treatment procedure that is extremely difficult to follow.

1. *Involvement.* The first and most difficult phase of Reality Therapy is the gaining of the *involvement* that the client so desperately needs but which he has been unsuccessful in attaining or maintaining up to the time he presents himself for treatment. Unless the requisite involvement develops between the responsible therapist and the irresponsible client, there can be no therapy, Glasser asserts. The guiding principles are directed towards achieving the proper involvement: a completely honest, human relationship in which the client, for perhaps the first time in his life, realizes that someone cares enough for him not only to accept him but to accept him in order to fulfill his needs in the real world.

"How does a therapist become involved with a patient so that the patient can begin to fill his needs?" (Glasser asks.) "The therapist has a difficult task, for he must quickly build a firm emotional relationship with the patient who has failed to establish such relationships in the past. He is aided by recognizing that a patient is desperate for involvement and is suffering because he is not able to fulfill his needs. The patient is looking for a person with whom he can become emotionally involved, someone he can care about and who he can convince cares about him, someone who can convince the patient that he will stay with him until he can better fulfill his needs."

Unless the client is convinced that the therapist genuinely cares about him, there can be no prospect for change. Glasser extends this thesis to all areas of human interaction, whether it be in marriage, school or work.

2. *Reveal yourself.* Glasser differs from Mowrer in terms of emphasis of confession as an essential ingredient for therapy, but he does insist that involvement cannot be obtained if the therapist maintains the aloof "stone face," the impersonal posture that is taught in conventional psychotherapy. On the contrary, the therapist must be prepared to *reveal himself* as a person, with a family, with a car, with his own ups and downs.

3. *Be subjective and personal.* Glasser feels that orthodox psychiatry, in its insistence on being objective and impersonal, is laboring under an almost impossible handicap. People simply do not change in that kind of interpersonal situation. Furthermore, not only should the therapist be subjective and highly personal, he must demonstrate this attitude by constantly speaking of himself, using first person pronouns. For example, in working with a student who is not handing in his term papers, the reality therapist does not say, "The school administration expects you to do your homework," but "I would like you to work."

4. *Emphasize behavior, not feeling.* Unlike conventional psychiatry, which is very much concerned with providing a forum for the expression of feelings, Glasser notes: No one ever explains what the therapist is supposed to do with these feelings once they've been expressed. Glasser, on the contrary, suggests that the person speak about concrete behavior and deeds rather than philosophy and rumination. He holds that feelings are beyond our control; behavior is not. We can't tell ourselves to start feeling happy, for example, but we can tell ourselves to *do something.* Best of all, if we can do something responsible rather than irresponsible, our behavior may help us feel better. The Reality therapist does not mind discussing this and other concepts of his craft with the client, rather than acting as though he were in possession of some great esoteric final truth that is beyond the comprehension of mere laymen.

5. *Force a value judgment!* The most important single component of Reality therapy as a method, next to obtaining involvement, is to so direct the conversation that the client makes a value judgment about his behavior. For example, to use a situation mentioned by Glasser, if a kid punches a teacher in the nose, we ask him, "Now, did that behavior do you any good?" If the student responds that it did, there is very little you can do about it. Drop the matter for discussion at a later date. But, Glasser insists, in ninety-nine out of one hundred cases, the boy will think for a moment and then respond, "Naw, I guess it didn't. Just made a big hassle and now I'm in more hot water than ever." The client must be pressed, again and again, to evaluate the responsibility of his behavior. Is it helping him meet his needs? Is it interfering with other people meeting their needs? Is it doing him or

others any good? These are the inquiries the Reality therapist throws at the client after a firm involvement has been achieved.

> Having looked over these excerpts, how would you say each approach is similar to what I've been saying in this chapter? How does each differ?

3. I suggested several situations in this chapter that might be characterized as counseling situations. To get the feel of the concepts I've sketched, look back over these situations, and think how you might approach each person from the stance of different counseling theories.

    For example, let's think about Jan (pp. 156-157). Her youth leader, Mr. Jack, had been aware that something was wrong. Let's suppose that, as Jan is approaching his office, he is thinking about how to handle the situation.

Jan's been so sharp. But these last few months——. She sure has lost interest. She was cheerful . . . so open, too. Now, she backs off from the others. Sure doesn't seem to respond to spiritual things, either. Maybe even close sometimes to rebellious.

The whole pattern seemed to fall into place a few weeks ago. Then Mr. Jack heard Jan had been dating an unsaved fellow, and taking a beating from the church gang and heavy opposition from her parents.

Looks like I'm finally going to have a chance to help. Glad she asked for that private talk. Could be she's under real conviction. Let's see, . . . what are some good Scripture verses to use with her? . . .

> In this sketch, Mr. Jack sounds as if he'll be a directive counselor, planning to tell Jan what to do about what he believes to be her problem.
>
> Write out a dialogue that represents what you think each will say and do if he does take a directive approach.
>
> Now, looking over the *identification* approach again, do another dialogue. What will each say and do if he takes the identification approach?
>
> If you wish, do the same with other situations described in the chapter, until you begin to "feel" the differences and the interpersonal implications. For even greater value, role-play these situations with a friend, taking turns alternating as counselor/counselee, and attempting to get the feel of each approach.

4. *For further reading*
    William Glasser, *Reality Therapy* (New York: Harper and Row, 1965).
    John D. Krumboltz and Carl E. Thoresen, *Behavioral Counseling: Cases and Techniques* (New York: Holt, Rinehart and Winston, Inc., 1969).
    Paul Tournier, *The Strong and the Weak* (Philadelphia: Westminster Press, 1963).

Part Three

PROCESSES OF MINISTRY

YOUTH IN SCRIPTURE

YOUTII IN BODY RELATIONSHIP

YOUTH IN LIFE

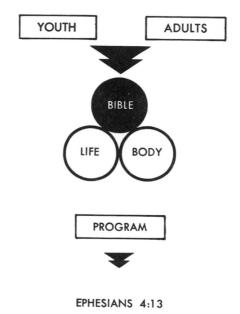

EPHESIANS 4:13

YOUTH IN SCRIPTURE

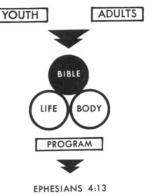

10

confronting reality

Dr. Charles I. Gragg, in evaluating the training given young people for careers in business management, has commented on the idea underlying most such training. The present approach, he says, which rests on the idea of giving carefully selected young men information and general principles others have acquired in years of business experience in order to give them a head start, "rests on a decidedly questionable assumption: namely, the assumption that it is possible by the simple process of telling to pass on knowledge in useful form. This is the great delusion of the ages. If the learning process is to be effective, something dynamic must take place in the learner."[1] The passing on of information — no matter how important that information may be — should never be mistaken for that dynamic something happening within.

The assumption that "telling" passes on knowledge in useful form is a delusion that has long plagued evangelicals. Convinced that Scripture is God's Word, containing information that we need and that has a vital meaning for us, we have been quick to emphasize communication of biblical content. But we have not been as quick to check and see if we communicate it in useful form — if our reading and teaching of the Bible has had God's intended impact on lives.

Probably nowhere in youth ministry as in our interaction with Scripture has our intellectual-spiritual orientation been more in evidence. And probably nowhere in youth ministry do we more need to involve youth as whole persons with the biblical Word which speaks out decisively about their whole lives.

Somehow we need to bring young people into that kind of contact with God's Word that carries them beyond understanding it to the place where the divine perspective permeates personality, reshapes values, and is expressed in decision.

---

[1]Charles I. Gragg, "Because Wisdom Can't Be Told" (address of the head of the Harvard Business School).

In a recent article in *Instructor* magazine, entitled "Swing Toward Decision-making," Dr. Theodore Kaltsounis evaluates the changing role of social studies in the public schools. "Teaching children how to make good decisions," he says, "is becoming a very important, and most likely the ultimate, objective for the social studies."[2] Dr. Kaltsounis goes on to explain that for years social studies have been primarily descriptive — an analysis of and explanation of cultures and conditions. Over the past few years, however, educators have become convinced that learners need to be "prepared to function now as well as later in this complicated society in which they are living."[3] As a result, the structure of teaching is shifting; and curriculums are being redesigned to reach new and different goals.

The following quote highlights what a secular educator sees as essential to an educational approach that focuses on decision-making; essentials distinctly parallel to approaches Christians need to take in communicating God's Word.

> *It should be made clear that decision-making does not minimize the value of concepts, generalizations, inquiry, social sciencing, and the like. It simply shifts their position from ends to means.*
>
> Decision-making involves three basic elements: knowledge, values, action.
>
> Values, which include the feelings, dispositions, attitudes and beliefs of the decision-maker, are just as important as knowledge in making decisions. *At times, value factors can be more important than knowledge.* For example, a person may inquire into the unfair treatment of the minority groups. He may conclude and declare that discrimination is evil. Yet, when it actually comes down to supporting an open-housing policy for his neighborhood, he finds all kinds of excuses to oppose it. He might say, for instance, that he does not object to having a minority person move into his neighborhood, but he is concerned about what this might do to property values.
>
> During the past, the school has done a great deal to increase children's knowledge. The more recent emphasis on concepts and generalizations has strengthened this function even more, but little has been done in the area of values. There is a need for the school to expand its role and devote more time to designing ways which will stimulate children to discover their inner world of values, to analyze them, and to modify or perhaps reorganize them.
>
> Finally, decision-making requires action. It is this step that has the potential of making social studies as exciting and useful to the indi-

---

[2]Theodore Kaltsounis, "Swing Toward Decision-making," *Instructor,* April, 1971, pp. 35-37.

[3]Ibid. pp. 45-56.

vidual as well as to society. It is in action that the child will see the relevancy of what he knows and is learning.

Taking action gives the child an opportunity and the stimulation to bring out his inner feelings and values. He can test their validity in the light of related information, and the feeling and values of his classmates and other persons closely associated with him.

Decision-making then takes the social sciences beyond simple intellectualization concerning the society and into the realm of positive social action.[4]

Each point made in this quote is directly relevant to our ministry with youth. Scripture has not been inspired by God for "simple intellectualization." Rather, God's Word bursts upon us with the demand that we submit ourselves to it, permitting God to reshape our personalities through His revelation. And the test of our commitment, as well as the process through which growth in Christ takes place, is decision. Decision takes the Bible and our faith out of the realm of "belief about" and into the realm of positive, obedient response — into the realm of action.

In chapter 2 I spoke of viewing Scripture in a reality framework rather than simply in a truth framework. By this I particularly meant to insist that the Bible's teachings are not merely to be believed (which is appropriate to an objective but impersonal truth) but also are to be acted on (which is appropriate to a confrontation with reality). There is a tremendous difference between these two teaching goals — and how they can be reached.

In school I have learned many things which I accept today as true — but which make absolutely no demand on me for response. In high school I learned (and passed tests to prove I had learned) that there were so many representatives and senators from our state, what the powers of the supreme court were, etc. In college I was forced to take botany and zoology, and in the process learned the parts of a flower, the make-up of cells, and even the body parts of some huge South American frogs which I had cut up with distaste. I accepted as true what I was taught, and in some cases even discovered in the laboratory by personal investigation that certain statements were true. *But the truths I learned and accepted had no impact on my life.* They called for no particular response and demanded no change in my values or my actions.

This kind of learning requires only a simple "acceptance of x as

---

[4]Ibid.

true" and normally has little impact on life — even when it potentially has implications for life. A study by Dr. Thomas D. Cook of the effects of confronting a belief with its implied action consequences is quite revealing here.[5] Cook and others communicated to a group of college students a message which had potential life implications. Cook showed the students that an untrained person has the ability to help mentally retarded children in institutions. Student groups were given this message, alternately with and without the information that they had easily available an *opportunity* to help in a local institution. With the added information, the message not only had potential action implications; it confronted the students with the necessity of decision.

What were the results? Students who were *not* confronted with a perceived action consequence (a demand to decide) accepted the information as true: they believed an untrained person could be of help. Students who were confronted with the action consequences (and forced to make a decision) *rejected* the information, refusing to believe an untrained person (now they themselves) could be of help, and "the costly action was totally resisted."

Somehow a "truth" which implied something for life but which did not demand a decision to act represented no threat, and so could be believed without cost!

It is important to understand that our present educational system is designed for the communication of cheap truth. It focuses on the transmission of information which can be accepted (believed) without any necessary change in behavior, without personal decision. In fact, the whole approach to teaching/learning that characterizes our schools is suited to just this kind of teaching.

The impact of Dr. Kaltsounis' article and the many like it is to point out that when an attempt is made to communicate costly truth — truth that demands decision — *an entirely different educational approach is required!*

Turning to Christian education, we note that our teaching/learning approaches are in fact largely patterned on and just like the secular — suitable only to the communication of cheap truth. But the Bible communicates a costly truth — the kind of truth that not only has potential implications for life, but which in fact demands decision.

[5]Thomas D. Cook, John R. Burd, and Terence L. Talbert, "Temporal Effects of Confronting Belief with its Action Consequences," report financed by a grant from the Council for Research at Northwestern University, Evanston, Illinois.

Thus the Scripture says, "Don't, I beg you, only hear the message, but put it into practice; otherwise you are merely deluding yourselves" (James 1:22 *Phillips*).

God's truth *can* be heard as a message that requires only assent. That involves no costly decision to respond. *But it must not be. For Scripture is by nature a revelation of reality, and with reality each human being must come to terms.*

Reality revealed

In *Psychology of Personal Constructs,* G. A. Kelly makes a point restated by many in many different contexts: our universe is open to interpretation, and our interpretation is important. In fact, decisions and choices in life are ultimately based on our perception (conceptual and affectual) of the world.

> The universe is real; it is happening all the time; it is integral; and it is open to piecemeal interpretation. Different men construe it in different ways. Since it owns no prior allegiance to any one man's construction system, it is always open to reconstruction. Some of the alternative ways of construing it are better adapted to man's purposes than are others. Thus, man comes to understand his world through an infinite series of successive approximations. Since man is always faced with constructive alternatives, which he may explore if he wishes, he need not continue indefinitely to be the absolute victim either of his past history or of his present circumstances.[6]

Looking at the world from different viewpoints, then, opens up new options to action which free us from various dead ends. For instance, the mechanistic physics of the 19th century set a pattern of determinism that spilled over into the social as well as physical science. Dr. Werner Heisenberg's work on atomic physics, leading to the replacement of deterministic concepts by those of randomness and probability, opened up exciting new avenues of research in the physical sciences, and led to drastic revisions of thinking in the social sciences as well. This new "construction system," or way of understanding the world, not only changed our generation's way of thinking about the world, but also our way of interacting with it.[7]

When an issue involves a reconstruction of our understanding of reality, our way of living must always change.

---

[6]G. A. Kelly, *The Psychology of Personal Constructs* (New York: W. W. Norton and Co., 1955).

[7]See particularly the following works by Dr. Heisenberg: *Philosophic Problems of Nuclear Science* (New York: Fawcett, 1963), *The Physicist's Conception of Nature,* trans. by Arnold J. Pomerans (Connecticut: Greenwood, 1958).

It is perhaps easiest to see how a perception of reality affects behavior by illustrations from the physical world. It is because of our reality-orientation that we look for doors to enter buildings rather than try to walk through walls. It is because of our reality-orientation that we hesitate to cross the street in the face of onrushing traffic. Our perception of reality tells us that we cannot walk into walls without bruising and that a mistake in gauging the speed and distance of an on-coming automobile is likely to be our last mistake. *When we are fully convinced that something is rooted in reality, we modify our behavior to harmonize with it.*[8]

This principle operates in the social and moral world as well as in the physical. If we lie, ultimately it is because we see reality as something we can manipulate by falsehood, rather than understanding life as truly under the control of a God who is sovereign, and who is involved in our lives. A biblical reality-orientation frees us to be finished with lying and to speak the truth with our neighbor (Eph. 4:25). If we adopt the playboy philosophy of sex, it is because ultimately we accept the animalness of man, and are willing to treat other persons as *things to use* to give us pleasure. Our response to people, to situations, to all of life, is based ultimately on our whole-person (conceptual and affectual) orientation to reality.

What is involved in a reality-orientation, then, begins to come clear.

First, there is the universe itself: the physical and social and spiritual world we live in. Secular thought sees the universe as "open to interpretation" and reconstruction. For to the non-Christian the universe is essentially impersonal, without meaning or purpose or goal. And so man can make of life what he will, and choose his own values on the basis of what seems to work best for him. But the Christian has a different view of the creation. He understands the universe as essentially *personal,* created and sustained and guided by a God who involves Himself with us human beings to infuse His own loving purposes and give life ultimate meaning. We joyfully proclaim that "reality" is *not* something for man to construct for himself. Reality is the physical and social and spiritual world as God has made it and knows it to be.

---

[8]Let me stress again that "fully convinced" is not merely a statement about intellection. I present no such argument as Plato, that the person who knows the good will always choose it. Rather, "conviction" here refers to a person's whole perception of a situation: his understanding and emotional commitment. In familiar terms, I'm talking about one's believing in something "with all his heart."

The secularist has only human experience to guide him in his attempts to approximate reality, and come to grips with life. But the Christian has an entirely different source for his understanding of *Amen!* reality: the Christian has revelation. God's own understanding of the meaning and purpose of life and the principles on which we are to operate is made available to us in His Word. Only God truly understands what men fumble with in their mean attempts to find meaning. "Who could really understand a man's inmost thoughts except the spirit of the man himself?" the Bible asks. "How much less could anyone understand the thoughts of God except the very Spirit of God? And the marvelous thing is this, that we now receive not the spirit of the world but the Spirit of God himself, so that we can actually understand something of God's generosity toward us" (1 Cor. 2:11, 12 *Phillips*). And the Scriptures go on to point out that God's Spirit has acted to impart God's grasp of reality to us "in words not taught by human wisdom but taught by the Spirit" (1 Cor. 2:13 *RSV*). The conviction that we have revealed in God's Word an accurate and trustworthy portrait of reality underlies our attitude to such biblical exhortations as this: "Live for the rest of the time in the flesh no longer by human passions but by the will of God" (1 Peter 4:2 *RSV*). Because the Gospel message is anchored in reality Paul says, "Whatever happens, make sure that your everyday life is worthy of the gospel of Christ" (Phil. 1:27 *Phillips*). The Gospel, as well as the entire Word, reveals reality, not irrelevant truth, and so demands that we live in harmony with it.

The Christian's conviction that Scripture is God's revelation of reality is central to our understanding of the role the Bible must take in Christian education of youth — and is determinative for our understanding of *how* to communicate it.

A second thing to note about a reality-orientation is that it involves a personal commitment that is reflected in behavior. Reality always demands a response and is hard on those who make a mistaken response. I read last winter of a snowmobile driver who dashed at full speed out onto a frozen Wisconsin river and plunged to his death through the ice. He *thought* the ice was safe. But in reality, it was only one-fourth of an inch thick.

We can play with ideas. But we can't play with reality. We live in harmony with it, or suffer the consequences.

Thus we need to communicate reality not only so that people come to understand it intellectually, but so that they subjectively

179

accept and act in harmony with it. To attempt to communicate Scripture in the way we attempt to communicate true but irrelevant information (so that it might be accepted as true without demanding decision and response) is to violate the essential nature of the Scripture itself. God's Word must always be communicated so as to demand and invite decision to act.

Dr. Cook's experiment (p. 176) gives us insight into what happens when we attempt to communicate reality in ways suitable only to the communication of true-but-irrelevant information. Remember that Cook succeeded in conveying information about the ability of the untrained person to help retarded children so as to gain acceptance of it as a belief — when that communication was framed as an undemanding truth. But when the same message was communicated in the same way with its reality-orientation made plain ("if you believe this, go to an institution and volunteer to help"), then the information was rejected.

Something more than true information is required to produce decision.

Communicating a reality-orientation is in fact distinctly different from communicating true information. It has different goals, and requires a distinctive approach. We should be very clear on this: the communication pattern appropriate to one is not appropriate to the other! Something very different is demanded of the learner who is coming to grips with reality from that which is demanded of the learner who merely masters and accepts information which has for him no reality-orientation.

Information inadequate

Earlier we saw that Dr. Kaltsounis thinks of subjective factors in teaching for decision-making as values. Values, he says, "include the feelings, dispositions, attitudes and beliefs of the decision-maker."[9] Garrison agrees, for he says, "Values refer to what we regard as important, rather than what we know. They are organizing factors within the personality and are especially important in relation to morals and character."[10]

Scripture presented in a reality-orientation brings a confrontation with values. "What we regard as important" may very well not be

---

[9]op. cit.

[10]Karl C. Garrison, *Psychology of Adolescence* (Englewood Cliffs, New Jersey: Prentice-Hall Inc., 6th ed., 1965) p. 183.

what God says is important. Man's essentially self-centered view of life is in direct conflict with the biblical teaching that in reality the route to fulfillment is self-denial. Human wisdom finds it difficult to accept the fact that the leader must learn to function as a servant. Yet when we are confronted by God's view of reality, we are forced to choose: to decide to reject the biblical, to relegate what the Bible says to the realm of true but unimportant information, or to explore and restructure our own values and way of life. If we take this last course, we involve ourselves in a painful reordering of our feelings, dispositions, attitudes, and beliefs — a reordering of our inner man to bring our values in harmony with the objective revelation of reality God has shared with us in Scripture.

"Teaching the Bible" or "getting people to study the Bible," then, demands that we pay attention not only to accurate transmission of biblical information and concepts, but also to what must happen within learners when they confront a reality that demands response and change. And this we must never forget. The Bible, understood as God's revelation of reality, contains costly (not cheap) truth. As such a revelation, God's Word must be taught for decision, not for "acceptance."

We need, then, to reject educational approaches that are designed only to gain acceptance of truth (as illustrated in the secular "classroom" approach to teaching/learning) and develop distinctive educational ministries which will free learners to explore and change their values.

If we continue to teach the Bible in old ways, youth may well accept its teachings as true, but file that truth away as irrelevant to life.

If we in old structures teach the Bible as a reality structure, demanding decision and action, youth may well reject its viewpoint as in conflict with their own unexamined but dearly held values.

If we teach the Bible in contexts where youth are confronted with God's revelation of reality (and thus are faced with the necessity of decision and action) *and* where they are free to explore, express, and change their values, then and only then can we expect transformed lives.

What context frees persons to change and develop new values? I pointed out in an early chapter that values are formed in and through interpersonal relationships — with parents, peers, and other significant persons. In the last chapter of the previous section I stressed the importance of the leader developing a *"person with"* relationship with youth. For the leader to have an impact he needs to be in a relationship with youth in which life-to-life communication can take place — a relationship in which the objective reality revealed in the Word can be seen incarnated; where God's truth can be perceived in the experiences, feelings, emotions, and behavior of a Christian example as well as in his beliefs and ideas. To deal with what Dr. Kaltsounis calls values we need to have honest sharing of affective as well as cognitive data. (I am using "affective" here as Parry does; he writes, "All messages meant to convey the quality of moods, preferences, values, emotions, hedonic tones, strivings, pleasant and unpleasant conditions, physical or mental, volitions and attitudes.") [11] Only where there is an open and loving *relationship* between the adults and youth in the teaching/learning situation, with freedom to share feelings as well as to discuss concepts in the study of God's Word, is there likely to be that kind of study that leads to decision, and the personal discovery that God's Word actually *is* Truth.

Guidelines

To this point, then, I have argued that our attempts to involve young people in Bible study must rest on certain understandings and presuppositions. These are, to summarize:

(1) God's Word must always be understood as a revelation of reality.

(2) As such, it must always be taught for decision, to produce action that is in harmony with the reality it reveals.

(3) Secular education is designed to communicate information as "truth to be believed"; *not* as a reality demanding decision.

(4) When action implications are specified in an "information" teaching/learning setting, the information itself is more likely to be rejected than is merely the specified action.

(5) The problem with the information-oriented teaching/learning process is that it does not deal with values, the "what's important to me" that is the basis on which most of us accept or reject various points of view.

(6) Only an approach to teaching/learning which seeks to deal with learners' values in a context of open, honest, and loving personal relationships is likely to bring learners to accept and live by a particular view of reality.

11 John Parry, *Psychology of Human Communication* (New York: American Elsevier Publishing Co., 1968) p. 65.

Understanding Scripture as God's revelation of reality — a revelation that demands decision and commitment — has many practical implications for youth ministry. We want to lead youth into God's Word. But we want to do it in such a way that they respond with a decision to live by it.

This understanding of Scripture provides criteria by which we can evaluate some of our present approaches for involving youth in Bible study. Are our classes and meetings information-centered? Is there a free expression by youth and adults of feelings and attitudes and beliefs in the study situation? Is there exploration together of the life-response that is demanded by taking this particular portion of God's Word seriously? Is there a shared expression of commitment? Is there actual life-change (observed and reported) taking place on the basis of a biblical understanding of life and an adoption of biblical values?

Although the answers to these questions may often be discouraging, the same questions give us guidelines for developing contexts in which meaningful study of God's Word with youth can take place. For God's Word does portray a reality that each of us is invited to experience in Christ. And the Holy Spirit, working in our lives through his Word and through one another is uniquely able to set young believers on the pathway to maturity and vital relationship with Jesus Christ.

PROBE
case histories
discussion questions
thought-provokers
resources

1. A friend of mine describes the Sunday school class of a seminarian. Look over his description, and see how successful you think he is in communicating God's truth in its reality setting. Can you see strengths and weaknesses in his approach? How might you teach differently? What would you do in the same way that he does?

Earlier this fall I talked with one of the grad fellows who is a Sunday school teacher; in the course of the conversation he shared some of his views about teaching. By the way, he is not a Christian education major, and has never had a C.E. course! At any rate, I wanted to talk to him some more but I didn't want to make it an interview in any way. Well, today we got together and ate lunch together — and the topic came up so naturally that I didn't even have to initiate it.
Rusty feels:
Content is very important. Bible knowledge is a must. Methods can never outweigh Bible knowledge.

We need to experience biblical principles rather than just read about them. We need to see what the Bible says and then put it into practice in daily life.

Curriculums which have students merely fill in blanks are not good, not teaching the student anything.

How he structures the Sunday school hour: The president of the class welcomes visitors, gives announcements, leads in prayer, then calls on Rusty. Rusty then has a "gossip time"; everyone has to share something. Then, Bible study. They're in Romans now. They're in small groups with a group leader. Rusty gives them assignments, so they have specific questions to answer. He supplies Bible dictionaries, atlases, concordances. Findings are written out; each student keeps his own notebook. Each student writes how the passage applies to his life. Groups come together to share at the end. Oh, he also has something special, a record, article, or something they discuss — some current issue.

He gives homework assignments, expects students to prepare at home. He feels it's wrong not to demand work. He keeps them busy all hour, tries to vary his "something special" every Sunday. He feels this is important. I asked if there would be any trouble getting a substitute teacher now when he's gone for vacation. Oh, no, he said, they don't need a sub. They have their assignment and know what they're supposed to do; they'll get along just fine without a teacher.

Rusty feels it's terrible how little our people know about the Bible. He thinks this may be because teachers have taught out of commentaries and quarterlies rather than getting right into the Bible. That's why he's so strong on Bible knowledge. Then he said that we need to train teachers to communicate Bible knowledge effectively. And with that lunch was over.

2. Like Rusty, I have some pretty strong ideas on how Bible content needs to be communicated. The concept of Scripture as a reality that demands response has definite implications for structuring the teaching/learning situation, whether for the traditional Sunday school hour or a small group meeting.

   I will not attempt to go into structuring the teaching/learning situation for the Sunday school in this book because I have an entire book, *Creative Bible Teaching* (Moody Press), that works this out in detail. For those whose ministry involves Sunday school teaching, I suggest you consider looking over *Creative Bible Teaching*.

3. In this chapter I suggested that we need to develop a Bible-study situation in which youth feel free to explore, express, and change their values and attitudes as they study Scripture. It seems to me that to a great extent this kind of freedom depends on two factors:

   (1) The interpersonal context. Only when we feel the love and acceptance and concern of others do we feel free to share honestly. When we are dealing with values, we are exploring the very roots of our personalities, exposing thoughts and feelings and experiences that are often heavily laden emotionally. The same context of mutual self-revelation that frees persons in the counselor/counselee setting is necessary in the Bible study situation.

(2) A second factor has to do with our sense of relationship with God, and with the "tone of voice" in which we hear Him speak in Scripture. One Sunday I heard a sermon in a Phoenix church exhorting members to witness for Christ, and constantly reminding them that they *ought* to share their faith. The tone was insistent and demanding; the "ought" framework destructive of positive motivation and very likely to produce a sense of guilt and inadequacy. *And the framework and tone were utterly unscriptural!* For biblical commands are not uttered in the demanding tone of "ought." They are uttered rather as the invitation of a loving Father who is eager to have His children experience the joys of discovering reality.

Freedom to respond to the Word seems to me to rest not only on the interpersonal context in the study group, but also on our perception of the tone in which God Himself speaks and relates to us.

These two elements (the interpersonal relationship context in which Scripture is studied and the believer's perception of God's tone of voice) seem so vital to me in freeing us to explore values when we come to the Word that I've devoted another book to them. This book, *Creative Bible Study* (Zondervan, 1971) is designed to help small groups develop facilitating relationships for "reality-based" Bible study, and to develop a healthier perception of Scripture itself, as well as sharpen skills needed to find God's answers to our problems in His Word. The following resumé, which I prepared for a class in youth ministry at Wheaton College, may give you an idea of what I mean by "tone of voice" of Scripture, and the kind of issues dealt with in *Creative Bible Study*.

TRAINING IN PERCEPTION

Imagine two persons asked to walk through an art gallery and, when they emerged, questioned about what they had seen and remembered. One of them has been trained by a teacher who constantly drilled into his students: "Think blue. Think blue." The other has been trained by a teacher who constantly repeated, "Think red. Think red."

It's pretty obvious that when the two are questioned after their tour, they will have noticed different pictures, and will emphasize different features. They have been sensitized by their training to think and perceive from very different standpoints.

The Bible is understood and perceived much as the pictures in the gallery. The message that comes across is not necessarily what is objectively there, but what we tend to perceive from our training and our very human way of looking at life and relationships. Unfortunately, and very unbiblically, many of us read and think "ought."

TWO STANDPOINTS

Two standpoints were illustrated in class by the tale of the two mothers who spoke the same words, in the same imperative: "Get away from there!"

The first mother was watching TV, and was angry when her three-year-old wandered between her and the screen. And her imperative was matched with a threat: "Or I'll let you have it!" The second mother was cooking, and uttered the command as her tot toddled with outstretched hand toward a hot dish on the stove. We noticed several differences between the same words uttered in the same imperative:

First Mother	Second Mother
1. Has a selfish motive.	1. Has only the child's good in view.
2. The tone conveys demand; insistence on subjection.	2. The tone carries urgency, but love.
3. Painful consequences of disobedience are threatened by the injured party—the mother (punitive).	3. Painful consequences would follow as natural consequences because of the realities of the situation.

And, of course, the question comes, which of these two mothers — these two situations — is God and His Word *most like?*

The answer (mine, at any rate) is: Like the second, and *not at all* like the first!

HOW THEN DO WE UNDERSTAND BIBLICAL COMMANDS?

They may be read either in a "law" or in a "love" framework. In the law framework, they seem to be a demanding voice that insists that we live up to standards to gain God's and others' approval. This legalism seems to me to be horribly unscriptural. The Bible says the law always relates to the sinner to create and demonstrate guilt (Romans 3:18-20), and "is not really meant for the good man" (1 Tim. 1:9). Paul explicitly calls foolish those who, becoming Christians through faith, try to go on in the Christian life by subjecting themselves to law (Gal. 3:1f) and he makes it clear in that chapter that "we are completely free" from the authority of a Law which he identifies in chapter 4 as "basic moral principles" — not just the "ceremonial law" as some would interpret it.

Romans 7 makes it clear why we *must* be free from law: one who looks at law as a standard he ought to keep finds his sinful nature energized by that very law to struggle against it! God's solution according to the continuing argument is to look to Christ, live responsive to Him, and so find oneself doing spontaneously all that law commands! (For an extended discussion of this, see the "youth asks" book, *Is God Necessary?* chapters 6-10.)

BASIC ELEMENTS OF THE TWO SYSTEMS

How do these two approaches work out? — one hearing Scripture as law (with its demand and insistence on achieving certain standards) and the other hearing Scripture as love (with its gentle but firm guidance away from what harms toward what is good and brings meaning with joy).

SYSTEM ONE — the Bible read in the framework of "ought"

a. *Puts God* in the position of insisting on performance, demanding change, nagging us to act and *be* different than we want to and are.

b. *Puts you and me* in the position of one who is expected to struggle and "do your best." It condemns us to feel our guilt and inadequacy, to feel worthless, because we often fail.

c. *Puts commands* between God and us, as though He would love us only when we've lived up to some demand.

SYSTEM TWO — the Bible in the framework of "invitation"

a. *Puts God* in the position of a loving Father who guides His children away from harm to what is good and most enriches life.

b. *Puts you and me* right where we are — as unable in ourselves to experience the good life God invites us to experience, but not disappointing God by our inadequacy.
What do I mean by this? Simply that God *knows* we can't obey and doesn't expect us to try to live up to standards that sin's warping power has put beyond our reach. "Without me," Christ said, "you can do *nothing*." So *nothing* is exactly what is expected! Instead of demanding that we try to do what we cannot do, God accepts and loves us as we are. And, coming into our lives, lives for us. So Paul's "not I, but Christ living in me" isn't mystical theology. It's the bluntly practical guts of Christian experience.

c. *Puts the imperative* in the light of invitation — invitation to turn to Christ in faith and say, "I can't; You can," and then to *act* in full expectation that He *will*. Commands do not come between us and God; the imperative read as invitation draws us closer to Him in full reliance and a trust that is freed from any question of condemnation for being what we are — able, apart from Him, to do just exactly nothing.

4. I have suggested in this chapter that revealed truth communicated in the formal "classroom" setting is not adequate for changing values and leading to decision and to that response that the nature of the Word as God's disclosure of reality demands.

The following is the report of a study of the impact of communicating truth about God in a classroom setting that further explains what I've been saying in this chapter, and to some extent may demonstrate that this point of view is correct.

If nothing else, this study seems to me to indicate that the church must seriously rethink the ways in which we try to communicate the Word of God to others.

Background

At present, institutional Christianity attempts to communicate religious faith to children primarily in formal learning situations. Programs of the Sunday school and other educational agencies are structured on the classroom model (teacher, time-bounds, content curriculum) and designed mainly for the communication of information. This is easily demonstrated by a review of curriculum materials, of books written to guide teachers, and by the admissions of critics of the system who confess that, while in theory they desire religious education to be of a different character than this, it is in fact essentially a belief-transmitting system.

Some research (notably that of Goldmann) has criticized religious education by questioning the appropriateness of curriculum content in view of children's cognitive development. But little or no research has been done on a far more basic issue: the question of whether the classroom learning model is an appropriate one for religious education in the first place.

Assumptions

It is assumed by the author that the "Christian faith" is neither understood nor to be understood as simply a system of beliefs about God, self, and the world. Thus, the New Testament links the concept of God as a God of love with both loving attitude and loving action by one who holds this belief:

> We know what real love is from Christ's example in dying for us. And so we also ought to lay down our lives for our Christian brothers. But if someone who is supposed to be a Christian has money enough to live well, and sees a brother in need, and won't help him — how can God's love be within *him?* Little children, let us stop just *saying* we love people; let us *really* love them, and *show it* by our *actions* (1 John 3:16-18 *The Living Bible*).

This linkage between knowledge, attitude, and behavior, so prominent in the biblical portrait of Christian faith, is held by the author to be essential to Christian faith, and the true goal of Christian education.

Although most Christians hold this goal in common, Christian education has not been designed to deal specifically with attitude and behavior, nor with their linkage with belief. Rather, the educational system of the church focuses on the teaching/learning of beliefs, and merely assumes that if one has the "correct beliefs," appropriate attitudes and actions will follow. It is this assumption that this chapter seeks to question and to examine.

Critics of this assumption have suggested various alternative religious education strategies to the classroom model strategy. One much talked-of is that of centering Christian education in the home. Here, it is felt, beliefs, attitudes, and behaviors are in fact already linked through a variety of operative learning mechanisms. In this view, the role of the parents in communicating the Christian faith is far more significant than that of the teacher, and the context of life far more determinative than the classroom, in fixing the child's attitudes and behaviors, if not his formal beliefs. Thus Christian educators might well focus on the training of parents as communicators of faith, rather than on the training of teachers and the creation of curriculum.

These two strategies (classroom and home) can hardly be tested empirically as wholes. But certain implications of the assumptions underlying each do appear to be testable. Thus, if the classroom teaching of "correct beliefs" about a religious object does in fact produce a corresponding and appropriate attitude toward that object, some indication of the possible validity of this approach to Christian education would be provided. If, however, individuals who were thus taught and who held (as testable knowledge) similar beliefs were shown to have significantly different attitudes toward that object, then the classroom approach to Christian education might reasonably be questioned. Finally, if the differences discovered could be partially explained by the functioning of the concept in intergenerational interaction in the home, the significance of a strategy focused through the home would be given empirical support.

Difficulties peculiar to this study

Several difficulties seem peculiar to the study of religious beliefs. One of the most significant has to do with the idea that religious beliefs are in fact learned in the classroom situation, rather than being assimilated from the culture. Thus Bose in an unpublished dissertation (1929) indicates that church school attendance makes little difference in the religious concepts of children! How then can we be sure that the beliefs studied are actually learned through formal religious instruction? Might not *any* religious belief tested have been learned informally in the home or be otherwise available in the culture?

Another difficulty has to do with the selection of an "attitude object" for study. Is any single religious attitude object central enough to serve as a valid indicator of the effectiveness of religious training? Would the selection of several religious attitude objects provide greater reliability?

Finally, another difficulty seems peculiar to the measurement of attitude toward a religious object. In the population to be studied (those who have received formal religious training) it is likely that "the affective attribute" will in nearly all cases be "good." Thus it may be extremely difficult to isolate and evaluate negatively weighted affect.

Because of a recognition of these difficulties, and in an attempt to limit their impact as much as possible, the following decisions were made as to the design of the study.

a. *The population* The population to be tested are all eighth graders in a Christian grammar school. Each student has not only received formal religious instruction in his church on Sunday, but also receives a common daily religious instruction as part of the school curriculum.

The school is situated in an upper-middle class suburb, with an excellent public school system available. The school does not accept disciplinary students and requires that at least one parent express agreement with the school's statement of faith before a student is accepted. Thus the primary motivation for sending a child to this school is a religious motivation.

This population then provides a definite congruence as to (1) parental religious motivation and conviction (as measured by willingness to pay heavy tuition costs above normal school taxes), (2) student exposure to formal religious training, and (3) the specific system of "correct belief" which is taught.

b. *The attitude object* After consideration, "God" was chosen as the attitude object to be studied. The reasons for this selection were (1) the centrality of God in the Christian faith, (2) the possibility of multiple differentiations of the beliefs within the concept, and (3) the certainty that much of the classroom instruction provided either directly or indirectly was concerned with the God-concept.

189

c. *The measurement of attitude* Within this population and the belief system itself, the affective attribute by which the students are enjoined to evaluate God is "good." Each item of belief about God can be, and is, within this system conceptualized under that attribute.

This factor makes it very difficult to measure "attitude toward God" on any positive—negative—indifferent scale. For nearly any belief about God which might be elicited from a subject, no matter how negatively loaded it might appear to another, can within the subject be so linked with other beliefs that it appears to him to have a positive affect.

Thus it is necessary to develop tools with which to measure attitude toward God without reliance on the weighting of beliefs about God as having in themselves positive, negative, or indifferent affective loading.

Two notions were adopted by the author to help isolate and evaluate the subjects' attitudes toward God. They are (1) centrality and (2) relational proximity/distance.

(1) *Centrality* Those beliefs which were central in each subject's concept of God were assumed to be the best indicators of his attitude toward God. To distinguish those beliefs which were central, a projective, self-interpreted test was given. The assumption here was that in creatively representing God the most salient beliefs would surface, and that these would then be identified when each subject interpreted his picture.

> Subjects in the school classroom were first given crayons and 8 x 11 sheets of paper, with the following instructions: "Use the crayons to show on the paper what God is really like. Colors can mean different things, or things you draw can have different meanings. Your only job is to get down on the paper what God is really like."

They were told they had twenty minutes to draw their representations. Following this period, they were asked to write on the back of their picture an explanation of it, so another person could see what they meant to express.

Descriptive and evaluative attributes were then listed for each subject's work, and centrality was determined by both dominance of an attribute in the pictorial representation and sequence of appearance in the written explanation.

(2) *Relational proximity/distance* While attitude toward God may be difficult to measure by weighting belief statements affectively, it may be possible to get at a person's underlying attitude toward God by weighting beliefs *relationally*. The concept of personal relationship with God is central to the Christian faith, not only as expressed biblically but also as expressed in the writings of contemporary Christian educators. The goal of Christian education may thus be at least partially conceived in terms of initiating and developing a close personal relationship with God, and responsiveness to God as a Person.

Thus it becomes significant to note that some beliefs about God have relatively little relational impact ("God is omnipotent"), while other beliefs about God have great relational implications ("God forgives"). Similarly, some have the potential of increasing the sensed nearness of God-in-relation-to-man ("God is love"), while others have the potential of increasing the sensed distance from God ("God punishes sin"). In terms of *relational proximity/distance* a belief might then be weighted plus (those beliefs which are perceived as increasing a sensed nearness to God), minus (those beliefs which are perceived as increasing sensed distance from God) and neutral (those beliefs which are perceived as having no relational impact.

While few Christian educators would desire that beliefs given negative ratings on a relational proximity/distance scale be eliminated from the God-concept, most would at the same time hope that those beliefs which were given a positive rating would have a central position in the belief system, in view of the relationship goal of Christian education discussed above.

Thus for purposes of this study, the beliefs which surfaced in the projective test were first listed, and then evaluated by the subjects as to positive, negative, or indifferent weight on a relational proximity/distance scale. This rating was then taken as an accurate and meaningful indication of attitude.

Hypotheses

Using the concepts developed thus far, along with other tools, the following hypotheses, which flow directly from assumptions underlying one or the other of the Christian education strategies previously discussed, were tested: (1) That formal (classroom) religious instruction can produce congruence of belief about God. (2) That formal religious instruction does not produce congruence of attitude toward God. (3) That attitude toward God is more dependent on integenerational interaction in the home than on beliefs communicated in the formal learning situation.

Results of the Study

Hypothesis one: That formal (classroom) religious instruction can produce congruence of belief about God.

The results of the Belief Congruence Test (p. 197) demonstrated a definite congruence of beliefs about God within the population of thirty-five subjects. Variance appeared on only two of the twenty items on the Belief Congruence Index: item 3 on the multiple choice section, and item 10 on the paired descriptive words. It seems possible that the confusion on item 3 results from either a lack of teaching on the specific topic, or the teaching of *both* the two answers chosen by the majority. Item 10 caused confusion because the subjects stated that "either" or "both" of the choices could be true.

If only the eighteen remaining items are considered, *only twenty-three of the possible 630 discriminations deviated from the majority choices!* Even more significantly, of the twenty-three, one subject deviated on five items, two subjects deviated on two items, fourteen deviated on one item, and *eighteen showed no deviation from the majority!*

Thus the first hypothesis, that classroom teaching of religions could produce congruence of belief as measured by a test, is regarded as proven.

Hypothesis two: That formal religious instruction does not *produce congruence of attitude toward God.*

The procedure designed to reveal attitude was to have the subjects (1) "draw God" to show what "He is really like," (2) give a written

191

explanation of the picture, and (3) indicate on a Relational Proximity/ Distance Scale the relational impact of each descriptive term used by the entire population of subjects. Drawings were rated as revealing a positive, negative, or indefinite attitude on the basis of a subject's own indication, on his RPD scale, of the relational impact of the descriptive terms he himself used in explaining his drawing.

In scoring, a significant difference in the pattern of responses on the RPD scale was noted, with some subjects ranking most descriptive terms as "making me feel nearer to God," and some ranking most descriptive terms as "making me feel farther from God" or "neither." It was decided to include the pattern of response on the RPD scale in the final rating of a subject's attitude.

The derived basis for assigning a subject a positive attitude was this:

> Only a subject whose drawing showed a clear predominance of *nearer* items, as determined by his own evaluation of the relational impact of descriptive terms he used, *and* at least *a majority plus six* of the items on the RPD in the "makes me feel closer to God" column is considered to have demonstrated a positive attitude toward God.

The derived basis for assigning a subject a negative attitude was this:

> Only a subject whose drawing showed *no* predominance of *nearer* items, determined as above, *and* at least a *majority plus six* of the items on the RPD scale in the "makes me feel farther from God" or "neither" columns is considered to have demonstrated a negative attitude toward God.

Maintaining these rigorous standards, nine of the thirty-five subjects indicated a positive attitude, and five of the thirty-five demonstrated a negative attitude. Strikingly, of the five showing a negative attitude, three showed *no* deviations on the BCI, one showed one deviation, and one showed five deviations! Of the nine showing a positive attitude, five showed no deviations, and four showed one deviation.

I thus conclude that the differences in attitude cannot be traced to beliefs taught in the classroom in and of themselves, and the second hypothesis, that "formal religious instruction does *not* produce congruence of attitude toward God," is regarded as proven.

> *Hypothesis three: That attitude toward God is more dependent on inter-generational interaction in the home than on beliefs communicated in the formal learning situation.*

This hypothesis is purposefully vague. Unfortunately, on further thought it appears also to be inaccurately stated, in that the term "dependent" might be taken to imply a direct cause/effect relationship. This study, however, makes no attempt to define the relationship it attempts to demonstrate. The intention is limited to the demonstration of *some* correlation between subjects' attitudes toward God and intergenerational interaction in cases where attitude variance cannot be explained by variance in belief. Thus there was no attempt to prove that belief is not a factor in attitude toward God, or that a particular style of intergenerational interaction is either sufficient or necessary cause for development of a positive or a negative attitude.

Thus the Intergenerational Interaction Index (I.I.I., page 198) was developed within a rather broad theoretical concept of the role of such interaction in religious development; a role which ought at this point to be made explicit.

Theoretical framework An examination of Old and New Testament documents indicates a striking reliance on family relationships and roles in the nurture of faith. In Deuteronomy, a pattern for the communication of faith that relies on intergenerational interaction is stated. Here the writer commands an adult generation:

> And these words, which I command you this day, shall be upon your heart; and you shall teach them diligently to your children, and shall talk of them when you sit in your house, and when you walk by the way, and when you lie down, and when you rise (Deut. 6:6, 7 *RSV*).

The elements of the system presented here are these: (1) adult commitment ("upon your heart"), (2) parents as the primary teachers ("you shall teach them"), and (3) the locus of teaching the informal context of daily life. It is here presupposed also that there is a content of faith, expressed in words.

Each of these elements in communication is picked up and amplified in various ways throughout Scripture. Both (1) and (2) are especially reflected in the New Testament concept of the minister as the model ("an example to believers" N.E.B.) and as one involved in the life of the people (cf. Paul's missionary method as shown in I Thess. 1). Christ's training of the disciples amply demonstrates the life context principle.

The biblical pattern just sketched thus provides the general theoretical framework from which the author worked to construct the I.I.I. It was postulated that the communication of faith would be facilitated when (1) the parents provided a positive model and were perceived by the subjects as experiencing a relationship with God; (2) when the parents accepted a teaching role and were perceived by the subjects as actively relating God to the subjects' lives, and (3) when there was interaction about God in a variety of informal contexts, covering a range of experiences and a variety of situations.

It was also considered, although not directly derived from the biblical pattern just stated, that there might be a relationship between the subjects' attitude and the situations in which a subject perceived the parents as most likely to introduce God (for example, if God is usually brought up in a discipline situation, does the child come to view God in a negative light?). Finally, it was also considered possible that a subject's perception of his parents' attitude toward him as a person might have an impact on his self-concept, and thus directly or indirectly on his attitude toward God.

Results Examining the I.I.I. and breaking down the impact of each of the elements just discussed — (1) parents as models, (2) parents as teachers, (3) a variety of contexts for interaction about God, (4) situations perceived as most likely to see parents introduce God, (5) the perceived parental view of subject's self — the following results were observed.

(1) *Model: subject's perception of the reality of God to the parents* A clear relationship between attitude and the parents' modeling of rela-

tionship with God was demonstrated on the I.I.I. Specifically, the open-ended sentences "I think my parents feel God . . ." and "In our home, God . . ." led to expressions by all positive-attitude subjects which indicate a clearly perceived reality of the parents' faith. This is so striking that the results are reproduced here.

| positive-attitude subjects | negative-attitude subjects |

I think my parents feel God . . .

N1 is always with them, that He guards and protects them and will always provide them with whatever they need.

N2 is real in their lives and He does answer prayer.

N3 is alive, real, and a great help in everyday life.

N4 is the greatest thing they ever knew.

N5 keeps us going.

N6 is a living person.

N7 is real.

N8 is real.

N9 has been very good to us and has blessed our whole family.

D1 is someone to escape to when they can't *stand* the kids anymore.

D2 is God.

D3 is far away.

D4 seldom.

D5 doesn't matter.

In our home, God . . .

N1 is always with us. This is what we feel because we always feel free to talk to each other about Him.

N2 is the ruler of all and is taken too lightly. He comes first.

N3 is the center.

N4 is a part of our daily lives.

N5 is real, but isn't overwhelmingly active.

N6 helps us in our problems.

N7 ranks first.

N8 ranks first.

N9 is respected

D1 is considered holy and just and someone who will eventually punish the nasty children and protect the poor, suffering old parents.

D2 is with us.

D3 is a tradition.

D4 has done a lot, but I'm not sure what they mean.

D5 is hardly ever talked about.

In addition, on "My parents and I talk about God most when . . .," all nine of the positive-attitude subjects reported, while three of the five negative-attitude subjects cited occasions. On "My parents talk to each other about God when . . .," again all nine positive-attitude subjects reported, but only two of the five negative-attitude subjects did so.

(2) *Parental acceptance of the teacher role*   No pattern was discernible.

(3) *Variety of contexts in which interaction about God takes place* No significant differences were discernible.

(4) *Situations in which parents perceived as most likely to introduce God* Both positive- and negative-attitude subjects perceived God as likely to be introduced in disciplinary situations (when I did something wrong; when I broke a rule), and to a lesser extent in enjoyment situations. Three of the five negative-attitude subjects and three of the nine positive-attitude subjects saw God as likely to be introduced *only* in the disciplinary situations.

(5) *Perceived parental view of the subject's self* No clear pattern was discernible. Of the five negative-attitude subjects, one had an unmixed positive perception (my parents usually are proud of me, satisfied with me, and really like me) and two had an unmixed negative perception (my parents usually are critical of me, disappointed in me, and don't really like me). Of the nine positive-attitude subjects, four reported an unmixed positive perception, and *none* an unmixed negative perception.

In summary, there seems to be evidence of a relationship between the subjects' attitude toward God and the parents' modeling of relationship with God; that is, *when the subjects perceive an apparent reality of God to the parents.*

To further test the significance of this factor, the papers of the twenty-one subjects whose attitudes had not been considered to be clearly revealed were placed in three categories: (1) those indicating a definite awareness of the reality of God to their parents, (2) those indicating awareness of a lack of the reality of God to their parents, and (3) those whose responses could not be so distinguished. The following chart reports the indices of attitude for the members of each of the above groups.

RPD		feel			belief		
		nearer	farther	neither	+	—	0
Those showing a definite awareness	1.	14	6	4	3	1	—
of the reality of God to parents	2.	14	7	3	2	—	—
	3.	18	2	4	—	—	—
	4.	14	7	3	2	1	—
	5.	18	6	—	—	—	—
	6.	9	4	11	1	—	1
	7.	11	5	8	3	—	2
Those showing awareness	1.	11	11	2	1	1	—
of lack of reality	2.	11	4	9	2	—	2
indistinguishable	1.	16	2	6	—	—	1
	2.	11	10	2	—	1	—
	3.	13	5	6	4	—	1
	4.	14	3	10	2	—	1
	5.	10	8	6	—	2	—
	6.	17	7	—	—	—	1
	7.	12	12	—	1	2	—
	8.	11	8	5	2	—	—
	9.	17	4	3	2	2	2
	10.	13	7	3	4	—	—

In view of the pattern and relationships thus demonstrated, there does seem to be strong evidence for acceptance of the hypothesis that a relationship does exist between subjects' attitude toward God and intergenerational interaction. While the tools used are not considered to be refined to the point where this hypothesis could be considered proven, the study has produced corroborating evidence.

Discussion

This study was undertaken to test assumptions that underlie two broad strategies of Christian education. One strategy, viewed by the author as the present approach taken in most Christian churches, focuses educational effort on the classroom teaching of correct belief, with the implicit (although not explicit) assumption made that such belief will In itself produce corresponding and appropriate changes in attitude and behavior. By discovering a population within which such a strategy has in fact produced a remarkable congruence of belief, and by demonstrating a distinct discongruity of attitude within it, the strategy as a whole has been called into serious question.

Clearly, religious attitudes (and probably behavior) are *not* totally dependent on religious belief.

The study also attempted to test an assumption underlying an alternate strategy, one which would relocate educational emphasis, placing it in the home. By showing a direct correlation between a subject's attitude toward God and certain factors in the home, the importance of the home to Christian nurture has been demonstrated.

Certain implications for Christian education may then be drawn from this study.

1. Reliance solely on a classroom style of Christian education is both unwarranted and dangerous. Although this approach to education may produce congruity of belief, it is not able to deal with the total personality of the learner. And the total personality is of concern to the Christian educator.

2. Parents do have a definite impact on the religious development of the child; specifically playing a formative role concerning attitudes toward objects of religious faith.

3. Although the study did not show that the classroom strategy of Christian education should be abandoned, it did demonstrate that far more concern must be given to helping parents fulfill their nurturing role.

4. If perceived reality of God to parents is a crucial factor in the development of a child's attitude toward God, Christian education should give primary consideration to *adult* education, encouraging the adult's growth in his faith and experience with God. Only thus can the model required be provided.

5. Further studies of the many factors not within the scope of this study are needed. For instance, in the present study beliefs concerning a religious attitude object were held constant. What if other groups (one of subjects who attend only Sunday school,

another of subjects who have *no* formal religious instruction) were included in a similar study? How would the belief and attitude systems of these populations vary?

Many other questions also deserve study. How much of the belief system congruity demonstrated in this study is traceable to beliefs available in the home? Can the home have as great an impact on belief system as it apparently has on attitude? Is Sunday school of any value at all?

None of these questions are answered by the present study, and certainly its results cannot be generalized to include such questions. But it does suggest several areas for further research.

Even with its limitations, however, the results obtained in this study appear to the author to speak significantly to Christian education, and to indicate a need for a thorough and scientific re-examination of present practices. And they indicate a need for a willingness in the church to radically restructure its educational ministry in those areas where it is found to be necessary to do so.

BELIEF CONGRUENCE INDEX
(see page 191)

I. From what you have been taught in school and at church, select the phrase which *best completes* each sentence.

___ 1. God is love means that (a) He never has any other feelings, like anger, (b) He feels love for all people, (c) He loves Himself, but not people.

___ 2. God's holiness (a) keeps Him from touching in any way this sinful world, (b) keeps Him from doing any wrong, (c) keeps Him from doing wrong on purpose.

___ 3. God forgives us (a) when we do what is right, (b) when we know Jesus Christ as Savior, (c) when we are sorry for our sins and never do them again.

___ 4. God is (a) a Person who pays little attention to people, (b) a Power who cares very little about us, (c) a Person we can think of as a Father.

___ 5. God can (a) do things in our world whenever He wants to, (b) never affect things in the material world because He is Spirit, (c) do very little to help us when we are in need.

___ 6. Jesus Christ (a) is God, so we can understand what God is like by learning about Him, (b) was a great teacher but not God, (c) was a very good man.

___ 7. God's way of dealing with sin in our world is (a) to punish everyone who commits a wrong, (b) to condemn to hell everyone who commits a wrong, (c) to send His Son to die for sin so He can forgive us.

___ 8. God (a) is talked about in the Bible, but what is said is only the ideas different men had about Him, (b) speaks to people today directly without using the Bible in any way, (c) had the Bible written so people could learn who He really is and what He is like.

___ 9. God (a) knows most things, but not everything, (b) knows what people plan to do, but can't do anything about it, (c) knows everything, and is able to do anything.

___10. God (a) has a plan for your life that is good, (b) hopes that you will choose to do good things, but doesn't have any overall plan for you, (c) isn't interested in what you do with your life.

II. From what you have been taught in school and at church, cross off the one word in each pair which does not describe God accurately.

1. fair	unfair	6. unforgiving	forgiving
2. loving	unloving	7. friendly	unfriendly
3. weak	strong	8. good	bad
4. wise	unwise	9. limited	all-powerful
5. sinful	sinless	10. invisible	visible

INTERGENERATIONAL INTERACTION INDEX (1)
(see pages 192, 193)

Please complete the following sentences with the first thought that comes to you.

1. My parents talk to me about God when . . .

2. My parents talk to each other about God when . . .

3. I think my parents feel God . . .

4. In our home, God . . .

INTERGENERATIONAL INTERACTION INDEX (2)

I. Circle the one word that best describes what happens in your home.

    A. My parents and I talk about God most when I am . . .

               happy

               sad

               angry

               thankful

               upset

           (other) _____

    B. My parents talk to each other about God most when they are . . .

               happy

               sad

               angry

               thankful

               upset

           (other) _____

II. Check *each* statement that is *true*.

    A. I can remember talking with my parents about God when . . .

        ___ I didn't understand a decision they made.

        ___ We were enjoying something beautiful together.

        ___ I broke a rule.

        ___ We were having fun together.

        ___ We were on vacation.

        ___ I did something that was wrong.

    B. I can remember hearing my parents talk about God when . . .

        ___ They were trying to make a hard decision.

        ___ They were planning something fun.

        ___ They had friends in to visit them.

        ___ One of them had hurt the other's feelings.

        ___ They were hugging and kissing each other.

        ___ One was angry at the other.

III. Circle the word or phrase of each pair which best describes your experience at home.

A. My parents are likely to bring God up when they . . .

      1. criticize me   praise me

      2. feel proud of me   feel angry at me

      3. seem to like me   seem to dislike me

B. Usually I think my parents . . .

      1. are critical of me   are proud of me

      2. are disappointed in me   are satisfied with me

      3. really like me   don't really like me

IV. Please check each item which is a regular habit for you and your parents.

    ___ Go to church

    ___ Go to Sunday school

    ___ Go to youth group

    ___ Read Bible at home together

    ___ Pray together at home

    ___ "Say Grace" at meals

11

involved, together

YOUTH   ADULTS

BIBLE

LIFE   BODY

PROGRAM

EPHESIANS 4:13

The Bible plays a central and utterly vital role in Christian ministry with youth. God's Word provides our only trustworthy guide to reality, for it is God's revelation in words of His own accurate knowledge of the meaning and purpose of our lives and how we can live them "in Christ." For anyone to live and mature as a Christian, he simply _must_ learn to see life from God's viewpoint, and respond to everything in life on that basis. In terms of what I suggested last chapter, youth must come to grips with God's Word as His revelation of reality, and learn to act on it.

In the preceding chapter I suggested that decision to act involves more than possession of accurate information. It involves opening up our personalities and our values to change. I also suggested something that will be developed in the next section of this book: the need for a distinctive context of interpersonal relationships to free us and motivate change.

Youth ministry then must confront young people with God's Word as a reality demanding their decision, and must permit them to explore this reality in open, supportive relationships with others.

How can we bring about such a confrontation in the local church and create the necessary relational context? Clearly this approach to Bible study demands very different skills, knowledge, motivation, and acceptance of responsibilities from those of the traditional approach, which requires little of youth except that they come to "class" and listen to an adult "teach." While more detailed guidelines to both Sunday school and small group Bible study remain the province of the two books noted last chapter (_Creative Bible Study_ and _Creative Bible Teaching_), we can perhaps sketch here the characteristics of study situations with which youth ministry must be particularly concerned.

Perhaps the most helpful approach to thinking about involving youth with God's Word is first to ask ourselves, What, specifically, do we want to accomplish? What are our goals in involving youth in Scripture?

201

There are a number of ways to state goals, but probably it is best to translate them from general statements to specific, observable behaviors. That is, to state what a person who has attained a certain goal will *do* that gives evidence of attainment. Simply making generalizations ("We want kids to trust the Bible") is not very helpful. We can't tell from such a statement what "trust the Bible" means. Many people "trust the Bible" in an abstract, impersonal way. Others "trust the Bible" in a deeply personal and committed way, and demonstrate their trust by acting in accord with God's Word even when alternative ways of response to a situation may seem easier or "safer." What we need to do, then, is to state goals in general terms, but go on to specify clearly just what behaviors we can accept as evidence that they are being reached.

There are several sources of evidence that we might want to consider. Probably the simplest is the kind represented in passing a paper/pencil test. This source of evidence is most appropriate for measuring achievement of knowledge goals. Does a teen know the books of the New Testament? Give him a paper and pencil and let him write them down. Does a teen know what it means to become a Christian? Sit down with him and ask him to explain the Gospel.

It should be clear that while this kind of test gives evidence of knowledge, it may indicate nothing about personal response. A young person may be able to explain clearly how to become a Christian without having a personal, saving relationship with Jesus Christ. Knowing about the Bible is *never* to be equated with response to God. Certainly such knowledge is basic. But, as we saw in the preceding chapter, we need to be concerned with more than knowledge. We care about *knowledge* and *values* and *decision*. Biblical knowledge is a means to our ends in youth ministry, but never the end in itself. The end is decision: action.

How can we measure decision? How can we tell if our young people have gone beyond acceptance of the Bible as information to respond to God's revelation of reality? Two sources of evidence seem open to us. The first is the young person's report of his own experiences. Does this teen in sharing his life tell of finding guidance or strength through Scripture? Does he report on looking in the Word for comfort or understanding? Normally, what happens inside a person, or how he acts when we're not with him, is something we can discover only as he reveals himself to us.

YOUTH/SCRIPTURE GOALS

	Goals stated in general terms	Behavioral statements	R	O	T
KNOWLEDGE	I. Have overview of the content of Scripture.	I. List with 80% accuracy the 14 periods of Bible history including (a) approximate times, (b) books of Bible written then, (c) major persons, and (d) major events.			x
		Match with 60 of the 66 biblical books a statement of the distinctive message or thrust.			x
		List for 20 of 25 basic Christian doctrines at least two passages of Scripture which express or define them.			x
		Etc.			
	II. Be able to approach the Bible as a reality revelation.	II. Given a list of 5 common youth problems, develop answers to four and express them in essays appealing to reality as revealed in Scripture.			x
		Take a passage of Scripture and show its relationship to his own life today, including its guidance for response to his own life-situations.		x	x
		Etc.			
SKILLS	III. Actually seek solution to personal problems and questions by searching the Scriptures.	III. When faced with uncertainty concerning a value-based choice, seek out guidelines for his decision in Scripture.	x		
		When feeling discouraged or unhappy, read Scripture for comfort and/or understanding.	x	x	
		Keep notes of at least four weekly times in Bible study that reveal probing for life-application.	x	x	
		Etc.			
ACTION	IV. Share responsibly in Bible study with others.	IV. Meet weekly with other Christians for prayer and Bible study.	x	x	
		Speak honestly and self-revealingly in the weekly meeting with other Christians.	x	x	
		Prepare, as required by the group, for sharing by personal independent study of Scripture during the week.	x	x	
		Etc.			
	V. Live in accord with the reality revealed in Scripture.		x	x	

sources of evidence of achievement*

*R: self report of experience
O: observation of behavior
T: test

Sample goals for youth's involvement with Scripture stated in general and behavioral terms

There's also a second test of decision: our observation of behavior. How does he respond in a Bible study group? What attitudes does he reveal? How does he behave in various situations? What values are expressed in choices we see him make? Is his life and character in harmony with the Word? Or, in Paul's terms, is his "everyday life worthy of the Gospel of Christ"? When a person's report of his experience and our observation of his behavior harmonize, we have evidence that he has gone beyond Bible knowledge — that he is using his knowledge to make decisions and as a basis for action.

Let's go back, then, to the question of what goals we want to set for youth ministry. What involvement with God's Word can we expect of youth, what does this involvement mean in behavioral terms, and how will we know if youth are growing in the ways we've said are important? On page 203 is a simple chart specifying sample goals and behaviors, as well as the most likely sources of evidence that goals are being reached. This is not an exhaustive set of goals, nor a complete specification of behaviors that might serve as indicators of achievement. But they do demonstrate (1) several basic goals which we must be concerned with in youth ministry and (2) how to move from general statements of goals to specify the behaviors they imply. Thus the chart shows a helpful way for a youth leader to approach goal-setting in this important area of his ministry.

Settings for involvement

The chart on the preceding page indicates that we need Youth/ Scripture goals in several areas. We need to set *knowledge goals, skill goals,* and *action goals.* The first two of these are actually means to reaching the third. Yet in practice the first two are normally products of the third! Only as a young person becomes convinced of the meaning of God's Word for his life, and begins to discover reality by living in obedience to Christ, is he motivated to learn more about the Word. And skill in Bible study develops through just that kind of practical, relevant searching of Scripture that reaching action goals implies.

Thus *involving youth in the kind of study of the Bible that leads to and demands response is our first concern in youth ministry.*

Where there is no decision-focused, decision-motivated Bible study involvement, there will be little growth in either knowledge or skills. Our priority, then, must be to develop a setting for reality-based, value-shifting study. Until this is successfully accomplished, little can be done to reach *any* of our Youth/Scripture goals.

So let's evaluate the potentials of various settings readily available to us in youth ministry for interaction with Scripture.

The "class" setting Most local churches consider the Sunday school the "Bible-teaching arm of the church" and see the ministry of the Word centered there. Evaluating objectively, we can see the class setting has both advantages and drawbacks as a teaching/ learning situation.

The drawbacks are those shared with other formal teaching/ learning settings. And the Sunday school does have much in common with the secular educational approach. Each operates within strict time boundaries ("We have 45 minutes for class today, so let's get on with it"); each tends to cast an adult in the role of teacher (giving him primary responsibility for preparation and presentation); each operates with a curriculum that specifies what will be studied that day or week.

The time boundary is one of the most serious drawbacks, for it tends to limit expression in class to the concept level. Put bluntly, it is very difficult to have free expression of feelings and honest exploration of values when time is so strictly limited. Meaningful expression of personal concerns and self-revelation takes longer than expression of thoughts and ideas. But this is vital for that teaching/ learning which leads to decision. Normally when freedom of expression does exist in the class, there is little time for facing action-implications of Scripture, and coming to decision. *At some point in the teaching/learning process the lack of time is going to keep teens from interacting at necessary depth.*

This drawback can be overcome to some extent by changing the traditional "teacher" role. As I noted above, the formal learning situation casts the adult in the role of teacher and makes him primarily responsible for lesson-preparation. Teens come to class unprepared, and unready to participate. Where teens have been involved as responsible participants, and have prepared through personal Bible study for class, the Sunday school hour can become a most meaningful time.

In *Creative Bible Teaching* I have suggested that four processes are required for meaningful interaction with Scripture in the class setting. These processes, successively, lead learners to —

1. Locate and define an area of life in which they sense needs, and become sensitive to ways in which the Bible portion to be studied is important to them.

2. Go into Scripture and study the selected passage, discovering the reality it reveals, so coming to understand God's point of view on the original issue.

3. Continue then to compare the life issue they originally explored with the Scripture, seeking to understand how the biblical revelation sheds light on their lives. How do the present values of each, and his behavior, match up with the Word? If a person takes the Word seriously, how might his life and values be changed?

4. On the basis of this last exploration, each decides to act on the Word — and returns to daily life to do so.

When students come into a classroom unprepared, each of the above four processes must either take place or be initiated in the class hour. So the class time may be diagramed as follows:

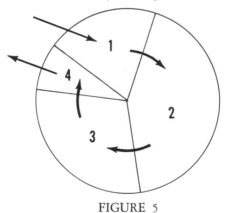

FIGURE 5

The teaching/learning process
limited to the Sunday school
class hour.

On the other hand, when young people take responsibility for study outside of class, the Sunday school hour can be used in a distinctively different way! Rather than attempt to squeeze all four processes into this limited time, the first and second processes and part of the third can be accomplished through individual preparatory study. Then when the teens come together, they can focus on the third process — that very process of exploring values and present experience in the light of Scripture which is not only essential for decision, but which requires the relational context that group study can provide.

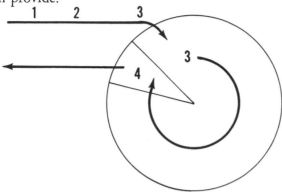

FIGURE 6

The teaching/learning process when individuals prepare by study of the Scripture before class permits class time to center on the third crucial process.

The Sunday school, then, *need not* be a formal learning situation just because it happens to meet at 9:30 Sunday morning. But for it to function as something other than a formal situation, it is probable that close personal relationships between class members will need to be developed before teens meet together as a class. (A fall retreat might be used to help members of new classes come to know each other as persons, and free them to share honestly with each other in the learning setting.) Meaningful exploration of life and values does require a level of trust not created by mere acquaintance.

Curriculums, although listed with time and teacher characteristics of the Sunday school as drawbacks, are not necessarily so. Today very excellent curriculums, designed to involve youth in just the processes I have noted, are available. It is true that, as some object, curriculums do not encourage opening up the class to discussion of immediate and felt needs. We can't simply sit down and say, "Well, what's bugging you today?" But we need to remember that *all* of Scripture is inspired by God and is profitable. We all need to expand our vision beyond those things our problems make us sensitive to.

It certainly is true that in our ministry with youth we must be sensitive to their life-situations and their concerns, and we must be ready to work with them to help each discover God's guidance in Scripture. But we need to do more: we need to start from God's viewpoint and expand our awareness of the meaning of our lives. Today's youth curriculums often feature studies that are carefully chosen for their importance to youth, and their relevance to adolescent concerns.

The Sunday school hour, then, while it has drawbacks which may hinder involvement of teens in reality-oriented Bible study, is nevertheless a potential center for such study.

There is another possible use for the Sunday school that many are exploring today. That is to recognize the formal characteristics of the hour, and take advantage of the strength of the formal situation. And that strength is the opportunity for the communication of information.

As I noted in the goals specified earlier, it *is* important for the Christian to have a working knowledge of the Word. Yet few in our churches have a firm grasp of Bible content. Knowing what the Bible talks about, its main themes and doctrines, the historical setting of the books and the distinctive message of each, is tremendously helpful for reality-oriented Bible study. Content knowledge indicates to us where we can best seek God's personal guidance, and keeps us from misinterpreting verses and paragraphs by tearing them from the context of the whole.

Thus many today seek to turn the Sunday school into a "school of the Bible," offering electives and knowledge-oriented courses, issuing notebooks and giving examinations, even providing certificates for those who enroll in a course and successfully complete it. This approach certainly has merit, *provided that somewhere else youth are being involved with God's Word as a decision-demanding reality.* Ultimately the Word of God must be approached as reality revelation, and to such a revelation only obedient response is appropriate. Studying the Bible for knowledge is valid as an aid to true Bible study: it can never be a replacement for it.

Small groups The small group setting[1] is receiving much attention in the church today — attention it certainly merits. As used today, the phrase "small groups" refers to more than size. Groups do usually include only a few (five to twelve is most common), but

---

[1]The nature and role of the small group in the church is explored in chapters 12 and 13 of my book *A New Face for the Church* (Zondervan, 1970).

the picture the phrase conveys is primarily one of close, intimate personal relationships. Size, in fact, is determined by this function: we can get to know well only a few others at a time.

These small groups are usually formed because Christians sense a need to get to know one another as persons, to move beyond the superficiality that marks so much of our contact with others, to find friends who will love and care about them.

Sometimes small groups fail to move beyond deepening relationships, and so have been criticized for "encouraging exclusiveness." But in this chapter we want to see the small group (that coming together of persons who are learning to know and accept and care about one another) as a setting for Bible study. When such groups are involved in meaningful Bible study together, sharing a commitment to the Word as authoritative for their lives, the potential dangers of the small group can be avoided, and the group setting can become a dynamic power for personal spiritual growth and effective witness.

Small group Bible study can perhaps be most clearly seen in contrast to the traditional Sunday school approach. In small group studies the time is usually open. Thus there is room for sharing and mutual self-revelation; the development of those close interpersonal relationships that are so vital for changing values and making decisions.

The format of the small group meeting thus differs significantly from that of the Sunday school. While there is no standard procedure, the following illustrates a common pattern.

1. "Temperature check" — sharing where members are and how they feel, experiences of the past week, any problems and concerns.

2. Bible study — reading, discussing, and exploring Scripture, chosen either by predetermined plan ("We'll study Acts 3 next week") or on the basis of group members' concerns ("Carol, you've been bothered by that too? Let's look and see if we can't find some help in Scripture.")

   The Bible study itself may take place before the meeting as an individual responsibility, during the class meeting individually, or as a group experience, by simply reading and talking over a passage.

3. The Bible passage which has been studied is explored for its impact on members' lives. Here what has been shared at the beginning often seems to be excitingly illumined by the Word, and definite guidance given.

209

> 4. A time of prayer for each member, asking God's enablement for planned responses expressed, showing and expressing mutual concern and commitment to live the Word, concludes the meeting.

The time of these meetings, as I mentioned, is best left open. But it is not unusual for them to take three hours and more, with up to an hour given to each of steps 1, 2, and 3-4.

Not all youth in our churches are ready for this kind of in-depth involvement. But it's important to provide such opportunities for those who *are* ready, and to encourage those who become involved to constantly demonstrate their love and concern for others who are not yet involved with them.

Personal Bible study Many reports of teen devotional habits bear out what we know intuitively. Few youth have regular interaction with God's Word. Yet I included in the goals on page 203 several items which imply personal and private investigation of Scripture.

There are many reasons advanced by teens for their failures to have "personal devotions." One typical group mentioned difficulty in concentration, interruptions, inability to stay awake, lack of interest, no place to be alone, lack of regularity, and inability to get up early enough.[2] Yet all these simply reflect a more basic failure. The root problem is that few young people today find the Bible interesting or meaningful.

The solution is not to resort to exhortations to "have a daily quiet time," but to provide in your youth ministry both motivation for study and opportunity to learn how to study. The solution is to make youth's involvement in Scripture meaningful and exciting.

Such motivation and meaning are best discovered through study with others. Linking what teens study privately to what they share when they meet with others (whether in Sunday school, a small group, or person-to-person with the youth leader) provides an important impetus to study. And sharing perceptions with others, learning to see fresh meaning in the Word, is the best way to foster awareness of the value of personal Bible study.

Motivating Bible study

There are several sources of motivation for involvement in God's

---

[2]From a survey taken at a YFCI convention in 1961 of youth from sixteen denominations, living in north central USA.

Word. These, in order of priority of introduction in a local youth ministry, are:

Responsibility to others   In the next section we'll explore in some detail what is called in this book "Body ministries." Underlying the concept, however, is awareness that God has joined us with others because we need them, and must develop commitment to them. Mutual self-revelation, a coming to know others as persons, so often alluded to in this book, is the way we come to know others in the body and sense our unity with them. When we have come to trust and accept one another in Christ, *this relationship itself is highly motivating.* A sense of responsibility, then, to those to whom we become committed, is a primary and initial motivation for personal Bible study. When studying God's Word is no longer viewed as the role of a "teacher," but when each person involved accepts his responsibility to share with and minister to others, individuals can be expected to study and prepare for group meetings.

Where no group yet exists, the leader himself can tie into this motivation by developing close personal relationships with individuals and meeting with them privately for prayer and Bible study.

Probably seeking to help youth become involved in this way with others, so they accept responsibility for personal study, is *the* crucial starting place in motivating teens in any youth ministry.

Awareness of relevancy   This is the second type of motivation. When young people discover how excitingly the Bible speaks to their individual situations, an important motive for study is created.

Such an awareness can be developed in either of the group settings discussed in this chapter. But we need to remember that one's underlying attitude toward Scripture is critical. In the preceding chapter (PROBE 3) I suggested that God's Word can be heard as Law or invitation. The way an individual perceives the tone of Scripture is unquestionably going to affect his responsiveness to a Word he learns is relevant to his life. Thus a nagging mother may be heard by a teen to say something relevant — but a nagging mother is hardly welcomed or responded to! In leading youth to see the Word as relevant, we *must* make sure that they view God's involvement in their lives in a positive way. (As I noted last chapter, this is just the issue that is taken up in my book, *Creative Bible Study.*)

Experience of reality   The ultimate motivation for continued involvement in God's Word is a person's own experience of reality.

Christ said to a disciple who questioned how He would make Himself real to believers after His death and resurrection; "If a man loves me, he will keep my word, and my Father will love him, and we will come to him and make our home with him" (John 14:23 *RSV*). Living by the words of God not only sets us free (John 8:31, 32); love-motivated response to God makes Christ real.

Just as our love for persons grows as we come to know them better, so our love for God grows as we come to know Him better. And the one pathway God has provided for us to know Him as a Person is through responsive obedience to what He says to us in His Word.

Our goal, then, in seeking to tap other motivations for Bible study is to lead youth into a vital relationship with Jesus Christ — a relationship which submerges other motives in an overriding desire "to know Him."

PROBE
 case histories
 thought questions
 discussion questions
 resources

 1. Put yourself in the place of a person called to minister with youth at *Typical Local Church*. The teens are not particularly enthusiastic about church. Half of those associated with the church come to Sunday school, fewer to Sunday Evening "Youth Group," — and more to the frequent socials the church has sponsored. After a few weeks you do locate two or three kids who seem to be honestly concerned about their relationship with God, but most have at best a superficial interest.
  In this setting, (1) develop a set of goals concerning the teens' involvement in the Word that you would set for the first six months; for the first year; for five years. Then (2) plan a strategy of approach you would take to reach the goals. What study settings would you use? What motivations would you try to establish? How would you do this?

 2. I mentioned that good curriculums are available for the ministry with teens. Evaluate several in terms of the processes discussed on pages 206ff. Include also in your evaluation the "small group" approach reported on pages 149-151. Watch particularly for what they attempt in respect to Scripture as a reality that demands response.

  Materials are helpful not only for classes, but also for personal devotional aids. A survey of 200 young people taken by some of my students at Wheaton shows that those who use printed helps are significantly more involved in personal devotions than others.

TEENS WHO USE PRINTED HELPS		TEENS WHO DO NOT USE PRINTED HELPS
39%	Have daily devotions	19%
52%	2 or 3 times weekly	25%
9%	sometimes	49%
—	never	7%

Printed helps, however, may either aid or hinder young people in interacting with the Word as a reality revelation. Devotional "thoughts" often totally neglect the need for personal response.

Following is an example of the kind of devotional guide that helps a young person confront the Bible meaningfully. It was developed by a student — something you might like to try for "starters" with interested kids in your own group.

#1

"I can't live the Christian life. I just can't do the things I should." Ever feel that way? What could you tell a person who feels that way? Search for an answer in Romans 8:1-9. (Use *Living Letters* if possible.)

    I. Using your own words and based on your own understanding, write the main thought of each verse.

    II. Think through these questions as you reread the passage.

        1. Can a Christian live a life pleasing to God? If so, how?

        2. What do you feel is the key to living this life?

As you studied this passage of Scripture, how did you feel toward your own possibilities of living a life pleasing to God? Ask yourself, "If I take this passage seriously, what will I do about it this week?" Talk it over with the Lord. Record any decisions you make if you wish to check yourself later in the week.

#2

"I so often feel pulled in two directions. I want to do what God wants me to, but I just don't always do it." Think of the last time you felt that way. What was the problem?

    I. Read Romans 8:10-16; take a pencil and jot down your insights, questions, and reactions.

    II. If there seemed to be no power to overcome the sin nature, and the person continually did what his sin nature bugged him to do without feeling the struggle mentioned in the above quote, what would you conclude about that person? Check your answer with the text.

III. Now turn to Galatians 5:14-26. As you read jot down answers to these questions.

    1. Is this struggle common to Christians?

    2. What does God advise me to do?

    3. What is God's part in solving the problem?

    4. What is my part?

Can I do my part? *Will* I do my part? (Need help? God's here — why not ask Him?)

#3

Linda lay on her hospital bed, staring at the wall. It has been a month and a half and the doctor said it would be yet another month before she could get out. Why did this have to happen to her — hundreds of kids go horseback riding and never get thrown. And two and a half months may mean a repeat of tenth grade. She hurt deeply inside at the thought of being put back a grade behind her friends. Linda picked up the card she had received from her best friend. It read, "All of us are praying for you, Linda. Please try to remember that 'all things work together for good.' " Linda tossed the card aside and covered her eyes which were wet with tears — "Who says all things work together for good," she thought.

Can you feel with Linda? Ever feel the same way about anything?

I. Read Romans 8:17-29 carefully and try to identify with Linda as you read. Try to work through this problem of why God permits Christians to have troubles and suffer.

II. Summarize each verse with one sentence, using your own words.

III. Reread, and stop after the verses indicated to answer these questions:

    1. v. 21: Any idea how sin, death, thorns, thistles got here?

    2. v. 23: When will things change?

IV. Does God allow the daily problems and troubles of the Christian? Why do they happen? Does He offer any present help to get us through them? Reread verses 26 and 27.

How do you feel about this whole question of trouble and suffering? Any doubts or questions? Any new insights? Talk them over with the Lord. Would your attitude be like Linda's in her present situation?

#4

"Who cares about me or my troubles or my point of view? Who cares?"

I.   Read Romans 8:29-39, and select one main idea from the passage to jot down.

II. Reread the verses and jot down related ideas or questions. In the light of this passage, how do you feel about your relationship with God? His relationship to you?

Can you think of recent situations in which you have felt alone, forsaken by people and God? Or in which you have doubted your salvation? What caused those feelings? How would you feel in similar situations now? Why?
Be honest with God. Tell your real feelings to Him.

3.   Here are other examples of study guides, developed for teens at Washington's Fourth Presbyterian Church by youth minister Rus Cadle. One represents interaction with basic doctrine; the other, exploration of a more personal passage.

THE RESURRECTION (Theories)

Senior High Team Meeting March 24, 1970

Mark 16

Other Prophecies!

1.   Mark 8:31; 9:31; 10:34 — Prophetic statements fulfilled in Chapter 16. Time was given in each prophecy (3rd day) and it was fulfilled to the exact day.

2.   *Direct evidence* — Jesus was gone.

Circumstantial — Stone was rolled away. Jesus was gone from the place they had laid Him.   (Details)

Contributory — Angel in white robe. Mary Magdalene, Mary the mother of James, and Salome. Jesus appeared to two of them (v. 12). Jesus appeared to the eleven (v. 14).   (Feelings invoked)

3.   Climaxes —
a. Jesus has conquered death and fulfilled prophecy.

b. Appears to disciples, restores their faith, and gives the great commission.

c. Ascends into heaven and sits at right hand of God.
(Climax to all these traced topics)

4.   Exciting climax that is reached. Precise, detailed account. Angel appearing — supernatural — so few verses describing such a momentous, significant event.

5.   Conclusive evidence that Jesus Christ is the Son of God, that He did rise from the grave, that He did appear to many people, and that now He sits at the right hand of God.

6. A. Theory that women went to the wrong sepulchre because it was dark. They were still dazed with sorrow.

    1. Mark states "the sun had risen."

    2. At least two of the women had seen where Joseph and Nicodemus had lain the body (Mark 15:47; Luke 23:55).

    3. If one mistook the path, she would have been corrected by the others.

    4. They had come on a practical mission; no sentimental sorrow brought them there.

    5. Why did Peter and John verify their story?

  B. Swoon theory — Jesus did not die on the cross, He fainted. He revived in the tomb, left it, and made Himself known to the disciples.

    1. Evidence contradicts this theory.

    2. Centurion assured Pilate of Jesus' death (Mark 15:44, 45).

    3. Joseph and Nicodemus took down His body, wrapped Him in the grave clothes, and laid Him in Joseph's new sepulchre.

    4. Inconceivable that after all He had gone through He was just in a swoon.

    5. How could He move the rock which covered the entrance to the tomb without disturbing the Roman guard?

    6. How could He perform all that He did after coming out of the tomb weak and having had no food, or no one to care for His wounds?

  C. Thieves stole the body.

    1. How could thieves have gotten past the Roman guard? How did they remove the rock?

    2. Why would thieves have left the grave clothes and taken the body?

    3. What motive would the thieves have for their action?

  D. Disciples stole the body.

    1. Rumor that Jews spread from the earliest days.

    2. In fact, the Jews did all they could to prevent the resurrection. Set up a guard, sealed the tomb (Matthew 27:62-66).

    3. Matthew records that when the soldier told the chief priests what had happened, they bribed him into telling the people, "His disciples came by night and stole Him away while we were

asleep." They promised to protect the soldiers if any problems arose. "So they took the money and did as they were told; and the story has been spread among the Jews to this day" (Matthew 28:11-15).

Considerations:

1. It is unlikely that a Roman or Jewish guard would fall asleep.

2. How could women get by the guards, roll away the stone, and remove the body?

3. Even if the disciples removed the body, there is a psychological factor which is hostile to the whole theory. Their whole message in Acts is based on the resurrection. How could they center their life work on a horrible hoax, a lie? Inconceivable that they would allow themselves to preach a falsehood, and then suffer beatings, torture, and even death for a hoax.
   If we get anything from Acts, it is the sincerity of the Apostles. *"Hypocrites and martyrs are not made of the same stuff."*

E. Roman or Jewish authorities stole the body.

1. Their only reason would have been to prevent trickery.

2. However, when the disciples in a few weeks claimed Jesus' resurrection, *all they had to do was produce the body.* They didn't. Instead they persecuted the disciples as violently as ever.

3. The authorities' silence is as eloquent a proof of the resurrection as the apostle's witness.

Proof of Christ's Resurrection:

1. The sepulchre was empty!

2. The grave clothes were undisturbed.

3. The Lord was seen.

4. The disciples were changed.

For and against Markan authorship

1. Mark was the author, interpreting Peter, dependent upon Peter.

   a. Clement of Alexandria
   b. Tertullian
   c. Origen   } External Evidence
   d. Eusebus
   e. Jerome

2. Mark abounds in details of time, place, circumstances, feelings, and manners of Jesus and others. All this indicates that Mark was an eyewitness or received his information from an eyewitness.

Team Meeting May 25, 1971

2 Timothy 3

The secret to a successful and productive life, is really no secret to a person familiar with the Scriptures. Psalm 1 says, "Blessed is the man . . . whose delight is in the law of the Lord and in his law doth he meditate day and night . . . whatever de doeth shall prosper."

What a fantastic promise! Paul has just mentioned that the Scriptures are the comprehensive equipment of the man of God and fit him fully for all branches of his work. So with these promises in mind, consider what you can give God in return. Notice that the promises are conditional: their fulfillment is to those who are faithful to them; this fulfillment is not simply given to Christians. Recognize the discipline associated with really getting something out of the Book. Make it your aim this week to master the passage we're studying.

Chapter 4 is the concluding chapter of 2 Timothy. You'll notice a lot of personal messages. Look them over to see the breadth of Paul's relationships with and trust in Timothy. Remember that this is a letter written to a young minister, but what can you learn from his charge that you can apply to your life? Here are a few guide questions:

1. What were the elements of Paul's charge to Timothy?

2. Think about the words "prove, correct, and encourage." Are you capable of doing these things? (Remember 2 Tim. 1:7).

3. Paul warns Timothy of things to come. What were characteristics of men in those times?

4. What are characteristics of Paul's advice to Timothy? List them.

5. What is the reward that Paul has received for his faithfulness?

As you are studying this week, ask the Holy Spirit to guide you through the passages. Remember that He is with you always. Also remember that your spiritual fitness is your greatest responsibility to both yourself and the people your life influences. Use the study method we learned last week. First write out the verse, and then your thoughts underneath. Have a good time in the Word!!!

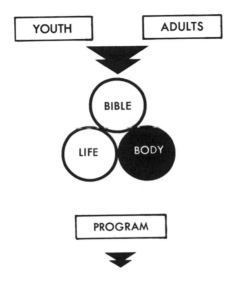

EPHESIANS 4:13

YOUTH IN BODY RELATIONSHIP

12

the new community

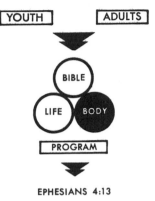

EPHESIANS 4:13

As I noted in earlier chapters, values are communicated and personality formed in the context of interpersonal relationships. But not all kinds of interpersonal relationships are helpful or effective conductors of values. The social sciences recognize several possible products of group influence, including compliance, identification, and internalization.[1] Only the last of these, internalization, implies the character transformation for which God has called believers together "in church."

The local church as an association of persons does not automatically or necessarily function as a transforming community. As in many types of associations, the influence of the church group on the believer may in fact produce only conformity — a situation in which the lowest level of acceptance of biblical values may produce a high degree of conformity in public statement.[2] Simply *having* a group we call our "church youth group" or "youth fellowship" is no guarantee that the purposes God has in mind for the church will be fulfilled. For a group of Christian young people to function as Christ's Church is intended, it must develop the kind of interpersonal relationships which are to characterize His Body.

And at this point, we can depart from all reliance on the social sciences for direction of the life of the Body. For God's Word gives clear and distinctive direction for our life together — directions we must take seriously in youth ministry if we are to tap the dynamic power of the Holy Spirit released when God's people come together as the Body of Christ: the new, and the transforming, community.[3]

---

[1]See Allen's discussion of Kelman's theoretical formulation in "Situational Factors in Conformity," in Leonard Berkowitz (ed.), *Advances in Experimental Social Psychology* (New York: Academic Press, 1965).

[2]See an interesting study of "Effects of Different Conditions of Acceptance upon Conformity to Group Norms" by James E. Dittes and Harold H. Kelley, which first appeared in the *Journal of Abnormal and Social Psychology,* Vol. 53, July, 1956.

[3]The implications of this truth for the local church as a whole are discussed in my book, *A New Face for the Church* (Zondervan, 1970).

At several points in this book I've emphasized relationships: in chapter two it was to note the impact of others on an individual's emerging self-concept; in the section on leadership the dynamic of Christian leadership was seen as example provided in a mutually self-revealing, open and honest relationship; and in chapter eleven where this same kind of relationship in a group is viewed as providing the most meaningful context for Bible study. Now, at last, it is necessary to go into some detail about Scripture's revelation of the quality and function of relationships that are to exist between believers in Christ's Church and, as part of that Church, in youth ministry.

Love, the first prerequisite

Jesus' words to His disciples pick up a theme that is reflected often throughout the New Testament. "I am giving you a new command — love one another. Just as I have loved you, you must love one another. This is how all men will know that you are my disciples, because you have such love for one another" (John 13:34, 35 *Phillips*).

It is tremendously impressive to page through the Scriptures and see the emphasis given to love in Christ's Church. At the risk of losing your attention (I find that my own tendency when I come to a string of quotes is to skip them!), I'd like to reproduce just a few of the many references to love. As you look them over, note the significance each passage invests in love. (All of the Scripture quotations are from Phillips' translation.)

"Now that you have," says Peter, "by obeying the truth, made your souls clean enough for genuine love for your fellows, see that you do love one another, fervently and from the heart" (1 Peter 1:22). Fervent and genuine love is a major theme of both Pauline and Johannine Scriptures. Paul writes,

> Keep out of debt altogether, except that perpetual debt of love we owe one another. The man who loves his neighbor has obeyed the whole Law in regard to his neighbor. For the commandments, "Thou shalt not commit adultery," "Thou shalt not kill," "Thou shalt not steal," "Thou shalt not covet," and all other commandments are summed up in this one saying: "Thou shalt love thy neighbor as thyself." Love hurts nobody: therefore love is the answer to the Law's commands (Rom. 13:8-10).
>
> Above everything else, be truly loving, for love is the golden chain

of all the virtues. Let the peace of Christ rule in your hearts, remembering that as members of the one body you are called to live in harmony, and never forget to be thankful for what God has done for you (Col. 3:14, 15).

You should be free to serve one another in love. For after all, the whole Law toward others is summed up by this one command, "Thou shalt love thy neighbor as thyself" (Gal. 5:13, 14).

John, particularly in his first letter, discusses in depth the love relationship that is to exist between Christians.

> We know that we have crossed the frontier from death to life because we do love our brothers. The man without love for his brother is living in death already. . . . We know and to some extent realize the love of God for us because Christ expressed it in laying down his life for us. We must in turn express our love by laying down our lives for those who are our brothers. But as for the well-to-do man who sees his brother in want but shuts his eyes — and his heart — how could anyone believe that the love of God lives in him? My children, let us love not merely in theory or in words — let us love in sincerity and in practice (3:14-18).
>
> The test of the genuineness of our love for God's family lies in this question — do we love God himself and do we obey his commands? For loving God means obeying his commands, and these commands are not burdensome, for God's "heredity" within us will always conquer the world outside us (5:2-4).
>
> To you whom I love I say, let us go on loving one another, for love comes from God. Every man who truly loves is God's son, and has some knowledge of him. But the man who does not love cannot know him at all, for God is love.
>
> To us, the greatest demonstration of God's love for us has been his sending his only Son into the world to give us life through him. We see real love, not in the fact that we loved God, but that he loved us and sent his Son to make personal atonement for our sins. If God loved us as much as that, surely we, in our turn, should love one another! (4:7-11).

There is something both vastly moving and extremely practical about the love God's Word describes as the essential mark of Christian community. This love isn't cast in Scripture as an impractical or abstract ideal. It's a motivating drive that finds constant and daily expression in interpersonal relationships. "Love one another fervently." "Serve one another in love." "Express love. . . ." "Love in sincerity and practice."

The same Scriptures that exhort love also leave us multiple examples of love in action. Some of the clearest examples of how love is expressed are found in context with a simple phrase: "one another." Here the command to "love one another" is illumined as various dimensions of the reciprocal relationship are etched in the most graphic terms. While a full-fledged study of every occurrence of "one another" in the New Testament is well worth our time, only a sampling can be given here of the many portraits of love in action.

"Welcome one another . . . as Christ has welcomed you" (Rom. 15:7 *RSV*) This instruction to the church in Rome, which Paul addresses as Christ's Body, highlights love as welcoming or "receiving" other believers into fellowship. The Greek word here is $\pi \rho o \sigma \lambda a \mu \beta \acute{a} \nu \omega$, which means "receive or accept into one's society, into one's home or circle of acquaintances."[4] This same word is used in Romans 14:1: "Welcome the man whose faith is weak — but not with the idea of arguing over his scruples" (*Phillips*). The Bible portrays everyone who knows Christ as Savior as "accepted in the beloved." In Jesus Christ every Christian has been welcomed by God into the community of the saints; every Christian has become a member of Christ's Body. Love recognizes this shared relationship to Jesus Christ, and eagerly welcomes other believers into the inner circle of friends who love and care for one another as members of a closely knit family.

Note that this welcome is not conditional. It is not dependent on a person's acceptance of our particular point of view, or of our scruples concerning doubtful practices (see Romans 14). Welcome is not, as a pastor friend of mine recently stated, dependent on his subscribing to exactly the same doctrinal statement we subscribe to. If a person knows Christ, he *is* a member of God's family, our brother or our sister, and love demands that we welcome him and love him wholeheartedly.

"In honour preferring one another" is the way the King James renders Romans 12:10. Phillips says it this way: "Let's have no imitation Christian love. . . . Let's have real warm affection for one another as between brothers, and a willingness to let the other man have the credit." The root idea of the word rendered "preferring," $\pi \rho o \eta \gamma \acute{e} o \mu a \iota$, seems best taken as "try to outdo one another." In this and other meanings, love is seen as creating a relationship which is marked by the opposite of competition and competitiveness.

---

[4]Source for the definitions of Greek terms in this chapter is Arndt and Gingrich's *Greek/English Lexicon*.

Here we have a portrait of Christians coming together eager to listen to, and to respect, the views of others as important. There's no attempt here to force others to our point of view, or our position. There's no "politicking" behind the scenes. Love finds expression in Christ's Church in the realization that each person is important — that each has a place, for God speaks through each. And so love seeks to help each find God's place for him, not through competition, but by encouraging everyone to contribute, and by hearing contributions with respect.

Christians are able "to admonish one another." This statement of Paul in Romans 15:14 points up a fascinating dimension of the love relationship that is to exist in the Church, and is to mark our fellowship today. The word "admonish" is the Greek word $\nu o \upsilon \theta \epsilon \tau \acute{\epsilon} \omega$, which means to warn, admonish, and instruct, with the general connotation of "helping through warning and rebuke." It is particularly striking that in a fellowship of persons who welcome and show respect for one another love is also expressed by rebuking. Here echoes of Paul's command to "speak the truth in love" are heard: family love often demands rebuke of a son or brother. So, too, in the Church of Christ love may demand warning and admonishing a fellow Christian. And even from this negative expression of concern love is not to draw back.

In our culture we hesitate to rebuke even those we are closest to. "If you can't say something nice about someone, don't say anything," is a proverb that is not normally applied to saying *about* — but certainly is applied to saying *to*. Confrontation is avoided — as the mouthwash ads that feature debates over "who will tell the boss about his bad breath?" illustrate. But real love is impelled to speak out even in rebuke when it is necessary for a brother's good. And it is this kind of risk-taking love that the Christian community is to know.

"Provoking one another" is an archaic phrase we find in Hebrews 10:24, which in the original means "to consider, notice in a spiritual sense, to fix the eyes on." The thought here is: Draw attention to and concentrate on that which needs to be done.

In the context of "one-anothering" we might better translate the thought as "to stimulate" or "to encourage." The meaning is quite clear. Christianity is an action religion. We are called to live our faith in Christ, not simply to "believe" about it. And so when Christians come together as the Church, one of the ways they minister is to encourage one another to act in faith. Love is expressed by stimulating other believers to step out and live the life of Jesus.

"Bear one another's burdens and so fulfil the law of Christ" (Gal. 6:4 *RSV*) is the last description of love we'll take time to note. This one is particularly important, for it is directly connected with the command to love (the "law of Christ" referred to in the text). And because bearing one another's burdens implies at least two corollaries: first, that we care deeply about the troubles and needs of other believers, and seek to shoulder them in prayer, in encouragement, in expressed concern. And second, that the burdens of believers are shared with others. The only way I can know of the needs of another person is if he tells them to me. If he shares. So this "one another" phrase tells us much about love in action. Trusting love honestly and openly expresses its needs and weaknesses and burdens to others: responsive love rejects criticalness and condemnation to express concern and care. Love takes the neighbor's burden as its own.

Now, whatever can be said about the love which the Bible speaks as central to life together in the Church of Christ, we must say this:

> This love is marked by in-depth involvement of
> believers in the lives of one another.

> This love is marked by an active sharing of one
> another's life and experiences.

Love in the Body encourages, bears burdens, welcomes, and admonishes, and performs a host of other simple ministries that cannot possibly exist without a deep knowing of others as individuals.

A "just as" love

So far in this chapter I have tried to sketch (all too briefly) something of what Scripture has in mind when it speaks of love, and how Christ's command to love calls us to involvement and deep personal relationship with other Christians. We need to note two other aspects of the biblical love: aspects which seem to stand in such contrast to each other that they appear almost to exist as a paradox. These aspects are rooted in Jesus' expression of the new commandment. There He gives us definite instructions as to the way in which we are to love each other: "even as I have loved you."

The standard of love between Christians is God's love for us. And so we find often in the New Testament directions like "Be as ready to forgive others as God for Christ's sake has forgiven you" (Eph. 4:32 *Phillips*). God's love is the pattern on which love in the Body must be modeled.

Here we must remember, as I discussed on page 84f, that God's relationship with us is linked to acceptance, and rooted in forgiveness. God "knows our frame." He operates under no illusions when He invites us into relationship with Him through Jesus Christ. Before our salvation, the Bible honestly portrays us as "spiritually dead" (Eph. 2:1; Col. 2:11ff). As "drift[ing] along on the stream of this world's ideas of living, and obeying its unseen ruler (who is still operating in those who do not respond to the truth of God.)" We were all "like that in the past, and followed the impulses and imaginations of our evil nature, being in fact under the wrath of God by nature, like everyone else" (Eph. 2:1ff *Phillips*). And this the Bible calls being "dead in our sins" (*KJV, N.E.B.*).

There was and could be no basis in ourselves on which God might say, "I accept you." No sincerity, no efforts of our own, no suffering or fleshly dedication, could give God grounds for saying, "You're trying — so I'll accept you for that." The Bible is utterly clear that Jesus died to provide the grounds of our forgiveness, and that God is One who "justifies *the sinful*" (Romans 4:5). God's love goes out to us *as we are,* and in His offer of forgiveness for Christ's sake He accepts us freely and fully for love's sake.

Most of our human relationships have had a performance-linked basis. An employee is valued because of the work he does. A husband or wife is appreciated when he or she meets the other's expectations — and may be rejected for failures. Young people are welcomed when their hair and clothing suit our idea of what is respectable, or when they seem to accept adult wisdom without question. Performance-linked acceptance says, "I value you for what you do. And when you displease me, I reserve the right to reject you."

This conditional attitude toward others is one that Jesus Christ decisively rejected in His life and in His death. His love went out to sinner as well as disciple, and only those who refused Him, as did the Pharisees, found themselves cut off — not by His choice, but by their own. Christ expressed the principle of unconditional love in His Sermon on the Mount in these words: "You have heard that it used to be said, *'Thou shalt love thy neighbor and hate thine enemy,'* but I tell you, Love your enemies, and pray for those who persecute you, so that you may be sons of your Heavenly Father. For he makes his sun rise upon evil men as well as good, and he sends his rain upon honest and dishonest men alike" (Matt. 5:43-45 *Phillips*).

No, an entirely different basis for relationship is seen in Christ's love: He accepts others *as they are* — and loves them anyway.

This is particularly important in Christ's Church. We believers are still human beings, still sinners, still flawed by the selfish drives and desires that bring us into conflict with God, with ourselves, and with others. Our flaws do bring us into conflict with other believers. (Otherwise the Word's many reminders to "forgive one another" would have no meaning. Only where there is injury and sin is there a need for forgiveness.) Our flaws — the sin that struggles to trip us up — often succeed, and cause us to fail our God and one another. It is particularly because we are sinners who are at the same time saints that we need assurance that other Christians love us *just as* Christ loves us — that other Christians accept us and welcome us and value us *as we are.*

Certainty that we are loved as we are frees us from the need to pretend with one another and lets us share our burdens and our inadequacies. "Perfect love casts out fear" (1 John 4:18). Where we are loved, we can open ourselves up to one another and cast off all hypocrisy.

Yet many claim to see a danger in this kind of acceptance-linked love. They fear (and not without reason) that a love that asserts, "I love you *as you are,*" gives license for all sorts of sin and looseness in living. But here the Bible speaks in an exactly opposite vein. The Bible presents a love that accepts persons as they are, yet insists on a disciplined, discipled life. In fact, the Bible suggests that a God-like love that meets and accepts people where they are actually energizes an amazing transformation. Accepting and loving people as they are implies no abandonment of them to present bondage. Instead, it is the first step toward their becoming.

So Paul exhorts believers to put their old life behind them. "No more evil temper or furious rage: no more evil thoughts or words about others, no more evil thoughts or words about God, and no more filthy conversation. Don't tell one another lies any more, for you have finished with the old man and all that he did and have begun life as the new man, who is out to learn what he ought to be, according to the plan of God." For the new man, "Christ is all that matters, for Christ lives in . . . all [believers]" (Col. 3:8-11 *Phillips*). The same thought is repeated over and over in the Word. "Finish, then, with lying, and tell your neighbor the truth. For we are not separate units but intimately related to one another in Christ" (Eph. 4:26 *Phillips*). "Live together in harmony, live together in love, as though you had only one mind and one spirit between you. Never act from motives of rivalry or personal vanity, but in humility think more of one another than you do of yourselves. None of you should think only of his own affairs, but each should learn to see things from other people's point of view" (Phil. 2:2-4 *Phillips*).

No, the experience of an acceptance-linked love — a love that accepts us, knowing full well all that we are — is no invitation to continue in sin. Instead, it is God's open door to transformation — to actually become in daily life what we are potentially in Him. Thus Scripture reminds us, "Consider the incredible love that the Father has shown us in allowing us to be called 'children of God' — and that is not just what we are called, but what we *are*. Our heredity on the Godward side is no mere figure of speech!" (1 John 3:1, 2 *Phillips*). So Scripture also urges us, knowing the completeness of God's love for us: "With eyes wide open to the mercies of God . . . as an act of intelligent worship, give him your bodies, as a living sacrifice, consecrated to him and acceptable by him. Don't let the world around you squeeze you into its own mold, but let God remold your minds from within, so that you may prove in practice that the plan of God for you is good, meets all his demands and moves toward the goal of true maturity" (Rom. 12:1, 2 *Phillips*).

Remolding lives

We can perhaps now see more of the concepts that underlie the titles of this section and this chapter. In youth ministry, we must see our young people in Body relationships, experiencing together the new community.

The Bible speaks much of the Body of Christ, focusing our understanding of the local church as well as universal Church through this figure. If we take the Body concept of Scripture seriously, we are driven to the awareness that Christians who come together in churches are to form no mere association of individuals who band together for a common goal or a common set of purposes. Instead, Christians are called together by God because a supernatural unity *exists*: individually we are members of Christ, together we are His Body (1 Cor. 12:27). The unity which exists because of our common share in Christ does not need to be created, but it does need to be "maintained in the bonds of love." *We need to experience the reality of a relationship which God's Word affirms does exist.*

The Bible is utterly clear on the cement which binds the Christian community together as a Body. That cement is love. Thus the constant emphasis in the New Testament on love among believers. Only when we love one another, become involved in one another's lives, care for one another, bear one another's burdens, and live openly and forgivingly, do we experience the meaning of the Body.

Christ's "just as" helps us see both the nature of the love we can have for each other, and the purpose of the Body. By nature Christ's love is forgiving love, accepting love — love that recognizes failures but joyfully asserts the worth and value of the individual. Jesus' love is a giving, self-emptying love. Jesus' love was expressed in His commitment to live, and even to die, for others. And it is just this kind of love — *love that commits us to live and even die for the benefit of our brothers* — that is to exist and be expressed in Christ's Church.

But even more, Christ's love reflects the purpose of the Body. The love of God is a freeing, transforming thing. Along with forgiveness God gives each believer a new heredity, a capacity to become the "new man." And so all of a person's life opens outward to newness once he comes to know Christ.

Life in Christ's Church has exactly this same impact. Through the Body, believers unified in love and commitment to one another, God opens and remolds our personalities. He transforms us into the image of His Son.

This must, in fact, be central in our understanding of the Church, His Body. The Body exists, and we are called together in unity, to be changed persons through ministries the Holy Spirit performs for each of us through the others. So the Bible says, "Serve one another with the particular gifts God has given each of you, as faithful dispensers of the magnificently varied grace of God" (1 Peter 4:10 *Phillips*). *Every passage in the New Testament that speaks of the*

Body speaks of spiritual gifts.[5] And, the New Testament is clear, *each* believer has one of these spiritual gifts; a capacity to be used in ministry to others and to be a means God uses to remold personalities. Spiritual growth individually and corporately depends on the active involvement in mutual ministry of each believer, for Scripture says that "the whole body, as a harmonious structure knit together by the joints with which it is provided, grows by the proper functioning of individual parts to its full maturity in love" (Eph. 4:16 *Phillips*).

Strikingly, study of Scripture leads to the conclusion that spiritual gifts are not exercised so much through organizational roles as in the context of interpersonal relationships. All the ministries mentioned earlier as practical expressions of active love — welcoming, preferring, exhorting, provoking, bearing one another's burdens — are occasions (in individual or group situations) when gift-ministry takes place. So, as the Scripture says, "let us think of one another and how we can encourage one another to love and do good deeds. And let us not hold aloof from our church meetings, as some do. Let us do all we can to help another's faith, and this the more earnestly as we see the final day drawing ever nearer" (Heb. 10:24, 25 *Phillips*).

Love, then, not only unites the Body through commitment of Christians to one another; love expressed (in welcoming, rebuking, encouraging, etc.) is the medium in which spiritual gifts operate. When Christians are involved in one another's lives in loving ways, God's creative and transforming power is unleashed for tranformation. "God works through different men in different ways, but it is the same God who achieves his purposes through them all. Each man is given his gift by the Spirit that he may use it for the common good" (1 Cor. 12:6, 7 *Phillips*). *The supportive, loving concern of Christians gathered in Body relationship is, together with the Word of God, the primary means God uses to remold us from within — a dynamic, divine power that growth in Christ demands we experience in life together as a new community; a community created and marked by love.*

---

[5]Spiritual gifts are best understood as particular ways the Holy Spirit works through believers to strengthen, motivate, and transform other Christians toward maturity and Christlikeness.

More than a peer group

In an earlier chapter we saw something of the influence of the peer group on youth in our culture. Reasoning from what is known through observation and the social sciences, many who are engaged in youth ministry have written compellingly of the power of the peer group and have suggested approaches for developing a strong peer group in the church. Usually one rationale for social and recreational activities in the church is drawn from the premise that doing things together socially is one way to build a peer group.

I hope that it's clear that what I'm arguing for in this chapter goes far beyond the "peer group" concept — and speaks of a far deeper relationship than can be established by "doing things together in a social situation." At best, in the local churches attempts to develop peer groups bring teens together in loose *association*. But what we must do in youth ministry is bring Christian teens together *as Christ's Body*. And for this, the normal activities on which we have tended to rely are tragically inadequate. The community of love to which we are called in Christ goes far beyond what most of us have dreamed of experiencing.

Summarizing, the community we need to build in youth ministry among Christian teens, the community which permits the experience of Christ's Body, is characterized by —

(1) deep involvement in one another's lives, sharing of concerns, caring, supporting, and encouraging.

(2) each person's seeking to minister to and help others in every way he can.

(3) honesty and self-revelation in all ministry situations, made possible by the conviction that each loves and is loved by the others.

(4) commitment of each Christian young person to the others in the group, to consider them and their needs before his own.

These are indeed necessary, for they constitute together the practical expression of Christ's love: that love which Christ commended to His disciples as a "new commandment . . . that you love one another; even as I have loved you, that you also love one another (John 13:34 *RSV*).

When this love fills and infuses our youth, and they begin to live with each other in love, Christ's Body becomes an experienced reality to them, and one of God's necessary conditions for maximum spiritual growth is met.[6]

PROBE

case histories
discussion questions
thought-provokers
resources

1. In the next chapter we'll explore ways of building the new community of love in youth ministry. But before we do, we need to get a better feel for the Body concept introduced in this chapter. To put the concept in biblical perspective, look over the following three Bible passages that deal with Christ's Church as His Body.

   You'll want to examine each passage for several salient features:

   (1) What is the nature of the Body revealed here?

   (2) What are the functions of individuals as Body members? What is the result if they do function in ministry? What is the result if they do *not* function?

   (3) What does each passage indicate about the relationship context in which gift ministries operate? Why so much stress here on interpersonal relationships?

   It's well worth taking time to explore these passages now, and to think seriously about the specified areas of examination. (All of the Scripture quotations are from Phillips' translation.)

I Corinthians 12 and 13 —

As the human body, which has many parts, is a unity, and those parts, despite their multiplicity, constitute one single body, so it is with Christ. For we were all baptized by the Spirit into one body, whether we were Jews, Greeks, slaves or free men, and we have all had experience of the same Spirit.

Now the body is not one member but many. If the foot should say "Because I am not a hand I don't belong to the body," does that alter the fact that the foot *is* a part of the body? Or if the ear should say, "Because I am not an eye I don't belong to the body," does that mean that the ear really is not part of the body? After all, if the body were all one eye, for example, where would be the sense of hearing? Or if it were all one ear, where would be the sense of smell? But God has

---

[6]In the long run, we need to build this same kind of community across the generations, to mark the life of the whole church. In such a church, many distinctions between youth and adult will be (and in several churches with which I am acquainted, *have been*) reduced, and youth and adult accept one another as valuable members of the Body, who need and love each other.

arranged all the parts in the one body, according to his design. For if everything were concentrated in one part, how could there be a body at all? The fact is there are many parts, but only one body. So that the eye cannot say to the hand, "I don't need you!" nor, again, can the head say to the feet, "I don't need you!" On the contrary, those parts of the body which have no obvious function are the more essential to health; and to those parts of the body which seem to us to be less deserving of notice we have to allow the highest honor of function. The parts which do not look beautiful have a deeper beauty in the work they do, while the parts which look beautiful may not be at all essential to life! But God has harmonized the whole body by giving importance of function to the parts which lack apparent importance, that the body should work together as a whole with all the members in sympathetic relationship with one another. So it happens that if one member suffers all the other members suffer with it, and if one member is honored all the members share a common joy.

Now you are together the body of Christ, and individually you are members of him. . . .

As we look at the body of Christ do we find all are his messengers, all are preachers, or all teachers? Do we find all wielders of spiritual power, all able to heal, all able to speak with tongues, or all able to interpret the tongues? No, we find God's distribution of gifts is on the same principles of harmony that he has shown in the human body.

You should set your hearts on the best spiritual gifts, but I shall show you a way which surpasses them all.

If I speak with the eloquence of men and of angels, but have no love, I become no more than blaring brass or crashing cymbal. If I have the gift of foretelling the future and hold in my mind not only all human knowledge but the very secrets of God, and if I also have that absolute faith which can move mountains, but have no love, I amount to nothing at all. If I dispose of all that I possess, yes, even if I give my own body to be burned, but have no love, I achieve precisely nothing.

This love of which I speak is slow to lose patience — it looks for a way of being constructive. It is not possessive: it is neither anxious to impress nor does it cherish inflated ideas of its own importance.

Love has good manners and does not pursue selfish advantage. It is not touchy. It does not keep account of evil or gloat over the wickedness of other people. On the contrary, it is glad with all good men when truth prevails.

Love knows no limit to its endurance, no end to its trust, no fading of its hope; it can outlast anything. It is, in fact, the one thing that still stands when all else has fallen.

Ephesians 4:1-24 —

As God's prisoner, then, I beg you to live lives worthy of your high calling. Accept life with humility and patience, making allowances for one another because you love one another. Make it your aim to be at one in the Spirit, and you will inevitably be at peace with one another. You all belong to one body, of which there is one Spirit, just as you all experienced one calling to one hope. There is one Lord, one faith, one baptism, one God, one Father of us all, who is the one over all, the one working through all and the one living in all.

Naturally there are different gifts and functions; individually grace is given to us in different ways out of the rich diversity of Christ's giving. . . .

His "gifts unto men" were varied. Some he made his messengers, some prophets, some preachers of the gospel; to some he gave the power to guide and teach his people. His gifts were made that Christians might be properly equipped for their service, that the whole body might be built up until the time comes when, in the unity of common faith and common knowledge of the Son of God, we arrive at real maturity — that measure of development which is meant by "the fullness of Christ."

We are not meant to remain as children at the mercy of every chance wind of teaching and the jockeying of men who are expert in the crafty presentation of lies. But we are meant to hold firmly to the truth in love, and to grow up in every way into Christ, the head. For it is from the head that the whole body, as a harmonious structure knit together by the joints with which it is provided, grows by the proper functioning of individual parts to its full maturity in love.

This is my instruction, then, which I gave you from the Lord. Do not live any longer as the gentiles live. For they live blindfold in a world of illusion, and are cut off from the life of God through ignorance and insensitiveness. They have stifled their consciences and then surrendered themselves to sensuality, practicing any form of impurity which lust can suggest. But you have learned nothing like that from Christ, if you have really heard his voice and understood the truth that Jesus has taught you. No, what you learned was to fling off the dirty clothes of the old way of living, which were rotted through and through with lust's illusions, and, with yourselves mentally and spiritually remade, to put on the clean fresh clothes of the new life which was made by God's design for righteousness and the holiness which is no illusion.

Romans 12:3-18; 14:5-15:7 —

As your spiritual teacher I give this piece of advice to each one of you. Don't cherish exaggerated ideas of yourself or your importance, but try to have a sane estimate of your capabilities by the light of the faith that God has given to you all. For just as you have many members in one physical body and those members differ in their functions, so we, though many in number, compose one body in Christ and are all members of one another. Through the grace of God we have different

235

gifts. If our gift is preaching, let us preach to the limit of our vision. If it is serving others let us concentrate on our service; if it is teaching let us give all we have to our teaching; and if our gift be the stimulating of the faith of others let us set ourselves to it. Let the man who is called to give, give freely; let the man who wields authority think of his responsibility; and let the man who feels sympathy for his fellows act cheerfully.

Let us have no imitation Christian love. Let us have a genuine break with evil and a real devotion to good. Let us have real warm affection for one another as between brothers, and a willingness to let the other man have the credit. Let us not allow slackness to spoil our work and let us keep the fires of the spirit burning, as we do our work for the Lord. Base your happiness on your hope in Christ. When trials come endure them patiently; steadfastly maintain the habit of prayer. Give freely to fellow Christians in want, never grudging a meal or a bed to those who need them. And as for those who try to make your life a misery, bless them. Don't curse, bless. Share the happiness of those who are happy, and the sorrow of those who are sad. Live in harmony with one another. Don't become snobbish but take a real interest in ordinary people. Don't become set in your own opinions. Don't pay back a bad turn by a bad turn, to *anyone*. See that your public behavior is above criticism. As far as your responsibility goes, live at peace with everyone. . . .

Again, one man thinks some days of more importance than others. Another man considers them all alike. Let every one be definite in his own convictions. If a man specially observes one particular day, he does so "to the Lord." The man who eats, eats "to the Lord," for he thanks God for the food. The man who fasts also does it "to the Lord," for he thanks God for the benefits of fasting. The truth is that we neither live nor die as self-contained units. At every turn life links us to the Lord, and when we die we come face to face with him. In life or death we are in the hands of the Lord. Christ lived and died that he might be the Lord in both life and death.

Why, then, criticize your brother's actions, why try to make him look small? We shall all be judged one day, not by one another's standards or even our own, but by the judgment of God. It is written:

As I live, saith the Lord, to me every knee shall bow,

And every tongue shall confess to God.

It is to God alone that we have to answer for our actions.

Let us therefore stop turning critical eyes on one another. If we must be critical, let us be critical of our own conduct and see that we do nothing to make a brother stumble or fall.

I am convinced, and I say this as in the presence of the Lord Christ, that nothing is intrinsically unholy. But none the less it is unholy to the man who thinks it is. If your habit of unrestricted diet seriously upsets your brother, you are no longer living in love toward him. And surely you wouldn't let food mean ruin to a man for whom Christ died.

You mustn't let something that is all right for you look like an evil practice to somebody else. After all, the kingdom of Heaven is not a matter of whether you get what you like to eat and drink, but of righteousness and peace and joy in the Holy Spirit. If you put these things first in serving Christ you will please God and are not likely to offend men. So let us concentrate on the things which make for harmony, and on the growth of one another's character. Surely we shouldn't wish to undo God's work for the sake of a plate of meat!

I freely admit that all food is, in itself, harmless, but it can be harmful to the man who eats it with a guilty conscience. We should be willing to be both vegetarians and teetotalers if by doing otherwise we should impede a brother's progress in the faith. Your personal convictions are a matter of faith between yourself and God, and you are happy if you have no qualms about what you allow yourself to eat. Yet if a man eats meat with an uneasy conscience about it, you may be sure he is wrong to do so. For his action does not spring from his faith, and when we act apart from our faith we sin.

We who have strong faith ought to shoulder the burden of the doubts and qualms of others and not just to go our own sweet way. Our actions should mean the good of others — should help them to build up their characters. For even Christ did not choose his own pleasure, but as it is written:

The reproaches of them that reproached thee fell upon me.

For all those words which were written long ago are meant to teach us today; that when we read in the scriptures of the endurance of men and of all the help that God gave them in those days, we may be encouraged to go on hoping in our own time. May the God who inspires men to endure, and give them a Father's care, give you a mind united toward one another because of your common loyalty to Jesus Christ. And then, as one man, you will sing from the heart the praises of God the Father of our Lord Jesus Christ. So open your hearts to one another as Christ has opened his heart to you, and God will be glorified.

2. Take a moment to compare what I've suggested in this chapter and what you've seen in the biblical passages above with your own experience in the church, or with the pattern of relationships that now exist among the youth with whom you minister.

   Describe briefly the relationship patterns you observed the last five times you saw or brought your teens together for *any* purpose. (This might include a Sunday school class, a "youth group" meeting, an officers' meeting, a social occasion, or just a chat with several kids, etc.)

   Now, compare what you have just described with the kind of relationships the chapter and the Scriptures speak of. How does what is actually happening in your group compare? How is it like, and in what ways is it unlike, what I've described?

   What conclusions do you draw from your evaluation and comparison?

3. I know that it's hard to visualize Body relationship — especially when so few have experienced it. The following is a report written by two girls about their relationship as roommates for a quarter. Both were in my class in Youth Ministry at Wheaton College and ran into some of the ideas I've been discussing in the chapter. I think you'll find their perceptions and their experience together helpful in communicating the emotional tone of what I've been trying to say. What they began to experience as their relationship grew is very much like the Body relationship that's been the main burden of this chapter.

ANALYZING A ROOMMATE SITUATION: PERSONAL RELATIONSHIPS

In this project, we — Karol and Jan — analyze a rooming situation. We tried to determine what kinds of things were really important to us in our relationship. We both sat down and wrote our reactions to each other from the first time we met to the last night of our being together as roommates. And then after reading each others' reactions we sat down together at the typewriter and reacted together to what we had written. Even in writing about each other we expressed our feelings in relation to how the other person had affected us. It was not only a great learning experience, it was a tremendous sharing experience and a wonderful way to end our quarter of rooming together.

KAROL

January 1971

The first time I met Jan was in March of 1970. I had just had my hair cut, and I guess that it was a release for my emotions, because I was crying. The girl in the room across from me had hurt her foot, so the two of us were standing out in the hall, crying, and neither of us could stop. This was when Jan tromped up. She was tall and seemed like the motherly type. Automatically she became sympathetic. I just had the impression of a very kind girl, very free with love and expression of it.

Our first real meeting was on the steps of Evans Hall. I was going out with a guy she knew and was concerned about spiritually. That whole evening (it was quite long) was very Christ-centered, and started off a friendship very deeply.

We were deep, but never close friends. Due to circumstances which developed in December, we were both in need of roommates. I thought it would be really fun to room with her, but I was afraid of pushing myself on her, because she was so kind that she would never refuse, and I didn't want her to have to feel pressured. One day I came to her room and presented the idea. She immediately squealed, and jumped up to give me a big huge hug, and I just knew that she meant it.

I went into the situation without reserve. My opinion of her at the beginning of the quarter was extremely high. She was close to Christ, outgoing, very pretty (I didn't think that she was very smart), but she was completely accepted. I felt that she had absolutely no interest in guys, and she seemed like such a strong girl that I figured she would never be able to be married happily, in a submissive sense. And she was super-spiritual.

I pretty much felt that there were things which she was above. Not snobbishly, but just not even concerned about such trivia that I (inwardly) was really interested in.

She was consistent with herself, and acted pretty much the same with everyone that she was with. She was very motherly, and when we were together she was always very sure to see that I was included in everything. This was really good, because I was so used to being the big advisor and mother. It felt good to have somebody looking out for me.

So began the first week of Winter Quarter.

February 1971

At the end of the first week I began dating a guy Jan knew pretty well, and this brought us closer. From my way of thinking we were beginning to develop a normal girl-girl relationship. We began to share concerns (small, picky things) which I had never really thought of expressing before, and which added bonds to a growing friendship.

Our big breakthrough, in our own lives, and in our relationship (based on humanness) came on the 8th or 9th of February. Within two days we were both torn down from pedestals, and one night we just began to really open up our lives to each other. We both gave impressions of being extremely mature, "spiritual," goody-goody, "hard to get," and to those who just saw us and didn't know us at all, we could both be mistaken for loose girls.

For the first time in my life, I opened up parts of my life, which were just icky, and she understood. One of us would say something and the other one would understand and be able to relate a very similar instance. We had come up different paths, and hit the same fork.

Together, we came to face the blackness in our lives, and it helped so much to have each other at a time like this.

I began to see Jan as an equal: equal, not somebody "super-spiritual." I had usually been a counselor and if I would start to share something with someone, would get something like, "You think you've got problems, you should hear about what happened to me!" And I loved that, but once in a while I just wanted to feel a hand that was just a little stronger and firmer than my own when it was faltering.

Jan was so much like me. We were up until 4:30, and we were both constantly sharing, because it was all the same. There was finally somebody who was standing very near me, and we were both pushing the other just a little. We were able to tell each other things which we've never told anyone before and it helped break down images on both our parts.

We've both grown up as "Miss Perfections." And that night we had to finally admit that we both had flaws. Jan and I both had guy problems — the problem of having guys flip, without our having any feelings. This had put both of us on the defensive, and we were beginning to harden towards the male sex.

I had always seen a beautiful, patient, near-perfection (just what I rebelled against) person in her, and to know that she felt some of the same defenses that I did, helped me to feel much closer to her again. Jan is so giving, and loving, but just like me, she can put up fronts of snootiness and cutting with guys who can be pains. Our being together has helped us to be able to see so much more of ourselves, and to talk about it, and admit it.

Our defenses were out of weakness not out of strength, and our putting up barriers meant just so many more to tear down. Super-strong Karol and Jan had holes in their armor — and we could finally see them.

Jan and I have not prayed together very often, but our lives together revolve around Christ. That is one very beautiful thing which I really treasure.

Here faith is in Christ and Christ's love — I get so tired of philosophical arguments and intellectual discussions. Just to be able to experience Christ's love with a person, and share it is one of the most beautiful gifts. Christ has given her more love and concern than just about anyone I've ever met — and I've seen it constantly. All I can do is praise Him.

March 1971

Tonight was our last night together, and I miss her. She has changed, in my mind, from a "spiritual Sally," who was just too involved with Christ to become upset, to a very real, beautiful human being. I used to think that she had just gobs of compassion, but no empathy, and I've been allowed to see the empathy, so much and so beautifully.

We've also become close as human beings, and girls. She really gives me encouragement, and love — she's always so willing and ready. Most evenings we would have at least a few minutes of sharing, and going through our days — just like girls.

We have to separate next quarter, but even in that I can see God's planning. We were put together for one quarter in order to learn from each other, and to support each other in some hard times. These hard times are very uncommon for both of us, and God provided us for each other.

Now He has taught us, and we have to learn to apply it, maybe we can stand that better if we're apart from each other.

We've developed a friendship, and a deep-rooted love has grown. She's even more than I ever imagined her to be, because she has weak spots and she's shared them with me.

I had a higher opinion of her than just about any other girl on this campus, and through the last quarter, and seeing the shakiness and humanness in her, my original opinion has been solidified.

JAN

My first recollection of Karol was at a dorm meeting early in January when she was part of a skit that was advertising the coming dorm banquet. We were both members of the freshman class here at Wheaton, but we had never met, even though we *were* in the same dorm. Perhaps it was because she lived up on the 4th floor and I was down on 1st floor. She played a really corny part in the skit and I remember asking the person next to me just *who* that girl was. I felt that she had to have a lot of nerve to get up in front of the whole assembled dorm with that stupid costume and makeup and do those silly things. I remember thinking that I had never noticed her before and to be quite honest, after that skit, I wasn't any too anxious to really make her acquaintance. I suppose that was really having a closed mind and attitude but it never *once* occurred to me that night that we would ever meet, much less become close friends and eventually good roommates.

My first actual encounter with Karol occurred up on her floor later on during that year in March. I had come up to the floor to visit her roommate whom I had met and gotten to know quite well at band camp, before the freshman year had started. When I got up on the 4th floor, a girl with short, brown, and curly hair was sitting in the middle of the hall, crying her eyes out. I immediately thought that something terrible had happened and I asked my friend what was wrong with the girl. She quickly told me that the person was Karol and happened to be her roommate and had just had her hair cut. She told me not to worry because Karol had informed everyone on the floor beforehand that she was going to cry as soon as she realized that her long, dark hair had been cut. I remember saying a few words to Karol but nothing really significant remains in my mind because of that encounter.

Our first *real* encounter as two individuals occurred within the dorm again around the middle of May, right before the baseball banquet. It turned out that I had found out *who* Karol was going to the banquet with and one night when we saw each other on the steps, I asked her about how she was feeling about the dating situation. That conversation turned out to be a real sharing time with both of us finding that we both had *real relationships* with our Savior and Friend, Jesus Christ and could turn to Him in times of frustration and worry. We prayed together and after that meeting I really felt that I had met a true "sister" in Christ. Even then I could sense that we had a lot in common as far as attitudes, spiritual insights, etc., were concerned.

When Karol presented me with her problem of not having a roommate I didn't at first think of the possibility of her moving in with me. I considered the problem to be a "dorm thing," and since I lived within another dorm, I felt like a friend listening to a situation with no real answer or comments to give. I think I *did* offer her a place in my dorm, but the *actual* possibility of that coming about didn't really hit me. For one thing, I never really considered that Karol would *want* to move out of the dorm with all her friends living there and also it just seemed like a *remote* possibility in many ways. But I was overjoyed the night that she came over and told me that the arrangements had all been made with Mrs. Hackman and that she'd be living with me 2nd quarter and "did I mind?" Of course not! I was truly happy, especially after having lost my other roommate, I was lonely for someone to live with me. So it was settled before Christmas that she would move in with me after winter break, until spring break when we believed Eunice, my other roommate, would be coming back.

When Karol first moved in with me in January, it was all new and fresh. We weren't really close friends but I knew that we were a lot alike basically. She was funny but could be serious and I enjoyed it, for I was a lot like her. Of course, there had to be some adjusting, but I feel that this was mainly due to our lack of knowledge about each other. I don't feel that either of us *really tried* to fake each other out concerning our own personalities but we just needed time to get to know and understand each other.

I suppose the point at which the "getting to know each other" period finally culminated into a deep, full understanding and friendship was during the first week in February. One night we just talked until four in the morning and let it all out. We seemed to discover so many things that were alike in our basic personality make-ups. Our spiritual ideas seemed to match as only God could match them and our lists of personal hangups, priorities, ideals, problems, etc., were almost awesome in their similarities. At times one of us would say exactly what the other person had been thinking or feeling. I felt completely on a level plane with Karol, that night with no personal barriers placed before me, so I could really see "Karol" and I think she really saw "Jan."

And so it's been basically since then. This winter quarter has been fantastic in so many ways. I personally have learned quite a bit. God has shown me so many things about myself and my relationships with those around me. Karol and I, I feel, can *and do* talk about almost anything, especially our own personal problems, which are usually the hardest points in our characters to reveal. I've grown to love Karol more and more every day and Christ is teaching me to love even more through her. My attitude towards her most definitely has changed, for before I didn't know *Karol*. And even during the first weeks in January, I didn't know her. I think that although we didn't try to fake each other out certain aspects of her personality were revealed a little later than others. I must say that I was relieved in one sense. When friends would find out that I was to have Karol as my roommate, they would invariably say, "Oh she's *so* funny — you'll have a riot!!" until I was almost afraid that I was going to have a comedienne on my hands. But as it turned out Karol's brand of humor is basically the same as mine — Praise the Lord! For I truly think that He gave me a prize. We *both* grew. And I think we both grew out of being on top of our lofty spiritual-social pedestals into a realization of what its *really* all about and where it *really is*. It, of course, meaning life, and life is only evident or possible through God — and *that's* where it really is. Karol and I, I think, finally not only knew this, but *really* knocked away some of that strangling pride. Praise the Lord!!

BOTH OF US

Well, we've just read each other's critiques and it blows our minds. What one of us meant to say and didn't the other one did. And we really think that both of us meant to say the same thing. As we were reading them, we both squealed or made some other kind of unusual noise. At the same points in our papers we would squeal. One thing that has really hit us both is that this roommate situation has not only shown us that we are two very similar people but that we've both grown together in the same direction and the same ways. And all the growth has been through Christ.

We both had rather narrow conceptions of each other which broadened slowly during the first four weeks of our stay together, and all of a sudden one night these misconceptions didn't seem to matter anymore, because we were seeing the real people and not the outer shells. It seems to us that both of our real personality hangups had grown from a good amount of spiritual pride, especially in the area of dating in which we thought that we were such "super-strong women" who are always looking down at these "poor weaklings" of men we were always tromping into the ground as they flipped over us. Live it up! We're living it up in just writing down right now what thoughts came into our conversations.

In reality these "poor guys" were the strong ones. They were putting themselves on the line for us, which really took a whole lot of strength, courage, and honesty. If in the course of our lives we had ever fallen over any guy we couldn't even admit it to ourselves, never mind anyone else and especially the guy! We were too afraid of someone doing to us what we were becoming known for. Do you want to know what we were? We were "strong, secure, dominant, idealistic, and-proud-of-it women with the most humble and modest attitudes." We didn't even *realize* that we were beautiful, kind, considerate, sought-after, admired, and *least* of all we didn't realize that we were up on pedestals. We kept wondering where those pedestal-cleaning bills were coming from!

One of our greatest defenses were our mouths. Sarcasm came quite easily whenever we felt we were in danger. This is something that wouldn't have hit us quite as hard if we hadn't roomed together last quarter. Tonight *is* our last night together as roommates and the full impact of what God has really shown and taught us *together* this quarter is really hitting us. We have tried too hard to be "like" Christ; and that is just plain stupid. There is no way that we can ever be "like" Christ for He, and He alone, is perfect. All we can do is look at Him. In Matthew 6 it says, "The lamp of the body is the eyes; if therefore your eye is clear, your whole body will be full of light." Only Christ has light which can penetrate into that inner realm of darkness. And only in this way can we really be living for Him. Trying to be like Christ puts too much emphasis on ourselves and our own efforts, but looking at Him, His glory is so overpowering, that we can't even see ourselves.

Within a two-day span two pedestals were knocked down. In the same hands that handed us hurt, we were handed balm. We had grown up being little Miss Perfectionists. We had heard so much of this that we were beginning to rely on our own strength, rather than just following at Jesus' feet. He didn't push us down; He gently and lovingly took His hand and laid on just enough pressure to help us down on our knees.

It's been a rather hard quarter because God's given us a speed course in human relations. But our identical end reactions were our desire and action of praising Him. We both grew so much and it was only through His goodness, His guidance, His grace, His loving care, and His perfect love. And it was only when we took our eyes off ourselves (where *all* problems have their beginning) and looked to Him, that He was *able* to teach us . . . praise the Lord!

4. Have you ever had a relationship with anyone like the relationship these two girls have described? — the kind that's helped you to be and see yourself, and stimulated real growth and change toward Christlikeness? If you have, why not take time to write about your experience even as the girls wrote about theirs?

   If you still have a hard time "getting the feel" of the Body relationship I've been speaking of, you might want to look at Pete Gillquist's book, *Love is Now* (Zondervan, 1970). It expresses in terms of a young man's growing relationship with God the attitudes and perspectives that are to shape our relationships with others in Christ's Body.

13

community, now

YOUTH · ADULTS

BIBLE

LIFE · BODY

PROGRAM

EPHESIANS 4:13

Jan and Karol (PROBE 3, pp. 238ff) broke through the barriers of super-ficiality that exist between persons and came to know the "real" Jan and Karol underneath. In the context of honesty and self-revelation that marked their sharing, weaknesses were exposed, as well as strengths. But even the "icky" was accepted: they discovered that they loved each other *as they were.*

The involvement in each other's life that they began to experience did more than bring them closer as persons. Both girls talked about "growth." Both discovered truths about themselves that they had been blind to; ways that sin had been warping their personalities and their relationships with others. Pedestals were knocked down, the girls related. And rejecting the discovered reliance on their own strength, they turned to "following at Jesus' feet." So God used each to minister to the other, and to "help us back down to our knees."

This is how Christ's Body is supposed to function — accepting and loving other believers as they are, opening up our lives to one another, discovering needs in each life and finding encouragement for change — with all of it gently turning our eyes back to Jesus, to follow Him. This is life together in and as Christ's Body.

How do we develop this kind of love between believers? Even if we could put the youth of our churches into roommate situations, like that of Jan and Karol, a Body relationship wouldn't necessarily develop. How then do we move toward developing Christian community? How do we build and maintain the unity of the Spirit in the bonds of love?

There's probably no more significant or challenging aspect of youth ministry than working toward Body relationships. Significant, because mutual ministry "in Body" is essential to the life together of Christians. Challenging, because in most situations development of Body life may be slow.

The slowness stems from several sources. Many teens will not be

245

far enough along in their own growth as persons to fit comfortably into mutually self-revealing relationships, though there are churches where junior high youth (ages 12 to 14) seem to have developed Body relationships. Yet the goal of involvement in Body life will seldom be reached with *all* teens associated with a local church. Another source of problem is the pressures on youth leaders to maintain a flurry of activities and programs for teens. Too often we fall into the trap of equating "keeping them busy" and having numbers of persons involved in our programs with "success." Unless the goal of building Body relationships is kept constantly in focus, the necessary building processes are likely to be displaced by efforts to maintain an inherited pattern of programs and activities.

It's helpful, then, to review briefly the essentials of Body Ministry. Chuck Miller, presently Minister to Youth at Lake Avenue Congregational Church in Pasadena, and one of the most effective in building a Body relationship in his work with youth, draws three priorities from Scripture that help him keep his ministry in focus.

The first essential (John 17:21) is personal commitment to Jesus Christ, that He may stand as the foundation of all unity. The second essential (John 17:22) is each believer's commitment to the Body, "that they may be one, even as we [Father and Son] are." The third (John 17:23) is commitment to the work, "that the world may know." Chuck's contention is that the second essential, commitment of Christians to each other, is the most neglected in the Church of Christ today, and that development of the Body organism through commitment of Christians to each other is crucial.

Thus when Chuck first arrived at Pasadena and found the normal "program-centered" youth ministry, he began at once to focus on building the organism. To Chuck this meant getting to know in-depth kids who were already committed to Christ, to teach them to love each other. He encouraged each to commit himself in these words: "I am going to give my life to people"; and he taught them how to pray for and love individuals. As the kids discovered in Chuck's example what loving others meant and began to get involved with others themselves, chains of love developed. These chains first involved other Christian kids, but then reached out beyond to communicate Christ to others.

One of the teens Chuck sought to help love in January of 1969 was Bob. Soon a core group of Christian young men, who went to the same high school and had opportunities to meet and pray together, developed. Working with Bob, Dennis, Brad, Mike, and Jon, Chuck helped them open their lives to one another and shoulder each other's burdens in prayer and loving concern.

As these kids grew in Christ, they began to contact non-Christians, reaching out to show Christ's love to them and share the Gospel. As a result of their witness on campus, Scott, Roy, and three Johns came to know Christ. Roy, who came to Christ in March, 1969, at Teen Breakfast Club — an outreach activity designed to give the kids a chance to share the Lord with friends — led Larry to Christ. Larry had both been on drugs and pushed them. Through Larry, John G. came to know Christ in May, and in June this John led John B. to Christ. In eighteen months, twelve to fifteen "generations" of believers had come to the Lord in Pasadena.

The outreach began with building the Body.

Personal commitment to Christ, expressed in commitment to other believers, overflows in love-motivated communication of the Gospel to the world around us.

What were the essentials of this Body ministry? Just what we've seen in the preceding chapter: *love* — a love that involves itself in the lives of others in mutual self-revelation and self-giving, love that commits itself unhesitatingly and without condition to care for others and seek their good.

Means God uses

There are three primary approaches to building Body relationships — or perhaps I should say, three contexts in which we can work toward its development. The first context is individual, and the means God uses is the person and example of the leader. The second context is the small group. And the third, the larger gathering of believers.

The leader's example   As we've seen in earlier chapters, Christian leaders always lead by example. *There is no other way to guide people into growth.*

I know that some of my writings on the church have been criticized by those who feel I've left no place for the pastor and other church leaders in my approach to renewal. I'm concerned about this reaction, because it's clear from Scripture that leadership *is* vital to the health and growth of the Church—and of every local church. But what I've suggested is not leaderless churches: *it is churches in which leadership functions in the biblical way. The church must have leaders, but it must have leaders who lead by example.*

Example-leadership is not demonstrated primarily in the sermon from the pulpit or in chairing committee meetings. Example-leadership isn't demonstrated primarily in the planning of programs and the making of plans and preparations. *Example leadership is demonstrated and exercised by personal involvement with people in ministry* — by talking with and listening and sharing. By teaching another person how to love by loving, and how to reveal himself by revealing yourself. Example leadership is an informal, interpersonal involvement with the *persons* to whom we minister.

In youth ministry, the first prerequisite for building the Body is that the youth leader comes to know and love individual teens. There will, of course, be times when he speaks to the group, and chairs committees, and makes plans and preparations. But nothing must be allowed higher priority than teaching kids to love by coming to know and love them. *Anyone working with youth who is not building this kind of relationship with individuals and small groups will never succeed in developing the Body relationship.*

The small group While many in the church are turning with enthusiasm to the small group, others associate the movement with "sensitivity training" and all sorts of excesses. Certainly by "small group" no implication of the latter is intended. What is intended is the notation of a simple fact. We can know on the intimate level implied in this and the preceding chapter only a certain number of persons. As time goes by, we find it easier to move quickly into Body relationship with other believers, and to function as a Body in larger, congregational-sized meetings. But there are compelling reasons for bringing Christians together to share with one another in small groups. I've expressed some of these in an earlier book.

> To learn to trust and to become trustworthy — to learn to love, and become loving — we must become deeply involved in the lives of others to whom we commit ourselves in Christ. To develop this kind of relationship we need to share ourselves with others, and they need to share themselves with us. All of this demands time. More than this, it requires a face-to-face relationship — a relationship we can have with only a few others at one time. And thus a church is forced to move to a small group structure.
>
> "Small," then, suggests a size which permits and encourages face-to-face relationship. It is not so large that any will be cut off from deeply and personally sharing himself with others, and in turn receiv-

ing from them. How large is this? Some research in group dynamics suggests that five may be the optimum number! But often groups of eight or twelve are suggested for church fellowship groups, and this range seems to have advantages.[1]

It should be noted here that often small natural groupings already exist among teens, on which we can build toward the Body. For instance, in many churches today youth attend more than one high school. Kids from each high school form a natural group, and we can work toward development of a supportive Body relationship among them as a base for witness in that school.

In most school systems a distinction is made between teens by grade level, with the tenth graders and the twelfth, for instance, carefully distinguished. Where such distinctions are also made within the church (as is normal in larger churches), groups can be established by age and grade level, thus corresponding roughly with Sunday school classes as well.

Although small groups will grow naturally as Body life develops, and can be used creatively to foster Body life, the example of the servant leader is still central and essential. It is, to me, a mistake to attempt to develop Body life in youth ministry wholly through the operation of small groups. The first foundation, and the continuing impetus to formation of the new community, is and must be the adult leader's involvement with individuals in the group: his teaching them how to love by first loving them.

Figure 7, below, illustrates a development pattern for Body life in a youth ministry, showing the central role of the leader's example, with *subsequent* development of small groups and change in the character of larger group meetings.

The whole group As more and more teens experience love and commitment, the character of the larger meetings of the group changes and takes on a distinctive Body character. There is freedom now to be honest with others who are "strangers," but whom we trust because we know them to be brothers and sisters in Christ who are committed to love us. The following description of a church service in California reflects what may happen as the discovery of our Body relationship shapes life together.

---

[1]L. O. Richards, *A New Face,* p. 153.

What kind of church service appeals to youth today? One answer comes from Peninsula Bible Church, Palo Alto, California. Seventy percent of the Sunday evening congregation of more than 750 are under twenty-five years of age. The traditional structure of the evening service — song service, announcements, Scripture, special music, preaching — was replaced by a time for sharing of needs and gifts by the people.

Pastor Ray Stedman explains: "We began with the question, 'Where are you hurting? Not where did you hurt ten years ago, but where are you hurting right now?' "

To give the people a chance to express this, a leader with a microphone roves through the congregation. People tell how they came to Christ last week, how the Lord supplied a particular need for food, about a relative who needs prayer because he's on LSD (another youth prays on the spot), how God spoke through a passage of Scripture, about the need for a car, and so on. Throughout, the rest of the people participate also, usually by enthusiastic applause.

The offering is different! People are told that if they have an immediate need, they may take up to $10 from the plate. If they need more, they are invited to come to the church office the next morning to explain their need.

After a hymn, there's a 25-minute Bible study, which includes questions from the congregation. Hands are joined for a closing chorus, "We are one in the Spirit, we are one in the Lord." For another hour people stay on their own, talking, praying, singing, and sharing in small groups.

Mr. Stedman attributes youth's participation to "a climate of honest realism" in the service. When long-haired, barefoot, strangely dressed young people began to appear, some "middle-class saints gulped," says the pastor, but "they welcomed the young people, listened to them, prayed with them, and opened their hearts. The kids did likewise."

And so the character of all meetings changes as Body life grows. Bible study takes on new meaning, as believers are freed to expose their lives to Scripture's searching light. And the reality of Body's Truth is experienced as each is stimulated and encouraged by others to step out in faith to *do* Christ's words.

Essentially, then, the roles that are most often in mind when a "youth director" is called by a church or when a "youth sponsor" is appointed, are *not* the crucial roles in youth ministry. The key to growth of the new community, and to success in youth ministry, is in the impact on persons of the leader as he himself proves the catalyst through which Christ draws the whole group together in and around Himself.

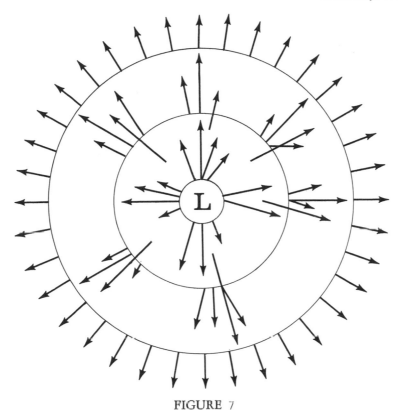

FIGURE 7

PROCESS OF DEVELOPMENT OF BODY LIFE
BEGINS IN THE CENTER AND MOVES OUTWARD

(1) The leader seeks out those who are committed to Christ and by example teaches them how to love and be committed to each other. (2) These in turn reach out to other teens, forming small and natural groupings of youth who begin to experience Body life together. (3) As more and more of the youth group become involved and experience one another's love, more and more freedom exists when the whole group is gathered for worship or study.

PROBE
case histories
thought questions
discussion starters
resources

1. The viewpoint expressed in this chapter is in fact a very simple one. The key to building the Body relationship in youth ministry is the person of the leader. Still, the practical implications are very hard to grasp, for few of us have ourselves been so led! To make the process as clear as possible, I'm including here the responses of a man in youth ministry whom I've asked, "How did you go about

building a Body relationship in *your* ministry with youth?" **Here
is his reply:**

TALKING ABOUT "BODY RELATIONSHIPS"
IN THE BODY OF CHRIST

J. Bristol

First let me share what is really behind our youth ministry, and
actually this is a principle that's not simply behind the youth ministry,
but behind all phases of our ministry in our church. I think that we
take as our goal (we as pastors on the staff are very much agreed)
the proclamation of Christ, as Paul says in Colossians 1:28, 29: "Him
we proclaim, exhorting every man (or admonishing every man) and
teaching every man in all wisdom that we may present every man
mature in Christ." This is the focal point — the underlying verse, the
underlying purpose, the underlying concept which guides all we do.
That's rock bottom, right there.

Now, we seek to carry this out by means of certain principles laid
down in the Scripture. First of all, I think we could build a model
from the bottom up. We have principles; we operate on what we discern
to be scriptural principles concerning how to go about the work of the
Church, the work being admonishing and teaching in order to present
men mature in Christ. And this we carry out through the scriptural
principle of equipping the saints for ministry. In Ephesians, Paul writes
that the Lord has given certain people to the Church — prophets,
apostles, pastors and teachers — for equipping the saints *for* the work
of ministry *for* the building up of the body of Christ. We who are
pastors see ourselves essentially as coaches in this.

We start off with principles and then we have above that the promise
that the Lord makes again in Ephesians, that the body will function
smoothly — each joint, each ligament becoming stronger so that the
body may grow qualitatively and quantitatively. This is the promise
He's made, that when we follow these principles, our body will grow.
And from this springs our program. So, we always put principles first,
then the promise that comes to us, and then the program will always
come from the principles. We think programs vary from church to
church as God leads men in different situations. But we feel the
principles do not vary.

With this goal in mind, let me speak with regard to what we're
doing in the junior high youth program at this point. We have on
Sunday morning approximately 200 to 250 junior high school kids in
our Sunday school department, and each class has two teachers. We
have a co-teacher arrangement. I'm always for this, because I like to
see the kids exposed to Jesus Christ through two different personalities.
What Sunday morning gives us is what we would term a "pool of
kids" — a large number of kids. Some of these kids are Christians;
some *have* to come because their parents make them; some are inquiring
kids, wondering about Christianity; and some of them simply aren't

Christians at all. I'm sometimes puzzled why some of them come, but at any rate, we have a large pool of, say, 200 kids. From that pool we draw anywhere from thirty to seventy-five kids on Wednesday evening, when from 5 o'clock to 6 we have what we call our time of "Bible Rap and Body-Life Sharing." This is a time when some of the more serious-minded kids come out. We don't offer any gimmicks; we simply say, "We're going to study the Scriptures; this time is for those of you who are serious in your relationship to Christ, and who want to spend time studying the Scriptures, rapping about different problems that you have on your mind, different questions that you come up against at school, or just in your own thinking. You come on out to our time of Bible Rap and Body Life."

Now this meeting that we hold from 5 to 6 on Wednesday has two emphases or thrusts to it. First of all, we have a time of praise. That's not exactly a thrust, but we have a time of singing, with guitars and ukuleles; we sing some of the more contemporary songs. Then we have a time of scriptural input. We always go through the Scriptures. The kids sit there with their Bibles and we go through the Scriptures. We've been working our way through *James* recently. But as we go through the Scriptures, we seek not only to learn what they have to say to us about Jesus and about our commitment to Him, about where we stand in relation to Him and to our brothers and those outside of Christ. We're also seeking to teach the kids to learn to feed themselves from the Scriptures. This is one key thrust of what we're trying to do — to get them to learn to feed themselves, so that they don't become dependent on a pastor, youth worker, or a Sunday school teacher, but that with just the Bible they can put spiritual food into their souls. This is one of our thrusts, then: a study of the Scriptures.

After that, we have a time of body-life sharing. This is a free time when we begin by asking, "What's the Lord been doing in your life?" and, "If there's something we can pray about, can we have some prayer requests"; and "We don't want to pray for your Aunt Suzie down in Tampa who sprained her ankle; we want to pray about *you,* where you're hurting. How can we, as brothers and sisters in Christ, bear your burden?" A scriptural mandate for this is Jesus' words in John: "By this shall all men know that you are my disciples, that you have love one for another." And then also Paul, in Galatians 6:2, said, "Bear one another's burdens and so fulfill the law of Christ" — which is the law of love. But we can't bear each other's burdens unless we are acquainted with each other's burdens. So this is the time when we share both our burdens and our joys. So we throw it open, and it takes time for real honesty — gut-level honesty — to develop. And I wouldn't say we've by any means arrived; we have a long way to go, but there are flashes, and I think honesty is contagious, and burdens are shared and hearts are opened up. We pray for unsaved parents and about the problems in their homes. Some kids have confessed that their moms and dads are fighting, and we need prayer for the healing of that relationship. Others have fallen out with their friends and they feel that this has been a blow to their witness — and they want to be effective witnesses for Christ, so will we pray for reconciliation between them and their friends? One boy was flunking English, and his dad's an English teacher — would we pray for him? Another girl wanted us to pray that she'd be able to control her tongue, because she's had a lot of problems with it. After we get a number of these requests, I write them briefly on the board and say, "Well, now, who'll pray for Meg here, or who'll pray for Ken, or who'll pray for Joe? If some request is particularly pressing or needful, several of us will pray for it. And the kids will raise their hands, and say, "I'll pray for him"; "I'll pray for her," and then we go to prayer. We also encourage spontaneous prayer, too, as the Lord leads. We simply take this time together to pray. It's really good; it's really rich to have these kids hear people in their own peer group praying for them, and bringing their petitions before the Lord. And of course the kids then really learn how to pray in a group. We also have sentence prayers sometimes — for different people or different outreaches of our church — different concerns. And this is our time of sharing. Now I've found that in the group, when these needs come up, afterwards kids will just put their arms around other kids (even in junior high) and say, "Boy, we're going to be praying for you this week, brother." And it's beautiful to see. Sometimes it even breaks me up. I think there was one time last year that was really something. There were about seventy-five kids there, and we had a season of prayer that lasted for forty-five minutes. A lot of it was spontaneous and beautiful and real. One kid would confess something and another one would pray for the person who had just confessed a fault — a prayer of encouragement, which showed acceptance and love and concern for this person. It was really beautiful. So this is why we call it "Body Life" — the body is alive to bearing each other's burdens. Now we don't only bear burdens; we praise the Lord for answers to prayer when a person becomes a Christian! I'm sure at least half a dozen of the kids will praise God for this. We'll just praise the Lord together and really make that Christian feel welcome, and accepted and loved. It's really great.

Now of course, from our studying of the Bible, questions come up and this is where some of our give-and-take of questions comes — some of our "Bible rap" time. The kids feel very free to invite non-Christians to our group. This past week, a boy came who had made the statement that he didn't *want* to go to heaven; he'd *rather* go to hell. He came to our group, and we just had a tremendous time talking about Jesus and what He's done for us. So the kids have this group then, as a type of environment where they feel free to bring their non-Christian friends. It's a little different from going to Sunday school. Oh, I think Sunday school — just the term sometimes has a stigma for non-Christian young people. But this Bible-rap time is a little more with it. At least, I think it appeals to the non-Christians in this way. Then after this time from 5 to 6, we usually just go en masse to MacDonald's and load up on hamburgers and fries. Then we come back and play all kinds of games for about and hour and a half in the gym. And the kids let off steam in this way.

Our discipline in the group is strictly under the guidance of the Holy Spirit. If the kids are getting noisy, we bow in prayer, and I ask them to pray that the Holy Spirit will keep us still and quiet and receptive and respectful of each other as we talk and share. And this has worked. This past year it's been beautiful; we pray that God will quiet our hearts. Then too, we know that we can let off steam in the gym later. But it's been rich and very real. Our program comes from this principle of building up in Christ, equipping the saints, not only to feed themselves, but also to witness to their friends and to share their faith. This is another thrust as we study the Bible; they ask questions about situations they have encountered the preceding week with their non-Christian friends.

So then, I want you to get the picture. We have this big "pool" that comes on Sunday morning — a couple hundred kids, then about fifty or sixty on Wednesdays, and then from this Wednesday group, I reach in again and I have a smaller group. This one is only of boys that I'm working with, and these are more intimate disciples. Jesus chose twelve that they might be with Him. Sometimes it might sound arrogant for a man to say, "Well, I'm taking these people to be my disciples." But we do have Christ's commission, "Go and *disciple* all nations." Bob Smith of Peninsula Bible Church recently pointed out to me that in Jesus' command there, the verb is disciple, and it's modified by three participles — going, teaching, baptizing. So that's what I'm seeking to do with this small, intimate group (it's just a handful of maybe five or six boys, depending on who can get together with me). We just do things for fun; there's no program, no set thing we study. But we'll go out and play pee-wee golf, go to a football game, or try to arrange an airplane ride for us. We'll get together and play monopoly or baseball, or just go do something else together. I just want to be with them, to *enjoy* them, to *fellowship* together. And it's amazing to me, that as we grow together like this, the kids do become committed to each other. And also, biblical things come up invariably and naturally. I don't bring them up. I don't say, "Okay, now we're going to study this book of the Bible together." No, I'm just with them to enjoy being with them, and to talk about where they're at. We hope to be going on a little camping outing this school year, too. I'm really expecting that to be good for our relationships. So I have this small core group. I see in Jesus' ministry how he preached to the 5,000 and then there were the 500 to whom He appeared as the resurrected Lord, and then He did send a smaller group out two by two — seventy people, and then He had a smaller group still — the Twelve, and a very intimate group in the twelve — Peter, James, and John. And my intimate group is these few kids, and within the group, there's even a couple that I'm closer to than to anyone else. I don't choose these boys because of any particular great leadership qualities I see in them; I just pray the Lord will direct me to them. I've got one boy who doesn't have very many leadership qualities at all; he was a real "cool guy," coming from a big family and needing attention terribly. The Lord's just been transforming his life in front of my eyes, and I'm seeing him grow into a beautiful Christian. But I don't try to pick out the "big men on campus," and make them my disciples; I just pray and select as the Lord leads. I don't always tell the parents why I keep asking their kid out to these special functions. Now we do run into resentment. Some kids who are left out feel, why doesn't John ask me out? But I simply can't handle more than a few in this intimate group. I'm sure it will come as no surprise to you that those who are most committed to each other are those in this intimate group, and what's interesting is that these kids have different backgrounds; they even go to different schools. And yet together, boy, we've got more commitment to each other as Christians in the body than anyone, and I can ask them to pray and I *know* they will. It's beautiful, and I keep them in my prayers before the Lord. So this is the thrust of our junior high ministry. I think this is where the most effective work is done — in the smallest group. This is where I'm most in touch with the kids. We have big things that we put on in the Deablo Valley here. For instance, this month we are having a big junior high Wing Ding at the Evangelical Free Church — bringing in a special speaker; we're having a hamburger-eating contest, a colossally huge volleyball game, and we're having a time of real singing and sharing. We're also having seminars on witnessing, on obscenity, on relationships, trying to offer some things to junior highs that heretofore had only been offered to senior high. I don't really look to these big things to have a great deal of effect on young peoples' lives. I think it's good that we offer them, because that shows we care, and the kids can pick up good things, but there are these few that I feel are being reached really in depth through my ministry. Now, of course I have these kids for only two years, and then they move on up into the high school department. In high school, our minister to youth, Jim Gordon, is following exactly the same principles that I'm following in junior high. He has his "pool" on Sunday morning. In the high school group we minister to about nineteen high schools, an adult couple being responsible for the Christians in each school — seeking to disciple them, to do things with them, to be with them. So we have this operating not only on a staff level as a ministerial staff working with the young people, but also on a lay level, where we're encouraging our laymen to disciple in this way. College students are discipling high school students, *older* high school students are discipling *younger* high school students. We're at a point now where some of the numerical growth is really becoming evident among those who are being discipled by others who *have been* discipled. This is following the teaching of 2 Timothy 2:2 — "What you have received from me," says Paul to Timothy, "commit to faithful men who will teach others." And actually this year now, I've sent some of my first group of discipled people on up into high school, and I'm not quite sure *where* they are now; sometimes they tend to get lost. Jim Gordon doesn't merely take up where I left off; he prays and selects his own kids as God leads him, and they're not necessarily the kids I've had with me. But it's an effective ministry, and a good one. I'm very thankful for learning these principles of ministry since I got out here.

I don't know of anything else I can add; this really says where it's at here in the work. We're continually learning; we don't feel we've arrived by any means, and we do have a long way to go. Ultimately, we're hoping for greater commitment to the kids on the part of Sunday school teachers — more people who will be *doing* discipling because they *have been* discipled. This is the goal, but you always start small before you ever get a great number involved. You have to grow, of course, and there's no substitute for time in developing quality of work with people. But it's a fun thing too. That's what's so rich about it. There's no work about this discipling. It's really enjoying relationships and friendships in Christ. I feel very privileged to be able to go out and do the work of ministry by playing miniature golf with my kids — thoroughly enjoying the gusto and zest they have for life.

2. I commented in this chapter that working through small groups *alone* is not sufficient, in itself, to build a Body relationship or to establish mutual ministries. Still, it *is* helpful to the development of the Body to plan retreats, Bible studies, etc., around small groups, and to use this form to support and stimulate the development of the Body.

The following retreat program is an example of the kind of thing that may be done to draw teens closer together as persons and help them come to know each other in deeper ways. A retreat like this can well be used over Christmas or Easter holidays with natural groupings that have already developed (using Sunday school classes or other previously established associations as the basis for group assignment), or it may be used at the beginning of a school year to introduce to one another persons who will be together in some such natural association.

The retreat plans were developed and carried out by four Wheaton graduate students, drawing from several sources for the ideas and plans.

YOUTH AND SMALL GROUP ACTIVITY

Results desired

Purpose: To initiate a once-a-week small group gathering of teens which will in its operation —
(1) provide mutual support and acceptance
(2) promote prayer and sharing together
(3) augment larger Bible study and evangelistic activities

257

Aims,
(long range): To meet together at least once a week
To share problems and experiences
To pray about and for each other

Aims,
(immediate): To provide in a retreat setting a positive experience
in small group meetings
To motivate establishment of continuing small group
meetings through the school year.

Program: A one-and-one-half-day retreat

SCHEDULE FOR SMALL-GROUP LEARNING EXPERIENCE

FRIDAY —

Arrival at campgrounds (time to get settled and get bearings)	7:00 P.M.
Meet in living room (brief song time)	8:00 P.M.
First group meeting	8:15 P.M.
Snack time	10:30 P.M.
Devotions	11:00 P.M.
Bed time	11:30 P.M.

SATURDAY —

Breakfast	8:00 A.M.
Clean rooms, devotions, visit, etc.	8:45 A.M.
Meet in living room (get directions)	9:15 A.M.
Second group meeting	9:30 A.M.
Break time (prepare for lunch)	12:00 M.
Lunch	12:15 P.M.
Clean-up (boys wash dishes, girls set and clear tables)	1:00 P.M.
Recreation time: snacks available (planned activities or freedom — your choice)	1:15 P.M.
Meet in living room (get directions)	3:45 P.M.
Third group meeting	4:00 P.M.
Break time (prepare for supper)	6:30 P.M.
Supper (boys set and clear tables, girls wash dishes)	6:45 P.M.
Meet in living room	7:45 P.M.
Fourth group meeting (stay as a whole group)	8:00 P.M.
Departure for home	9:30 P.M.

FRIDAY EVENING

First Group Meeting — *Depth Unfoldment*

Estimated time: 2 hours, 15 minutes

PURPOSES:

Develop respect for self and others
Get acquainted quickly (works 5-6 times as fast as the usual way)
Get rid of social masks

ACTIVITY:

Play "emotional charades"

Two teams. A person from each team acts out to his own team an emotion that the other team has chosen. Five times for each team. Team with the lowest time in guessing the emotion wins.

Divide up into small groups of 5-6

Use egg timer. Person holds it in his hand while talking. Time for each person is six minutes.

Each person shares the most important events or situations which have contributed to his development.

Question the person should answer is — What and/or who influenced your life so far? (with 3 or 4 illustrations)

During the last minute of the six, the person is to relate the happiest moment of his life.

Question the person should answer is — If you were given one wish to come true what would that be?

(Note: If he doesn't use all his time, the group may ask him personal questions.)

IMPORTANT: THE GROUP LEADER SETS THE TONE AND DEPTH BY STARTING THE PROCESS WITH HIS OWN SHARING.

At the end of the evening join hands and sing, "We are one in the Spirit." Dismiss for bed!!

SATURDAY MORNING

Second Group Meeting — *Success Acknowledgment*
Estimated time: 2½ hours

RE-ENTRY EXPERIENCE:

Meet in the same groups as the night before. Have each person vocalize the things he remembers as the most interesting about the person to his left.

PURPOSE:

Conscious awareness of one's own personal success patterns.
Become sensitive to potential in self and in others.
Inspire action toward greater achievements.

METHOD:

Identify with our own successes.
Knowing and understanding the attitudes of the group to myself.
Sharing freely, being truthful and honest with others.

ACTIVITY:

Each person jots down what he considers his success on a large paper taped to the wall (one for each person in the group.) The question should be stated like this: "What are your successes and why are they so important to you?" Then the group discusses each individual's sheet. This process could better be facilitated by having each individual share his successes with his group.

On a second sheet of paper placed on an easel before the whole group someone records observations made by the group about each individual in the group. *THAT PERSON MAY NOT COMMENT UNTIL THEY HAVE ALL FINISHED.* Question asked is, "What do you see about _____? Observations should be person's trends, principles, concepts, and patterns, which are inherent in these successes. Group should then conclude by formulating a definition of what success is to this person. (Does it show personal relationships, self-fulfillment, emphasis on material gain, or what does it show?)

SUCCESS, WHY?	OBSERVATIONS:
	SUCCESS TO _____ IS:

SATURDAY AFTERNOON

Third Group Meeting — *Strength Recognition*
Estimated time: 2½ hours

INTRODUCTION:

Exploring gifts and talents aids one to recognize and assess his God-given personal potential. Most people see their own strengths and resources as very limited; unfortunately we can see our own weaknesses more easily. Therefore, we must increase our self-knowledge (which raises our estimates of our own gifts and talents and changes our self-image).

PURPOSE:

To help us recognize our gifts and talents as others close to us see them. To begin group encouragement.

ACTIVITY:

Each person lists on a small piece of paper his own strengths.
(Dimensions are: sports, hobbies, arts, spiritual strength, work, intellect, inter-personal relationships, organizational ability, humor, perseverance, etc.)

Then the group lists on sheets of paper taped to the wall and bearing the person's name, the strengths they see in each person.

The person then compares his list with the group's list, and reports to the group how close they came.

The group then discusses the question for each of the individuals: "What do you observe in my personality, that may prevent me from using my strengths?" Jot down key words on a sheet on the easel for each person.

Have the group predict about each person. What will he be in ten years? *PERSON MAY NOT SAY ANYTHING DURING THIS LISTING.* When they finish he may react.

STRENGTHS	AVOID:
	IN 10 YEARS:

SATURDAY EVENING
FOURTH GROUP MEETING — *PUTTING IT ALL TOGETHER*
Estimated time: 1 hour, 15 minutes

PURPOSE:

Reaching a solution as to how best to utilize our strengths in living for Christ.

ACTIVITY:

This will be an entire group meeting. Everyone should be in on this. Open with prayer and ask for a time of sharing in "what has this weekend meant to me." (Hopefully many will share).

Questions to be asked are —

What can hinder us from utilizing our strengths as we go back to campus?
What keeps us from living for Christ?
How can we best overcome these problems?
(The group should decide these solutions.)

DISMISSAL

3. In this chapter I've suggested that the role of the person ministering with youth that is most crucial is that of *example*. And that this requires personal involvement with kids, loving them, and teaching them to love each other.

If you are presently ministering with youth, it might be helpful to do an analysis of your *contacts* with your teens. The chart on page 264 will help you analyze the pattern of your ministry in terms of the kind of contacts, the roles, the purposes, and interrelationships it supports.

If you agree with the priorities in youth ministry which I've suggested in this book, you will perhaps be interested on completion of the chart to ask, What are my priorities? What do my activities indicate my priorities are? Do any changes in my approach to ministry and investment of my time seem to be needed?

INTERPERSONAL CONTACT EVALUATION CHART

Occasions when I am with the youth (in class, committee mtgs, socials, counseling, etc. *in order of* amount of time spent.	I. Describe briefly what happens in the contact situation. State, specifically, the *goal* of the contact (study, decide plans, etc.)	II. What is my role in this contact situation? Am I teacher, leader, coach, motivator, "person with," or what?	III. To what extent do I get to know the teens as *persons* in this contact?	IV. To what extent do they come to know me as a person — in self-revealing depth?

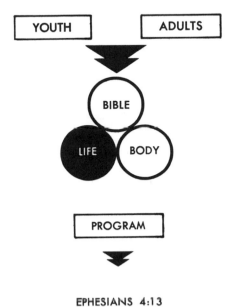

EPHESIANS 4:13

YOUTH IN LIFE

YOUTH   ADULTS

BIBLE

LIFE   BODY

PROGRAM

EPHESIANS 4:13

14

committed to life

In his excellent book, *Young People and Their Culture,* Ross Snyder makes an important point. Our faith comes to life, and takes on meaning, in life itself. He reports,

> "At a conference of 300 youth leaders — both Protestant and Catholic — held in 1965 in Minnesota there was almost unanimous agreement in checking as "very true" this item: "The great words of the church are not the words that young people whom I know use to choose and think with."

So we better translate the great words into words and imagery that young people can use to choose and feel with. And demonstrate that the words are usable — more so than any others — in the difficult situations of life.

For nobody understands a word — or makes it one of his "speaking words" — unless the word has been used in situations that are important to him. How does a child (or anybody) learn the meaning of a word? He learns it as the "utterance occasion" of someone significant to him. A little child hears his mother and father talking, and he hears them use certain words. He begins to imitate the words; he accidentally uses the word in the right situation and he gets "Ohs" and "Ahs." So he gets a glimmer of the meaning of the word. Then he begins to use the word in his own expressive spontaneity and to speak it in the kind of situation in which he ought to use it. He doesn't sit down at the dictionary and learn words. He really never learns the meaning of a word when mother and father sit down and try to "teach it to" him. He has to hear the word *in situation.* (This is what is meant by "utterance occasion.") And then *he* has to use it in situations and have people recognize what he is talking about.

Young people have to learn to use theology by hearing people use its words when they are struggling with life. They have to learn to

267

use the great words of Christianity by hearing people use them as they talk about current events. As they are in the process of trying to make sense out of "what happened to me."[1]

Life is the arena of our faith. Failure to link our experience of life, our values, our feelings, our patterns of response, to the reality of who we are and are to become in Christ, leads to a distorted and inadequate Christianity and to distorted and inadequate persons.

I have several adult friends who are eagerly seeking God's healing today because they never examined and brought life into harmony with God when they were young. For youth, as a time of transition from childhood to adulthood, from dependence to independence, is *the* crucial time for becoming. Attitudes and personality traits that take shape in adolescence often persist as deep-seated roots of the adult identity. So it's particularly important as we minister with youth to lead them to respond to this biblical imperative: "Brace up your minds, and, as men who know what they are doing, rest the full weight of your hopes on the grace that will be yours when Jesus Christ reveals himself. Live as obedient children before God. Don't let your character be molded by the desires of your ignorant days, but be holy in every department of your lives, for the one who has called you is himself holy" (1 Peter 1:13-15 *Phillips*).

The phrase that seems particularly important to me here is the simple one, "as men who know what they are doing." In the first chapters of this book I noted with concern that the tendency in youth culture is toward existentially oriented, hedonistic *in situation* choices. That is, youth tend to make decisions on the spur of the moment, on the basis of what they feel will be pleasant or pleasing to them then — without reference to long-range implications of the decisions, and without concern for the basic meaning of their lives. This, as I've noted in another book,[2] is of particular concern because it is the little decisions we make that fit together to create the pattern of our lives and personalities. The little decisions, not the big ones, shape us as *persons*. The tendency of youth to live *unexamined lives* is one of the most disturbing facts that we need to face in youth ministry. And one of our main concerns in ministry with youth should be to help them live *examined lives* — to help

---

[1]Ross Snyder, *Young People and Their Culture* (New York: Abingdon Press, 1969) p. 101.

[2]*What's in It for Me?* (Chicago: Moody Press, 1969).

them take an honest and close look at themselves and their experiences, and evaluate them in the light of Scripture. Questions such as "Who am I?" "How do I respond to others?" "How do I respond in this situation or that?" "How do I react to problems and pressures?" "What is the meaning of these responses?" "How does 'God's obedient child,' who knows what he is doing and rests the full weight of his hopes on Christ, see these issues and respond?" — these are the questions we need to help teens raise, and find answers to through living God's Word.

Examining life

I've attempted to explore the process of examining life in another book, *Creative Bible Study*. After giving a simple outline of the process, I'll provide a PROBE excerpt from that book which may illustrate the process and make the concept underlying the thoughts easier to grasp. But first, the process of "examining life."

Raising life to a conscious level   This is the first step in becoming Christian persons who "know what they are doing" and so respond obediently to Christ. Raising experiences and attitudes and feelings to a conscious level seldom happens "alone." Examination of life in most cases requires a Body relationship with other Christians (or a counseling relationship like that described in chapter 9). In relationship, certain of love and acceptance, we open ourselves up to one another.

It is doubly important, then, to build toward Body relationships in youth ministry, so that ideas and attitudes and feelings that are often repressed and hidden from others (and thus usually from ourselves!) can be expressed. Only what we expose to one another can we examine. Only what we can expose can we deal with on a conscious level.

Isolating concerns and issues   I suggested a bit ago that examining life involves asking probing questions about meaning. "How do I respond to this?" "Why?" "How am I as a Christian to understand this experience and respond?" As we begin to expose our lives and experiences to each other, we soon discover that we have many such concerns in common. Each of us, even though we are unique individuals, is bound up with others in a common bond of human experience. The Bible puts it this way: "No temptation has overtaken you that is not *common to man*" (1 Cor. 10:13 RSV). Individual situations may differ, but at the root are basic questions about life and meaning that are common to all. And so (as the PROBE excerpt will illustrate), one person's revelation of a need or experience is quickly seen by others as being *like* their own, and so stimulates their own sharing. As sharing and self-revelation take place, the basic questions that concern us can be isolated and defined. When we have formulated questions, then and only then can we come to God to seek His answers.

Explore reality as revealed in Scripture The Christian's conviction that God has revealed the meaning and purpose of life in His Word, and provided certain guidelines to experience of that meaning, directs our attention to the Word of God. When a shared concern has been expressed, a question about meaning formulated, we turn together to find answers and guidance and understanding in Scripture.

I've noted this earlier, but it's worth repeating. In ministry with youth we must help teens explore Scripture in a reality — or life-focused — context. For the Bible isn't merely a fund of facts to be mastered: it is God's unique revelation of the meaning and purpose and pattern of life in this world and the next.

Commitment to respond to God in faith When a shared concern has been expressed, and the biblical revelation searched to discover the reality which helps us understand its meaning for us, only obedience is an appropriate response. Not that the Christian sets out to "try" to do or feel what the Bible says he should do and feel. Rather, the Christian hears God's Word as invitation (see chapters 10 and 11), and with full confidence that Jesus Christ is able to do *in us* all that He commands *of us,* the believer responds to do God's Word — in faith.

These four processes (raising life to a conscious level in shared discussion of our experiences; isolating and defining concerns we have in common; seeking understanding and meaning in God's Word; and finally committing ourselves to respond as God's obedient children by acting in faith on His Word) are all involved in guiding young believers to a Christian involvement in life.

Programming involvement in life?

It should be clear from the above that youth are, daily, already involved in life. Thus, in one respect we do not need in youth ministry to "program" life-involvement. Instead, we need to provide opportunities for youth to explore the meaning of life as they are already experiencing it, to reshape their understanding and responses to the routine by God's Word.

At the same time, there are times that we want to provide an involvement in life as youth are *not* experiencing it. When we want to break out of the routine, to explore something which may be vital to a balanced understanding of life and its meaning. So we may program a trip to an Indian reservation, an opportunity for our teens to tutor inner-city children, a get-together with youth in a nearby mental institution, or (for some in the group) a summer overseas serving with a missionary of our church. In these experiences, too, the processes of exploring are important. And examination of the experiences is as vital as involvement in the experience itself.

In the next chapters we'll look at two special areas of youth's involvement in life that are linked closely with the uniqueness of the Christian faith (witness and service). But we should never overlook in our ministry with youth the central fact that our teens *are* involved in life, daily — and that a major concern of our ministry should be to help them explore and discover the meaning of their life as Christians, to experience the reality and freedom found only by bringing "every department of our lives" into full harmony with God.

PROBE
case histories
discussion questions
thought-provokers
resources

1. The following is an excerpt from my book, *Creative Bible Study*, (Zondervan, 1971) pp. 195-198, that may illustrate the process I've been suggesting. Several chapters in this book deal with the particular skills and approaches to Bible study needed to move from expressed concerns to discovery of meaning through God's Word.

   Life for all of us falls quickly into familiar patterns: patterns that become habits. But every now and then something happens that jolts us from our comfortable and familiar ways of life. We're forced to make new decisions, to respond to something unexpected. Or perhaps something we read makes us wonder about a pattern in our life.

   It's at times like these we need to define our experiences — into concerns.

   * * *

   There it was when Carl walked into the drive-in grocery! Right on the counter, where the kids from the nearby high school — and everyone else — couldn't miss seeing it. A whole stack of those magazines, with naked and near naked girls seductively posturing on the cover.

Upset, Carl grabbed the carton of milk he'd come into the store for, picked up an evening paper and paid the woman, wife of the middle-aged man who'd just taken over the franchise. Looking rather grim, uncertain about what to say or how to say it, Carl simply hurried out the door.

* * *

Exhausted, Mary slumped in her favorite chair beside the FM radio. She reached back to massage her neck: one of those horrible headaches was beginning. She felt its familiar probing; knew how easily it would become a pounding up toward the top of her head.

How many times had she and Amy argued this week? That girl! At sixteen she knew everything — and how she resented rules. Or even advice. "But she's young. So immature. She's *got* to listen. . . ."

It was so hard to know how to communicate. Even to know when a parent should set rules. Or the kind of rules. Kids had to learn to make decisions for themselves sometime.

Not everyone should be parents, Mary thought wryly. *Not people like me.* She reached over and turned on the FM, then leaned back, rotating her head rhythmically, hoping the headache would go away.

Life Stays With Us

Sometimes headaches do go away. But life doesn't. Life stays with us, and brings with it the unexpected situation — or the all-too-common one — that leaves us disturbed and shaken. How are we to respond to them? How do we handle uncertainty, doubt? The easy way is to try to avoid painful experiences, or to struggle to ignore them. Carl simply won't go into that store again. Mary, who has to live with her problem, will turn to soothing classics on FM in an attempt to forget the recurring arguments with her daughter, and dull the physical pain they cause.

Run away from it?

Ignore it?

We can try, of course. But life with all its realities rushes in on us again and again — and reminds us that, as Christians, we're called to live Christ's life *in* the world. In this world. This world of sin, of stress, of injustice, of pain, and of the unexpected experience that leaves us uncertain and confused.

Somehow the Christian can't afford to treat the painful as an occasion for retreat. To the Christian, each fresh experience is an invitation from God to learn more of Him, and to live more of Him.

The Bible is God's unique resource, given to help us transform uncertainty to opportunity and tragedy to triumph. Experiences like Carl's and Mary's are often given us by God to stimulate our growth; to lead us to Scripture and fresh discovery of reality as God knows it and as He wants us to express it in our lives. Rather than withdrawing from life's jolting experiences, we need to see them for what they are: God's invitations. Invitations we need to accept if we're to grow to maturity.

Invitation Accepted

How do we accept the invitations that God extends to each of us through the experiences of life? Basically, by defining our experiences as a concern, and bringing our concern to God, to search out His help in the Scriptures.

Defining experiences Experiences like Carl's and Mary's normally flood us with feelings. It's these feelings, feelings of frustration and futility, that we try to reduce by flight. Usually we're so busy trying to get away from them that we resist thinking about the experience that caused them. It was an unpleasant experience—too painful to dwell on.

But if we're to handle our feelings effectively, we need to face them. By coming to understand situations that give rise to such feelings, we can learn to respond positively, to reduce frustrations by creatively expressing God's will through our lives.

It's necessary, then, to relive painful experiences. I don't mean the way we often relive them — simply rerunning them to berate ourselves for supposed or real failures. I mean to relive them *in search of understanding*. To rethink the experience, to ask "why" of our feelings, to pose the kind of questions that will help us pierce to the core issues which the experience has raised.

Take a look again at Carl's experience. It's easy to see why he was upset and concerned. The moral deterioration of our society is all too obvious; the flaunting of sin as "personal freedom" and a "right" of the "mature adult" is all too common a hypocrisy. But there were other things that had added to Carl's jolting shock. He'd never seen that kind of magazine in the drive-in before. In fact, the last couple to run it, now returned to the laundry business in Denver, had chatted with him of their determination to keep the store a "family" one. Then, too, Carl felt some responsibility for his community, and for the high school (attended by his own son) just two blocks from the store. Still, he didn't feel free to infringe on the rights of the owners. He couldn't *demand* they remove the magazines. Or picket the store, or do any of the other things people do today to try to force their ideas and ways of life on others. And then, too, he wondered about a chance to witness to the new owners. He'd known the old ones well — even given them a couple of Christian books. Would his witness be helped or hurt if he said something about the magazines? Was it better to ignore them, with the intention of trying to become a friend first, and perhaps winning the owners to Christ?

All these thoughts flickered through Carl's consciousness, and, uncertain about the answers, blocked by his uncertainty from any positive action, Carl felt frustration — and ran. And the feeling of futility created by that frustrated retreat made the experience too painful to think about later.

But later is just the time to think about it. Later, when there's no pressure for immediate decision to frustrate us. Later, when there's time to sort out the issues and, with our questions defined, to search the Scripture for guidance.

As concerns If Carl had thought over his experience as we just have, and isolated some of the questions on which he needed God's viewpoint before he could work out his response to the new situation, his experience would have jelled into a *concern*. By a "concern" I mean a *formulated question about reality which can direct our search in Scripture for God's guidance in life*.

From Carl's experience at least two *concerns* arise: How am I as a Christian to relate to non-Christians? How am I as a Christian to respond to sin in my society?

We could follow the same process in Mary's experience with her daughter Amy. The swirl of questions about guidance, communication, rules, etc., that have overwhelmed her and so many others in our day may also be expressed as concerns: How am I as a parent to live with and guide my children?

In fact, *all our experiences,* as we grapple with them in search of understanding, can be defined as concerns. And this definition can lead us into fruitful, purposeful Bible study.

2. **Ross Snyder has spoken of exploring and interpreting experience in the book quoted at the beginning of this chapter. Here are two excerpts that may be helpful in adding meaning to the concepts I've expressed in this chapter (emphasis added).**

A lived moment is not just frantic activity, a rushing from one situation of programmed sensations to another. Nor is it identical with working ourselves up till we and those around us are "high."

A lived moment is a peak experience. Where we experience, somewhat intensely, "I AM." And creation — rather than mere excitement — is coming off. Something new is coming out of everyday mud, so at the moment I am no longer on my way to becoming a clod or froth.

A lived moment is *lived*. Someone is within it — enduring it, tasting it, being expanded or shriveled, enlivened or deadened by it. And — interpreting its meaning. That someone is you.

For *what* happens is not so important as how we interpret it, i.e., what it means. The issue always is, not that nobody waved goodbye, but, "What does it mean? What does it mean to be *me* — this particular fellow — to whom nobody waved goodbye when I ran?"

A lived moment always involves a *selfed* body. It is not a happening of startled molecules, but an event in which *a person* is manufacturing meaning. To be filled with undigested "experiences," with lived moments that never had a chance to grow up, is a self-imposed version of the rat race so prevalent in our civilization.

Interpreting a firsthand experience is an important part of living it.

We are built to process moment into meaningful moment. A *human* being has to have a meaningful world in which to exist, and meanings to select out and tune his actions. He has to be the *poetry* of the present, not just the present. Spelling out implications of this emphasis on not only having lived moments, but developing meaning out of them, is much of this book.

At a time when masscomm's flood — radio, TV, the movie, the printed page — is replacing *primary* experiences (those we have in face-to-face encounter and in bringing off enterprises *we* plan) with secondary encounters consisting of blips on a picture screen and page, *lived moments* become overwhelmingly important. For otherwise we live deprived lives, with contrived feelings and packaged interpretations we have been sold. The images and symbols which master our behaviors will not bubble up out of our own creative springs, but will be inserted by him who sells and therefore masters us. And we will never know what *is* real.

Our creative imagination must be stirred by the lived moments of *our* living. Then we will be all one piece, and a work of indigenous art. *Our* lives will be saturated with meaning.

Phenomenologizing

We also find it very helpful to acquire the skills of phenomenologizing. Which is a disciplined way of doing what we are doing most of the time in a very fragmentary way — i.e., trying to grasp what *really* happened in an experience, and what it tells us about ourselves and what life is about.

Some experiences seem unusually full of "more than meets the eye." Such lived moments are worth nurturing in such a way that we develop what is *within* them.

The first step is to describe as fully as possible exactly what happened as it happened. Don't put any judgments upon the good or bad of what happened or the people involved. Just be a scientist and describe this *particular* lived moment.

But do include what went on "inside" you. For that is a crucial part of your story of what happened. It is being honest enough to make clear that your story is always the lived moment *as you saw it, as you experienced it. Your story is not — and cannot be — an impartial, objective account that everyone would know about. And therefore, you must include what feelings you had as the situation developed, the flow of attitudes and intendings you were acting out. You try for the fullest and most accurate account of the lived moment as it was experienced by you, as it appeared to you within it.*

You can do this by writing it out, or by telling it to a "receiving" listener, whose function in the conversation is to help you clarify to yourself what went on — particularly within you.

The second step is this. With this documentation of its immediacies before you, you try to determine, *"What kind of transaction was going on here? What would I name it? What made this the kind of lived moment it was? What processes were going on?"* You are still sticking to what was really within this particular experience. You are trying to comprehend what was here — what its pattern and line of development was. Was it, for instance, really an act of injustice? Was it love — or naive excitement?

From looking at and naming this particular experience, *you are forced to work on "What is love, anyway? Just anything anybody calls 'love'? No." As best you can, from this experience and that of other people, you try for a picture of the processes which love is — anytime, anyplace.* So that you can understand and handle *many* situations, novel situations you have never before been in. So that you will not be sold the spurious article and be played games with.

Working along the lines of this first and second step of phenomenologizing, Gabriel Marcel did a memorable job on "what is involved in being *with,* rather than *alongside* another person?" Kierkegaard worked out what dread is, and the process of becoming an authentic person rather than a phony.

Max Scheler's analysis of the process of resentment is a famous achievement of this second step of phenomenologizing. It enables us to understand many things that happen in this world. And to heal resentment in ourselves and the social scene — if healing is desired (most of the time it isn't).

Step two, then, is an attempt to see the *basic* processes that are at work in the lived moment. To discover what processes *make* certain kinds of life worlds — loneliness, communion, expansion of consciousness, the lived moment of choosing, of celebrating, of arting. Always, phenomenologizing is penetrating into *what is.*

In this second step, we also reflect upon what this experience reveals about us. About our dynamics and the way we are organized. Such as catching —

> the particular mixture of good and evil, of defeat and success that I was here;
>
> what I really want out of life — as revealed by what I did here;
>
> the kind of sensitivities I have, as revealed by the way my conscience hurts and thrusts me toward fresh growing;
>
> what I am true to: what is true to me;
>
> what is my truth? When does it come out?

3. It is of interest to note that what I've suggested in this chapter gives us a distinctive *starting point* and approach to Bible study. Good Sunday school curriculums do focus study on issues that are particularly relevant to the life of teens. And the process in good materials begins with an effort to help the youth feel the "concerns" that will be spoken to in the selected Bible passages. Yet the passages are necessarily chosen before the learning situation develops, and without reference to the *particular* present concerns and experiences of the group or class.

The process outlined in this chapter, however, begins always with the present and particular concerns of each group or class. Life itself raises the issues, demanding that youth struggle with them to frame definitions of what concerns them. For this, a facilitating Body relationship is important, and the motive for searching the Scripture highly personal and compelling.

Both of these approaches have a valid place in our ministry with youth. It is important, however, to be aware of the fundamental differences that exist between them, the limitations and the particular skills and approaches needed for each. If you are interested in exploring the concepts underlying each approach, and the techniques appropriate to each situation, you may want to look at my *Creative Bible Teaching* (communicating in the class situation) and *Creative Bible Study* (communicating in the small group, life-focused situation).

15

the sharing life

From the earliest days of the Church, believers in Christ "went throughout the country, preaching the good news of the message" of the Gospel (Acts 8:4 *Phillips*). And each new company of believers established by the early apostles became "a sort of sounding board from which the Word of the Lord has rung out" (I Thess. 1:7 *Phillips*). Paul's awareness that God had in Jesus Christ "reconciled us to himself" was accompanied by a deep conviction that this same God had made him—and us—"agents of the reconciliation." (2 Cor. 5:18 *Phillips*). Central to the meaning of the Christian's life is the experience of sharing Jesus Christ with others.

Young people in evangelical churches are aware that witnessing is not only expected of professional Christian workers and adults — it's also expected of *them*. But our young people, for a variety of reasons, are not sharing Christ. The enthusiasm, the spontaneity, the naturalness of talking with others about a relationship with God that has deep personal meaning for us, isn't part of the normal experience of our Christian youth.

And this is of deep concern in youth ministry. Part of the meaning of being a Christian is found in identifying ourselves with Christ's great purpose, to bring persons into relationship with God, discovering in the Savior forgiveness of sins and freedom from bondage to sin's warping power. Because God reaches out to others to offer a great and free salvation, we, as God's children, are called to reach out to them also, sharing with them God's invitation to the present experience of eternal life.

The Gospel is reality. Our call as agents of reconciliation is reality. So youth cannot know life in its full abundance until they find identity with the divine and compelling reality that is the good news of Jesus Christ — for all.

In a three-year study involving over 3,000 teens and twenties in evangelical churches in this country and Canada, a number of barriers to personal evangelism — this sharing of Christ's life with others — were discovered.[1] Over 95 percent of the teens indicated

---

[1]The study was done under my supervision by a number of successive graduate and undergraduate classes in youth ministry at Wheaton.

279

that *they* (not just adults) ought to witness. But most of them honestly admitted that they were not, in person-to-person confrontation, speaking with others about personal relationship to Jesus Christ. The young people had been *told* they *ought* to witness; but rather than responding to the church's exhortation, they found a number of reasons why they could not. The demand of "ought" was unable to motivate response, even when youth accepted the demand as reasonable and right.

What were some of the reasons youth advanced for failure to witness? The reason most often mentioned was fear. There was a deep concern for what other kids would think. Potential ridicule, fear of making a fool of oneself, uncertainty about acceptance if they should speak of Jesus Christ in personal relationship terms, all loomed large in youth's decisions to remain silent. Knowing the power of the peer group (see chapters 2 and 5), and youth's need to belong, we can be sympathetic with such doubts and fears.

A second reason youth advanced was lack of "know-how." "I wouldn't know how to begin," or "I wouldn't know what to do if someone asked questions," or "I don't know enough Bible verses," appeared on the majority of papers. While teens could point to training classes in the church, to role-play experiences in youth group, and even to Sunday school units on "how to witness," they felt totally inadequate for the task. The concept of witness as a simple sharing of what Christ means to them as persons, of an introduction of one friend to another, seemed foreign.

A third problem that loomed large was a lack of relationship with non-Christians. Few teens who responded spoke of non-Christian *friends.* Many explicitly said they "didn't know any unsaved kids well enough to speak to them" about Christ. Like their elders, the associations of Christian young people were often circumscribed by the church crowd. Knowing others than these as friends — the kind of friends who come over to your home or who you hang around with when you have free time — was unusual.

A final problem was a sense of aloneness. Nearly all the teens expressed a belief that other Christian young people ought to witness, too — but nearly all said also, "If I were to witness I'd be the only one around doing it." The obligation of involvement in personal evangelism is something all give lip service to. And something most do *not* carry over in action.

280

Each of these barriers is a serious one. Together they cut our young people off from an experience that is part of the meaning of a Christian's life. God has called us to Christ, to know Him and love Him, and to invite others to know and love Him, too. We find part of our identity as Christians through participating in Christ's own love for others, and expressing that love to them in witness to our Savior and Lord. Anyone concerned that youth become involved as Christians in life must, then, seek to involve them in personal evangelism.

But as we minister with youth we need to recognize the barriers that exist. Rather than urging and demanding, "Witness!," we need to find ways to guide teens into a healthy experience of the sharing life.

How can we overcome the barriers? What's involved in leading teens to witness?

Motivation I've suggested before in this book that the "ought" motivation is both ineffective and unchristian. What is capable of motivating teens to share Christ with others — and what motivation is appropriate?

In the first place, our motivation is to be Christ's motivation: *love*. Christ died for us, because He *cared*. A few of the kids who responded to the study on which this chapter is based mentioned a love motivation: "I want to witness, because I want my friends to have what I have." When witnessing is seen as meeting the deepest need of a person we've come to care about, it's removed from the realm of "duty" and becomes "desire." And to the extent that we care about the persons we share Christ with, we begin to operate with the motivation of God.

Sometimes we can "care" for people in the abstract. "Everybody ought to know," is a chorus we've often sung. And who can deny it? But God hasn't placed us next to everybody. He has placed us next to certain individuals and called us to care concretely for *them*. So we are to develop concern for the people we know, and come to love them more as we get to know them better. Love not only *calls for* involvement with others; it *is called out* by involvement with others. So one of the first effective steps toward helping teens witness is helping them come to know, as friends, unsaved persons. Rather than fighting against involvement with non-Christians — as many evangelical churches still do — we need to encourage involvement, and train our teens to develop love for kids still outside of

Christ. This approach, taken by Chuck Miller (see pages 246 and 247) led to twelve to fifteen *"generations"* of believing teens in just eighteen months!

The suggestion that the church encourage Christian kids to develop friendships with non-Christians reflects a basic concept of communicating Christ. For all the impact of mass media on communication in our modern world, few young people are reached for Christ by impersonal, one-way communication. The older "Youth For Christ" rallies of the fifties that emphasized mass evangelism have been replaced by an "each one reach one" strategy. Today the most effective communicator of Jesus Christ to a young person is another young person, who will love him and in person-to-person relationship share the reality of Christ. Thus all that I said earlier about the importance of a model, of someone to incarnate the reality of biblical truths so they can be tested and seen to be real, is totally relevant to evangelism. And the primary context for communicating Christ is one formed by friendship.

Motivation for sharing Christ, then, grows out of developing personal relationships with non-Christians and learning to love them for Christ's sake.

The love motivation in witness is, however, as much vertical as horizontal. Love for others takes on evangelistic meaning only when it is balanced by love for Christ as well. Thus an effective witnessing emphasis in youth ministry presupposes that, through involvement in Scripture and Body relationships, young people are growing in their own relationship with the Lord. As one of my friends emphasizes, "Witness must be the overflow of a life that Jesus has filled up." Jesus said, "The man who believes in me, as the scripture said, will have rivers of living water flowing from his inmost heart" (John 7:38 *Phillips*).

A third aspect of motivation for witness is found in the fact that motivation grows *through experience.* In most cases involvement in an experience is a precondition for motivation. Thus, as I tried to illustrate in PROBE, Chapter 3, we need to take teens out to witness with us, not tell them to go out and do it on their own.

Part of the freeing power of experiencing God's truth is that, as we become involved in reality, the Holy Spirit's touch testifies that this is the life — that this is "where it's at" for us. To many young people and adults, motivation for witness has come through being in a situation where you somehow *had* to speak out — and discovered in the speaking the excitement and joy that sharing Christ brings. Thus Dave Roper in the PROBE report of helping kids start witnessing found that their response to the experience was, "Hey, that was great! Let's do it again!" In their speaking out for Christ, the Holy Spirit authenticates the fact that this is one source of meaning and purpose in the life of believers.

A final aspect of motivation is found in group support. The knowledge that others are witnessing too, the opportunity to share experiences, the chance to pray together and encourage each other in this expression of the Christian life, is vital. And so once again we're driven back to the Body relationship, *the* context for support and encouragement and stimulation to live Christ's life in the world.

We can begin to build motivation for witness as a natural expression of the Christian's life, then, by (1) developing a balanced ministry in which Christian young people are growing in their own relationship with God, (2) encouraging personal involvement and the development of friendships with non-Christian kids, (3) providing opportunities to share Christ by "going along with" others, gradually becoming involved, and (4) providing a supportive Body relationship with other Christian kids who are committed to and personally active in sharing Christ themselves.

Know-how The basic solution to lack of witnessing know-how is also found in experience. One philosophy of education has it that persons should be provided with knowledge and information *before* they become involved in situations where they need to use it. Another philosophy suggests that knowledge and information should be provided as necessary, concurrently with involvement. There's little doubt that the latter is usually best for developing skill in witness. Training classes that focus on providing "techniques" before involvement in witnessing experiences often prove *demotivating*. It's best to seek, as Roper did, to let witness experiences provide a "need to know" motivation that blends the learning with the living.

Lack of friends I've already spoken of this final category. One of our greatest needs in youth ministry is to encourage the development of friendships with non-Christians on the campus and in the neighborhood — friendships which, when the teen is a growing believer, become the context for sharing Christ.

The need to encourage development of such friendships raises many questions of programming in the local church, which we'll look at in the next section of this book and in PROBE. But for the

283

moment it is important to note that the church definitely needs to correlate its programming of youth activities with those of the school and community. And the church needs to plan ways to support individuals in their campus involvements — ways that will help them find opportunities to share Christ with their friends.

Helping young people witness, and so become involved in a vital dimension of living the Christian life, is one of the basic goals of effective youth ministry. There are many barriers to witness that cut evangelical youth off from this rewarding experience, and thus from balanced growth as Christian persons. But the barriers can be overcome. Supported by a balanced ministry which meaningfully involves teens in Scripture and in Body relationships with one another, our young people can be guided into the sharing life.

PROBE
case histories
discussion questions
thought-provokers
resources

1. One area touched on in this chapter is that of structuring activities to support the sharing life. The following letter, written by Dave Roper, youth minister at Peninsula Bible Church in Palo Alto, California, describes an approach he developed and used through the 60's. It gives a valuable picture of a broad approach to programming to encourage outreach and evangelism.

    Dear Marshall:
    Thanks for your note and your interest in our ministry here at Peninsula Bible Church. I hope that we can be some help in supplying information for the project that you mentioned.
    In order to save time and cover all the bags, it would probably be best to use the same outline and categories you suggested. So here goes . . .

    I. Description of special evangelistic projects

    A. *Best Deal.* We take over the Young Life clubs in the area during the summer and operate under the name of *Best Deal.* We change the format somewhat, have swim parties, barbecues, hootenannies, what have you. We call them "parties with a purpose." We try to flex with the crowd, and do whatever interests them currently. Right now surfing is the fad, so we are planning a "seminar in the sand" (the kids call it a "screech at the beach"). What we do is immaterial. The purpose is to expose non-Christian kids in the area to Jesus Christ.
    During the winter we try to have two or three reunions before our *Best Deal Retreat* after Christmas. Actually, this year we have been pressed for time and could have only one re-

union. We feel that we should have had more, to keep our contacts hot.

We have to depend on the kids to bring their friends. We discourage coming alone, but it happens anyway. We encourage them to be frontal and tell their non-Christian guests what it is all about. We have found pagan kids don't mind coming to a "religious" meeting if they are forewarned and if they expect to have a good time anyway, but they resent being brought under false pretenses.

Teenagers will put up with a lot if things are done on their level and in a *qualitative way*. I can't stress the latter too much! Everything has to be up to snuff with the high school crowd around here. Perhaps Mr. Hendricks has told you of the unique community that we serve. We draw predominantly from the Stanford community and kids here are used to the *best*. I feel that this is true of the high school community across the country these days. Kids are bone tired of the half-hearted attempts of the church to reach them. They simply are not impressed. So, at least here on the coast, they stay away from church. It's tragic, but the simple fact of life. In order to reach them we have to win their respect and the right to tell them of Christ. In short, the principle seems to be   keep it at their level and keep it sharp!

The program of *Best Deal* is flexible, but our messages *are consistently on the Person of Christ and His ability to meet every need that these kids face in their world*. We don't try to be brief or breezy, but to lay the facts on the line. Again, Marshall, I am convinced that teenagers do not want to be entertained and pampered. They want to know how to get the most out of life. We just tell them which way the Lord is going, and if they want to have complete realization in their lives, they need to go with Him.

B. *Young Life*. During the school year we encourage our church kids to get behind their *Young Life* clubs in their own schools. *Young Life* has done a tremendous job here, and we want to support them in any way possible. We are not interested in peddling P.B.C. (Peninsula Bible Church), and it is immaterial what church they land in, as long as they are getting fed. So we encourage our youngsters to bring their friends to *Young Life*, support their campaigners, and find that our kids have really rallied around the thing. It seems silly to me to try to crank up a competing evangelistic effort in a high school where *Young Life* is already working. If they are weak, we can give them help, and I have found that they really appreciate it.

C. *International Dinners*. We have had these on the college level and decided last year to try one for the high school students (exchange students) in the area. This is not strictly an evangelistic effort, as we did not present a Gospel message at the dinner, but it is an opportunity for our kids to form friendships that lead to opportunities. International students cannot be pushed, and there has to be a prolonged friendship before they open up, so we want to provide some sort of time where these friendships can be started. We are planning another next month; this one to be a dinner, but one prepared by the internationals for us. It is shaping up to be real exciting. We keep them small and hand pick our sharpest, more mature high school kids to be there.

D. *Snow trips.* A fellow here in the area has given us the use of his cabin in the Sierras for short week-end snow trips. We take along 15 or 20 kids and spend the time skiing and loafing around the cabin. We try to take up several non-Christians for exposure to the other Christian kids and personal contact. We have two of these planned for this winter.

E. *Wilderness camps.* I wrote an article on this in the March, 1963, *Christian Camps and Conferences* magazine. It will give you more detail than I can in the letter. It's called "Rewards of Wilderness Camping." I can tell you that there are plenty!! I wish that I could do this full time. It's really simple. We take a handful of fellows and spend a week with them in the Sierras. We try to pick young people that are in need of some personal follow-up and move in with a special invitation to go fishing with us and then *make hay*. Ray Stedman and Bob Smith started this here at P. B. C. about four or five years ago, and we are becoming more sold every year. The article will fill you in on the details. I'm sure that the library has a copy. If not, CCCA can send you one.

F. *Retreats.* We have high school retreats every winter. This year we held an outreach conference: *Best Deal* Retreat. It is nothing new or novel. We asked every Christian kid coming to bring a non-Christian buddy and, if possible, to pay his way. We have a few scholarships available, if they need help. However, we use these only as a last resort. We feel it is a part of their ministry to these people to fork over the cash. These retreats run over a long weekend and are pretty much like any high school conference. We keep them free and uncluttered; usually have only two meetings a day, but plenty of time for counselors to move in on a personal basis. They are *some fun* and highly productive, as they often seal decisions that have been on the back burner for months. Again, we try to get top resource people. Most of the counselors are kids from our college class or the *Young Life* volunteer staff. We import speakers from outside. There are a number of excellent camp sites in the Santa Cruz Mountains behind Palo

Alto and, of course, Mount Hermon is right up the hill and is very good for this sort of thing.

G. *Backyard conferences.* We are doing some thinking now on a new approach for this Spring, utilizing what we call "backyard conferences." We got the idea from International Christian Leadership and their work with Christian businessmen and leaders in government. We are putting together a team of sharp high school kids to bring to breakfasts and evening meetings where they can give their testimony in an informal way, and then have a free-for-all discussion afterwards. Mr. Robinson could probably fill you in on details and the way that these groups work. We are very active in ICL here, and it seems that this approach is workable with high school kids. We'll be giving it a little more definition as we work together on the idea.

II. Evaluation of evangelistic projects

A. *Purpose and Goal.* We call these approaches "evangelistic aids," because we realize the real work of evangelism is done on a man-to-man basis, not by blasting away in a crowd. This is true at all age levels, but particularly so with the high school gang. We want our own church kids to *use these programs as springboards into personal discussions about the Christian faith.* As they drive home, or see their friends during the week, they may have an opportunity to refer to something that was said or a personal testimony or something similar, and then relate to their own experience. In short, we want to make it easier for our own kids to witness to their friends. Some teenagers make a decision for Christ through a message delivered to the group, but the largest percentage of decisions come from personal follow-up either by one of our kids or an adult leader.

B. *Problems.* Man . . . where do I start?

1. Gaining support of teenagers in the church. They are scared silly at first. Afraid of all sorts of things, but primarily afraid of failure. They think the program will be a flop and that they will be embarrassed. They think that no one will come. At least at first this is true. The key, of course, is to gain their involvement. Let them plan the programs, suggest speakers, etc. They have terrible ambivalence, however. They think that they can do everything, and therefore thousands of kids will come and have a great time. On the other hand, they don't think that they can do anything, and the thing will be one big flop. So they must be involved, and they must have lots of adult help and reassurance. I won't belabor the point. I'm sure that you know this as

well as I do. Anyway, involve them and teach them how to walk by faith.

Our biggest problem is that we just don't *really* expect God to do anything. (Since . . . they can see through adults like a pane of glass, it doesn't take them long to be unbelieving believers, as well.) So you walk by faith and teach them that God is expecting them to move out and be used.

2. Attitudes of parents. If you start evangelizing, you are going to have pagan kids all over the church, and most Christians don't really want that. The natives get contaminated. Actually, we don't have this problem here. We can thank the Lord for a group of people dedicated to the idea that God put us in this community to build bridges to non-Christian folk and bring these people into a relationship to Jesus Christ. It is refreshing, Marshall. I hope that you men get into an outfit where you will have the freedom to move and experiment and know people are behind you and praying for your kids.

3. Leadership. We have a real need for dedicated, training leadership. I'm not talking about bow-tie cuties. We have a bunch of those here on the West Coast. I mean men who are willing to sweat and pray over high school kids; who will take the time to get on their wave length. I don't really know, Marshall, what makes a good youth worker. I usually go to a prospective worker with two lists of qualifications: one a list of *absolute* prerequisites, such as faithfulness, teachableness, harmoniousness, and personal spiritual experience; the other a list of *desirable* qualifications, such as training and experience. I think, Marshall, we can teach a person anything, but only the Holy Spirit can motivate. We look for the man who wants to move and has the necessary spiritual qualification first, and then go from there.

4. Quality. I mentioned this before. There's always the tendency to let down our guard and get sloppy. It's the beginning of the end when we do. Did you ever listen to kids comment on one of their own? Almost everything they say, has to do with appearances. "That looks good" is a favorite expression. Things have to *look good* to a teenager. He is not so concerned with reality (we are) as with appearance. So we show him how the two are related. Things look good because they *are* good. This is hard to sell when we just slam something together at the last minute.

5. Church relationship. This is not really a good definitive

term for what I have on my mind. What I am talking about is the ability to maintain an aloofness to your own church groups when you go out to reach pagan kids. I stated earlier that our public image may smell. So we have to divorce ourselves from any local church and just go after kids as interested members of the community. We never mention P. B. C. at these programs, unless someone asks us where we come from, or who is sponsoring the event. We are not trying to be devious, but just want to allay any suspicions. We have to instruct our kids on this, as well. We are not interested primarily in getting kids to come to P. B. C. *We want to win them to Christ first.* Our allegiance is to Him, not any local church body. *We sell this hard.*

There are a couple of things that run parallel to this. We have found that kids do end up here at P. B. C. as a result of these evangelistic activities. In fact, right now the hard core of our high school group is made up of kids who met the Lord the last couple of years. However, in order to integrate these raw kids into a church environment, we have to make several adjustments. We don't soft-pedal the teaching ministry, but we do try to be as non-churchy as possible. We call our group the Koinonia Kampus Klub (not the P. B. C. High School Group.) We have little calling cards printed up with the name of the group. (I've enclosed one.) We pass them out to kids, if they are interested. We call our evening group "The Huddle," not a training hour. We don't get together and entertain each other on Sunday evenings. We meet to plan for action (hence the name "huddle"). We prepare for assignments — planning *Best Deal,* working on creative projects, preparing a children's church program, visiting kids that are out on the fringe, doing work around the church, such as maintenance, etc., preparing a program for a rest home. The whole idea, Marshall, is that we want to challenge kids — not entertain them. We have a great big banner on the wall of the high school room. The thing reaches from one wall to the other, and in bright red letters three feet high it says, "THE EXTRA MILE." That's our theme this year. We want to stretch these kids all over the place. Give them realistic, honest-to-goodness opportunities to minister, and not just play church.

I'm sure there are other things I might say along these lines. There are plenty of problems, not the least of which is the initial inertia that you have to overcome. I think it is essential in youth work that we be flexible and keep our programs terminal. By that I mean that we give everything to one program for a while, and then shake everything up and start over to rethink the whole system. We want to be free to try new approaches and allow the Lord to lead us into new areas of experience. I think unless we do that, we tend to get swept into some little eddy and miss the main stream of God's purpose for us. Frankly, we want to know where He is going, and we want to be part of the program He has mapped out. In short, we want to follow Him. To do this, I feel we must stay alert and be willing to flex as He directs.

III. Our thinking concerning:

A. *Fundamental need of high school group* (I assume you mean outside of the church?).

1. Acceptance by Christians for what they are! They smoke, drink, and in general, raise hell. So what! So would I if I did not know Christ. Let's love them (which is really what the Lord commanded us to do first) and gain the right to expose them to Christ's love.

2. A relevant faith. Most of our presentation of the gospel is so irrelevant that they never see any need. Most of our kids out here are jaded and disillusioned by life. They need to know of the "saving life of Christ" and His willingness to make them all they know they should be.

3. Challenge. I've already commented on this.

4. Dedicated adult leadership. I wonder if you saw the questionnaire that Scripture Press circulated on why teenagers have dropped out of churches across the nation. One answer that kept cropping up with embarrassing consistency was, "There was no reality in the lives of our leaders." I am speaking of leaders who are willing to go where they are and do what they do in order to win a hearing.

B. *Basic problem of reaching high school group.* I think it grows out of the natural antipathy of adults and youth. They live in two different worlds. Each one thinks of the other as a problem. The adults are trying to foist their standards on the kids. The kids are just faceless idiots racing down Middlefield Road. Neither tries to take the trouble to get to know and understand the other. The kids can't, the adults won't. I feel we have to take the initiative and build the bridges. We have to find out who they are and what they want and why, and then win their respect. I really think, Marshall, that young people are nothing but a big problem to most Christians. They wring their hands and talk and write books and forget the basic principle that the Lord employed when He chose twelve to be *"with* Him." How can we hope to do His work unless we do it His way? How in the world can we share our lives with kids without getting next to them and getting to know them and their real needs and problems?

C and D I think I've covered in earlier portions of this letter. It's hard to evaluate spiritual success. You sure can't do it by numbers. I think we equate size and success too much. The Lord said the really significant group is where two or three are gathered together. I feel the Lord has been teaching us this here. We have large numbers of kids out to some of our meetings, and we have an opportunity to expose a lot of kids to the Gospel. But the really significant work is being done by individuals and couples and small groups who are taking time to work with a few kids on a qualitative and quantitative basis.

2. Campus Life (Youth for Christ) has been very much concerned about development of a contemporary and personal approach to penetration of the high schools of our country. The following expression of this strategy, developed for the Fox Valley, Illinois, area, is included because it speaks to several signficant issues.

    My own observation of the program is that success of the strategy depends on the amount of *personal involvement time* given by leaders. The greatest weakness in practice seems to be too much reliance on the Insight and Impact group meetings, which cast the C.L. personnel in "leader" and "meeting director" roles rather than as the "person with."

IN-DEPTH PENETRATION OF THE HIGH SCHOOL THROUGH CAMPUS LIFE

There are nearly fifty public and private high schools in the Fox Valley area, each with its own unique personality and character. Each has its own traditions, its strengths and weaknesses, its own set of problems. But all of the high schools share one common denominator — the American adolescent. He may enjoy the benefits of his father's executive salary, or he may be struggling with his parents to gain indentity with the affluent. Usually he is active in some level of the school's society. And, in Fox Valley, he is at this point unaffected by Campus Life.

Let's say that the average high school population for any given school might be around 2000 students. In the fifteen or so clubs in Fox Valley, the average attendance runs between 20 and 30. Simple arithmetic tells us that no more than 1% of that school's population is coming in contact with the message of Campus Life. That's not what Campus Life is all about. So, let's attempt to examine the campus more closely so that we can have a basis for devising an effective strategy for campus evangelism.

One convenient way might be to analyze the school on the basis of its social groups: the "rahs," the "greasers," the "jocks," the "nobodies." That sort of stereotyping has its drawbacks, so let's look at the campus from another perspective. Let's divide the school into *interest* groups, for it's here that we find the basis for much of the school's social organization and for much of its *organized* activity.

A very easily identified group would be the sports crowd, all those guys who concentrate on athletics as their primary activity and the gals who associate with them. Along with them we have the cheerleaders and pep club gals many of whom are social leaders. Musically-oriented students make up another interest group as well as those Thespians who secret themselves on rehearsal stages. We might also consider the producers of the school newspaper and the yearbook as a publications group. Also apparent is that group of students either elected or appointed to positions in student government. And, in the 70's, we must also consider the rise of organized student minority groups striving to assert their identity in the campus world, particularly blacks and Chicanos. On the average campus of 2000 students, these interest groups might represent the number of students shown in the following table:

Interest Groups in the Population of the Average High School

GROUP	#	GROUP	#
Sports	200	Cheerleaders, Pep Club	50-100
Music	400	Student Government	50
Publications	50	Drama	25
Minority	(?)		

The important thing to remember about these groups is that they are often the influential groups on campus, and they are often led by highly influential and socially capable students — the kind of students that we need to involve in Campus Life. Therefore, any strategy we project must take into consideration these interest groups and their leaders if we are to effectively reach the populace of our area's high schools.

THE STRATEGY

Our strategy begins with and depends on the efforts of both paid and volunteer staff. Without their leadership and commitment to the exciting goal of in-depth penetration of the campus with the Gospel, we cannot succeed. Therefore, our efforts should first be directed toward recruiting volunteer staff who will be able to infiltrate these campus interest groups. We recruit by saying to the administrators of Wheaton College and to its students something like this:

> "We need three more guys in the Glenbards who can make meaningful contact with the wrestlers on that campus."
> "We need two gals at Willowbrook, one to build rapport with

the cheerleaders and the other to develop a ministry with some of the music students."

"Could you help us as a guy with ideas about student government and a commitment to sharing your faith? We need your help in developing a ministry with the kids in Student Council at Wheaton North."

Fox Valley should recruit volunteer staff with skills and abilities in the interest groups we have discussed, and those staff members should be assigned to the campus where they will be most effective.

STAFF AND CAMPUS CONTACT

As you would suppose, our efforts should be directed to penetrating every interest group on the campus. Obviously there will be overlap among these groups; but each campus will have its prominent interest groups, and we will have to tailor our staff to align with those interest groups. Let's break this down to see how it should work on one campus. At Glenbard East, a school of nearly 3,400 students, Campus Life has had a checkered history of modest success and glaring failure. The club suffers from real image problems and in the past has had strained relationships with school administrators. Last spring, however, a renewed effort was made to build the club and its image. By the end of school, relationships with the administration had been improved, and the club gained momentum with a noticeable attendance increase. Looking at the staff we see that the leader, Bill, has a special interest in both student government and dramatics, while Jim is particularly interested in the Insight crowd. Jean is a college cheerleader, while Jan has no specific interest group. A quick sample of the core group reveals that several list music, sports, and drama as their primary interest, a couple list pep club, and one mentions publications. No one indicates a primary interest in cheerleading, student government, or minority groups. On another level, the group can be characterized by largely evangelical-church-oriented kids (environmentals) with a subsidiary group of Catholic teens who are vitally interested in the success of the club.

Obviously, the staff must begin to make contact with students involved in cheerleading, student government, and minority groups. Bill could develop a ministry with student government kids, and Jean could build a relationship with the cheerleaders. For Bill this would probably mean contacting the student body president and sharing with him the club idea, and then possibly setting up an appearance at the next student council meeting to talk to all of its representatives. Contact with the sponsoring faculty member is vitally important, for as we gain his confidence in who we are and what we're doing to help kids, that confidence will spread to students in that interest group and other faculty members. It will also be necessary for Bill to develop a good rapport with the class leaders, so that he will have a well-balanced source of contact with those students involved in student government, key kids on any campus. Jean will probably begin with a casual contact with one of the cheerleaders or be introduced by one of the club core girls who has a friend in that group. She could work out with the cheerleaders and perhaps offer her services to be of assistance to them at games. Building a good relationship with the faculty women who sponsor the cheerleaders is important here, too, and she will need to overcome any threat that she might be to the authority position of the sponsor. Since only from five to ten minority students attend East, contact has been more difficult. Yet, the recruitment of one black volunteer staff could be instrumental in involving these students in Campus Life. This same staff member could also develop a ministry with some of the sports crowd if he is able. And, perhaps one more staff person would be needed to strengthen the contact with the music group at East. What we have attempted to show is that a new level of in-depth penetration can be reached when staff members are conscientiously chosen on the basis of their ability to relate to and have a ministry with a particular interest group. The quality of that ministry must be characterized as person-to-person.

How do members of the staff make contact with students? There are several tried and proven ways for them to make contact with students on their assigned campus. The WALK THRU is perhaps the most basic and useful of all the campus contact techniques. The staff member picks his time to visit the campus at the time when he will see the largest number of students, usually directly after school. He will probably arrive just a few minutes before school ends so that he can drop in to see the principal or other administrator, or perhaps visit a teacher. Through an appointment card signed by a teen at club or because he has called a particular student, the staff member arranges to meet individual students at appointed times after school. Sometimes it will be a CHECK-UP in which the staff member checks up on the progress of a new Christian or core kids in the club. Often, he will be meeting with some teens to simply share with them about Campus Life in an effort to gain their involvement. Eventually, he will know many students by sight and give them a casual "hi." The important thing to remember, however, is that with each contact the staff member makes on campus, students become more and more aware that here is an adult that cares enough to try to get the feel of their world and to be available to them in their world, the high school campus.

SPORTS ACTIVITIES of all kinds provide a natural setting for contact with teens. Many staff members will probably take one of their club guys with them to the game and join right in with the screaming crowd.

The staff member's contact routine must also include occasional visits to the pastors of local churches where club kids attend. Important aims of his church contacting are to build the church's confidence in him, to gain contact with their teens, and to provide a vital communication link between the Campus Life program and the church.

Another source of contact with teens is appointments made with key guys and girls as you drive them to club or take them home. Much ground can be covered as you have a casual and private conversation en route to or from club.

THE CLUB

An examination of a club like that of Glenbard East and many others in Fox Valley reveals an interesting fact. As you can see in Figure 8, essentially the same core kids provide the bulk of attendance at both Insight and Impact. Nearly all of the twenty-five or so core kids attend Insight and only about five more students other than core kids attend Impact. In other words, we have a secret meeting of the saints called Campus Life that doesn't attract any more than five or ten non-Christian or, at least non-Campus Life, students, to its major evangelistic thrust, the Impact meeting.

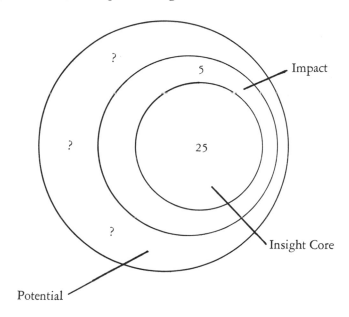

FIGURE 8

As we have said, that isn't effective penetration. Admittedly, our person-to-person contact with various kids in the interest groups will considerably help the response we get in the Impact meeting. Yet, the character of the meetings themselves must be of such a nature that they will both attract a large segment of the campus non-Christian crowd and eventually win the right to be heard. We have a good kick-off approach for the school year in the Organizational meeting and the Burger Bash outlined in Manual III. Yet, those subsequent early meetings must be designed to continue the *image-building* that will be needed to strengthen our campus ministry. This might be better accomplished by the year II "Super-Muscle Party," and other more action- and social-oriented meetings, i.e. Bath-Tub pack, and Bigger and Better Hunt.

Insight, on the other hand, continues to be the meeting designed for the Christian and non-Christian student interested in a small, serious discussion about Christianity and its application to everyday life. This year, Insight is especially geared to help the Christian guy and gal stand alone in their faith, independent of pastor, parent, or even Campus Life leader.

The difficulty we must overcome is the "rut" of having two meetings with essentially only the same core group in attendance. There is on the one hand a need for "Impact" such as the Campus Life meeting. And, we also have this other meeting known as Insight for that small group of kids really interested in what we're doing there. So, we have essentially two *different* meetings. The core group attends Impact because they have brought non-Christians or students previously unacquainted with Campus Life to that meeting. Many non-Christian students will attend Campus Life simply because they know or have heard about the fun and sharp activities that just a lot of kids on campus enjoy at Campus Life, or because we as staff have built rapport with them in their interest group. Non-Christians and Christian core kids attend Insight to "dig in" to learning to stand alone in their faith under the guidance of a staff leader who gives them individual attention as he builds them up.

Much of the effectiveness that we have in our club efforts will depend on the kind of "image" that we build for Campus Life. In the past, many clubs have been viewed by faculty and administrators as a sort of "Bible club" that meets secretly with ten to fifteen kids. Unfortunately, many students still may have that conception. It is our responsibility, therefore, to give the school an accurate image of Campus Life so that it will have confidence in who we are and what we're doing. It must be positive, it must be sharp, and it must be real. That's the kind of image that attracts kids to clubs.

How do we build that "image" that is so vital to our ministry? We have talked about the staff member's campus contact and have shown how vital a role his contact plays in developing the school's confidence in him as a person who cares.

But the design of the club meetings and the strategy we use in presenting them, especially the early meetings of the year, are fully as important. After our CORE and ORGANIZATIONAL meetings, in which we mobilize our core kids and other interested students for the year's activity, we put on the BURGER BASH. This is a tremendously important event, for it is the first public appearance of the club in the school's activity calendar. Here's where we can say to a large group of students, at least 150, that "Campus Life is here, this is what it's about, and here's how you can be involved." And, it's out of the contact that we make through that meeting that we find most of the kids who will be involved with us through the year in Campus Life.

Immediately following the BASH we have our first CAMPUS LIFE meeting. This will vary from year to year as the manuals give us new resource ideas. Yet, the first meeting should continue to build image and involvement. The design should be built around lots of action *with only a passing stress on the spiritual.* We still need more time to win the right to be heard. The second Campus Life meeting two weeks later can be more closely aligned with the manual format of crowd-breakers, entertainment, and discussion. As we put our best efforts into building a club program that strives for a maximum of group enjoyment, group involvement, and group expression we will see success in building a good club image.

Fox Valley HAPPENINGS play an integral role in building the individual club image. For, here is the event in which all clubs get together in an informal setting to experience together a Campus Life "happening." The elements of group involvement and entertainment blend together into an exciting evening of fun. The staff designs the program to involve the kids in singing, skits, and dialogue. The first semester HAPPENINGS are designed to build image, to provide an atmosphere of involvement that individual club leaders can use to build their own club program. The "campus spotlite" section of the HAPPENING is particularly helpful. We begin with a fall kick-off HAPPENING in late September, which will usually follow a week of assemblies in featuring one of Youth for Christ's nationally known singing groups. The assemblies themselves help promote the club's start for the year, and the group will be available for BURGER BASHES the evening of the day that the individual school has its assembly. That first week then focuses attention on Campus Life and channels a mass of interested students into the kick-off HAPPENING. In October, SCREAM IN THE DARK provides a week of involvement in the wildest haunted house ever seen by most kids. And November means a SPORTS HAPPENING hosting varsity squads and lettermen from the schools, plus a "battle of cheerleaders" and an appearance of a well-known Christian athlete. Holiday Teen Convention, our Christmas conference designed to communicate to teens, follows in December. All these events reinforce that Campus Life is a first-rate organization which does unusual and fun events geared to high schoolers.

SUMMARY

What we have developed then as a strategy can be seen in figure 9.

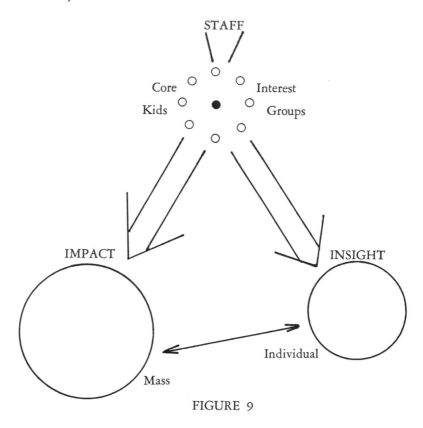

FIGURE 9

A selected staff develops a person-to-person ministry with students from representative interest groups on the campus. He spends time with them, builds rapport, and seeks opportunities to share Christ with them. He also spends time building up the lives of core kids, challenging them to meet their responsibility of influencing the students of their campus for Christ.

As non-Christian students are led to a personal relationship with Christ, the staff leader channels them into the Insight program where they can receive individual attention in a group experience designed to help them stand in their faith.

3. While we're speaking of contexts for communication of the Gospel, we have to include the coffee house as a setting particularly adapted to contemporary youth culture. The following article, reprinted by permission of *United Evangelical Action* magazine, gives helpful insights in the approach and the mechanics of setting up coffee houses.

Perhaps the greatest value of this approach is that, while it does not develop an initial friendship base, it does operate in a two-way communication pattern. The witness is given as sharing, involving listening as well as speaking.

A NEW BRAND OF COFFEEHOUSE

By Ian Kerr as told to Kendal Smucker

Mike, a product of a broken home, at twenty years of age was on probation for aggravated battery. One day, after weeks of aimlessness, Mike dropped in to a coffeehouse to try to make a date with one of the hostesses.

While he was waiting to strike up a conversation, fellows and girls, dressed and not so dressed, and with hair — more or less — drifted in for coffee, Pepsi, music and talk. A folk group performed and then a Youth for Christ team member took the mike and straightforwardly told how the Lord Jesus Christ could make a miracle out of a mess.

The words got through to Mike. For the first time in years tears began to roll down his face. He asked Christ to take over his life.

That critical step led to a severe beating by several of his old cronies, but Mike went back to the place of his conversion, this time to pass on to other young people what he had found there.

It is not so strange that the place of Mike's conversion was a coffeehouse. The name may be the same, but it is a new brand of coffeehouse from the communist-tainted image formed by the radical-talking beatniks of the 1950's or the communal "trip" depot of the "turned-on" hippies in this decade. Music and entertainment, discussions and public expression, a place to talk and meet people and ideas — this is the coffeehouse. A Christian coffeehouse adds to this a Christian perspective on life and its problems and needs.

A Pasadena, Calif., church youth group has, for several years, operated a coffeehouse on the Tournament of Roses parade route. Hundreds of students swarming to the annual event find a mug of hot coffee and a warm place to wait out the chilly late night hours before the parade begins. The youth group members fan out at coffeehouse tables and engage the visitors in conversation about contemporary concerns. Eventually they offer Jesus Christ as the Person who makes life supremely meaningful now.

Suburbanite and city-dweller, young and old, student and worker, skeptic and inquiring, all are being reached through the Christian coffeehouse. It has been especially effective with the high school and college-age group. Southern Baptists have instituted a student program designed to be an influence for Christ on the troubled campus of San Francisco State College. A major purpose of their coffeehouse ministry is to expand dialogue sessions with the more than 20,000 students.

The coffeehouse is an unusually effective means of evangelism and a relatively easy method to incorporate. A coffeehouse can be adapted to almost any situation, any locale, any group, any budget, any schedule.

Have you been wanting some vehicle as a Christian contact with the world? You can start a coffeehouse in your own community. There are four simple steps: organize, train, finance and locate, and program.

1. Organize

A Christian coffeehouse project, as a legitimate service to the community, needs to have a recognized sponsoring group. This may be a denominational board, an individual church, a laymen's group, or a committee of local churches. Regardless of the sponsoring body, the basic purpose should be evangelistic. If there are different doctrinal traditions represented in the churches sponsoring the project, there should be an understanding that only the basic, essential Gospel of Jesus Christ must be presented, without peripheral doctrinal emphasis. The fundamental purpose of a coffeehouse is to present Jesus Christ in meaningful terms. One interdenominational group spent a great deal of time in fitting out an old warehouse. The sponsors worked right along with the young people in painting a large mural on the wall, building a small stage and coffee bar, and arranging dim lighting to give it atmosphere.

The sponsoring group has the responsibility of hiring a manager to coordinate the project, and the manager in turn recruits and trains team members in the coffeehouse method and work.

What should the manager look for as he interviews and screens potential team members? He should seek persons within the age-group for which the coffeehouse is intended. A youth-slanted coffeehouse should not have a team member over twenty-five. Coffeehouses with different age slants can be more flexible.

One twenty-eight-year-old wife and mother, whose husband's ministry kept him away from home a good share of the time, became part of a local outreach to win teenagers to Jesus Christ. Soon 30 teenagers were coming regularly to the old barn and many of them gave their hearts to Christ. They wrote a play about a teenager being converted in a coffeehouse and presented it in other coffeehouses, civic halls, fairgrounds, etc. When they outgrew the barn, they fixed up an empty grain warehouse. In this case it became a meeting place between young people and the church, where each could grow to understand the other.

A coffeehouse team member needs a knowledgeable spiritual depth and willingness to listen to others. He needs emotional and intellectual stability toward what he believes. He should be adaptable to youth situations, have a sense of personal worth, and be able to view himself as others see him. He should be sensitive to his relationship with others as he converses; and he ought to be interesting because of what he is, not what he says or does. This requires, of course, that the team member have interests in many areas in addition to a vital Christian faith.

2. Train

Once a corps of team members has been selected, the training begins. An important aspect is becoming accustomed to each other. In the training period the team should learn and work together as a group in love and openness. Members must be free with each other before they will be able to be free in personal dialogue in the coffeehouse. As the team makes out policies for the operation, it learns how each member thinks. The crisis of being in a new situation and solving initial problems will draw the members together. A spiritual unity, born of Bible study and prayer together, will build a group bond and individual growth of team members.

A coffeehouse effort in a medium-sized city was planned six months ahead of the scheduled opening. During this time praying together was an integral part of the briefing session. Because the team members discovered that the spiritual rapport they gained was so beneficial, they continued their prayer meetings through the year, with the young people praying for specific individuals they had met and witnessed to at the coffeehouse.

The other half of the team's training is to practice the evangelistic skills that members will use in their contacts. The same methods they use to open up to each other in dialogue are the ones they will use in talking to customers. At the training courses for the coffeehouse team mentioned above, Billy Graham counseling tapes were listened to and discussed. A solid ground in personal evangelism is necessary, but flexibility should be stressed. Fixed formulas for salvation are out; a different approach is needed for each person. Consider what might happen to a drug user listening to the horrors of his lostness and damnation when he is still under his drug's effects! Adaptability to each situation is very important.

Also of concern in the training program are discussion-leading skills, ways of dealing with specific spiritual problems, and know-how of following-up a relationship outside the coffeehouse.

The coffeehouse can and should be more than just a ministry to the unsaved. Christians have problems and questions, too. In a college-town Christian coffeehouse a coed team member approached another girl and talked with her awhile. She soon realized the girl was also a Christian. She checked an impulse to leave and seek a more "profitable" person to talk to. She stayed to draw out the girl's inner goals in life.

Some time later the second girl applied to become a team member, revealing that the coed with whom she had spoken on her initial visit to the coffeehouse was the first person who had shown her an openness and honesty. Through their discussion she had come to see how much her own life was lacking in purpose, and subsequently she had allowed Christ to remedy it.

3. Finance

Collecting finances and locating a room or building seem to go hand in hand, with finances determining the choice of site. Start raising funds toward the expenses by encouraging direct giving. Mobilize prayer support, and interest your own church members in the project. Keep in mind that the average coffeehouse can cover only 50 percent of its expenses from sales of concessions or from a cover charge.

Our "chain" of coffeehouses has found the following expenses about average:

decorations (spent only once)	$50-$200
rent	up to $250 per month
manager's salary	$100 per month
advertising (only periodically used)	
maintenance	$25 per month
utilities	$50 per month

This budget is prepared from frequently operating coffeehouses; most of these expenses may be sharply curtailed by selecting a less expensive site, such as a church basement or meeting hall.

Part of the coffeehouse's costs may be raised by instituting a cover charge for all who enter. How much is enough? Fifty cents is considered standard. Soft drinks and coffee are then on the house; other concessions may be sold extra.

. . . and Locate

Scouting for a good coffeehouse location will bring up a variety of interesting prospects, but the final choice probably remains tied to the budget and the purposes of your coffeehouse as outlined by the sponsoring group. The ideal location is near, but not too close to, your specific target group. Putting the coffeehouse in the middle of the group tends to transfer control of attendance to the group. But it is equally important to locate within reach of your target group. If you are going for the after-school crowd, locate near their after-school hangouts. Or locate near their evening school and community activities, where they can drop in afterwards. A Christian coffeehouse seeking a college crowd would naturally locate near the campus.

A word about size: it is better to be too small than to be too big. Young people especially like cramped quarters and dark atmosphere with lots of noise. Noise provides privacy of conversation and a small, packed room looks better than a spacious room only three-quarters full.

Originality may yield an unthought-of but highly successful accommodation. For a summer project, a nondenominational group pitched a tent at the edge of a tourist town. They set up tables, pop art, candles, a coffee machine, and a platform for their folk group and guitarists. After a slow start, it crammed in hundreds of teen-agers from miles around all summer long.

Another group approached a local snack shop proprietor and got permission to take over his shop one night a month. He got a profit on the coffee and provided heating, etc. The Christian group made sure there were plenty of customers and, in turn, stipulated that they could speak and sing when they wanted to. All this without paying him a penny for using the premises!

But basically there are four types of housing arrangements that you can use for your Christian coffeehouse — a church basement or hall, a community building, a leased room or a part of a private house.

Each has its advantages and disadvantages. The church room will have the stigma of being in a church and may not be conducive toward some freedoms more readily allowed elsewhere. It has the advantage of being the least costly to operate. Decorations usually need to be removable and storable.

A community building, such as a youth center, public recreation room or Junior Achievement building, offers a more neutral element, but costs more to rent. Scheduling for both these locations may be difficult, as the coffeehouse will have to compete with other groups for time.

If you intend to operate frequently or full-time, probably the best — but also the most expensive — is the storefront coffeehouse or leased room. Sound systems may be installed for public addresses and stage performances as well as for recorded music entertainment and background music. Decorations can be permanent as you like.

A modified version of a storefront coffeehouse can be created in the basement of a private home. Decorations may be either permanent or portable. Rent may be less expensive, and the location will still carry a neutral atmosphere.

During the time of locating, organizing, and decorating, the manager and team should be training and setting the specific coffeehouse policies. These policies may vary according to location and age-group of the average customer. Hours may range from afternoon to after school to late at night.

Alcoholic beverages and drugs are off limits in any coffeehouse. Persons who have been drinking or taking drugs may enter if they do not bring their paraphernalia in with them and are reasonably composed.

Such controls are usually respected. A hippie dope user at a Christian coffeehouse asked a fellow user if he could smoke pot inside the room. The second told him, "No, go outside." A Christian coffeehouse is in essence a ministry of service and hope, and it is to such as these that the team members are eager to introduce the offer of abundant life.

PUBLIC RELATIONS

Although the grapevine is your usual best advertiser, insert an ad now and then in your local newspaper (advertisers also rate special consideration in public relations news releases). Put posters in the local storefronts — let the community young people know your coffeehouse is open to them. Present invitation cards to nearby schools, welcoming the students.

To publicize the opening of their coffeehouse, one inventive group organized a community parade with posters, car floats, a folk group playing on a truck, and young people handing out invitations. This publicity was too good. Their premises couldn't cope with the 400 young people who turned up!

Invite the local police to drop by frequently. They probably will anyway, so take the initiative: invite them before they come. Get them on your side. Police have been known to thank Christian coffeehouses for working with students and youth. A friendly attitude toward the police inside the coffeehouse will encourage customers to police the coffeehouse themselves, aiding the team workers in preventing house rule violations.

4. Program

The final step in getting your Christian coffeehouse under way is to program. What do you plan to do there anyway? Listen to music? Sit around and talk? What about? Have a guest lecturer in for a talk and open discussion? Bible studies? Public forum? Contests? Artistic expression of all sorts? Debates?

Some coffeehouses feature gospel beat groups, some folk performers. One in a Baptist church uses only community singing accompanied by a piano and guitar, and straight gospel solos. But 250 young people, most of them unchurched, listen and applaud.

But whether a "square orthodox approach" or geared to the "now" sound, your choice of program should be coordinated into an effective program that will allow your team members to accomplish their basic purposes of entering into worthwhile dialogue with the customers.

While the main thrust of the Christian coffeehouse is to introduce others to Jesus Christ, it should not end there. Don't fall into the fallacy of poor follow-up of coffeehouse contacts. A west coast church has special monthly meetings for their coffeehouse contacts, as well as home Bible study groups.

Christian coffeehouse workers often take an individual interest in customers they are praying for. More than one team member has spent his time out of the coffeehouse hunting down a job for a friend gained over a cup of coffee. One British worker, just before he left for the United States, worked earnestly with a British hippie for only two weeks. The hippie was on drugs, was a runaway from home and was living in a cave. That the worker had made some impact with the fellow was evidenced by the letter he received after he came to the States. The hippie wrote that he was off drugs and was reading his Bible seriously.

Young people who venture into the Christian brand of coffeehouse across the nation are often antiestablishment, antichurch, and anti-Bible. Many go out the same way. Some are puzzled, their preconceived ideas of Christianity perhaps shaken somewhat, at least tested. A few — a worthwhile few — discover inside that coffeehouse what life is all about and walk out knowing where they are going.

NOTE: For information on the Christian coffeehouse ministry, read John Perry's book, *The Coffee House Ministry,* and Lyman Coleman's *The Coffeehouse Itch.* If possible, visit a coffeehouse already in operation for some valuable first-hand insights. Tape lectures and further information on the coffeehouse may also be obtained by writing to Mr. Ian Kerr, The Coffee House Ministries, 313 North Blanchard, Wheaton, Illinois 60187.

4. A final PROBE feature is from Jack Armant, of Warren Park Presbyterian Church in Cicero, Illinois. Jack used a project approach

to involve teens in initial witnessing, and to provide motivation for preparatory study. There was a definite carry-over of witness into the high school campus after the kids returned from the H.I.P. experience.

H. I. P.
(HIGH SCHOOL ITINERANT PROJECT)

WHAT IS THE PLAN AND PURPOSE OF H. I. P.? To provide an opportunity for Warren Park young people to participate in a program which will involve active service among children, youth, and adults who need to know Christ, thus stimulating interest and understanding of modern day missions and the Great Commission of Christ.

It will provide a means of putting to practical use that which has been learned through prior training in the home and in the church Christian education program.

The following information provides a broad outline concerning the program.

WHY SUCH A PROGRAM FOR WARREN PARK PRESBY-TERIAN CHURCH? It is vital that the church develop expanded means, doing whatever is expedient, to present to its young people the need for finding and following God's will, the importance of each individual in the fulfillment of the Great Commission, and the need for furthering the cause of Christ. Overall, such a program will stress the importance of being "sold out," or totally involved with God's purpose for the individual. Beyond this, many of our young people could effectively use this time during an otherwise idle summer, efficiently and prayerfully planned, for spiritual growth and development as well as setting new goals for their lives.

WHO MAY PARTICIPATE? This will be open to all young people who have completed the ninth grade, through college youth. Participants must know Jesus Christ as personal Saviour. They must have wholeheartedly committed their lives to Christ and must show evidence of a good measure of spiritual and emotional maturity. The program is open to both young men and women.

HOW MAY A PERSON APPLY? Application should be made by completing the prescribed application form, giving prayerful and careful consideration to the questions and criteria set forth, providing concise and adequate information concerning oneself, thereby giving the candidate committee an accurate appraisal of applicant's aptitude, capabilities, qualifications, strengths, and weaknesses.

WHO WILL BE SELECTED? A candidate committee wthin the church will select a maximum of twelve (12) young people who have made application to participate in the program. . . . During the training those applicants demonstrating greatest proficiency and ability and whom the candidate committee feel would best represent the church in the project will be notified of their selection.

WHAT IS INVOLVED IN THE TRAINING PROGRAM? The program, though not burdensome, will nonetheless be challenging, and will require discipline of purpose, a desire to succeed, and near perfect attendance at special classes and seminars, scheduled at frequent intervals from March to June. A regular curriculum will be followed. The study will be both general and specific, covering many phases of teaching, and leadership training. Reading assignments will be an integral part of the training program. Areas to be studied include: study of the Gospel of John, personal evangelism, teaching skills, storytelling, song leading, and specific training in one or two different age levels of the Vacation Bible School materials we will be using. There will be an emphasis on growth in the areas of personal devotions and Christian fellowship.

HAS THIS TYPE OF ENDEAVOR BEEN TRIED ELSEWHERE AND WITH WHAT RESULTS? Short term missionary projects have been and are in operation under the auspices of several churches, schools, and mission boards. Specifically, the First Baptist Church of Wayne, Michigan; the Wheaton Bible Church; and the Park Street Church of Boston, Massachusetts, have carried on successful programs. Wheaton College, under the direction of the Christian Service Council, each summer carries on quite an extensive short-term mission project. It is our intention to seek aid from those who have operated similar projects and then to tailor our program to our needs and to the abilities of our young people, hoping to provide the best possible project commensurate with our resources.

WHAT ABOUT COST? This project will be done with the cooperation of the churches in the area. We will ask that all of the expenses for the trips be underwritten before we leave on the project. We would like the churches in the area of ministry to help bear some of the expense as well as to arrange for housing and meals for the young people. We would like for our own church to share in the travel expenses and we would like some of our members who are interested in this type of ministry to assist with donations to make this possible. The young people themselves will be responsible to help in the promotion and reporting of this endeavor. If time would permit we would even like the young people to help in raising part of their support. APPROXIMATE COST: $1200.

HOW WILL THE GROUP TRAVEL? Transportation will be in the new church van. We will always have a competently trained driver.

WHAT DO WE EXPECT FOR END RESULTS? The program is to be carried out by the Warren Park Presbyterian Church and we expect greater spiritual growth, more insight into the responsibilities of the Christian believer, and more active participation in the work of Warren Park and the ministry of Christ. Our prayer is that as God blesses the program nearly all who participate will forever after have the cause of missions branded on their hearts. The scopes of all participants will be broadened to the extent that personal effectiveness in all areas of life are expanded.

WHAT WILL BE THE RESPONSIBILITIES OF THE PARTICIPANTS IN THE PROJECT? Each young person will be adequately trained to teach a small group of children. Our objective will be to have each participant take an active leadership position on the trip. There will be opportunities for each to give testimony of what Christ is doing in his or her life. We will form a team which when not working in the Vacation Bible School will function in other areas such as special programs in churches, special youth evangelism, and other areas of Christian service.

(The program as described has been suggested on an experimental basis, allowing the completion of one training period, and one 2-4 week itinerant period.)

DESCRIPTION OF PROGRAM: Our objectives will be to work in rural areas in cooperation with 2 to 3 small churches. By previous correspondence we will ask the churches in the area to make arrangements for our young people to stay in homes (usually in pairs). The churches will also arrange publicity for us in advance. Our plan will be to arrive in the area on Saturday, to get settled in the homes and to become familiar with the particular area in which we will be working. On Sunday we will attend one of the cooperating churches in the morning and explain our objectives. In the evening we will attend one of the other churches. We will have prepared as a team to present music, testimonies, and to speak in these churches.

16

the serving life

YOUTH   ADULTS

BIBLE

LIFE   BODY

PROGRAM

EPHESIANS 4:13

The evangelistic imperative is particularly clear in Scripture. But to many God's call to service in the world, to "do good to all men," is not so clear. Denying that the church was called by God to be a social agency, they have little interest in ministries which are not directly evangelistic.

It's true that the church, as an organization, is not called to provide social services to the community. The Church of the New Testament is an organism, Christ's Body, and as such it exists for believers, a context in which they grow toward maturing in Christ. *But the individual believer is called to involvement with others.* Like the Father, who makes His rain fall on godly and ungodly alike, because He is love, the children are to care about people. We are to reach out to help them . . . because the God we represent is love.

In evangelism we need to take very seriously the concept that believers are to represent Christ in the world. That we are to be, as the very word "Christian" originally intimated, "little Christs." We are to live "so that the life of Jesus may be plainly seen in our mortal lives" (2 Cor. 4:11 *Phillips*).

Being like Jesus necessarily involves us in the lives and concerns of others. The Bible says that we have "no high priest who cannot be touched with the feeling of our infirmities" (Heb. 4:15). Jesus *is* touched, and in His life on earth He was constantly touched, by human need. We may validly see His healings and miracles as divine acts which authenticated Him as God's messenger. But we dare not take them as cold, calculating acts in which the needy were *used* for His own purposes. The Bible constantly reminds us, "Jesus had compassion on them." "Jesus reached out His hand and touched the leper." "Jesus wept." God's loving heart was expressed in acts of mercy, in reaching out to others to become involved, to meet need.

Today, as representatives of His love, we too must be a people who can be touched — who have compassion, who reach out to others, who become involved, and who meet human need.

The impersonal "service project" is inadequate. I think most of us understand the kind of thing I mean. Things like collecting cans of food for a rescue mission we've never seen and never will see, except perhaps for a brief hour sitting on a platform in front of rows of tired and dirty men. Things like making up a thanksgiving basket to be delivered by an embarrassed adult and a "teen representative" to a family who, while thankful, find the "charity" as painful to receive as it is awkward to give. Things like the traditional visit to the local old folks home, where a small group of kids cluster together to sing for the assembled elders and give a testimony or two, and then, after short and smiling farewells, to hurry back again to the world of youth.

These are terribly inadequate as expressions of God's love — not because the motive in planning them may not be right, nor because what is given may not meet a need. They are inadequate because such activities don't bring involvement with the others as persons.

I like far better, as examples of ministries of God's love, things like these:

Steve Cory, son of Scripture Press' editorial director Lloyd Cory, announces to his dad that he's decided to give up track so he can spend two more afternoons each week with the inner-city kids he's come to know while counseling at a summer camp.

As high schoolers, my wife and a friend gave up every Sunday afternoon to spend them with children in a children's ward in a Brooklyn, New York, county hospital. There they spent hours with the children, reading to them, talking, playing games, and telling flannelgraph stories.

Marlene LeFeaver, as a teen, joined several other girls from her church to spend Saturday afternoons in a home for delinquent girls, talking and listening, letting them know someone cared.

A ministry of caring

These last examples seem to me to include vital and necessary ingredients for Christian involvement in the serving life. What ingredients?

Personal involvement   In each of these cases, young Christians came face to face with persons whom they came to know and understand as they served them.

Involvement is important for both giver and receiver. So much of our "service" for others is impersonal and condescending. Giving "things" is often (and rightly) felt as a threat to the receiver's integrity, and the attitude of the giver is often (and rightly) questioned. But when a person gives *himself,* when he builds a relationship in which he communicates his respect and concern for the other as a person, love is communicated. Persons who receive desperately need to feel love. For love is a great assertion of worth. A gift given in love does not subordinate the receiver to the giver. It exalts him. For it is evidence of his value as a person in the eyes of the giver.

Certainly this is what Gospel love communicates to us. Whether we respond in faith or not, the Gospel tells us that we are loved — that to God we are worth the price of Christ's own blood. If we are to represent this God adequately to others, we desperately need to affirm the value of the persons we contact and serve. We need to love them as we serve, and so assure them that they are worth caring about — with no strings attached.

Personal involvement is also important for the giver. The Bible often speaks of Jesus as having been moved with compassion. Jesus *felt with* people in need. He understood their feelings and He involved Himself with them.

One of the benefits to the Christian of his service to others (while surely not a primary motive for service) is that in coming to know and to feel with persons in need, his own heart is opened up to compassion. The Scripture says that "the love of God is shed abroad in our hearts." And this is unquestionably important. As "God's obedient children," we are to be like our Father. We are to open ourselves up to experiences that are like the experiences of Jesus Christ, and we are to identify our own goals and purposes in life with His. "Impersonal service" is tragically crippling to both the one who serves and the one who is served. Giving without love degrades the receiver. And serving without understanding and identifying with the one who is served is a hollow mockery of the love that Christ, our example, calls us to experience and to express.

Cost In each of the "good" examples of servant-ministry, expressing care for others was costly. It demanded a decision to give up personal comfort, time, or something else which was important to the giver.

Such cost is a necessary evidence of love. We know the love of God because He gave His Son. Real love demands demonstration, and the most meaningful demonstration involves a personal sacrifice on the part of the lover.

In the long run, of course, love means gain. We can never outgive God; the more we spend for others in His sake, the greater the blessing and joy we experience. But denial of self, accepting our share of the cross, is felt as sacrifice before we discover it is gain. It wasn't easy for Steve to give up his place on the high school team for the sake of the inner-city kids he'd come to care about. It wasn't easy for the teenage girls to give up Saturday or Sunday afternoons, and give themselves at the children's ward and detention home. It is never easy to make the decision to surrender something that is ours for the sake of others. But it is just this kind of decision that meaningful service demands.

Understanding I've already mentioned this above, but it's important enough to deserve separate emphasis. Serving others demands that we seek to understand them — that we learn to feel with them. Serving others is a two-way transaction. In it both give, and both receive. Only service that involves us with others and leads to identification with them in their total situation approaches the servant ministry of Christ.

Involving youth in service

As with many of the elements of youth ministry described in this book, it is difficult to *program* for involvement in service. While the PROBE features following provide illustration of kinds of "service projects" teens may be involved in, and suggest resources, it is difficult to "plan" the kind of person-to-person ministry that our faith demands.

So what can we do? I believe that, as we minister with youth, we can be aware that the living of Christ's life calls us to care for other people, and to express our concern in servant ministry. Each community, each situation, has its own unique opportunities and needs. And it is important that we make our young people aware of human need — that we involve them as persons with persons in need, helping them interpret the experiences involvement brings (see chapter 14), guiding them to discover in servant ministry who they are as Christians.

And I'm also convinced that that servant ministry which is participation in Jesus' kind of life with people is marked by person-to-person involvement, by a costly giving of ourselves, and by a deepening understanding of and concern for persons.

Guiding youth into this involvement is part of our ministry with young people who are, after all, intended by God to grow toward the image and likeness of their Savior Jesus Christ.

PROBE
case histories
discussion questions
thought-provokers
resources

1. Books on youth ministry often provide lists of possible service projects teens can undertake. Here is one such list, from the book *Ways Youth Learn* by Clarice M. Bowman (New York, Harper and Row, 1952). Look through the listing and, as you do, ask yourself which of these have potential for involving young people in an experience of the servant-life as proposed in this chapter?

   a. *Helping in the church* —

   (1) Improving the church grounds and building.
   (2) Participating in youth choir.
   (3) Being an active member of the youth fellowship — helping in all activities; practicing friendliness; striving to reach unreached.
   (4) Equipping a game room in the church.
   (5) Assisting the pastor by distributing materials, flowers, bulletins; making telephone calls; running errands.
   (6) Issuing invitations to strangers.
   (7) Drawing or mimeographing a map of the community giving directions to the church, and distributing to strangers.
   (8) Visiting shut-ins; doing kind deeds for them such as reading to them or bringing music to them.
   (9) Volunteering to drive cars to pick up shut-ins or others who could not otherwise attend. Baby-sitting for parents to go to activities in the church.
   (10) Assisting with secretarial work of the church.
   (11) Holding services in institutions.
   (12) Writing up stories of church events for local newspapers or church papers.
   (13) Preparing some little-used room in the church as a chapel for individual prayer and small services.
   (14) Keeping the church building clean and attractive.
   (15) Caring for church hymnals and Bibles and books of worship.
   (16) Providing flowers.
   (17) Starting a costume wardrobe, collecting and classifying costumes for different types of dramatic productions.
   (18) Starting an art library — sorting, mounting, and filing pictures for ready use for teaching and worship purposes.
   (19) Making movable screens for church school rooms, particularly for children's rooms.

(20) Assisting children's workers (under their supervision) in storytelling, preparing equipment, gathering materials, and caring for children.

(21) Maintaining fellowship with persons away from the home church, through letters, bulletins, recordings, devotional aids, newssheets.

(22) Faithfulness as a group in participating in the worship and general work of the church.

(23) Etc.

b. *Reaching unreached persons —*

(1) Finding who and where the unreached are. Making a house-to-house canvass or other type of community or school survey.

(2) Publicizing church events (through personal word, telephone, posters, newspapers, bulletins, radio).

(3) Making provision for recreation regularly for youth and possibly also children's and/or adult groups, with a variety of activities, including the quiet and the active to appeal to different tastes and moods.

(4) Making provision for transportation of unreached persons.

(5) Co-operating with youth fellowships of other churches and faiths.

(6) Providing for services in closed churches.

(7) Starting neighborhood prayer groups.

(8) Starting outpost Sunday schools (under supervision of trained adult workers).

(9) Developing an "enlistment" service to help newcomers find niches for participation.

(10) Providing a lounge in the church building for reading, writing, or listening to music and for meeting friends under worthy auspices — for individuals who have no such places to go.

(11) Visiting unreached persons in homes; assuring them of sincere, friendly interest, following up by bringing them to church activities.

(12) Arranging outdoor sing on Sunday afternoon in summer, especially for unchurched people, or in sections where such opportunities for friendly participation are rarely offered.

(13) Arranging neighborhood gatherings for unchurched people to meet with friendly church people — for candymaking, packing boxes for relief, preparing for Christmas, etc.

(14) Caroling — not necessarily only at Christmas but at other times as well.

c. *Activities for building brotherhood and world friendship —*

(1) Using special missions materials in denominational and inter-

denominational publications (units, stories, activity ideas, party suggestions, music, drama).

(2) Providing bibliographies of missionaries and peacemakers who have worked for brotherhood.

(3) Encouraging hobbies that help to build world-mindedness, such as pen pals, stamp collecting, language study, making or collecting dolls of the nations, trips.

(4) Setting up an "overseas workshop," a place where youth can meet to mend clothes, collect goods for relief, repair and make needed items.

(5) Securing for showing among church people visuals or recordings to help deepen concern for others and build world-mindedness.

(6) Inviting persons from other countries and missionaries within reach to counsel with the young people about world relations and possibly vocational missions work.

(7) Setting up a world friendship library or corner or shelf in youth room, or somewhere in the church, or in a basement.

(8) Securing the interest of the librarian of the public library in arranging a special section or shelf of books dealing with international questions.

(9) Getting in touch with commissions on world peace of the denomination for up-to-the-minute suggestions and materials, such as radio scripts that can be used to build confidence and inspire peace action among the masses.

(10) Securing informational materials, including visual and auditory materials, from United Nations and possibly its branches such as UNESCO. Forming a United Nations club for securing needed information and discussing and disseminating it.

(11) Starting a personal campaign to rid one's own speech of slurring words or phrases or jokes ridiculing other people.

(12) Generally living as if all were one brotherhood, speaking that way, thinking that way, praying that way.

(13) Etc.

d. *Christian service action in lifting moral standards* —

(1) Seeing what recreational facilities and guidance are offered in the community to give youth from lower economic levels opportunities for fun and fellowship under worthy auspices, and fostering higher ideals within them.

(2) Getting the facts as to attitudes and practices of youth in the community, schools, etc., as to cheating, stealing, boy-girl friendships, gambling, drinking, use of narcotics.

(3) Calling together for consultation those likely to be most concerned and capable of offering help (church groups, civic agencies, character-building agencies, parents).

(4) Making the total church program for youth so alive that it

will help attract and hold the interest of unreached young persons; offering them jobs to do when they come so that they will feel needed, and thus gain a foothold in becoming better selves; surrounding them with wholesome group relationships, strengthening their ideals; guiding them in understanding better Jesus' teachings, and leading them to commitment.

(5) Etc.

e. *Christian service action in the local community* —

(1) Arousing interest in a community-wide recreation program for children, youth, and adults (including hobbies, crafts, outdoor activities, hikes, nature lore, folk games, other games, music, drama, intercultural festivals).

(2) Working in institutions (typing, general work, leading games or crafts, playing piano, assisting with children, telling stories, coaching drama).

(3) Conducting a Sunday afternoon sing each week.

(4) Growing flowers.

(5) Supplying reading materials to jails and other institutions.

(6) Helping harvest or gather perishable crops.

(7) Having a "Lord's Acre" project.

(8) Co-operating in a community survey.

(9) Presenting plays or visual aids dealing with social problems.

(10) Supporting a community project, such as a milk fund for babies (perhaps doing without refreshments at youth meetings, and giving the money that would otherwise have been spent).

(11) Investigating the treatment of criminals and delinquents — particularly of the younger ones — in the community.

(12) Working to overcome juvenile delinquency.

(13) Visiting the jails and detention homes and holding services.

(14) Analyzing the liquor problem in the community and organizing strategically to work on it.

(15) Encouraging citizens to vote.

(16) Helping foreign-born people to secure naturalization papers.

(17) Helping provide places for living and working for displaced persons.

(18) Working for safety.

(19) Helping prevent forest fires; replanting under direction.

(20) Sending youth teams to needy small churches.

2. There are several ways of building toward the *understanding* (the "feeling with") dimension that is to mark service to others. One of the most fruitful is through simulation, a technique which involves young people in "like real" experiences which closely parallel real situations. Simulation is a very helpful tool for Christian education, and may be effectively used *before* a direct experience, to sensitize young people to the feelings of others with whom they will be becoming involved.

To give you a feel for simulation, I've included the following report of a simulation experiment developed and conducted by Albert Zehr, of Baden, Ontario.

PROJECT ECONOMY

An Experiment in Simulation

The Purpose

Simulation as an educational tool is an attempt to imitate or parallel an actual situation or experience so closely that many of the effects of the "real thing" may be realized in a much shorter time than the real experience would take. A good experience in simulation can give its participants a vicarious experience to the extent that the dynamics and sensations realized may be very similar to those which the real situation would generate. Thus to have a simulation experience can often teach one what another person in the real situation is experiencing, or it may also help the learner to avoid a tragic real-life situation.

In the example which follows it was hoped that participants might experience the dynamics at work between rich and poor, and the emotions and feelings at work when one is caught in the rat-race of today's economic system.

The Implementation of "Project Economy"

It was decided that a certain group of youth would be brought together for a period of several days at a camp site or retreat center. Upon their arrival they would all engage in playing a game of Monopoly. There would be four players per game and each game would be played until one player was completely bankrupt.

When all games were completed the players would then keep their respective monies as their cash for the rest of the time together. This means some would be very rich and some would have adequate money, some would have very little and one out of four would have nothing.

The entire camp property would then be sold by auction to whoever would be able to buy such and the buyer could then in turn sell various units to the other participants, employing others if and when needed.

This means that the meals, the sleeping blankets, the cabins, the beds, the swimming pool, the washrooms, the ping pong, shuffleboard, etc., would all be sold. The purchasers would in turn hire others to assist them in renting the various facilities or entertainments.

When all properties were sold, the owners would then offer jobs to those who needed to work for a living.

There would not necessarily be enough jobs for all, and thus some would not be able to afford sleeping indoors, eating regularly or indulging in certain extras.

As this situation would develop and exist for several days and nights, many dynamics would begin to work and feelings should run high.

The one guide line would be that anything which is considered acceptable in our present society would be regarded as legitimate in our little economy.

Implications in the Actual Experience

On Thursday evening August 28, 1969, twenty-three youth, (aged 16-22) met at Hidden Acres Mennonite Camp, near New Hamburg, Ontario. The above instructions (see implementation) were made very clear. All sleeping bags and other gear were turned in and all agreed that anything which is acceptable in present-day society would be our only guide lines.

All began to play Monopoly with a mixture of fear and determination. Tension and frustration became evident as gradually some were squeezed into bankruptcy and others sagaciously benefitted. The losing players tended to become suspicious of others and some made attempts to quit while they were ahead.

Eventually the games ended with various amounts — from nothing up to $12,000 — in the hands of the respective players. This money then became the cash assets of each for the continuing experiment.

After all games were concluded, the bank government (in this case, the present writer) offered the facilities by auction to anyone interested and financially able. (Approximate figures which would set the cost of living at about $4,000 were suggested as general guidelines.)

The meals, sleeping blankets, washrooms, etc., were sold. Each purchaser had an eye to making a profit from the resale or rental of his property.

The poorer waited patiently during the above procedure, anticipating work so that they too could afford at least some of the necessities. Some were given "advance pay" by their employers so that they could afford at least a sleeping blanket for the first night.

As might be expected, the first night proved to be more of a lark than a hardship, but the realization that there were two more nights to worry about had its sobering effect.

It became very obvious that a tax scheme would be necessary to bring reality into the situation, for things were being given away freely and little care shown about frugality.

Thus, the following tax scheme was implemented. 1) 10% tax on original income over $2,000. 2) 10% property tax per day on the value of the property which the buyer had purchased from the government. 3) Luxury tax, $50 on swimming and $10 for all other entertainment to be collected from owner of each facility. 4) 30% gift tax, collected from anyone who gave money or other value to another. The tax scheme put the squeeze on everything. The rich groaned and raised their prices. The poor moaned and often did without.

The government auctioned tax-collecting jobs to any who wanted work. The government also accepted sealed bids for "F.B.I." agents. The agents were later secretly employed and served very effectively since no one was sure who they were. It was their job to report any irregularities in tax collection or other financial transactions.

By late Friday evening and early Saturday morning the dynamics resulting from poor sleeping conditions, lack of meals, etc., became quite clearly evident.

By Friday noon there was considerable discontent because of the high price of meals, ($300.00) which led to an attempt to boycott the noon meal. Those who could afford it gradually broke down and thus the boycott became ineffective, much to the dismay of the poor.

A mild brawl on the part of a number of the discontented resulted in the dismantling of the ping pong table which was owned by an especially aggressive businessman. Since the action seemed to have general "public" approval the government felt it wise not to attempt punitive measures.

An enterprising and creative person made a contract with the government to supply the camp house with "window holder-openers." She then in turn sub-let various parts of the job to sub-contractors. Such an effort helped to stimulate the economy.

When jobs were offered by the government, the middle class who wanted just a little more money, so that they could have another swim, or play more shuffleboard, etc., would usually under-bid the poor who then despaired, for, since the meals were $2-300, what sense was there in accepting a job for $50 or $75.

A complication which caused us some considerable difficulty arose in that we did not seem to have a built-in hoarding or saving drive. Many "citizens" began to plan to spend all their money seeing that it lasted only until the end of the experiment. After much thought, we decided to offer $1.00 in actual currency for every $1,000 which the players could produce at the end of the experiment. This seemed to do its work, for from that moment on the drive to get and keep money began to operate.

By Saturday it became apparent that taxes were draining the economy and the poor were just not getting enough work. A general mood of despondency prevailed. At this time the government instituted a "Government Make Work Project" (W.P.A.!).

The terms for the "Government Project" were that the Government would pay $50 each time a picnic table was carried around the lake. While the task itself was obviously nonproductive, a number of fellows began to work very hard at it. This in turn brought considerable hostility and ill-will from those who despised the "coolies" and "peasants" who would stoop to such demeaning labors.

After the workers carried the tables for a few rounds, they discovered a farm trailer and began to use it. They then loaded three tables onto it and four boys began to pull it around the lake. You can imagine their chagrin when they were informed that the government would charge $20.00 rental for the trailer for each round. When they could not prove any private ownership they finally concurred that it followed that it must then be the property of the crown and thus they worked all the harder paying "Caesar" his due. They hauled the tables around the lake (about 1/4 mile) some twenty times.

About Saturday noon a group of harried tax collectors and some irate citizens declared that they had enough of a certain fellow who was evading taxes and swindling various other people. The accused was brought before the government and although he denied all charges, the general public declared him guilty. When given a choice to pay a $500 fine or be imprisoned, he defied the court and was thus sentenced to four hours in solitary confinement.

His jail was a small confection booth which was securely locked and guarded. (During this time the government learned the high cost of confining prisoners.) After three hours the prisoner was released for good behavior, but he immediately faced the problems of the ex-convict. Where should he go? Should he admit his guilt? How would people accept him? Would anyone trust him?

At first he avoided facing others, swimming by himself and sunning alone. Finally, with some difficulty, he was again accepted by "Society" but not without some suspicions.

While the government did subsidize some "cultural entertainment" (poetry reading), by and large there was by design no extra activities or program, so that the poor would have to face idleness and boredom.

On Sunday morning everyone was given a free breakfast, the savings were traded in for real money (one player had $13,000). We then spent the next several hours evaluating the experience. Participants shared their various feelings and emotions. To hear them report with real feelings "what it's like to be despised" or "why I had to charge high prices" made it obvious that this had been a deep learning experience.

A questionnaire was administered to help determine further facts and evaluations.

Conclusion

Since some of the conclusions and dynamics are quite obvious in the foregoing we will not repeat them in this conclusion.

1. It became obvious throughout the experience and in the questionnaire that there was considerable feeling and some open hostility toward the government. Some of this was no doubt justified, in that the government was run quite arbitrarily and taxes and other assessments were levied after investments were made. Suggestions that the government should have been elected by the people have real validity, although this would consume much time and could almost be a "Project Government" in itself. Since hostility toward government is a very part of the common man's lot, it may have been realistic to have such. We would simply suggest that for a true democratic government to be set up would greatly complicate

the experiment and would hardly be feasible unless the total experiment would last a week.

2. Almost all (twenty-three) of the participants felt it would be advantageous to have a larger group.
3. All but three felt it was a success and all expressed an interest in participating in such an experience again.
4. About half admitted defrauding others or the government — mostly in tax evasion and using certain facilities without paying.
5. About half missed at least one meal, although only five people missed more than two meals.
6. Fewer than half were able to determine who the "secret agents" were; this prevented many irregularities.
7. Kids noted that they learned much by way of seriously weighing priorities, in light of scarcity.
8. Several noted that they became sick and fed up with the money obsession. Everything was so money-oriented that no one would do a thing without pay, and one almost had to pay for friendship.
9. One youth told an adult later, "It makes you feel low down and ugly after you sneak some leftovers from someone else's plate. It made me feel like a dog."

PERSONAL REFLECTIONS

1. More insights might have been gained if a serious study bringing Christian values and their implications for an evaluation of what had occurred, would have followed.
2. We would suggest that at least three days are necessary for such an experiment and a week might be preferable.
3. A group of from twenty to fifty would appear feasible.
4. The success of such an experiment will depend to quite an extent on the on-the-spot creativity and ingenuity of the kids and the leadership. One must play it by ear, rather than to try to rerun a pre-planned program.
5. A police-force, a welfare program, and a rescue mission were among other ideas which did not materialize in the experiment, whereas others not anticipated did take place.
6. A person trained in social work or group dynamics could find this an excellent opportunity to observe and help the group evaluate later.
7. The local news media took a real interest and gave us excellent coverage, resulting in a number of inquiries locally and in nearby cities.

Final Word

It is hoped that the foregoing may stimulate many creative projects. The sky and your imagination are the limits.

We do not presume a copyright on the above; however, since the idea was original with us, and since we have invested many hours, much energy, and some money, we would ask that those who implement an experiment from the above please send at least a brief report of the same to the present writer.

September 25, 1969

Albert Zehr
Baden, Ontario

3. **How can youth be sensitized to the needs of others and to opportunities for servant involvement? Here's one approach, developed by several graduate students, each of whom has had experience in ministering with youth in local churches. It is reproduced as an example of a possible approach which may be appropriate at different junctures of youth ministry in a local situation.**

YOUNG PEOPLE AND SERVICE PROJECTS

Basic Objectives: We want our youth —

1. to study together the scriptural relationship between faith and works.

2. to express a concern for a group of people outside of their own circle of friends by participation in a service project of their own choice.

3. to experience personal growth by participating in a service project.

4. to develop capabilities of working together as a *body* toward a specific task.

Basic Needs of youth which must be met before they can accomplish the above goals:

1. to be motivated to service.

2. to know the Scriptural content and principles relating to faith and service.

3. to become aware of opportunities in the area of service.

4. to experience oneness in a group situation.

5. to know how to relate to the people being served.

6. to learn the mechanics of setting up and carrying through a service project.

Input Characteristics and capabilities of the learners as related to the above needs:

1. Motivation
    a) sharing of those who have had previous experiences in service projects
    b) group experiences such as skits, films, or role plays
    c) field trip to expose youth to the need of an area

    d) leader, through various means

    e) church support of project and awareness of need

2. Scriptural knowledge — we will assume they know nothing in this area; so input will be mainly by —

    a) leader

    b) group exploration of specific passages

3. Awareness of opportunities

    a) resource persons from specific areas of need

    b) films, tapes, records, etc.

    c) own knowledge of needs

    d) church needs

    e) magazines, books

4. Group experience

    a) own previous experience

    b) take group through an experience together

    c) evaluate group dynamics (both leader and participants)

5. Specific skills related to particular projects

    a) resource people (e.g., hospital manager, tutor, etc.)

    b) own previous experience

System

We have designed a four-month program consisting of specific activities centering around a weekend retreat. The main purpose of the "pre-retreat" is to expose a core group of young people to a specific area of need in their city. These young people will be used during the retreat to share their experiences and act as motivational agents. The retreat itself will be primarily motivational and provide opportunity for the whole youth group to decide what service project they would like to work on (the option must be left open not to choose any project at all if they so wish). Post-retreat activities are participation in the service project and regular evaluation.

Before the retreat, leaders should —

1. contact various places to see if service projects are feasible. They should have a tentative list already formulated to present, such as:

    nursing homes

    orphanages

    home for unwed mothers

    inner city (social welfare)

    park ministry

    day-care center

    tutoring

    baby-sitting service

    caring for older folks (getting groceries, painting homes, etc.)

2. meet with core group to train them for their role during the retreat.

They should be informed as to the purpose of the retreat, and equipped with discussion leading skills.

3. invite resource people from various types of areas to be available for the Saturday evening discussion.

On page 325 is a schedule of the activities to take place in each of the three periods.

4. Where do you find help for moving into some of the areas suggested in this chapter?

On *simulation,* read a 30-page section on "Simulation in education and training" in the October, 1969 *Educational Technology* magazine.

On *community study and service,* see *Where It's At,* a research guide for ·community organizing, published by the New England Free Press, 791 Tremont Street, Boston, Mass. 02118.

September	Beginning of October — RETREAT			POST-RETREAT October - December
	Friday	Saturday	Sunday	
At the beginning of September choose 5 or 6 kids to be the core group. Choose an inner-city church that will work with you on this project.	Retreat begins after school	8:00-9:00 a.m. — Breakfast	8:30-9:30 a.m. — Breakfast	After the retreat the following things should take place.
	7:00-8:00 p.m. — Dinner	9:00-11:00 a.m. — Speaker: Relates the film to Christian service, then guides small groups to examine Scripture relating to Friday evening discussion. (Romans 12, James, Acts 2; 5:4. etc.). Groups reassemble and report: leader pulls ideas relating "faith and works" together.	9:30-11:00 a.m. — Free time; individual or partner devotions encouraged.	1. Each person should be involved weekly either as part of the group or individually in some sort of service.
Saturday	8:00-8:30 — Free time		11:00-12:00—Worship Service; theme should emphasize and draw together discussions of church and social responsibility.	2. The service project group should meet once a month to share and evaluate.
Young people spend the whole day with a cooperating inner-city family. The assignment is to live with the family in every way. The young person is to find out all he can about inner-city life-style and attitudes.	8:30-9:00 — Film showing a social need in an area familiar to the young people.	11:00-12:00 — Recreation	12:00 — LUNCH	3. Once a month each group shares activities, feelings, etc., to the whole group.
	9:00-9:30 — Divide into small groups to discuss: "Does the church have any responsibility to these needs?"	12:00-1:00 — Lunch	Go home	4. Bible study groups should be set up for anyone within the group who feels the need. (Study will emphasize their area of service and related concerns.)
Sunday	9:30-9:45 —Group reassembles to report what small groups have concluded.	1:00-3:30—Core kids share with group their experiences in inner city. Other resource people may be called on to speak briefly. Leader then conducts an interview with the core kids. Interaction session where group can share and ask questions to core group or resource people.		In January the leaders will meet for evaluation.
The young people conduct the worship service in the inner-city church. Lunch together back home and a debriefing session. What happened? What did you learn? (Optional) On Sunday evening share the experience with the adults of the home church in the service.	10:00—Fellowship sharing time LIGHTS OUT	3:30-5:30 — Recreation 5:30-6:30 — Supper 7:00-9:30 — Create a list of possible projects. Divide into groups according to interest. Each group prepares and presents a creative skit (recreational or dealing with project). LIGHTS OUT		Also the leaders and young people will meet for evaluation and will at that time decide whether to continue or not.

Part Four

PLANNING FOR MINISTRY

PROGRAMMING YOUTH MINISTRY

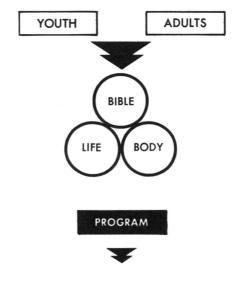

EPHESIANS 4:13

PROGRAMMING YOUTH MINISTRY

CHAPTERS

17

structuring for ministry

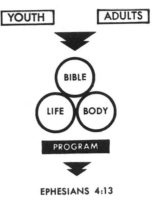

EPHESIANS 4:13

In a recent telephone interview[1] pastors told about their youth ministries and the dissatisfaction and failures which led to changes and experiments in nearly every church. New meeting times, new materials, new formats, and new group names were tried. The traditional time of the youth meeting was shifted from before to after evening services, settings changed from churches to homes, etc. Some had dropped Sunday youth meetings altogether, while others held fast to the traditional approach. Speakers, films, packaged programs, discussions and "tell it like it is" sessions were all being tried. In some churches socials had even replaced study and discussion.

The survey illuminates the common experience of many ministering with youth. Without clear concepts of goals, lacking a well-defined philosophy of ministry, experiment after experiment with programming is undertaken. And usually the result, after a brief surge of enthusiasm, is deeper discouragement and disinterest — followed by another desperate attempt to find something "new," "different," and hopefully, "successful."

But successful youth ministry isn't built on program or gimmicks. Successful youth ministry requires involvement of youths and adults in the three primary processes of ministry, and the development of programs that *facilitate involvement in these processes.*

The crucial issues in programming for ministry can be resolved into three: knowing the needs of the group and individuals, adopting a functional approach to youth programs and activities, and understanding the capabilities of available structural elements. The first of these is to be discussed in the following chapter on organization. The other two, functional programming and the capabilities of various structures, are the main concern of this chapter.

---

[1]Unpublished survey by Don and Martha MacCullough. Don is presently teaching Christian education at Philadelphia College of the Bible.

I've just stated what seems to me the underlying, the basic, the utterly crucial central principle that is to guide us in programming for, or in structuring, youth ministry. This prime principle can be stated simply in the form of a question which we ought to ask ourselves about every activity or program we plan: *How does the proposed activity facilitate involvement of youths and adults in the three primary processes of ministry (Scripture, Body, and Life)?*

Program planning criteria

Too often youth activities in the local church simply happen, without clear purpose or function. Or the purpose may be a questionable one, which has a negative impact in relation to the essential nature of Christ's Church. Socials and recreational activities are one part of the youth ministry in nearly all church programs, and a part which often is continued without thought of function. So the use of the proposed criterion, "Does the planned activity facilitate the three primary processes of ministry?" can be illustrated by an examination of different approaches to socials and recreation.

To illustrate this to my college classes I've obtained tape recordings from youth ministers in various parts of the country who have distinctively different approaches to social activities. Let me sketch three of them, each of which is represented in the practice of a particular church.

(1) *The 100% philosophy* This viewpoint, expressed in the practice of a church in Maryland, regards meeting the social needs of Christian youth as one of the church's responsibilities. Christian teens, as all youth, are developing socially. They need to learn to relate effectively to the opposite sex; they need fun times together. They need to see that being a Christian doesn't cut them off from the fun things of life.

Thus this church plans regular weekly social activities for its own teens, with the specific purpose that Christian kids might have fun together, thus meeting their social needs and, by encouraging boy-girl contacts in the context of the church, promote dating within the Christian community. In this church no "devotionals" or other spiritual emphases are "tacked on to the end" of socials. Socials are viewed as valid in themselves and as an integral part of the church's total ministry to the young people.

(2) *The 70-30% philosophy* This approach was adopted by a friend who ministered in a larger church in Phoenix, Arizona. He

determined to use socials creatively to involve more of his own teens in spiritual growth activities, and to build the group's status in the youth culture. He planned sharp and exciting weekly recreational and social evenings. These activities lasted about three hours, and featured sports, games, swimming, etc. The last hour of the evening was given to poolside Bible studies or films or special speakers.

Over a three-year period the program drew more and more kids from the church and outside it. And the reputation of that church for having class activities carried over to actually give teens who attended it higher status in the campus world! And, of course, the more kids that were attracted by the social activities, the more were present for the spiritual.

In this church, then, socials were not viewed as ends in themselves, but as means to several definite ends: to attract greater numbers for Bible study and other spiritual activities, to build the status of the group in the community, and, as a result, to help members of the group feel a sense of pride in belonging.

(3) *The 0% philosophy* This philosophy, represented by a church in California, states flatly that the meeting of social needs is not a primary responsibility of the spiritual leadership of the church. Rather than planning socials, the youth leadership encourages parents to accept this responsibility and open their homes to groups of their children's friends. Although this stand has brought pressure from parents who want social activities provided by the church, it has been firmly maintained.

For one reason, in this church there is a consistent emphasis on involvement with non-Christian youth. The leadership *doesn't want* Christian kids to develop friendships *only* with other Christians. So it refuses to compete with public school social and recreational programs, feeling that these are part of the "world" that Christians are to be "in" while not "of." Rejection of responsibility for the social life of youth, then, is balanced by acceptance of responsibility to help them live Christ "in the world" in which they are challenged to become involved.

There are, however, infrequent socials, of two types, and for distinct purposes.

One type of social is evangelistic, and for this all stops are pulled out, as the church plans exciting and unusual activities to attract non-Christians. Christian kids are encouraged to invite their friends,

331

there is a Gospel presentation, and the main burden of follow-up evangelism rests on the kids themselves.

A second type of social is simple, inexpensive, and also functional. It is designed to bring youth and their adult leaders together in a relaxed and informal atmosphere where they can get to know each other as persons as they play and talk together. The focus of this social is "getting acquainted."

From these descriptions, there are several things we might note before going on to a general evaluation.

In each case, the leader is *aware of his purpose in providing the activity.* There's no "let's do it because we've done it before," or ". . . because the other churches do it." The function of the activity is determined in providing and planning it.

Each of these approaches might be valid in a given local situation. That is, to some extent the approach one takes is conditioned by the needs and present state of growth of the kids in the group.

Then too, each approach has broad implications for the overall direction of the ministry. For instance, what are the long-range implications of the first, the 100% philosophy? — the one that sees the church as "responsible to meet the social needs of Christian teens." What happens if more and more the contacts of Christians are focused on and limited to other Christians?

In many churches such ingrownness develops with adults as well as with youth. All of life revolves around the church and church activities, and all friendships are with other Christians. But when the church becomes our world, contact with the world for which Christ died is too often broken! Our "separation" easily becomes a semi-monastic *isolation.*

I must confess that my own idea of the Church as God's transforming community is that it must function to equip the believer to live in the world and to communicate Christ to the world. I have seen too many young people from evangelical churches whose social lives have been so focused on Christian friends and church activities that they have not come to know non-Christians as persons and are, in fact, uncertain and frightened about relating to them. In the long run, I'm deeply concerned about the impact of this first philosophy on the direction of our ministry.

However, we can perhaps agree on these three thoughts. Each approach may have a valid role in a given ministry at a particular stage in its development. The role given to a particular activity (whatever it may be) should be understood and purposefully planned by the leadership. Each activity must be evaluated in the light of its long-range implications and its relationship to other elements in the youth ministry. (Thus, for example, the 0% philosophy, which encourages involvement in school activities, may not be appropriate if steps to help the kids become involved in Scripture and Body relationship have not been taken, and if they are thus unready to share Christ.)

With this said, let's return to the main issue in programming, which I stated earlier. In everything we must ask ourselves the question: "How does the proposed activity facilitate involvement of youth and adults in the three processes of ministry?"

We can apply this approach to social/recreational activities as to any others. Looking at the three primary processes broken down into the elements I've indicated in earlier chapters, we see:

Process Area	*Process Elements*
Scripture	being open and self-revealing
	being honest
	grasping the meaning of Scripture for our lives
	making response to God
	in worship
	in faith/obedience
	etc.
Body	intimate knowing of others
	being self-revealing
	bearing one another's burdens
	praying for, showing love to one another
	accepting and encouraging one another
	motivating
	etc.
Life	evaluating experiences
	expressing shared concerns
	seeking to grasp reality (Scripture)
	responding in obedient trust
	sharing Christ (witness)
	serving others
	etc.

Our question, then, becomes: What process elements can be facilitated by socials/recreation? And, What kinds of social activities are facilitating?

I think it's clear that the social philosophy presented as the last of the three, the 0% philosophy, is directly related to sharing Christ, and that socials can, as used in the California church, also give support to kids in witnessing efforts. It's also possible to see an indirect relationship to Body processes. While the deep sharing and coming to know one another as persons that is at the heart of Body ministry doesn't normally happen in the social/recreation context, it is still true that Christians need to see and know each other in many different situations. Sharing good times with others is one way of getting to know them as persons, and of sharing life.

So again, as in the California church, socials may have a function in providing informal settings where youths and adult leaders can get acquainted with each other. But while socials, which tend to maintain relationships on a rather superficial level, may have an indirect Body-building function, they are not central or crucial to that process.

Centrality I've suggested so far that we begin to think about elements in youth ministry by first attempting to relate each proposed activity to our model of ministry. That is, by asking whether or not a particular activity or structure or program actually involves young people and adults together in one of the three basic processes of ministry.

I've also suggested that we break down each process area into process elements: specific activities which characterize or constitute involvement in the processes.

Finally I suggested that some things we do in youth ministry have a direct impact on primary processes, while other things have an indirect impact, and still others have no impact at all. In making this last distinction, we move to the question of the *relative importance* of the things we plan and do in youth ministry. My suggestion here is a simple one: that our primary concern is to provide for and involve our youth in those activities which have the most direct relationship to elements of the three processes.

On this basis, it's easy to say that socials are *relatively less important* than, for instance, retreats at which teens are involved with each other in mutual self-revelation and welcoming (Rom 14:1). This is not, of course, to suggest that in planning a retreat we leave no time for games or fun. It is simply to point out that in planning *any* youth activity, we need to have its purpose clearly in mind, and to relate that purpose to the controlling concept of the nature of our ministry. Socials for socials' sake hardly fits this conception of youth ministry.

Specific activities   It's important here to note that the full range of things done in any youth ministry is available to the leader who seeks to minister in the pattern developed in this book. Youth leaders may still use films, or drama, or service projects, etc. Youth meetings may at times feature speakers. *But the function of these activities may very well differ from their function in the "normal" youth program.*

For example, films are often used by church youth groups. Too often a film is merely shown, and after it is over comments are made about it, or applications drawn from it. But films, like drama, have the unique capability of capturing and crystalizing a life issue so that youth can sense it, and, seeing it portrayed in the film, grasp and begin to deal with it. Too often a film attempts to deal with the issue in a cloture pattern. That is, the film seeks to present a problem, and then to present in its conclusion the Christian "answer." Rather than creating an open-ended situation which can stimulate the kind of probing and sharing that characterizes both Body and Life ministry processes, the film-maker feels compelled to make a presentation and then give his answer.

But in youth ministry we're much more concerned about bringing teens to explore their own lives and experiences, to discuss and define issues, and to find their own answers in Christ, than we are that they hear what a filmmaker has to say. When these purposes are kept in mind, when we have as a goal the use of a film to launch teens in one of these processes, then we *use the film differently than it is used in most churches.* When the film approaches a climax, and the life issue has been stated but not resolved, we stop the film. And we challenge our teens to explore the issue, its relationship to their own lives, to suggest a possible range of solutions, to relate them to the Christian revelation, and to make personal decisions and commitments.

Having specific goals in mind helps us evaluate the function of each youth ministry activity, and to plan how to use resources creatively and purposively.

In summary, then, I've suggested that in structuring youth ministries we have several clear guidelines to follow, and that all of them are derived directly from our philosophy of youth ministry itself. These guidelines are:

1. Plan activities and programs with a definite purpose in view.

2. Measure the purpose by this test: How does this planned activity facilitate involvement of youth and adults in the three primary processes of youth ministry?

3. Determine carefully elements that are integral to involvement in each of the three processes (see p. 333).

4. Give priority to activities which directly facilitate involvement of youth and adults in these process elements.

5. Use resources (such as films) creatively, to involve youth and adults actively in the process elements.

Program structures

By program structures I am thinking of those situations in which youth and adults get together — in the most simple terms: "meetings." In most churches the program is developed around several continuing, or permanent, meeting structures. Thus, a church will have a regular Sunday school program, a regular Sunday evening youth meeting, a regular youth choir, a regular Wednesday night youth prayer meeting, regular monthly or weekly socials, etc. The tendency even in churches with limited youth programs is to center the ministry around the regular continuing programs (usually Sunday school and Youth Group), and to supplement these with infrequent or irregular retreats, camp programs, and/or service and evangelistic projects.

I'm convinced that in general this approach to ministry is unhealthy. We ought to be constantly evaluating and constantly flexible in our programming. To a great extent this means that the major weight of our ministry may better be carried by *short-term program structures.*

Let's say, for instance, that we determine that *the* primary need of kids in Community Church is to come to know and trust one another, building toward a true Body relationship. So, for the first quarter of the church year, September-November, we're going to focus on involving kids in process elements that contribute to Body development. How might we do this?

Let's start off with a three-day "before school" retreat. Sort of as a last fling and launching combined. We go off to a camp with our adult and college-age leaders, and plan rather intensive "getting-to-know-you" activities (perhaps along the lines suggested in the retreat on pp. 259-263). For this we break the kids down into groups that correspond to the Sunday school classes they will be meeting in during the new school year.

Back home, we want to continue to build relationships in these groups, so we replace our regular Sunday school curriculum (for this quarter) with Lyman Coleman's *Serendipity,* a renewal-oriented program that helps kids get involved with each other by building on familiar Bible stories and concepts (see pp. 150, 151). Also for this quarter we plan *Body* meetings for the whole group (all who will attend), meeting together Sunday evenings. In these we focus on discovering from Scripture how Christians are to love and support each other, and then we invite the kids to share needs and perceptions right there, and to receive from others in the group those ministries they have been reading about.

These two programs are open to all the youth in the church, though not all kids will take part.

At the same time, the youth leader wants to begin building leadership in the youth group, and so he gives an open invitation to kids who want to meet with him at 6:30 one morning a week before school. They meet at a selected spot, perhaps a coffee shop or restaurant, and on different mornings he meets with groups from the different high schools group members attend. In the meetings he seeks to get to know the kids, to encourage them to pray for each other and share needs, and leads a short Bible study for which each is asked to prepare and to which each contributes.

The youth leader also spends time with those who will lead the Sunday morning group discussions, talking about and praying about individual teens in each group, planning how to help each individual in the coming week's study and sharing. Much time is spent during these months with the youth leadership staff, to build with them the same kind of Body relationship that is being worked toward in the youth group itself.

If special needs are seen, short term programs can be developed to meet them. Normally these will grow out of the expressed and thus-discovered needs of the teens. Are a number of kids concerned about dating relationships, or parent/teen conflicts? Perhaps a Friday evening, Saturday "overnight" at the church, using films and role plays to help focus issues and stimulate sharing and discussion will be appropriate. Or perhaps a series of five Wednesday night studies based on a book like my *How Far Can I Go?* will be planned for those who are particularly interested. It's not necessary in a program like this that *all* the youth show up: it's enough that we are providing for those who sense a need and desire to respond.

The next quarter we may shift our emphasis. Say that during the Sunday school hour we return to our regular curriculum for the quarter. Sunday nights we continue the Body meeting approach, which the kids who come are appreciating, and this develops into a team meeting (like that described on pp. 215-218). Because the kids have become enthusiastic about sharing Christ in the high school, you switch the early morning prayer breakfasts to afternoon sessions where you have more time with the kids, and work with individuals and groups from each high school to plan outreach strategy. Part of your strategy involves a New Year's retreat that focuses on how relationship with Christ can "overflow" to touch others' lives. And among the things you plan on the retreat is a four-day Easter evangelistic camp, the "ticket" to which is at least one non-Christian friend to accompany each attending teen from your group.

And the next quarter? Perhaps something else: elective doctrinal and "how-to-study-your-Bible" classes during Sunday school hour, Sunday evening outreach team meetings to continue evangelism, special small group "counseling" sessions with all the teens of the church, in which leaders meet with three or four at a time, perhaps a preparatory program for a Summer Missions program, etc.

The particular program, activities, and approaches any youth leader develops will be dependent on the growth and the needs of the youth, as a group and as individuals, at a particular time. In fact, all I've tried to illustrate with the foregoing is simply this: youth programming must be *flexible* and it must be *responsive* to the needs of youth. For flexible, responsive programming, it's important to think in terms of short-term — not long-term — structures.

It's important to be ready and willing to change — as long as all changes are related (1) to the needs of the youth with whom you are ministering, and (2) to the basic philosophy of youth ministry which provides theologically derived direction for ministry.

PROBE
  case histories
  discussion questions
  thought-provokers
  resources

  1. Several terms are used in specific and special ways in this chapter.
     If they are to prove serviceable tools for programming, they should
     be understood clearly.
     To check your grasp of the concepts expressed in each of the
     following, jot down a brief definition of it now, expressing your

present understanding. Then check back over the chapter and develop revised definitions.

    (1) the "prime principle" in program-planning
    (2) the three primary processes
    (3) process elements
    (4) central activities
    (5) program structures
    (6) flexible and responsive programming

2. I provided on page 333 a rather sketchy chart, showing some of the process elements in each of the three primary process areas. You'll note in looking at the chart that the process elements listed are actually *activities youth are engaged in which lead to growth in the process areas.*

    This chart is not an exhaustive one by any means. There are additional activities that may be said to be characteristic of involvement in each process area. In planning youth ministries, we need a clear idea of variety and range, as well as type, of process elements in which we should seek to involve our teens. So it should be particularly helpful for you to develop your own chart of *process elements.* For help in developing a more comprehensive list, you may want to reread the sections of this book that deal with each of the three primary processes (Scripture, Body, and Life).

3. One final practical task may help you evaluate the present state and direction of your current ministry with youth. Why not complete the following chart (including additional process elements developed in the PROBE 2 study)?

This chart (p. 340) lets you see visually the process elements for which your present structures seem to provide.

In the next chapter we'll have more to say about evaluating the effectiveness of involvement in the processes. But at this point, we'll only ask, Are youth given opportunity for involvement in key elements of the three primary processes through your present program?

PROCESS AREAS

LIFE BODY SCRIPTURE

PROCESS ELEMENTS
(from p. 333)

being open being honest etc.

LONG-TERM PROGRAMS

SHORT-TERM PROGRAMS

18

organizing
for growth

EPHESIANS 4:13

In the previous chapter we looked at some of the program structures which can support youth's involvement in the three primary processes of ministry. It was suggested that we need to view programs and structures in a distinctly functional way, always testing what we are doing against our purposes in youth ministry and always ready to respond flexibly to meet developing needs in the group and in individuals.

This last thought is a particularly important one. For it implies a feedback system that keeps us informed of where teens are in their growth as Christians and as persons. It implies an organization that uniquely facilitates communication within the group, and that has as its main concern *persons* — not the planning of programs.

How do we organize our ministry for this kind of growth — the growth of youth as Christian persons? What concepts and principles can guide us here?

There are several kinds of organization structures for church youth groups that are currently popular. One approach has the youth elect officers who represent them and who, with the youth sponsor(s), plan activities and programs. In this *representative form* of organization, as in our representative form of government, the assumption is that interests and needs will be communicated to the leaders by group members, who then act on their behalf. This assumption is usually unwarranted in both situations. Too often teen officers are not in close touch with other kids in the group. Many will even develop negative feelings about them when they fail to respond to the plans made for them, and when their "spirituality" may seem to flag. Even in the best of circumstances, the officers' concerns are focused on planning and motivating others for involvement in program activities. And as the officers represent the group, involvement with the officers in fact seems to blind adult leaders to the need for contact and communication with all group members.

A second approach to organization features a *planning group* system. In this popular form of organization, the group is divided into teams, each of which is responsible to plan and put on programs for the others in the youth group, and perhaps to plan other activities. The idea here is to involve the whole group by spreading responsibility for group meetings, and giving everyone a chance to develop various "leadership" skills by taking different roles in the teen meetings.

This approach, pioneered by a Christian education publisher and currently the organizational base on which a number of published youth materials are planned, also has a number of weaknesses. For one thing, once again the focus of the organization is on programs and meetings. And planning group leaders are cast as motivators, to urge others to take part in the meetings. And very seriously, as publishers of such materials are presently becoming aware, high schoolers are not any longer responsive to this approach. While there may be values in taking this approach with young teens (junior highs), most older teens (particularly those who have been organized on this plan as young teens) are openly disinterested.

Because in practice this form of organization channels the attention of the gathered planning groups toward programs (rather than into the three primary processes of ministry), little meaningful communication takes place in the planning group settings. If you doubt this assertion, check the suggested time allotted and the tasks to be accomplished in such meetings, as outlined in published materials.

Often the program materials themselves as provided by publishers give excellent seed thoughts and helps for involving youth in exploration of various significant issues. Such materials ought to be purchased and be made a part of the youth leader's resource library. But attempting to build a youth ministry on a steady diet of such programs week after week is tragically self-defeating. And organizing the youth to facilitate the production of such programs (the planning-group approach) is also, in the long run, self-defeating.

A third approach to organization brings adults and youth together in a "youth council." Although still a representative system, youth councils often function on a policy level, seeking to consider the broader needs and directions of the ministry. Still, communication channels are seldom clear. Though youth members may be elected from various organizations (one from each Sunday school class, two from the Youth Group, one from Youth Choir, etc.), they are too often viewed as representing these organizations rather than as being channels between persons. And little opportunity is given in classes or groups to hear reports of council members, or to request information on the feelings and needs of the kids. Even when such opportunity is given, the topics of concern are normally: "How do you feel about this program," or ". . . that plan" or ". . . our Sunday school classes," etc.

Somehow each form of organization that I've mentioned seems (1) to view as adequate communication from youth through *representatives,* (2) to put elected leaders in roles where they make decisions about and seek to gain general support for programs and meetings, and (3) to focus attention on the program plans rather than on persons.

Strikingly, none of these characteristics seems related to the nature of spiritual leadership as discussed in chapters 7-9! Even when these approaches to organization do "work," they tend to train the most concerned of our Christian youth for organizational roles rather than for spiritual leadership.

I'm aware that many will disagree, some violently, with what I've been saying in this chapter. They'll object, "But it isn't *necessarily* so! Elected officers, or planning group leaders, can be trained to function in the spiritual leadership way. This criticism of the ways we've organized youth groups isn't really valid."

To this objection I must express both agreement and disagreement. Theoretically, elected officers or group leaders *can* be trained to function in different ways — just the ways I'm going to suggest in this chapter. But practically, they are not. The fact remains that these organizational forms are *primarily oriented to programming, not to personal ministry.* No one who has sat in on meetings of youth group officers can help but be aware that the focus of conversation and concern is group meetings, what to do in them, how to gain the cooperation of the group to attend them, which teen will call so and so, or take this or that responsibility, and so on. But youth should not be taught to focus their concern on planning and maintenance of youth programs. They should be taught to love and minister to persons. They should not be trained to see the church as an organization, but to experience the Church as an organism.

What I suggest, in fact, is that we do away with officers and elected (or appointed) teen leaders, and that we organize the youth group on entirely different principles than the representative, program-oriented, organizational role patterns the discussed forms imply.

An organic approach to organization

I've just suggested that we reject contemporary organizational patterns for the youth group and reorganize on entirely different principles. It's helpful to spell out some of the principles on which this reorganization is to be based, particularly to make more clear the contrasts between organic and contemporary forms of organization and thus the compelling reasons for reorganization.

Contrast one: responsive vs. representative leadership It is true that one of our tasks in ministry with youth is to develop Christian leaders. We must provide a context for maximum growth, so that the spiritual gifts God has given each believing teen may surface, be recognized, and develop. It should also be realized that not every one of the youth in a church will respond to the opportunities to grow that a youth ministry provides. A number will remain untouched.

There are a variety of reasons for this. Some teens may be "verbal Christians." They've heard the Gospel from childhood, they know all the right words, but they have never responded personally to Jesus Christ. With others, a lack of response may simply be un-readiness. Some Christian teens who avoid opportunities for full dedication to Christ in high school respond enthusiastically as collegians or in young adulthood. God has His own time for each of us. And there are other reasons. But whatever they may be, the fact remains that in any youth ministry there will be some youth ready to respond, and others who remain on the fringe, involved minimally, but seemingly untouched and unready for discipleship.

These two groups are represented in the diagram at the right. As indicated, in most churches the *core group* will, particularly in the beginning of a ministry, be considerably smaller than that of the fringe group. This latter group, labeled the *contact group,* is made up of teens with whom the church has regular contact through one or more programs, and for whom church activities must be

provided, but who have not yet responded to the invitation to full discipleship.

In most churches *the primary strategic error in youth ministry is to organize to minister primarily to the contact group, and to largely ignore the core group.*

One of the reasons for this is that in most churches leaders still naively expect to have a spiritual impact on kids in and through *meetings* — not in and through persons. Thus programs and the organization of the group itself focus on gaining hearings with the contact group, and much of what the officers and adult leaders discuss decides what kinds of programs will motivate and interest the fringe kids.

The fact is, however, that the most significant group is the core group — the teens who are already responsive to the Lord, and who can be led into disciplined lives. *And the most effective way to reach fringe kids in the contact group and lead them into the core is by the impact of loving contacts with the core teens.* Contact group teens are to be *drawn* into the core, not *dragged* in by more and better programs.

An organic organizational structure recognizes, then, that life is most effectively communicated through life, and it focuses on building up kids in the core group in order that they may spread dedication through the group by the kindling power of their own love for Jesus and one another. In a very real sense, *the core kids are the teen leaders.* But their leadership is not going to be of an "elected representative" type. It's going to be the servant-leader, example type, discussed in chapters 7 to 9.

Thus we now can see something of what is meant by a *responsive* leadership rather than a *representative* leadership. We need to view those kids who respond to Christ in true discipleship as our leaders, not those who are elected by members of the group.

This responsive leadership is not exclusive. It is open to everyone in the group. That is, anyone in the contact group should be able to move into the core group *at his own choice*. We make provision for this by inviting all to core meetings—but, at the same time, insisting on a level of dedication and discipleship that makes membership both costly and meaningful. (By this I mean spelling out clearly our expectations for those who choose to take part in our core sessions. In some cases we may consider an early prayer/Bible-study breakfast a core meeting. Or perhaps an evening session where kids share what they have discovered in personal Bible study that each member of the group is expected to complete before attending.) As I mentioned, much of the time and the majority of the personal contacts of the adult leadership should be invested in core group activities and development of relationships with those who respond by choosing to accept the disciplines of core group membership.

This, then, is one of the principles on which our organization of the youth in youth ministry is to be based. We seek to develop a responsive, not a representative, leadership.

Contrast two: person vs. program orientation   In the new organizational structure, we seek to orient those who respond to the invitation to leadership to persons, not to programs. By this I mean that we do not try to make the kids responsible for the programs we plan (though individuals may be invited to take various planning responsibilities). The development of programs, the planning of retreats, etc., is the responsibility of the adult leadership, in response to needs that youth reveal.

Instead, we seek in our core gatherings to develop in teens a sense of responsibility and a love for other teens. This love is not exclusively exercised in the core group. But the teens are encouraged to love and get to know, to share with and pray for, kids in the contact group and non-Christians on the campus.

In keeping our focus on encouragement of core teens to love others, we are helping them see that the Christian is only indirectly concerned with church activities — but deeply concerned with the persons who make up Christ's Body. And thus the major topic of conversation, and the major burden of prayer, as far as the group as a whole is concerned, is the persons that make it up. By taking responsibility for programming and motivating attendance at meetings off youth, we're free to help them develop a concern and sense of responsibility for persons. And never think that there is no difference between *indirect* concern for persons ("we want to get everyone out to this retreat so they'll grow closer to Christ") and *direct* concern for persons ("Ken's really shook about school just now. He wants to come, but he's afraid he'll flunk out if . . ."). There *is* a difference. A tremendous one.

Contrast three: communication vs. control patterns Each of the organizational patterns I criticized earlier was essentially a control pattern. Youth were involved as leaders and given control functions, if not to make final decisions about programs and plans, at least to influence other teens and gain their cooperation or attendance.

The organizational form I am suggesting is concerned that the youth be given a communication function — not a control function. That is, that the primary function of kids in the core group is not to make decisions about "what next" (although they will have the *greatest* impact on decisions, in providing needed feedback), but to share with each other and the adult leadership all they know of the needs and concerns of one another, and contact group kids.

I just noted that the organizational pattern I am suggesting is oriented to persons, not programs and that the kids in the core group (the true leaders) become involved in knowing and loving contact group kids. What is learned of their needs and interests, their ideas and attitudes, their suggestions and criticisms, is shared in core meetings with a view to loving and praying for them, and finding ways to draw them closer to the Lord. As needs are shared, the adult leaders (who are also involved with individuals in the contact as well as the core group), develop quite an accurate impression of the needs of the larger group, and seek to meet these needs in a variety of ways and through a variety of program structures. *It was only because I envisioned this kind of feedback through the youth organization that I could suggest last chapter that we think in terms of ministry structures that are responsive and flexible, and thus short-term.* Only where there is a communication system that lets us know where the group as a whole and individuals are as persons can we hope to minister to needs, guided all the while by our overall concept of the nature of youth ministry.

The organization we need for youth ministry, then, is one which provides for open communication lines, not for youth's involvement in programming control.

347

Organic organization outlined

With some of the assumptions about the nature of our organization explained, we can turn to an overview of organic organization itself, and the function of the various elements. The organizational pattern is diagramed in Figure 10 on page 437, and shows the position of the youth leader, the adult leadership core, the teen core, the contact group, and the world/setting in which the group is placed.

The leader As I suggested earlier in this book, the leader in any Christian ministry is central to its development. This is true whether the leader is a pastor, one of several elders in the New Testament pattern of multiple-lay-leadership, a youth minister, or a "head sponsor." The leader is central, because in the biblical pattern he sets the tone for the group, providing the example, and demonstrating in "going before" the others in love and self-revelation the realities of the Christian life.

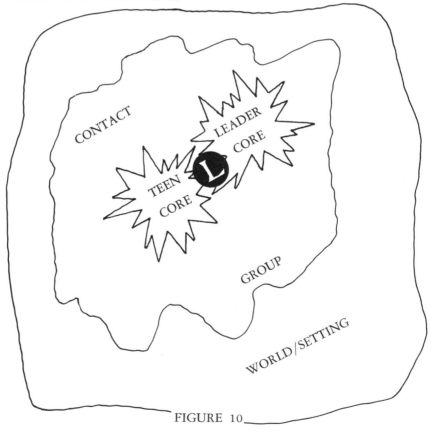

FIGURE 10

Elements in an "organic organization" pattern

As leader, he needs to set the example both for the adult leader core and for the teen core, as well as maintain relationships with kids in the contact group and non-Christians in the youth world/setting.

The leader's time is spent investing his life in others, in motivating and encouraging discipleship primarily in his leader core and teen core. Strategically, he seeks to reach the whole group and the world around by igniting response to Christ in these two key groups.

Although it helps if the person who is the leader has an awareness of the many resources and options open to him in terms of materials and activities and structures for youth ministry, it is essential that he have a clear grasp of the principles and processes of youth ministry. For, ultimately, the guidance of the program and the development of its structures in response to discovered needs is his responsibility.

Teen core   The teen core, as noted above, is formed of youth who respond to the open invitation to go on in discipleship with Christ. Through the example of the adult leadership, core teens are guided to focus their love for one another, for others in the contact group, and for kids in the world. Through sharing in the core meetings, they come to sense their responsibility for all the others in the Body, and provide the kind of information about the group and individuals in it that is necessary to guide the adult leadership in planning the overall program.

The leader core   The leader core is made up of all adults (and in many cases college students) who minister with youth. Ideally, this includes all associated with youth ministry in any agency, as youth ministry should be considered as a whole in the local church, not divided into "Sunday school" and "youth group" organizations with separate staffs and, usually, separate philosophies.

While members of the leader core may have different roles in the ministry, such as "teacher" or as "leader" of kids going to a particular high school, they are still to function primarily in the biblical servant-leader pattern. That is, they are to be examples, involved in the lives of the youth, sharing themselves with the teens, involved with them in the three primary processes of ministry — in Scripture, in Body, and in Life.

Here, I may stress again, the role of the overall leader is crucial. For much of his time will have to be spent with the adult leader core, helping them to think in terms of persons, not programs, and leading them to the kind of Body relationship with one another that they seek to foster among the youth.

Finally, I might note that the leader core shares with the youth director or head sponsor responsibility for developing the program structures through which the needs of the group and individuals are to be met.

Contact group As noted, this group is the "fringe group" — teens who are associated with the church and attend some of the youth activities, but who have not responded to the challenge to discipleship as have the core kids. The failure to respond in no way indicates that they should be disregarded in planning the youth ministry, or that the activities they do attend should be discontinued. In fact, as the core group is developed, the contact group becomes the primary recruiting ground for disciples. So at all times a concern for the contact group kids as individuals, a love for them, and an attitude of honest welcoming and acceptance of them needs to be maintained. Also the adult leadership will show concern by seeking to develop personal relationships with contact group kids as well as encouraging core kids to build such relationships.

World/setting The world/setting of the youth group is the campus and neighborhood world in which the young people live daily, and in which they meet non-Christian teens. Thus the world/setting, although shaped by the general attitudes and values of youth culture, is viewed primarily as the *persons* who move in it. And so the goal of the church youth ministry is clear: to reach out into the world/setting, to share Jesus Christ with teens, and to draw them into His Body as they respond in saving faith to Him.

The primary approach to teens in the world is the same as the approach to kids in the contact group at church. Young people who are growing in the Lord reach out with His love to them. To share themselves, and to care.

At times, as discussed in chapter 16, individuals or the group may minister love in service. But always, in individual contact, each will seek to love others and so share Jesus Christ with them.

This very loose organization, then, *is designed for communication of life by reaching out to persons with love.* Reserving program-planning for the adult leadership, organic organization of youth ministry frees youth to focus the concern of a responsive teen leadership on persons, communicating the needs of individuals to one another and to the adult leaders, while communicating in turn to individuals in the contact group and world/setting the love of God.

Evaluation

One final advantage of the organic organization as developed in this chapter resides in its provision for constant evaluation of the ministry.

Evaluation in Christian education has historically been conducted on two levels, while in fact the truly meaningful level of evaluation is a third. This means that we have had no truly meaningful way to evaluate what we have been doing in our church for many, many years.

Level one evaluation is in terms of "programs provided." You may have seen guides of this type, which are often used in denominational evaluation booklets (and even, with some slight modification, in this book!). This guide simply asks, "Do you have a departmentalized Sunday school?" "Do you have one teacher for every six children in Primary through Junior High departments?" "Do you have a children's church program?"

It's obvious that questions of this kind simply do not speak to the *effectiveness* of programs, but rather assume that if a church provides certain activities and conditions, effective ministry will take place.

I noted that a chart of this type exists in this book. Look back on page 340, and you'll note that you were asked to analyze (another word for evaluate) the programs you provide in your present youth ministry by checking process elements which presumably take place in your various long-term and short-term programs. It should be clear that, while such a chart can help you see what you may *not* be doing, it can tell you very little about what you *are* doing. Simply because an opportunity to interact with Scripture in a particular way, for example, is provided, does not mean that anyone in that situation is so interacting. Or that any are responding.

Evaluation on this level tells one nothing either of the present state of the practice in an organization, or of the results in persons' lives.

Level two evaluation is in terms of "good practice." You can also find examples of this kind of evaluation guide in Christian education materials and publications. "Does the teacher provide opportunity for the student to talk?" "What percentage of the time is teacher talk and what percentage student talk?" "Are questions open-ended to stimulate discussion, or simply 'yes or no' in nature?"

This kind of evaluation is also carried out by observation, as when a supervisor in the public school system watches a "practice teacher," or a consultant visits a Sunday school to observe.

At best this kind of evaluation can point up weaknesses in practice, and suggest methods and techniques for improving the quality of the teaching or leading. But again this kind of evaluation says nothing about results. One can't tell what is happening in the life of an individual by observing class or group practices. And because this kind of evaluation cannot give us answers about effectiveness, or needed changes in our ministry, it is not what we need.

Level three evaluation is concerned with what is going on in persons. It involves a revelation of needs, and a revelation of growth.

There have been some attempts to assess needs and changes in persons, normally through self-report questionnaires. Although these may be helpful at times, they encourage response only to the questions that are asked. And too often these may be the wrong questions! Also such forms do not provide for continuous appraisal.

Both a broader self-revelation and continuous appraisal are very important for youth ministry. Too often the only way we learn the questions we should ask of youth is *after* they have told us their experiences and concerns. If we are to attempt flexible and responsive structuring in youth programs and activities, we need continuous feedback. We need to know when something we've done has helped, and how much it has helped, and we need to know when we've failed. We need to know what needs are surfacing *now,* and how deeply these are felt, and by how many. We need, in short, a continuous flow of deeply personal information that can be gained only by a sharing of lives in response to love.

The organization I've suggested, then, has the advantage, in maintaining the kind of *personal* communication lines discussed, of providing youth leadership with a unique flow of the kind of data that permits constant evaluation of the state of the ministry.

Other contemporary forms of organization simply do not provide for effective, *level three* evaluation.

Does organic organization work?

Many raise very practical and, on the surface, valid objections to ministry concepts that I've presented in other books. I'm sure these same objections will be raised to this book, and to this chapter in particular. "But," they say, "does it work? Isn't this all 'ivory tower' stuff?" And others comment, "If only he'd work with youth in a church instead of in a college, he'd find out why it's impossible to do what he's talking about."

I appreciate these objections, and the element of validity they contain. I am not now serving a church as pastor or youth minister, and so I can't point with pride to a particular success of "my method." I do, however, have several reasons for believing that these particular objections are not actually valid, and in fact make nothing that I have said in this book or others of less value than if I were presently ministering in a church. But because, as I said, the objecttions are raised and do seem to have some validity, it seems to me worthwhile to take a moment to answer these objections.

First, the pragmatic test is hardly a final one. Because something "worked" for me doesn't mean it would "work" for you. Each of us has different gifts, each ministers in different situations. Therefore I could hardly promote a particular system just because it worked for me. That would be totally insufficient reason to argue that you ought to adopt my approach. (And, by the way, if I did argue this way, the same persons who object now would have good grounds to complain, "But my situation is different. I can't do it the way you did.")

Second, what I've tried to present in this book is *principles*. This is, in the technical sense of the term, a "theoretical" book. It develops a philosophy of youth ministry — it does not give you five easy steps to success with youth!

As a theoretical book, a book on philosophy of youth ministry, it pays more attention to *why* we develop our ministry in certain ways than to *how* we do specific things. I have tried to provide practical ideas and resources in the PROBE sections, but this is definitely not a book with 40 gimmicks that will increase your attendance at the youth group.

As a theoretical work, then, it has to be judged on theoretical grounds. Simply saying, "I don't think it will work," or "I think you'd have a hard time doing it yourself," is hardly a basis for rejecting or accepting a philosophy of ministry. No one, in fact, suggests that *any* approach to youth ministry is easy. Or that any guarantees success. God is the great Actor in our ministries, and His Spirit the One who touches lives and hearts. The basic question we

353

need to ask of a philosophy of ministry is not, "Does it look easy?" but *"Is it in harmony with the way God works?"*

Third, then, is this: Is it theologically and biblically sound? To me, this is the most significant consideration of all. For in all I have written I have tried to understand and explore God's written revelation, and to express what He has shown us of His Body and the nature of the ministry to which we are called.

I am, I confess, very much disturbed by people who ask only, "Are you doing it?" and overlook the central and crucial issue: Is this the pattern of ministry which God has revealed?

How long must we evangelicals, who pride ourselves in our high view of Scripture, resist seeking in God's Word direction for our ministries while querulously complaining that anything which does seek to explore Scripture for guidelines "looks hard"?

I must confess that as a fallible and limited human being, I cannot guarantee that in this book I have at all times caught and expressed the thoughts of God. That is far beyond me. So I am and must remain open to correction on the basis of possibly having misunderstood or misapplied what Scripture is saying. But at the same time I must decisively reject objections that excuse failure to examine one's own ministry under the authority of Scripture by suggesting that, since another is not currently involved in a particular ministry, his view can be automatically rejected.

Finally, I must also say that the basic approach to youth ministry developed in this book *does* work. I know personally men in youth ministry whose works are built on the biblical principles developed here, and whose impact on young people, some of whom I also know, are among the most exciting and vital renewals in our country. A few of these men are quoted in this book, or used as examples in PROBE features. Each of them is building his ministry on what he has seen in the Word of God as guiding principles and each has discovered both that a biblically based youth ministry *is* hard and that God is a faithful and a trustworthy leader.

May we all be willing to trust Him.

Summary

In summary, then, I have developed in this chapter an organizational pattern that is closely linked with what has been said in the rest of the book about the nature of leadership and the nature of the three primary processes of ministry. In a very real sense, this chapter and the rest of the book depend on each other. Only when a ministry is designed to involve youth in Scripture, in Body relationship, and in Life, will the organization I've suggested prove effective. And, conversely, only an organic type of organization will support and encourage the three processes of ministry.

PROBE
case histories
discussion questions
thought-provokers
resources

1. As in the preceding chapter, certain terms and concepts are crucial for understanding the approach I suggest. So take a moment to jot down your own definition of the following, and then work back through the chapter to develop sharper, final definitions.
   (1) representative leadership
   (2) responsive vs. representative leadership
   (3) person vs. program orientation
   (4) communication vs. control pattern
   (5) core group
   (6) contact group
   (7) *level three* evaluation

2. I suggested in this chapter that teen "leaders" in most organizational settings do in fact focus on program concerns, not people concerns.

   If you are presently ministering with youth, check me out by listing, right now, the *topics of conversation* in your last three meetings with teen officers. Also jot down an estimate of the time given to the discussion of each.

   How much of the interaction was oriented to program-planning or ways to get kids to cooperate with programs, and how much to considering group members as individuals and showing concern for them?

3. In this chapter I suggested that there are two core groups with which the youth leader needs to invest himself. The first is the adult leader core, and the second the youth core, made up of kids who respond to the challenge to discipleship.

   In most churches, this latter core group will be small. In your church, who do you think would be ready to respond now? List names, if possible.

   How might you go about developing them into biblical servant-leaders? Got any ideas?

4. It's probably difficult to grasp just what I am suggesting when I recommend that we take various responsibilities off youth and accept them ourselves. This is particularly difficult when so much of youth ministry literature seems to suggest the opposite — *giving* youth responsibility — and when good business management practices insist on delegation.

But I believe that what I have suggested is important, and that we should at least understand what is involved. Perhaps it's easiest to make the distinctions needed in terms of *kind* of responsibility we give youth. In youth ministry literature, the usual responsibility that is given to youth is *program* responsibility. In this setting the leader acts as a coach, and helps the youth do their jobs. But the kind of responsibility we need to be concerned with is *people* responsibility, and this is not directly related to "jobs."

It's probably easiest to see what I'm suggesting by looking at the two approaches in operation, in the planning of a retreat in the normal "delegate responsibility" pattern, and then in the suggested "adult accept responsibility" pattern.

Retreat planning: approach one

At the beginning of the year, the group's officers had laid out an annual calendar, and a retreat was scheduled for Easter vacation. In November at a biweekly officers' meeting, several committees were appointed to prepare for the retreat. There was a transportation committee, a program committee, a site committee, an entertainment committee, and a publicity committee. Committee chairmen were invited to meet with Mr. Swanson, the youth minister, before December to get help for starting on their jobs.

Ted, chairman of the transportation committee, was given places to check for bus rental, and he and Mr. Swanson discussed the advantages and disadvantages of using cars. Ted was then expected to determine costs, and also to poll the kids and their parents to see how everyone felt about using cars and if adult drivers might be available. He could then make recommendations to the full committee.

The program committee gathered at Mr. Swanson's home and went through his resource files. They checked materials from several publishers and looked over books that others had used as bases for retreats. Finally they decided on a topic presented in some of the sharpest-looking materials. The chairman was then given the job of working with Mr. Swanson to choose kids for the various parts that teens would have, signing the selected kids up for their parts and seeing to it that they were prepared.

Entertainment and publicity committee chairmen also had their turn, and in the chat with Mr. Swanson, what they were to do was laid out and a calendar of due dates was set up. The site committee chairman was given a list of eight camps and retreat centers within a few hundred miles of the church, and told to write or phone each for brochures and to check availability. He was to be ready with his recommendations by the next scheduled meeting, because time was slipping away fast.

As a good delegator, Mr. Swanson checked up regularly on the progress of his committees, and repeatedly told his kids that if they had any problems they should be sure to see him. He also praised them liberally when they were working well. But, as usually is the case, there were some who just didn't get the job done. Disappointed but not dismayed, Mr. Swanson worked especially hard the last week and a half before the retreat to catch up on the loose ends, and everything seemed to go off pretty well.

Retreat planning: approach two

Spring was the traditional time for a retreat at Staub Memorial Church; so in early September Carl, the youth minister, had reserved a camp in lower Wisconsin for the Easter break. Now in January he was sitting around his living room with the fifteen kids who made up the committed core he'd been building toward since he came to Staub a year and a half before.

He brought up the subject of the retreat casually, and asked the kids what they felt the retreat ought to accomplish. They had some of the usual ideas at first: a "deeper walk," maybe a focus on personal evangelism, maybe something on getting involved in better Bible study. But Carl led them to probe for needs. What did they feel their own greatest needs were just then? How about the other kids in the group? As they talked, he encouraged them to think of individuals they knew. What were their needs? Where were they spiritually? And how about the group as a whole? What did the whole group — not just the gang gathered there that night — really need?

It was amazing how the time went, but about an hour and forty minutes later some things were beginning to come clear. And the whole gang was agreed that what everyone needed — they themselves as well as the others who were not so involved — was to experience more of the unity the Bible says we have in Christ. The fringe kids needed to be drawn in and to know the love and acceptance that was beginning to mean so much to those who had responded to Carl's ministry. And the core kids needed to be reminded that they were *all* one in Christ, and they needed help to resist the temptation to look at kids on the fringe as "outsiders."

With the need defined, they spent nearly half an hour praying about what had been discussed, looking to God to meet the needs they felt.

Carl resisted the temptation to set up "committees." Instead, he began in the coming weeks to encourage all the kids to get closer to the others, in preparation for the retreat. And to pray for individuals, both that they'd come, and that God would meet each one there. Carl took on responsibility to plan the program himself. This wasn't to be a packaged program. He dug into his resource files, and tried to tailor the program to fit the specific needs of his group and to fit the activities to the kinds of things they liked and responded to. This kind of expertise was something none of the kids he worked with had as yet developed, and he didn't expect them to take on responsibilities for which they were not prepared. (After the retreat Carl planned to sit down with three or four of the key kids and evaluate. In the evaluation, he would take them through his planning process, and consider with them why some things had been effective, and some had not.)

Although he had made arrangements in September for the retreat center, Carl drove up one Saturday with Roger to look it over. On the way they stopped off at two other camps, and talked about the advantages and disadvantages of the different settings. While Carl didn't make Roger responsible to select a site, he did want some in the group to know how to select a retreat center, and to understand the criteria that were important to use. What is more, on the trip he and Roger had hours for getting to know each other on a deeper level.

While publicity was primarily handled through person-to-person contact, Carl knew the importance of creating excitement and group expectancy. About a month before the retreat he invited several of the most creative kids (fringe as well as core) over to his home for a poster party. Carl shared with the guys and gals what they wanted the retreat to accomplish, and they talked over how to appeal to most of the gang, and then they set to work creating ways to communicate and "sell." As the posters took shape, three of the girls spontaneously developed a hilarious skit, and were asked to put it on in Sunday school. Pizza and prayer climaxed the evening, and the dozen who exited Carl's house that night were now enthusiastic retreat boosters.

Carl did more work than Mr. Swanson had done. And it took him more time. But the retreat had greater impact, not only on the weekend itself, but in all the times of preparation and the ministries with individuals they'd occasioned.

Evaluation

These two sketches illustrate the differences that I feel are important in the two approaches to leadership. And they illustrate what I mean when I say adult leaders should *take on* rather than *delegate* responsibilities in planning and programming.

Note that in the first setting, teens were given jobs to do that had only indirect relationship to people. They were jobs to do — "for the Lord" perhaps — but with the connections to *ministry* difficult to sense.

In the first setting, teens were asked to do jobs for which they were inadequately prepared. The best of explanation and direction falls far short of the kind of training that the "do-it-with-them" approach of apprenticeship provides.

In delegating, Mr. Swanson forced his relationship with the kids into a performance-based pattern. He was not and could not be viewed as "friend and example" in this leadership role, where he was setting himself up as "boss" and demonstrating the boss role in checking up on their performance. (While checking up on others *is* necessary and valuable in ministry, it is important initially to make the checking up in terms of spiritual growth and responsibility. The performance ("job") relationship is best held off until a deep personal relationship is firmly established.)

In the second situation Carl involved his kids in the deepest concerns in planning: discovery and statement of need, prayer that God might work in meeting needs, and sharing the responsibility to draw others toward the Lord. Carl's focus was not on involving teens in the "job" responsibilities, but in the "people" responsibilities.

Carl took responsibility for planning and programming elements which only he was equipped to do well. But he worked to equip others — not by having them *do*, but by involving them with him in evaluation and on trips like the one he took with Roger.

Carl did *not* try to "do it all himself," but instead he attempted to do *with* the kids. He did not just delegate and check up, forcing preparations into the "job" category. He involved himself, and by being there, set a tone and directions, and demonstrated his desire to associate with the group.

Carl had extra time with various individuals and groups and, by keeping his own focus on persons, further developed his ministering relationship with them.

5. In the PROBE features in other chapters I've provided a number of examples and illustrations of program activities. Why not go through them all now, and then, thinking in terms of your group as you know them, see which activities might be appropriate for core and which for contact group gatherings.

Part Five

THE PRODUCT OF MINISTRY

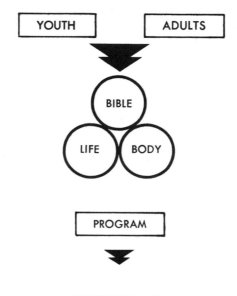

EPHESIANS 4:13

THE PRODUCT OF MINISTRY

CHAPTER

19. Growth, Together

19

growth, together

Ephesians says it. Christ's " 'gifts unto men' were varied. Some he made his messengers, some prophets, some preachers of the gospel; to some he gave the power to guide and teach his people. His gifts were made that Christians might be properly equipped for their service [ministering work], that the whole body might be built up until the time comes when, in the unity of common faith and common knowledge of the Son of God, we arrive at real maturity — that measure of development which is meant by 'the fullness of Christ.'

"We are not meant to remain as children at the mercy of every chance wind of teaching and the jockeying of men who are expert in the crafty presentation of lies. But we are meant to hold firmly to the truth in love, and to grow up in every way into Christ, the head. For it is from the head that the whole body, as a harmonious structure knit together by the joints with which it is provided, grows by the proper functioning of individual parts to its full maturity in love" (Eph. 4:11-16 *Phillips*).

Yes, Ephesians says it. The product, and the goal, of youth ministry is *growth, together, to maturity.*

In a real sense, this short passage brings together nearly all that I have been saying in this book. It focuses God's philosophy of ministry on its goal — growth toward maturity in Christ.

Note the various thrusts of the passage. God gives His Church men, men who are to function as leaders to guide and teach His people. But these leaders are not bosses or dictators. They are servants who exist to equip and activate believers for *their* ministering works. It is through the functioning of all believers, of each as an individual part of the Body, that the Body of Christ grows to its full maturity in love.

God has grouped Christians together, called us to union with each other as a Body. It is "in Body" that we grow. It is in the unity of a common faith and common knowledge of Christ that we are built up toward real maturity.

Thus the Christian leader seeks to develop love between believers — love, that gift which frees us to experience our unity. Not all respond immediately. So he works most closely with those who do respond, that they may grow and by their love draw more toward Christ and into unity.

The Body is a harmonious structure, growing as each individual makes his contribution. So the Christian leader seeks to develop openness and honesty, the context in which love can be given and received, the context for gift-ministry. Because believers are to hold to the truth in love, he seeks to involve the youth in Scripture. Because we are to express "the fullness of Christ," he leads them to share and explore their daily lives, that they might grow up into Him "in every way." And because a "full maturity in love" means expressing the fullness of Christ to others, he guides them to share the good Gospel news with others, and to live as Christ lived in the world — a loving servant.

Youth ministry is concerned with persons and seeks to help individuals grow in Christ in company with other growing believers, for so God has ordained. And our approach to ministry must reflect both the divine purpose and the divine pattern.

Only when we understand the goal to which Christ calls us, and grasp the tremendous resources He has provided in His Word, His Body, and His Spirit, can we conform our efforts to Him, and know the joy of those who live and minister in full accord with His will.

PROBE
case histories
discussion questions
thought-provokers
resources

— One final suggestion. Now, at the end of this book, try "putting it all together" by developing a ministry strategy of your own. Here's how:

Suppose that you have been invited to a typical local church as minister to youth. Briefly describe (drawing on your own experience) the situation you find: size of the group, present structures, attitudes of kids and adults, etc. Then write out a tentative three-year plan, stating goals for every six-month period, and giving details on how you expect to move to reach them. Feel free to go back over any section of this book, but develop *your own plan* as thoroughly, thoughtfully, and carefully as you can.

SUBJECT
INDEX

SCRIPTURE INDEX